ALSO BY ETHAN MORDDEN

NONFICTION
Better Foot Forward: The Story of America's Musical Theatre
Opera in the Twentieth Century
That Jazz! An Idiosyncratic Social History of the American Twenties
A Guide to Orchestral Music
The Splendid Art of Opera: A Concise History
The American Theatre
The Hollywood Musical
Movie Star: A Look at the Women Who Made Hollywood
Broadway Babies: The People Who Made the American Musical
Demented: The World of the Opera Diva
Opera Anecdotes
A Guide to Opera Recordings
The Hollywood Studios

FICTION
I've a Feeling We're Not in Kansas Anymore
One Last Waltz
Buddies
Everybody Loves You

FACETIAE
Smarts: The Cultural I.Q. Test
Pooh's Workout Book

"The School For Scandal."

THE FIRESIDE COMPANION TO THE THEATRE

*Featuring photographs from the Lincoln Center Library
of the Performing Arts' Theatre Collection,
New York Public Library*

ETHAN MORDDEN

*A Fireside Book
Published by Simon & Schuster Inc.
New York   London   Toronto
Sydney   Tokyo*

FIRESIDE
Simon & Schuster Building
Rockefeller Center
1230 Avenue of the Americas
New York, New York 10020

Copyright © 1988 by Ethan Mordden

Published by the Simon & Schuster Trade Division
FIRESIDE and colophon are registered trademarks
of Simon & Schuster Inc.

Designed by Kathy Kikkert
Manufactured in the United States of America

10 9 8 7 6 5 4 3 2 1

Library of Congress Cataloging in Publication Data
Mordden, Ethan, date
  The fireside companion to the theatre.
  1. Drama—Dictionaries.   2. Theater—Dictionaries.
I. Title.
PN1625.M67   1988   809.2'03   88-18444
ISBN 0-671-67188-X
ISBN 0-671-62553-5 (pbk).

All photographs save four are from the Lincoln Center Library of the Performing Arts' Theatre
Collection. The publisher and author gratefully acknowledge this contribution, especially those
photographs taken from the Van Damm Collection.

The other sources for photographs were Wide World Photos for Oh! Calcutta!, Kabuki, and
Nicholas Nickleby; and Martha Swope for the photograph taken of the production of Hurly-
burly, © 1984 Martha Swope.

Special thanks to Richard Goodbody for photography and printing.

FRONTISPIECE *Louis Calvert and Grace George in Richard Brinsley Sheridan's* The School for
Scandal *at* The New Theatre, *New York, in 1909.*

ACKNOWLEDGMENTS

The author wishes to acknowledge his allies and conspirators. Richard Lynch and Louis Paul of the New York Public Library at Lincoln Center kindly expedited that make-or-break moment in the production of books like these, the Gathering of the Illustrations. At Simon and Schuster, Liz Cunningham served as house enthusiast and sympathizer and Kathy Kikkert patiently bore my vague but insistent ideas on design. Warm thanks to all.

On July 11, 1988, while this book was in production, Tim McGinnis died at the age of thirty-four of heart failure. Tim was a fine, humorous, adventurous man and an editor of great generosity and loyalty to his writers. He was a writer himself. The publishing world will not see his like again, and this book is dedicated to his memory.

INTRODUCTION

This is an encyclopedia without birthplaces, middle names, and other nuts-and-bolts trivia. My intention is to provide the reader with a solid understanding of the world of theatre, both in its history and practice. This is a book of concepts, not of data. I have written it because other encyclopedias seem to me to have too many characters and too little character: facts without comprehension. My selection of entries is narrow in order to concentrate on essentials. However, to open up the scene somewhat, I have included not only the major figures, developments, and backstage terms but also a certain number of plays. Obviously, a book of this size cannot encompass the entire run of masterpieces, artifacts, and popular classics. Instead, I have chosen works to expand the discussions of playwrights, forms, and trends—specific examples, for instance, of expressionism, the chronicle play, farce, the star vehicle, and the theatre of the absurd; or the most explanatory works by such dramatists as Euripides, William Shakespeare, Molière, Johann Wolfgang von Goethe, Anton Chekhov, Eugene O'Neill, Bertolt Brecht, and Tennessee Williams.

I have not tried to impose a strict consistency of organization on the entries, to make the book readable as well as informative. It is my hope that some readers will use the book not only for reference, but to browse through its pages for pleasure. An asterisk (*) before a name or term denotes a separate entry on that subject, to facilitate one's personal research; but I have used these sparingly, to

be helpful rather than intrusive. It would be silly to hit, say, Eugene O'Neill with an asterisk on his countless mentions in these pages, hit after hit after hit. The asterisks appear, then, only when pertinent to the revelation of extrapolative matter.

The years cited in parentheses register the first public performance of a play, not its year of composition or publication; where this occurs more than two years before the premiere, it is noted by its own date. (Years for American and English productions, because of their unique "out of town" tryout system, refer to the New York or London premiere, respectively.) The translations of foreign titles are given literally or in the spirit of the originals, as opposed to the off-kilter reproductions we sometimes get in English. (Consider for example, Luigi Pirandello's *Cosi è {Se Vi Pare}*, variously rendered as *Right You Are if You Think You Are*, *And That's The Truth!*, *It Is If You Think So* —none of them a correct translation of the Italian.) Where these "false" titles have become acculturated, they are mentioned as such.

Playwrights, actors, directors, producers, designers, and so on are listed as they are generally known—Richard Brinsley Sheridan, for instance: but Sam Shepard. My transliteration of the Cyrillic alphabet is closer to the sound of the original Russian than the standard English spelling is, though in this book I have modified my usual system in the interest of legibility. Last, all translations of foreign language dialogue, unless otherwise noted, are my own.

THE FIRESIDE
COMPANION
TO THE
THEATRE

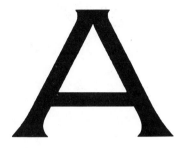

THE ABBEY THEATRE

In joint direction, the poet *William Butler Yeats, the benefactor Lady Augusta Gregory (1852–1932), and the playwright *John Millington Synge opened what was to become Ireland's *national theatre in 1904. As James Joyce has taught us, Dublin is the most conservative city in Europe, and as much of the leadership class opposed the theatre as encouraged it. Even many of its partisans expected the repertory to flatter rather than honestly reflect Irish life, and loudly protested such "defamations" of national character as Synge's *The Playboy of the Western World (1907). There were internal problems as well, first in assembling a capable troupe of Irish actors (there seemed to be none, and local amateurs had to be bolstered by ringers brought back from London), next in balancing the three founders' poetic bent with sound theatricality. For if Synge was splendid and Lady Gregory's folk comedies were delightful, Yeats was more the poet than the thespian, and leaned toward a gestural, not naturalistic, art. But the very naturalistic *Sean O'Casey joined the Abbey (as actor in 1919; as playwright soon enough), and O'Casey wrote of Dublin as Dublin is.

A great deal of history was made in this tiny house and some imposing literature heard; the spirit of adventure never surrendered to commercial demands. Granted, the Abbey has always been conservative in production technique, avoiding the avant-garde experiments of such directors as *Jerzy Grotowski and *Peter Brook, though Tom MacIntyre's *The Great Hunger* (1983), a symbolistic *pantomime directed by Patrick Mason, spurred controversy for its postmodernist approach. After a fire destroyed the old Abbey in 1951, the company moved to temporary quarters, finally taking over the present Abbey in 1966.
(See also The Gate Theatre.)

GEORGE ABBOTT (1887–   )

Actor, director, playwright, and producer, "Mister Abbott" (as everyone calls him) followed George M. Cohan in asserting a slick, fast, sassy American style in comedy, especially *farce. A typical Abbott hit was *Broadway* (1926), a gangland melodrama merged with a cabaret backstager, all speed and smarts—typical especially in that Abbott not only directed but rewrote Philip Dunning's script. (The two men shared the copyright.) Abbott got nowhere very quickly as an actor, and his writing was rudimentary. But he was an able executive, as director and fixer (during out-of-town tryouts). Most of his best work lay in musical comedy. In old age, he became fascinating less for his record —the 1987 Broadway revival of *Broadway* was his

Right, one of the most basic items in the absurdist repertory: Samuel Beckett's Endgame, *in a recent production at, symmetrically enough, the Samuel Beckett Theatre in New York, with (left to right) Alice Drummond, James Greene, Peter Evans, and Alvin Epstein (who also directed). Let us balance the opulently dreary emptiness of Beckett's ashcan wasteland with the dizzy, more articulate emptiness of Eugène Ionesco's satiric city in* Rhinoceros *(below), on Broadway in 1961 with Zero Mostel and Eli Wallach. All mankind is turning animal. Wallach will be the last man on earth, Mostel one of the next rhinoceroses. As we look on, he's already crossing over into . . . well, what is the derivation of Ionesco's symbolism? Nazism? Communism? Bourgeois zombie-ism? The absurd is seldom politically instructed, but it counts some cautionary tales.*

one hundred twenty-first show—than for his recreations. "When he's not working, he's golfing," his secretary remarked when he was ninety-five, "and when he's not golfing, he's dancing." At the 1987 Tony Awards show, Abbott explained, "It's because I love the theatre so much that I thought I'd stick around."

ABSURDISM

Critic Martin Esslin coined the term *The Theatre of the Absurd* in 1961 (in his book of the same name) to describe certain approaches to playwrighting developed in the post–World War II years. *Samuel Beckett, *Arthur Adamov, *Eugène Ionesco, and *Jean Genet, among others, seemed to treat the senselessness and lack of purpose in life in senseless dialogue and apparently purposeless action. As Esslin pointed out, the absurdists were not the first to view the world as bizarrely illogical—only the first to depict it in a bizarrely illogical style.

Because the absurdists were so different from each other, absurdism was not a movement or even an alignment, as its forerunners, *surrealism and *dada, somewhat were. Critic and translator Maurice Valency regretted Esslin's term, because it suggested to the popular mind that the absurd constituted a genre rather than a collection of experimental forms. Still, Valency had to remark "a certain family resemblance" and "an evident desire to strike out in new directions, wherever they may lead."

Indeed, the differences among the founding talents of this schoolless school are telling. Beckett increasingly purged his stage of effects, motion, color; Genet was always flamboyant. Genet constructed tensely political plays on specific issues; Ionesco's politics hid in ambiguous parables. The major absurdists did share a common location, Paris, for even the emigrés Beckett and Adamov wrote in French. Then, in the third edition of his book, Esslin added *Harold Pinter to his group of prime absurdists, officially endorsing the internationalism that absurdism had already developed in such other practitioners as *Edward Albee and *Friedrich Dürrenmatt. However, we give the last word to Ionesco, who thought the term *Theatre of the Absurd* meaningless. "All theatre," Ionesco explained, "is Absurd."

(See also *Aria da Capo, The Bald Soprano, The Dumb Waiter, Exit the King, Rhinoceros, The Visit,* and *Waiting for Godot.*)

ACTOR-MANAGER

The heavyweight thespian from about 1600 to the early 1900s: star, producer, and director rolled into one.

(See also Manager, Jean-Louis Barrault, Dion Boucicault, Mrs. Fiske, John Gielgud, Henry Irving, and Molière.)

ACTOR'S STUDIO (See The Method)

ARTHUR ADAMOV (1908–1970)

The only major *absurdist playwright to renounce the style in mid-career and try to redeem himself with more "positive" forms. Adamov was virtually nationless, a European: an Armenian born in Russia, raised in France and French Switzerland, and educated in Germany. He arrived in Paris in the 1920s, at the height of *surrealism's era, and fell naturally into absurdism's disenchanted fantasy, just as surrealism itself did. The short *La Parodie* (1950) is just that—a parody of forms, especially *expressionism and the *Theatre of Cruelty. Adamov's full-length *Le Ping-Pong* (1955), however, has been hailed as a key work of the absurd, the various influences of the anti-realistic theatre recombined in a darkly comic pageant of futility centered on the symbol of a pinball machine: the game that gets one nowhere.

Then Adamov shifted style, blending absurdism's disjunct dialogue and grotesquerie with the more realistically mimetic *epic theatre of *Bertolt Brecht. The pivotal work was *Paolo Paoli* (1957), a satire on capitalist society eagerly preparing for World War I. *Le Printemps '71* (Spring of 1871,

1960) goes well beyond absurdism and Brecht in a *chronicle play (about the Paris Commune) that, like *La Parodie*, pulls in various elements of the avant-garde, this time on the grandest scale possible. Increasingly radical, Adamov despaired of changing the world through art and died, an apparent suicide, of a drug overdose.

MAUDE ADAMS (1872–1953)

Nina Boucicault, daughter of the famous playwright *Dion Boucicault, created the hero of *James Barrie's *Peter Pan* in its 1904 premiere in London. But Maude Adams played it in New York the following year, and Adams immediately became the classic Peter. She became as well America's Barrie specialist, having already performed leads in *The Little Minister* and *Quality Street* and going on to *What Every Woman Knows* and *A Kiss for Cinderella*. Barrie's heroines tend to the fey, the impulsive, the pathetic—sometimes by turns but occasionally all at once, in moments of almost defiantly elfin charm. Clearly, Barrie's was a strange talent—but it utterly suited Adams's narrow range. Within her field she was apparently without rival, but most parts were beyond her. Like her colleagues, she made her obeisance to Shakespeare, but—contrary to what we read in most theatre encyclopedias—she was scarcely acceptable as Juliet and was so disastrous as Portia (to Otis Skinner's Shylock) that they disbanded their tour before the New York engagement. Besides Barrie, Adams favored the sort of French *trouser parts that *Sarah Bernhardt often played, most notably in Edmond Rostand's *L'Aiglon* (The Eaglet). But then these were modified Peter Pans. Or at least they were in Adams's hands.

A *Charles Frohman star, Adams took his advice in keeping herself unseen and unknown except on stage in his productions—took it so well that when Frohman went down on the *Lusitania,* Adams retired. She made a comeback in 1931, but by then her vogue, and Barrie's, had ended. Others had finally taken on Peter Pan, considered inviolably Adams's in her prime. *Eva Le Gallienne triumphed as Peter, as did, much later, Jean Arthur. Old-timers invoked the legend of Adams,

compared and sighed. But the 1954 musical version, staged by Jerome Robbins for Mary Martin, invigorated the play, pulled it out of the antique beauty of the old fashions into the slick techniques of state-of-the-art Broadway. Adams had reigned in legend for decades. Now, though she died just the year before Martin's Peter, her legend was over. She is nothing more than a name in books like this one.

THE ADDING MACHINE

Satiric fantasy by *Elmer Rice, prem. New York, 1923.

This is Broadway's outstanding entry in the style of German *expressionism, a funny and terrifying look at the dehumanization of society in the technocratic age. Imagine a Carol Burnett–Harvey Korman–Tim Conway comedy sketch played against the sets of the film *The Cabinet of Doctor Caligari* and you'll have some idea of the piece. Or consider the character list: Mr. Zero (the *protagonist), Mrs. Zero, Zero's co-worker Daisy Diana Dorothea Devore, the Boss (who callously replaces Zero with a machine; and whom Zero murders), Messrs. One, Two, Three, Four, Five, Six, and their wives (the jury at Zero's trial), Shrdlu (Zero's fellow murderer, whom he meets in the graveyard after they both rise from death), even A Head (yet another executed murderer, who is awakened by their talk and throws a skull at them). Or simply imagine the shock, in 1923, of Rice's first scene, bedtime in the Zeros's apartment. Hapless Dudley Digges, as Zero, lies in bed; tough Helen Westley, at the dresser, takes down her hair. She goes on about movie stars, her friends, money, him. Her aimless chatter turns into a brutal harangue, and she's still lambasting him as she climbs into bed and the lights dim. Zero hasn't uttered a word.

ADVANCE MAN

Dated American show-biz slang for "PR man," so termed because he made the approaches—the advances—on behalf of a manager, actor, or play.

AESCHYLUS (?525–456 B.C.)

The first playwright—the first, at least, whose texts have survived. Aeschylus supposedly wrote about twenty-two daylong tetralogies, of which only three-fourths of one, four complete parts of others, and a few isolated fragments are extant. He is the oldest of the Big Three of Greek tragedy, apparently more concerned with developing the conventions of tragedy as they were than, like *Sophocles and *Euripides, with bending or even changing the conventions. It is sometimes said that Aeschylus is a more admirable poet than his two successors but that they have the edge as dramatists, at least partly because the form of tragedy that Aeschylus inherited still counted only one actor (playing several characters, by turns) and the chorus. At some point, Aeschylus began writing for two actors and chorus, and later adopted the young Sophocles's use of a third actor. But even in Aeschylus's later plays, such as *The Suppliant Women* (date unknown), his dense deployment of the chorus relates back to tragedy in its primitive form, rather than looking forward to the more dialogue-oriented character conflicts of Sophocles and Euripides.

So powerfully does Aeschylus work within his tradition, in fact, that till recently scholars believed that *The Suppliant Women* must be an early work. But then Aeschylus's scope is vast, almost too vast to home in on the uniquely characterized *protagonists of Sophocles and Euripides—the former's Ajax or Oedipus; the latter's Medea or Helen. Aeschylus seeks out a sense of the world, of ontology and community, more than a sense of individuals' drives and choices. Discord, in Aeschylus, is apocalyptic; harmony blesses all. His *Prometheia* tetralogy (date unknown), then, seems to deal with the relationship of the world to Prometheus, rather than how Prometheus acts and feels himself. I say *seems* because only the first play, *Prometheus Bound*, has survived. We have sections of (and contemporary comment on) *Prometheus Unbound*, but the final story play, *Prometheus Fire-Bringer*, and the obligatory *satyr-play (title unknown) have vanished. Although in *The Persians* (472 B.C.) Aeschylus gave us the only extant Greek tragedy to treat real-life events of its own age, he was more often the timeless, universalizing giant

of his form. The Athenian state so appreciated his work that Aeschylus was the first dramatist whose plays were honored by revival at the annual spring play contest. Oddly, in composing his epitaph, Aeschylus mentioned his exploits in battle but said nothing of his art.
(See also Greek Theatre and *The Oresteia*.)

AFTERPIECE

A short comic work performed after the main play of the evening. The practice was especially favored on English stages during the seventeenth and eighteenth centuries, but the word *afterpiece* itself, according to the Oxford English Dictionary, was apparently not used before the early 1800s.

AGITPROP

From "agitational propaganda," denoting plays designed to influence the audience's politics in a coarsely aggressive manner. Most such works favored by fringe theatre groups are too timely to survive their day. But at least one has become a kind of neglected classic, always mentioned and seldom performed, *Clifford Odets's *Waiting for Lefty* (1935).
(See also *Newsboy*.)

AGON

In *Greek theatre, the "contest," or central conflict of the action. The antagonists may be chorus versus an actor (as in *Aeschylus's *The Suppliant Women*), chorus and an actor versus another actor (as in *Euripides's *The Trojan Women*), or between two actors (as in Euripides's *The Bacchae*: Pentheus and civic order confronting Dionysus and savagery).

EDWARD ALBEE (1928–   )

*Arthur Miller was the moralist, *Tennessee Williams the poetic sensualist, *William Inge the tidy naturalist. All three were in apparent decline when Albee came to Broadway from off-Broadway in

The climax of Odets's Waiting for Lefty, *easily the greatest moment in American Depression—era agitprop. The theatre becomes a union meeting hall, the audience turns into the union members, and the actors assume the job of activists exhorting their fellow members to strike for higher wages and a clean union. "Strike!" the audience cried in response. "Louder!" "Strike!" "Again!" "STRIKE!" Note *Elia Kazan (foreground, third from left) among the exhorters.*

1962 with *Who's Afraid of Virginia Woolf?* It was the most shocking uptown debut a playwright had enjoyed in as long as anyone could recall. Old memories thought back to *Eugene O'Neill's arrival on The Street (after comparable experience with one-acters in small theatres) with *Beyond the Horizon* in 1920—shocking in its intensity rather than in its revelations. Miller's Broadway debut was a flop that didn't last a week, Williams's was the gentle *The Glass Menagerie,* Inge's the mildly melodramatic *Come Back, Little Sheba. Virginia Woolf's* dissection of a sadomasochistic marriage, seen in the night-long drinking party of two college professors and their wives, was truly shocking in the American sense of shocking: confronting the public with unattractive truths. Critics were bewildered, unhappy, thrilled, astonished. Albee was offering marriage with the devil, it seemed. The

Pulitzer committee declined, withholding its drama prize that year—proof that Albee was on to something. But even the *New York Times* said yes; and *Times* critic Howard Taubman caught the parallel with *Strindberg.

There was a great honoring of masters in Albee, not only of Strindberg but of *Ionesco (in the *absurdist echoes and mocking facsimiles of *naturalism that relate Albee's *The American Dream* [1961] to Ionesco's **The Bald Soprano*) and of *Pinter (in a certain oblique twirl in the conversations, a noise in the pauses). This made Albee historical and contemporary at once—and Broadway needed a new king. Albee was crowned.

One read respect but sensed distaste in the reviews for *The Ballad of the Sad Café* (1963), Albee's adaptation of Carson McCullers. After all, Albee had given the bourgeois journalist the thing he fears the most, a flat-out gay play: Amazon heroine loves dwarf who loves Amazon's white-trash husband. Thus the establishment-baiting grotesquerie and bent heat that would characterize the outcoming gay world came to Broadway—albeit in a southern Gothic—and Albee barely got away with a *succès d'estime*. Boldly, he followed this with *Tiny Alice* (1964), an extravagant and ingenious but absolutely impenetrable allegory. The action is plain—the richest woman in the world buys a lay priest from the Church and leaves him in her mansion to die in a ritual sacrifice. The details are fetching—Alice is both the woman and a larger, deeper "being," and Alice's mansion contains a spectacular scale model of itself that contains a spectacular scale model . . . and so on. The symbolism is obviously pointed—pointed at what? To my knowledge, no one has solved the rebus, yet Albee repeatedly refused to explain it. This was a fatal mistake. *Tiny Alice* is rich and resonant, and there probably is a key to it; but to state, as Albee did in the published text, that "the play is quite clear," is something between impishness and a swindle.

So began Albee's decline in critical appreciation—and Albee's theatre, notwithstanding his off-Broadway origin, is Broadway theatre, where the critics are lawyer, judge, and jury. The Pulitzer people, eager to redeem their lack of chic on *Virginia Woolf,* gave *A Delicate Balance* (1966) their prize. But the reviewers became more and more skeptical, especially when Albee went on to backpedal in second-rate Albee or adaptations from other writers. Arrogantly, he dared a *Lolita* (1981), claiming that Stanley Kubrick's film version of Vladimir Nabokov's novel had offended Albee. The film, written by Nabokov himself, is fair Nabokov. The play is a shambles. Autobiographically, Albee railed at opinion makers in *The Man Who Had Three Arms* (1982), like most late Albee (and late Miller, Williams, and Inge) a very fast flop.

The best of Albee was a fearless questioning of American values, as in the feelingless beauty of the title character in *The American Dream,* carried over as the imaginary child of *Virginia Woolf*'s George and Martha (Washington). The best of Albee was innately stageworthy, seeking, vital, the theatre of a "natural son," as they put it down south: born to the art. The worst of Albee was imitative, vapid

showboating. Maybe some day he'll tell us what *Tiny Alice* is about, then apply himself to the task of supplying more fearless seeking. More plays on the order of *Virginia Woolf* and *The Zoo Story* (1959). More of the natural son.

Not that it matters, but Albee is the adopted grandson of E. F. Albee, the vaudeville impresario. (See also *The Zoo Story.*)

IRA ALDRIDGE (1804–1867)

As the first American black actor of note, Aldridge is more famous as an encyclopedia entry than as a historical figure, for he died so long ago he scarcely even casts the shadow of legend. At that, he spent the bulk of his career in Europe, playing the great tragic heroes from Belfast to Petersburg as "the African *Roscius." Supposedly stage-struck when working as *Edmund Kean's valet, Aldridge eventually played Othello to the Iago of Edmund's son Charles.

ALEXANDRINE

The characteristic verse line of classic French drama, iambic hexameter with a caesura understood at the half point. For instance, from Don Diègue's famous soliloquy in Corneille's *Le Cid*:

> O rage! ô désespoir! ô vieillesse ennemie!
> N'ai-je donc tant vécu   que pour cette infamie?

> (Oh anger! o despair!   Oh enemy old age!
> Have I but lived to come   to this pathetic stage?)

ALIENATION EFFECT

Verfremdungseffekt: the "distancing" of the audience from the action, in the *epic theatre principle of *Bertolt Brecht. Thus, rather than suspend our disbelief and identify emotionally with the characters, we are to retain our intellectual awareness and allow the players to identify the author's theme for us. It sometimes works.

SERAFÍN (1871–1938) and
JOAQUÍN (1873–1944)
ÁLVAREZ QUINTERO

As brothers and collaborators, this Spanish play-wrighting team put forth some two hundred plays, virtually all sweet-toned comedies in which any problem is solvable. Specialties of the house include the charming of tense old aunts by disorderly nieces, the taming of rakes, and a generally rosy view of Andalusian life. Helen and *Harley Granville-Barker translated a number of these comedies for production in England and America, most notably *Papa Juan, Centenario* (1909), about a wise old Mr. Fix-it, a Broadway hit for Otis Skinner as *A Hundred Years Old* in 1929.

ANAGNORISIS

"Recognition," in Greek tragedy—the moment, for instance, in which Sophocles's Oedipus realizes that the culprit whose sin has brought plague to Thebes is he himself, murderer of his father and husband of his mother. More recently, Maxwell Anderson defined it as an essential factor in imposing drama: "A play should lead up to and away from a central crisis . . . a discovery by the leading character which . . . completely alters his course of action."

And this leads us on to:

MAXWELL ANDERSON
(1888–1959)

"I believe with *Goethe," he wrote, "that dramatic poetry is man's greatest achievement on earth so far, and I believe with the early Bernard Shaw that the theatre is essentially a cathedral of the spirit, devoted to the exaltation of men, and boasting an apostolic succession of inspired high poets which extends further into the past than the Christian line of St. Peter."

Thus Anderson explained his decision to establish the verse play on Broadway; and against all possibility he succeeded. *Elizabeth the Queen* (1930); *Mary of Scotland* (1933); *Valley Forge* (1934); *Win-terset* (1935), the first modern American drama to dare poetry in a contemporary rather than historical setting; *High Tor* (1936), a verse comedy, even a verse *farce; and *Key Largo* (1939), a verse crime thriller, were among the plays that made the 1930s almost as much Anderson's decade as official heavy hitter as the 1920s had been Eugene O'Neill's. Anderson had the *Lunts, *Helen Hayes, *Katharine Cornell, and Paul Muni to bolster his appeal. Still, in all, his triumph was one of text, not of production, even considering *Jo Mielziner's staggering view of the eastern end of the Brooklyn Bridge that opened *Winterset* (originally entitled, in fact, *The Bridge*). For a decade, Anderson entranced American theatregoers with a form they usually forgave only in Shakespeare.

Versatile, Anderson also worked in melodrama and comedy and even wrote two musicals—lyrics as well as book—with Kurt Weill, *Knickerbocker Holiday* (1938) and *Lost in the Stars* (1949). Anderson first drew notice collaborating with Laurence Stallings on the war play *What Price Glory?* (1924), as romantic in its view of male bonding as cynical in its treatment of male aggression, and a cause célèbre in its—for the day—earthy diction. There is also a sentimental and shocking Anderson, the first in *Saturday's Children* (1927), a loving look at newlywed marriage, the second in *The Bad Seed* (1954), *grand guignol* about an adolescent murderess, so chilling (she gets away with her crimes) that little Patty McCormack regularly came out for her bow to a mixed review of applause (for her talent) and sullen resistance (toward her character).

The most genuine Anderson is political, roving through the past in *Elizabeth the Queen, Mary of Scotland,* and *Valley Forge* for the sources of power and the truths of nationhood, fighting for conservationism in *High Tor,* for anti-welfarism in *Knickerbocker Holiday* (which poses fascistic Pieter Stuyvesant as a parallel to Franklin Roosevelt), for racial tolerance in *The Wingless Victory* (1936) and *Lost in the Stars.* Anderson wanted nothing for the world but freedom. He fought as well to improve Broadway's reviewing system, denouncing the dull intellect and lack of artistic reference in the bulk of The Street's journalists. In response, the critics waited till Anderson produced a weak (though worthy) piece, *Truckline Café* (1946), and slammed him to pieces: *pour encourager les autres.* It brought

on one of Broadway's most notorious rumbles between artist and reporter and was unfortunately never resolved. There are fewer playwrights now; but there are still critics, and they're still as stupid and vicious as Anderson said they were—"a Jukes family of journalism" was his term. In *Gods of the Lightning* (1928), a fictional account of the Sacco and Vanzetti case, from arrest to execution (written with Harold Hickerson), Anderson put forth what may be his most characteristic view of the world, of politics, system, business-as-usual, critics . . . of everything. "There is no government," one character asserts. "There are only brigands in power who fight for more power! Till you die! Till we all die! Till there is no earth!"
(See also *What Price Glory?*)

ANNA CHRISTIE

Waterfront drama by *Eugene O'Neill, prem. New York, 1921.

Lynn Fontanne, of all people, played the heroine in the first version of the play, *Chris Christophersen*, tried out in 1920 in Atlantic City and Philadelphia, where it closed. O'Neill blamed the failure on the sluggish production, but also on his text—though when this was first published, in 1982, it read surprisingly well. But it is unoriginal, in shape, character, tone. An old sailor, railing at "dat ole davil sea," opposes the romance of his daughter and an intelligent but womanizing sailor. At length the old man gives in, the couple plan their life together, and, for a happy curtain, father gets a promotion.

In the authenticity of O'Neill's view of waterfront life, *Chris Christophersen* reflects the *naturalism developed on Broadway in the preceding twenty years. It's not unlike *Salvation Nell* without all the picturesque bit parts. In its hunger to communicate a worldview, *Chris* is worthy of O'Neill's *Beyond the Horizon,* the play that established his reputation that same year. But it lacks *Horizon*'s sweep and fierce power. And virtually nothing in *Chris* suggests the experimental O'Neill who pursued his destiny with *The Emperor Jones, Diff'rent,* and *Gold* in the months that preceded the premiere of the revised *Chris,* now centering on Chris's daughter and retitled *Anna Christie.*

In this final version the sea remains a menacing symbol. But now Anna is no prim young lady but a man-hating prostitute, and the sailor who loves her is no thoughtful Swedish idealist but an Irish brawler. (Ironically, this was how O'Neill had first envisioned the character in the planning outline of *Chris Christophersen.*) *Anna Christie* has proved one of O'Neill's most enduring works, though he came to loathe it because his carefully open-ended ending was mistaken for the kind of happily-ever-after he had tacked onto *Chris Christophersen.* Anna and her seaman do come to terms romantically, but it's O'Neill's point that their troubles aren't over. They're just beginning, with "dat ole davil sea" looming and storming in the background. A great success in 1921, *Anna Christie* made a star of the delicate Pauline Lord, cast against type, and nicely served Celeste Holm, Ingrid Bergman, and Liv Ullmann in later revivals. The performance of the 1921 Chris, George Marion, is preserved in two film versions, the silent with Blanche Sweet and the talkie with Greta Garbo.

JEAN ANOUILH (1910–   )

Along with *Jean Giraudoux, Anouilh stands among the few important French playwrights of the twentieth century who didn't deal in some form of the *absurd. In the 1950s, avant-garde critics accused Anouilh of becoming a *boulevardier, going for charm rather than ideas. But Anouilh himself has said that the theme is the starting point of his composition—plot, characters, and setting all come after.

Certainly, Anouilh is versatile, having bunched his texts under antagonistic groupings by type: *pièces roses* (sweet plays), *pièces noires* (dark plays), *pièces brillantes* (glittering plays), *pièces grinçantes* (grating plays), *pièces costumées* (chronicle plays), and *pièces baroques.* Anouilh is an accomplished thespian, a director, adapter (into French: of Shakespeare, Heinrich von Kleist, Graham Greene), and the husband of an actress, Monelle Valentin, who created the title role in the premiere of Anouilh's *Antigone* (1944). One element is constant in his work: wit. This has energized his critics. Surely Anouilh is too clever to be major. His one-acter *L'Orchestre* (1962) is virtually an exercise in cleverness. We look in on a third-rate Palm Court band, all women but for the pianist. Little happens. The players bicker about sewing and cooking. Two of them battle for the rights to the pianist. One of the two runs into the women's room and shoots herself. This is all. But Anouilh's deadpan whimsey and spoof are everything, not least in the rendition of "Cuban Delights," for which the orchestra players don Caribbean hats and sing "Delights, delights, Cuban delights!" at intervals.

On the other hand, Anouilh set down a most earnest document in *Antigone,* after *Sophocles. Submit to immoral practicality or defy the system idealistically? This is *Antigone*'s theme, vastly relevant to the German-occupied France of *Antigone*'s premiere. To compare *Antigone* with *Léocadia* (1940), the most gossamer of romances, is to see how varied is Anouilh's palette of colors, tones, personalities. Within the framework of an omniscient, one-person chorus, *Antigone* pursues profound questions of human responsibility: to family, honor, the state. *Léocadia* is a fribble of the clever Anouilh, about no more than a young man's morbid fancy for a dead beauty, and his aunt's fussy attempt to bring him out of it by reenacting the affair. Known in English as *Time Remembered,* the play charmed Broadway in 1957 with Helen Hayes, Susan Strasberg, and Richard Burton, the last most amusing in Anouilh's burlesque of the *tirade of the classic French theatre. But are we to seize the heroic moment or pine for lost love? Veering from one to the other of these two central themes, Anouilh confuses the annals. On what does he focus? Even his tone varies greatly—from the debonair banter of *Le Bal des Voleurs* (The Thieves' Carnival, 1938) to the sentimental historicism of *L'Alouette* (The Lark, 1953). Glittering plays or grating plays?
(See also *The Lark.*)

ANDRÉ ANTOINE (1858–1943)

As *actor-manager, Antoine championed *realism, founding the Théâtre Libre (Free Theatre) in 1887 specifically for the presentation of Ibsen, Strindberg, Hauptmann, and other realists. Impressed by the detailed acting ensemble and evocative decor of the *Meiningers, Antoine never-

theless emphasized lifelike sets over acting, perhaps because it was easier to redesign the performing area than to reeducate the performers. Antoine's influence was far-reaching; in France he is regarded as the key figure between *Molière and *Jacques Copeau.

GUILLAUME APOLLINAIRE (1880–1918)

Like his fellow playwright of the early avant-garde, *Alfred Jarry, Apollinaire wrote several plays but is famed for only one, *Les Mamelles de Tirésias* (The Breasts of Tiresias, 1917), the first and best of the *surrealist theatre pieces. Apollinaire is also known for his poetry and for his rascally charm. He was, among other things, a pornographer, a tireless gallant of the boudoir, and—it was generally believed—an art thief.
(See also *The Breasts of Tirésias.*)

ADOLPHE APPIA (1862–1928)

This extremely influential Swiss designer based his theories on the music theatre of Richard Wagner, where Appia found a mythopoetic intoxication of theatre more telling than that in, say, Shakespeare, Molière, or Goethe. Appia's theatre was music and light: it was in the technology of lighting even more than in his majestically simple set designs that Appia left his mark on twentieth century stagecraft. Appia's lighting not only shaped his pictures, not only gave them atmosphere, not only changed color and focus within a single scenic setup: Appia's lighting reinvented the very function of scenery, from background into environment. None of Appia's published Wagnerian set designs was in fact employed in the theatre; ironically, Wagner's grandsons Wieland and Wolfgang drew heavily on the Appia style in their trend-making post–World War II productions at the Wagner family theatre in Bayreuth, Germany.

ALEXEI ARBUZOV (1908–   )

One of the very few Russian playwrights of the Soviet era to succeed in the West, Arbuzov built his career on the tenets of *socialist realism. His stories are simple, his forms respect tradition, his take observes the Party line, and his outlook is happy. The slightly feminist *Tanya* (1938) has been called a lighter complement to *Ibsen's *A Doll's House*; and *Irkutskaya Istoriya* (The Irkutsk Story, known in English as *It Happened in Irkutsk,* 1960) has been likened to *Thornton Wilder's *Our Town.* Arbuzov also treats more overtly "relevant" topics, as in *Dalnaya Doroga* (The Long Road, 1935), on the building of Moscow's subway system. By far his most popular play in the West is *Moi Byedni Marat* (My Poor Marat, known as *The Promise*, 1965), a look at the relationship of three people in Leningrad, from the Nazi siege to the post-Stalinist cultural relaxation.

JOHN ARDEN (1930–   )

Of the political playwrights in Britain today, Arden is the most poetic, imaginative, theatrical. He is phenomenal: veering from naturalism to pageant from work to work, sometimes within a single piece; "flubbing" his supposed political agenda with characterological ambivalences—distracting flaws in his heroes and engaging quirks in his villains; adopting some of the principles of *Brechtian epic theatre but abjuring the essential Brechtian *alienation effect, to let his audience *feel* the action as it considers its implications. Thus Arden seems at once essential and irrelevant to his times. Important British theatre today (aside from *Simon Gray and *Alan Ayckbourn) is predominantly socialist inquiry, and Arden's social motivation is very broad. But his characterological and pictorial vitality outsings his message.

Thus, in the strictly *naturalistic *Live Like Pigs* (1958), Arden shows the clash between two classes of English domestic life, the sedately lower-middle Jacksons and the virtually barbaric Sawneys, thrust among the Jackson kind in a state housing project. The show is lively, funny, shocking—but whose side is Arden on? Progressives resented the Sawneys's lawlessness; was Arden defaming the welfare state? Conservatives resented the Jackson's airs and hypocrisy; was Arden defaming the respectable citizenry? In fact, Arden clearly takes no side, or

rather he takes a third side, the side of life. His worldview is too rich for a cartoon version of the problem in the style of *socialist realism, and his sympathies are huge. Similarly, in his best-known play, *Serjeant Musgrave's Dance* (1959), the eponymous hero is both attractive and repellent, admirable yet terrifying. He is a kind of gangster in military uniform, but he is a moralist. Indeed, it is Musgrave's sense of justice that impels him to the use of force in the first place.

Arden's early association with the ecumenically fecund *Royal Court Theatre was his strongest link with his fellow playwrights; his constant employment of poetry and song to comment on his dialogue scenes is his flagrant distinction. Arden went even further in *Armstrong's Last Goodnight* (1964), subtitled "An Exercise in Diplomacy." Based on the case of a sixteenth century Scottish noble, hanged for freebooting raids across the English border, the play is written, Arden says, in "a sort of Babylonish dialect" akin to the Puritan New English of *Arthur Miller's *The Crucible,* suggestive of rather than literally reviving an old dialect. This, combined with enough songs to outfit a musical and Arden's typical extravagance of characterization (the titular *protagonist, once again, is as dangerous as he is charming), yields a rich mix, all the more so for its confrontational interpretation of the politics of chronicle.

In the late 1960s, Arden began collaborating with his wife, Margaretta D'Arcy, most delightfully in *The Royal Pardon* (1966), a children's show based on the bedtime storytelling sessions in the Ardens's own household; and most impressively in *The Island of the Mighty* (1972), in many ways the summit thus far of Arden's unique form. A trilogy, *The Island of the Mighty* explores the Britain of Arthur and Merlin, blending Arden's sophisticated theatrical rituals with the rituals of primitive peoples. The three-night epic does not quite sustain interest. Certainly Part One, *Two Wild Young Noblemen,* is the most colorful in its look at two brothers parted and tragically reunited in a fight to the death among the matriarchal Picts. Worse yet, Arden and D'Arcy's disenchantment with establishment theatre organizations led them to picket the *Royal Shakespeare Company's production of *The Island of the Mighty.* Since then, the couple has withdrawn from the main stages to practice among

the more community-oriented groups of the fringe theatre.
(See also *Götz von Berlichingen*.)

ARISTOPHANES (?448–?380 B.C.)

The master of Athenian "old comedy"—contemporary, satiric, ribald . . . and dangerous. The state's capital case against Socrates for sedition is thought to have been encouraged by Aristophanes's savage portrayal of Socrates (by his real name, and bearing, in the typical actor's mask, his features) in *The Clouds* (423 B.C.). One wonders how Aristophanes stayed out of trouble, despite his popularity, for the Athens he wrote for was in decline, its democratic structures toppling and the endless Peloponnesian War against Sparta draining the city's sense of tolerance. Yet nothing escaped Aristophanes's spoof—especially the politicians and intellectuals of the leadership class. *The Acharnians* (425), *The Knights* (424), *Peace* (421), and *The Frogs* (405) all attack the Athenian government for neither winning the War nor calling it off, and *Lysistrata* (411), perhaps Aristophanes's most enduring work, presents a radical solution: the Athenian women go on a chastity strike until the men swear off war.

Aristophanes is much less frequently performed than the three great Greek tragedians, the older *Aeschylus and Aristophanes's coevals *Sophocles and *Euripides, because the comic's constant references to details of Athenian life are lost on modern audiences. Any readable text is stippled with explanatory footnotes. Then too, Aristophanes's outspoken sexuality embarrasses all but the most sophisticated spectators, as when, in *Lysistrata,* the heroine starts to outline her antiwar plan and Kalonika thinks she's speaking of something else:

KALONIKA: What is the matter?
LYSISTRATA: Something big.
KALONIKA: Oh? And is it *thick,* too?
LYSISTRATA: Yes, it's big and important.
KALONIKA: You'd think all the women would come running!
LYSISTRATA: Oh, if it were what *you* think it is, they'd all be here. No, this concerns something I've been turning about this way and that for many a sleepless night.

KALONIKA: It must be something very delightful for you to have turned it about so much.
(See also Greek Theatre.)

ARIA DA CAPO

One-act harlequinade in verse by Edna St. Vincent Millay, prem. New York, 1919.

A typical *little theatre opus, first staged by the *Provincetown Players and popular with other avant-garde troupes, later a staple of the American high school dramatic club. Millay deliberately opposes comedy to tragedy, opening with the bizarre chatter of *commedia dell'arte* figures at dinner:

COLUMBINE: Pierrot, a macaroon! I cannot live without a macaroon!
PIERROT: My only love, you are *so* intense. . . .

Two shepherds interrupt them for a pastoral that erupts in pointless violence. A fifth player hides the corpses under a table, and Columbine and Pierrot finish the playlet as it began, mirroring the ABA structure of the old Italian opera seria aria—thus Millay's title. Like *Ubu Roi and *The Breasts of Tirésias, Aria da Capo,* in its dainty way, prefigures the era of *absurdism.

ARISTOTLE (384–322 B.C.)

The first critic, and the last fair one. Writing, in the *Poetics,* about Greek tragedy considerably after *Aeschylus, *Sophocles, and *Euripides had died, Aristotle attempted simply to describe what they had created. Thus Aristotle took the art itself as a model for art, rather than judge art by his own external set of value judgments. At that, Aristotle seems to take the Sophoclean style as tragedy's highest form, perhaps fearing Aeschylus's epic grandeur and Euripides's disturbing realism. Commentators do not agree on exactly what Aristotle said on a number of matters, and his most influential point of discussion, the "three unities" of time, place, and action—barely touched on in the *Poetics*—became the critical establishment's ogreish blackmail in later years, especially in France in the days of *Corneille and *Racine.
(See also The Unities.)

FERNANDO ARRABAL (1932–   )

This prolific playwright suggests an *absurdist *Theatre of Cruelty. He says theatre must be "dangerous and revelatory," and calls his style "Theatre of Panic"—though his definition of this term is not very specific. Perhaps that's the point: for Arrabal's world is a grotesque labyrinth of images, historical, autobiographical, psychological. A child of the Spanish Civil War (the young Arrabal's father, sentenced to thirty years' imprisonment by the Fascists, escaped from a hospital in his pyjamas and was never heard of again), Arrabal is a refugee, a traveler, a permanent emigrant. He writes in French, the mother language of absurdism and personally preferable to his native Spanish. He recalls the repression and terror of the Civil War but eventually turned to the student rebellions of the 1960s, the black power movement, and even the Manson murders as subjects. *Le Jardin des Délices* (The Garden of Delights, 1969) typifies the mature Arrabal in its *surrealist exploration of an actress's memories and drives, while the brutally sadomasochistic *Le Ciel et la Merde* (Heaven and Shit, 1970) typifies the political Arrabal, obsessed with the disorders he has lived through. His best known play is *L'Architecte et l'Empereur d'Assyrie* (The Architect and the Emperor of Assyria, 1967), set on a tropical island in which the title characters—the survivor of an air crash and a native, the "architect" —undergo savage rituals of transformation till they wholly trade "selves" and the work starts over as it had begun.

ANTONIN ARTAUD (See Theatre of Cruelty)

PEGGY ASHCROFT (1907–   )

One of the classiest of actresses, not to put too fine a point on it. Dame Peggy somehow skirted the fascination for commercial hits and film work that drew many of her colleagues away from the center of their calling. Nor has she cooperated with the media. She has made very few Broadway appearances, concentrating on the *West End and, especially, the major British rep companies, the *Old Vic from the 1930s through its transition into the National Theatre of Great Britain, and the *Royal Shakespeare Company. Ashcroft has played Shakespeare, Wilde, and Ibsen (an honest, utterly shocking Hedda Gabler), but also Maxwell Anderson, Edward Albee, and Samuel Beckett.

THE ASTOR PLACE RIOT

New York: May 10, 1849. So intense are the feelings that theatre stars inspire in this era that the feud between the American *Edwin Forrest and the English *William Macready breaks into a full-scale riot while Macready is appearing at the Astor Place Opera House. Irish-American hostility toward the British is said to have energized the rumble. Twenty-two are killed and thirty-six injured, and the theatre, but two years old then, is considered cursed and goes out of business.

BROOKS ATKINSON (1894–1984)

It says something about Atkinson that he is the only critic who has a Broadway theatre named after him. Thespians generally regard critics as enraged schmucks; but in his thirty-four years at the *New York Times* (barring time out for war coverage), Atkinson built credibility as a kind of unadorned savant, an intellectual who knew little of theatre yet was strongly stimulated by it. Unlike, for instance, *George Jean Nathan or *Kenneth Tynan, Atkinson lacked background. But he also lacked Nathan's haughty self-display and Tynan's star-chasing chic. Atkinson was earnest, honest, and— above all—fair. He was quite something, given the nature of his calling, and he is much missed.

AUNTIE MAME

Comedy by Jerome Lawrence and Robert E. Lee, prem. New York, 1956.

The heroine of Patrick Dennis's novel is harder and sexier than she became in Lawrence and Lee's

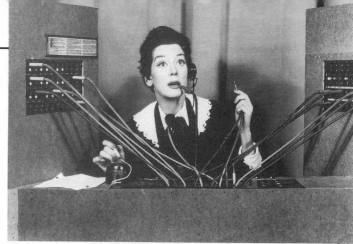

A kaleidoscope of star diva facets in Auntie Mame, perhaps the most astrocentric star vehicle in Broadway history. Clockwise from top left: the star entrance, the star in love (with James Monks as the poet Brian O'Bannion), the star comically frazzled on the job during the Depression, the star ever so grandly touched when the servants pay the bills, the star in adversity (inadvertently sabotaging Polly Rowles's Boston opening night) and triumph (winning a southern beau, Robert Smith, in a fox hunt), and the star in fashion (to the designs of Travis Banton, from the star's Hollywood days). The star is Rosalind Russell, and the facets of her fabled performance show us how definitively a vehicle can compose itself around a personality more than an idea.

adaptation, which emphasized the lovably madcap raising of her orphaned nephew to set off star Rosalind Russell as a kind of screwball Sister Kenny. From her entrance, trotting down a staircase dressed as a mandarin, Russell was seldom offstage, for there is almost nothing in the show but her capers: disrupting a play in the merest of walk-on parts, taking on the Old South on *its* terms, writing her memoirs while staving off a phony Irish poet, and humiliating various babbitts and bigots.

Such other divas as Greer Garson, Bea Lillie, Constance Bennett, and Sylvia Sidney played Mame Dennis, but the role belonged to Russell (through the film version) till Angela Lansbury reinvented the character in the musical, *Mame* (1966), a portrayal that survived yet another film version (with Lucille Ball, a wrong Mame) and even Lansbury's shortlived Broadway revival in 1983. Notwithstanding the story's immense appeal, the show is historically notable as the prototype of an equation of American commerce, from best-seller to star vehicle to film to musical to musical film. There are other examples—Margaret Landon's novel *Anna and the King of Siam,* counting film (Irene Dunne and Rex Harrison), musical (Gertrude Lawrence and Yul Brynner), and musical film (Deborah Kerr and Brynner), or Christopher Isherwood's *Goodbye to Berlin,* which went to the stage and screen as *I Am a Camera* (both with *Julie Harris as Sally Bowles), then to Broadway and Hollywood as the musical *Cabaret.* However, Patrick Dennis's book and its offshoots offer the most lucrative combination in all stages as well as the most purely star-oriented construction: from Russell to Lansbury to Lucille Ball.

AWAKE AND SING!

Bronx *naturalism by *Clifford Odets, prem. New York, 1935.

Isaiah 26:19: "Thy dead men shall live, together with my dead body shall they arise. Awake and sing, ye that dwell in dust: for thy dew is as the dew of herbs, and the earth shall cast out the dead."

On the other hand, listen to Odets's Berger family at the curtain's rise, just finishing supper:

RALPH: Where's advancement down the place? Work like crazy! Think they see it? You'd drop dead first.

That's Jules Garfield, later John of the movies. Here's Mother Bessie and grandfather Jacob:

BESSIE: You gave the dog eat?
JACOB: I gave the dog eat.

Stella Adler and Morris Carnovsky. Not to mention Luther Adler and Sanford Meisner, all of the original *Group Theatre production, directed by *Harold Clurman. *Waiting for Lefty* may be Odets's most famous title and *Golden Boy* his most enduring work. But *Awake and Sing!* is surely his most finished piece, an extremely honest and moving look at "dead men" struggling to survive, one of them—young Ralph—heartened by Jacob's self-sacrifice (he kills himself to subsidize Ralph's future), beginning his struggle to change the world for the better: "so life shouldn't be printed on dollar bills."

ALAN AYCKBOURN (1939–)

Because he treats bourgeois values comically, he has been called "the English *Neil Simon." But Ayckbourn's sharp social observation, insistently *farcical structures, and devious scenic plans set him apart—as does his cozy relationship with the Scarborough theatre company, where Ayckbourn launches his works in a smalltown atmosphere while Simon sticks to the big commercial houses. With Simon, we notice the wisecracks that build the characterization; with Ayckbourn, we notice the juxtaposition of characters that builds the action. Thus, Ayckbourn gives us the simultaneous development of two different dinner parties in *How the Other Half Loves* (1969), three *different* kitchens on successive Christmas eves in *Absurd Person Singular* (1972), three *different* bedrooms *at once* in *Bedroom Farce* (1975). *The Norman Conquests* (1973) is Ayckbourn's most typically quirky event: three full-length plays, each with the same three couples, each taking place *at the same time* as the others, and each connected to the others by congruence of location: from the garden to the living room to the dining room. In effect, there is no first, second, or third play. All are equal, and one may take them in any order.

More important, Neil Simon, at least until his deeper works of the 1980s, is easier to play than Ayckbourn because so much of Simon's humor is founded in situation rather than in character. "To play Ayckbourn properly," says director *Peter Hall, "you have to dig deep, be serious, and then get laughed at. It wounds the personality."

BAAL

*Expressionism in praise of the outlaw personality by *Bertolt Brecht, prem. Leipzig, 1923.

Brecht claimed that the title character, a sociopathic poet, was based on "a certain Josef K." who generated a series of unsavory rumors—in one he supposedly stabbed a companion to death—in Augsburg when Brecht was growing up there. Brecht had another model for his *protagonist, in Hanns Johst's play *Der Einsame* (The Loner, 1918), on the life of the nineteenth century poet Christian Dietrich Grabbe. Baal was intended as a "contradiction," a rebuttal of Johst's sanitized view of a corrupt and brilliant artist. Yet we wonder if Baal is not a self-portrait. Is the guitar-strumming, amoral, sensualizing genius poet something of an idealization of the man Brecht was trying to be, Brecht as a savage god of Augsburg?

This much Baal unquestionably is, seducing women then tossing them aside, exploiting and insulting, living entirely through his appetites, taking his innocent friend Ekart as his lover apparently through a sudden whim for possession and power, and finally killing Ekart and dying like an animal, crawling on all fours in a woodcutter's cabin. *Baal* is Brecht's first play, written in 1918, when he was twenty; and I wonder how many twenty-year-old playwrights have equaled the mastery of form that Brecht displays here. *Baal* fascinates for its wildly liberated dialogue, its nightmarish *naturalism, realistic yet distorted, its utterly confident tour of the shifting landscape of Baal's adventures. The anti-hero himself is a unique figure, as ugly as he is attractive, a "natural man" of primitive urges and sophisticated apprehensions: Neal Cassady as rendered by *Georg Büchner. Indeed, there is more than a touch of Büchner's *Woyzeck* in *Baal,* and Brecht's play is so unlike everything else he was to write—and so irrelevant to the politically didactic Brecht of the epic theatre—that it has been neglected. This is a sad loss, for *Baal* is possibly Brecht's most poetic script, and we must remember that Brecht was a poet as well as a dramatist. Here's a taste of *Baal,* in a scene early in the hero's relationship with Ekart. The two are in a green field of blue plum trees:

EKART: Why do you run away from the plum trees like an elephant?
BAAL: Lay your fin on my skull! It swells with

every pulse beat and then bursts like a bubble. Can't you feel it with your hand?

EKART: No.

BAAL: You know nothing of my soul.

EKART: Should we go lie in the water?

BAAL: My soul, brother, is the moaning of the cornfields when they waltz in the wind, and the sparkle in the eyes of two insects who want to eat each other.

EKART: A guy going crazy in July, his insides immortal, that's you. A dumpling that will some day leave heaven flecked with grease stains!

BAAL: Silly talk. But that's all right.

EKART: My body is as light as a little plum in the wind.

THE BACCHAE

Tragedy by *Euripides, prem. Athens, 405 B.C.

Two young men strive for domination. One represents reason and order, the other the sensual, the irrational. The reasonable one is a king—but the irrational one is a god. Thus Dionysus defeats King Pentheus of Thebes, luring him to the Dionysian revels where Pentheus's mother Agave, maddened by the god, will tear her son to pieces.

This is Euripides's last play, produced posthumously, as was *Sophocles's *Oedipus at Colonus.* But where Sophocles bids farewell to art believing in a world in which most things seek harmony, Euripides shows us a world in which terror and chaos are the overwhelming forces. Dionysus is not merely Pentheus's rival but the destroyer of all who deny him, bloodthirsty and implacable. The use of the chorus to play Dionysus's devotees marks one of the most colorful exploitations of the Greek singing-dancing ensemble; during the "group grope" era of the late 1960s, *The Bacchae* was a favorite subject for improvisational revision, most notoriously by Richard Schechner's gang, the Performance Group, as *Dionysus in '69* (1968). Much closer to Euripides is John Bowen's *The Disorderly Women* (1969), set in Pentheus's Thebes but written in modern English, with contemporary references.

BACK TO METHUSALEH

"A metabiological pentateuch" by *George Bernard Shaw, prem. New York, 1922.

The customary Shavian preface recalls to us the notion of evolution, before and after Darwin, with a great deal of debunking of various scientists and philosophers, especially Darwin. The notion of chance in the development of species, Shaw contends, is suicidal; thus the world sits back and lets things like World War I occur. No. Evolution must be *willed*. We have to decide what we need to become and then become it: wise. And in order to become wise we must live longer than the customary seventy years, for only ancients are sage.

Back to Methusaleh is "a bible for Creative Evolution," five plays starting in the Garden of Eden and ending on a summer afternoon in the year 31,920 A.D. in a new Eden wherein children are hatched out of eggs, enjoy a curtailed adolescence, and immediately assume the gravity and contemplation of the wise. Passion has been put by; flesh and blood are no more than a structure for existence:

THE NEWLY BORN: What is your destiny?

THE HE-ANCIENT: To be immortal.

THE SHE-ANCIENT: The day will come when there will be no people, only thought.

This possibility may be attractive to Shaw, who apparently regarded sex as an irritation, but it is not difficult to see why few if any people have taken Shaw's Creative Evolution seriously. Shaw thought of *Back to Methusaleh* as his masterpiece, and it does make for intriguing reading. But it is rather talky theatre, even for Shaw. As with most of his middle-period plays, the *Theatre Guild mounted the premiere, and, as Shaw refused to allow any cuts, each performance ran to three nights. This further blunted the play's influence. Later, truncated one-night performances also failed to establish it.

Incidentally, the play's title comes from Part Two, *The Gospel of the Brothers Barnabas,* which takes place in Shaw's own time. As one of the biologist brothers explains, "Political and social problems raised by our civilization cannot be solved by mere human mushrooms who decay and die when they are just beginning to have a glimmer of the wisdom and knowledge needed for their own government." The brothers are prepared to politicize their theory, trying it before the voters on the slogan, "Back to Methusaleh!"

BACKDROP (See Scenery)

FRANK BACON (1864–1922)

Bacon is a legend among American character actors, for after plugging away at supporting roles and bits all his life, he collaborated with Winchell Smith on a *vehicle designed to set Bacon off in his usual character of the wily, tall tale–telling scalawag. The character was "Lightnin' " Bill Jones, the play was *Lightnin'* (1918), and Bacon, at the age of fifty-four, became a star. He was enjoying the first anniversary of his Broadway glory in late summer of 1919 when the very young and powerless Actor's Equity called a strike against the producers. Some actors joined the action; others opposed it. But when Bacon threw his weight behind the union and walked out of *Lightnin'*, the strike was absolute and Equity earned its colors. When new contracts were signed and the shows reopened, *Lightnin'* went on to break Broadway's long-run record at 1,291 performances. The joyous Bacon was in Chicago on the play's national tour when he died.

GEORGE PIERCE BAKER

(1866–1935)

A surprising number of important American dramatists took Baker's workshop in playwrighting, Harvard's famous English 47, later transferred to Yale. *Edward Sheldon, *Eugene O'Neill, *Philip Barry, and Sidney Howard were among those present. However, O'Neill, at least, registered mixed feelings about Baker's effect. The professor seemed as admiring of tradition as he was ready to encourage innovation. Still, Baker was virtually the mentor of the generation of writers who led American drama from about 1910 into the 1950s.

THE BALCONY

Anti-fascist masquerade by *Jean Genet, prem. London, 1957.

The (Grand) Balcony is a brothel trying to carry on business as usual during the highly Interesting Times of civil war—Franco's Spain, perhaps, in the 1930s. This is Genet's miniature of society: nonentities come to the bordello to fulfill fantasies of power, of sadism and submission. The genuine authorities are on hand as well. But, given the masquerade, what difference does it make whether the authority of power is true or false? It is the costumes of importance, not important people, that run society. Roles, no matter how crucial, may be "distributed" at will. Thus it has become a convention of productions of *The Balcony* to build up the costumes of the "bishop," the "judge," the "general" to emphasize their anti-realistic nature. At the final curtain, the brothel keeper Madame Irma declares herself ready to prepare the studios and outfits for the next day's work, though the city is rent by revolution. She dismisses the audience; their homes, she warns, are even more artificial than The Grand Balcony of the role players. She directs the public to a side exit, through an alley, for their safety: the revolution is real. Ideally, there should be no curtain calls—and Genet would like a little machine-gun fire, from somewhere outside the theatre, to usher his public out.

THE BALD SOPRANO

One-act *absurdist "anti-play" by *Eugène Ionesco, prem. Paris, 1950.

Ionesco was originally going to call it *L'Anglais sans Peine* (English Without Pain), because he wrote it after running through an English primer made of extraordinarily banal sentences. Mr. and

Four views of the original production of Shaw's Back to Methusaleh, *by the Theatre Guild in 1922. Above, Part One,* In the Beginning, *closes in Mesopotamia, East of Eden, where "Adam delved and Eve span," as our photograph illustrates. Eve (Ernita Lascelles), the First Creator, bitterly observes to Adam (George Gaul) that "death is gaining on life. Already most of our grandchildren die before they have sense enough to know how to live." The human lifespan needs to catch up to the venerability that brings humans to wisdom. But lo, we move on (bottom left) to Part Three,* The Thing Happens, *set in 2170 A.D. in the parlor of the President of the British Islands (A. P. Kaye, center), here in conference with Confucius (Claude King) and the Archbishop of York (Stanley Howlett)—who is, at the time this photograph was taken, 283 years old. Taking seventy-eight as the typical lifetime, Confucius notes that the government owes the Archbishop "two and a half educations and three and a half retiring pensions." Center, Part Four,* Tragedy of an Elderly Gentleman, *takes us to the year 3000, by which time the capital of the British Commonwealth is Baghdad, though our shot gives us a pier on the south shore of Galway Bay in Ireland (Lascelles again, left, with Albert Bruning). Note that the tradition of costuming spokesman-like characters as Shaw himself is already underway. By Part Five,* As Far as Thought Can Reach *(right), we are well into outright science fiction—the two posing figures (Gaul, Lascelles) represent "the very highest living organism that can be produced in the laboratory." So boasts their creator, Pygmalion (Kaye, with upraised hand). Yet five minutes after their entrance, one of the artificial humans has killed Pygmalion. This suggests a cyclic structure, from the First Murder to what Shaw implies is the Last. And he closes his five-play pageant with the ghosts of Adam, Eve, Cain, and the Serpent, leaving us with the promise that death can be mastered. And what is beyond eternal life? Even Shaw cannot guess. "It is enough that there is a beyond."*

Mrs. Smith discoursed on where they lived, how many children they had, what he did in the office . . . then along came Mr. and Mrs. Martin to multiply the uncommunicative communications. And there, worrying over the profound vapidity of language in a vapid age, Ionesco found his first play. The Smiths begin it, the Martins continue it, a maid and an intruding fire chief do a little of this and a little of that, and, after a full-cast explosion of words, syllables, letters, and sounds, the Martins close the play with the lines the Smiths had used to open it: "There, it's nine o'clock. We've drunk the soup, and eaten the fish and chips . . ." Though *The Bald Soprano* is commonly taken as a revelation of the frailty of human intercourse, Ionesco meant it as an assault on the emptiness of bourgeois life. The original mounting was a failure, but a revival later in the decade became as much a mainstay of the theatre scene in Paris as the Agatha Christie mystery *The Mousetrap* did in London. At the present writing, *La Cantatrice Chauve* has just passed its nine thousandth performance.

AMIRI BARAKA (1934–   )

America's culturally revolutionary 1960s found reflection in the theatre: in antiwar plays like *The Serpent,* in sexually liberated plays like *Oh! Calcutta!,* and in plays by black writers exploring the failure of American race relations. Some of these were belligerently separatist, obsessed with "getting Whitey," raping his women, and burning his cities. LeRoi Jones was the outstanding member of this group, for the power of his anger if not for the quality of his language. Jones arrived on *off-Broadway with *Dutchman* (1964), set in a subway car, in which a white slut seduces then murders a young black bourgeois. Jones pursued his program: *The Slave* (1964) gloats over a black victory in a race war of the future; *The Toilet* (1964) romanticizes the beating of a white boy by his black schoolmates; *Slave Ship* (1967), less representationally, juxtaposes the title's historical setting with modern times in a collage of vignettes and ritual enactments. At the time of *Slave Ship,* Jones, now a Black Muslim, threw off the "slave name" inherited from his parents and the past and became Amiri Baraka, "Blessed Prince."

JEAN-LOUIS BARRAULT (1910–   )

Barrault may be the most gifted French thespian of the twentieth century. Certainly, his talents—as actor, director, and mime—benefited from exposure to many of the major forces in modern French theatre: producers *Charles Dullin and *Jacques Copeau, Etienne Decroux (Barrault's tutor in mime), and even Antonin Artaud, captain of the *surrealist lunatic fringe and developer of the *Theatre of Cruelty. Barrault started off with a bang, giving a mime adaptation of William Faulkner's novel *As I Lay Dying* as *Autour d'une Mère* (All Around a Mother, 1935). The staging was extreme, entirely in dumb show but for two speeches, costumed in the near-nude (though "costumed" is not precisely the word), and stylized far beyond the harlequin pathos that most spectators expected from the very concept of the word "mime." Town jesters dubbed it *Autour d'une Merde* (All Around a Turd), and Barrault's first master Dullin cried, "Compared with this, Artaud is *Boulevard!"

Yet now Barrault was to pursue his career at the most conservative of theatres, the House of Molière itself, the *Comédie-Française. As actor, Barrault suffered a disaster when he took over Don Rodrigue in *Corneille's *Le Cid,* but as director he did handsomely by *Racine's *Phèdre* and soon enough made his reputation with the very first mounting of *Paul Claudel's *Le Soulier de Satin* (The Satin Slipper), in 1943. The play had been published twenty years earlier but was thought unstageable—too long, too big, too serious. Barrault talked Claudel into extensive cuts and enlivened the pageant with bizarrerie and comic *business. The production was a very rich mix—but then so is the play.

Thus established as a director, Barrault formed his own company in 1946 with his actress wife Madeleine Renaud (1900–   ), a noted comedienne, especially in Molière and *Marivaux. At the Théâtre Marigny, the Compagnie Renaud-Barrault balanced classics with new work, *Chekhov with

*Cocteau, *Aeschylus's *Oresteia* and Racine's *Bérénice* with *Feydeau's *Occupe-toi d'Amélie* and *Ionesco's *Rhinocéros* in its world premiere, Barrault directing and playing Bérenger. The troupe so distinguished itself in the 1950s that the French Minister of Culture, André Malraux, invited Barrault to head a second *national theatre at the Odéon. Here Barrault stressed the contemporary, with more Ionesco, *Samuel Beckett, and the first production of *Jean Genet's very controversial *The Screens* in 1966. Two years later, during what was known in Paris as "les événements" (the events), rebellious students occupied and trashed the Odéon, and Barrault disgraced himself trying to join the Revolution. (The disgusted Renaud refused to take part in this offense to everything she stood for as artist and citizen.) When the smoke cleared, Barrault was dismissed. But then he seems as comfortable free-lancing as he does when institutional. He has toured extensively, to India, Alaska, Vietnam, Israel. But perhaps his most famous performance is that of the mime Debureau in that staple of revival house cinema, *Les Enfants du Paradis* (1943).

JAMES M. BARRIE (1860–1937)

As novelist and playwright, this Scotsman worked a unique territory in wistful fantasy. Biographers have revealed a man of bloodless appetites, a worshipper rather than a lover of women and a chastely avuncular devotee of little boys. No wonder, then, that Barrie's theatre dotes on skittish, adolescent-seeming women, on dull men, and on dream episodes in which we fly from reality into wish fulfillment. Typically, *Peter Pan* (1904) is Barrie's classic: its *protagonist is a young hero, but so tender a hero that Barrie insisted that only a woman could play it. Framed by scenes in the nursery of the Darling family, the play is essentially a voyage into a young boy's idea of fairyland, where instead of growing up and marrying, one befriends Indians, frolics with mermaids, and battles pirates. In *Peter Pan,* even Captain Hook is tolerable, vicious but amusing. The sole danger is erotic love. Peter is quite happy to retain Wendy's services as Neverland mother; but when, back in London, she

suggests they become affianced, he callously repulses her. Only innocence enjoys citizenship in Barrie's dream world.

Barrie did leave one interesting social comedy unlike his other fare, *The Admirable Crichton* (1902), a somewhat hard-edged look at England's class structure. Crichton, the austerely resourceful butler, becomes the king of the island on which he and his employers are shipwrecked because they have no survival skills and he can do anything. All defer to him. But, once back in England, everything resorts itself into the conventional pecking order, and Crichton, butler again, rejects the noble woman who loves him. "You are the best man among us," she insists. "On an island, my lady," he agrees, "but in England, no." Barrie isn't supporting the system; he is exposing its reckless rigidity. It is clear that he admires Crichton. Crichton *is* admirable. Still, such intrepidity Barrie normally preferred to discern in feyer personalities. "Pan!" cries Captain Hook, bested in the climactic swordfight. "Who and what art thou?" "I'm youth, I'm joy," cries Peter. "I'm a little bird that has broken out of the egg!" An enchanting notion, enchantingly developed. Think of it: pirates and Indians, the public clapping to revive Tinker Bell, and the delightful Lost Boys, all little birds broken out of the egg. Nevertheless, novelist Anthony Hope, author of *The Prisoner of Zenda,* was heard to remark as he left the theatre, "Oh, for an hour of Herod!"

PHILIP BARRY (1896–1949)

For most of his career, Barry balanced his forte, light social comedy, with more ambitious works in fantasy or allegory. Yet the public did not enjoy the serious, questioning, nonrealistic Barry. He was the poet of the "carriage trade," the Knickerbocker wit, and it is for his entertainments that he is remembered: *Holiday* (1928), *The Animal Kingdom* (1932), *The Philadelphia Story* (1939)—all about the need to defy convention and take life impulsively. This thesis in fact formed the thematic information for one of Hollywood's unique genres, screwball comedy. Barry supplied the setting, the characters, and the salient aperçu. Hol-

Two quite different Broadway versions of Barrie's Neverland hero Peter Pan: (above) in 1905, Maude Adams is farouche and ethereal, even in duel with Captain Hook (Ernest Lawford), though we sense genuine worry from (left to right) Wendy (Mildred Morris), John (Walter Robinson), Michael (Martha McGraw), Nana the dog (Charles H. Weston, behind Lawford), and the Lost Boys, all but one, like Martha McGraw's Michael, a young woman travestita. The *pantomime dog and the *"trouser roles" look back to old theatre traditions. But (right) in 1950, Hollywood refugee Jean Arthur is trim and bold, even given her famous crackly vocal delivery, halfway between incredulity and sass. It was a sassy production in general, in rather informal modern dress—note the very contemporary Howdy Doody doll hanging on the right corner of the blackboard. Barrie was so determined on women playing Peter that not till 1982 did a major troupe, the *Royal Shakespeare Company, dare Peter Pan with a male lead.

lywood added mobility, energy, oddball assistants —and a verbal cleverness that *Holiday* and *The Animal Kingdom* lack. Yet Barry, in his turn, learned from the movies. When Katharine Hepburn, a Hollywood washout, commissioned a hit from Barry—it *must* be a smash—he reclaimed his screwball format, absorbing some of its Hollywood emendations. Above all, Barry waxed clever this time, and placed Hepburn like a perfect jewel in an inevitable setting: *The Philadelphia Story.* This was the apex of Barry, his best and most enduring play. Those in search of the alternate, the weighty Barry, should investigate *Hotel Universe* (1930), considered shocking because it observed the *unities to the point of denying its public an intermission; and *Here Come the Clowns* (1938), riddle-of-life symbolism redolent of 1930s forced naiveté. These plays indict, explore, encourage. *The Philadelphia Story* captivates.

THE BARRYMORES (See The Drews)

LILIAN BAYLIS (See The Old Vic and Sadler's Wells)

THE BEARD

Post-"beat generation" one-acter for two players by Michael McClure (c. 1935–   ), prem. San Francisco, 1965.

Shocking in its youth for its bold language and even bolder finale, *The Beard* anticipates hip *Sam Shepard's use of American archetypes in its cast of Jean Harlow and Billy the Kid. (McClure was a founding member of San Francisco's "beat" scene in the 1950s.) Hostile yet flirtatious, the two "stars" pace around each other verbally, trading in images of self-love, star-worship, and sex till the three ideas intertwine. *The Beard*'s opening lines,

constantly repeated throughout the piece, set it up neatly:

HARLOW: Before you can pry any secrets from me, you must first find the real me. Which one will you pursue?

THE KID: What makes you think I want to pry secrets from you?

HARLOW: Because I'm so beautiful.

THE KID: So what!

HARLOW: You want to be as beautiful as I am.

THE KID: Oh yeah!

At the finale, he goes down on her as she screams out, *"Star! Star! Star!,"* the major reason why authorities and police harassed productions in San Francisco, Berkeley, and Los Angeles, forcing the intervention of the American Civil Liberties Union. It is also, no doubt, why devilish *Kenneth Tynan called *The Beard* "a milestone in the history of heterosexual art."

BEAUMARCHAIS (1732–1799)

Pierre-Augustin Caron. Beaumarchais represents French *farce halfway between *Molière and *Feydeau: more heavily plotted than his predecessor and more humanistically philosophical than his successor. Beaumarchais was a number of things besides dramatist, and his output is not large. However, it does include the *Figaro* trilogy, *Le Barbier de Seville* (1775), *Le Mariage de Figaro* (written 1781, prem. 1784), and *La Mère Coupable* (The Guilty Mother, 1795), famed beyond the spoken stage for operatic settings by Rossini (of the *Barber*) and Mozart (of *Figaro*). Beaumarchais's style is impudence, velocity, ingenuity, especially in *Figaro,* one of the most active but also one of the most politically defiant plays written during the eras when the Western stage suffered censorship. The gap between *Figaro*'s composition and premiere, in fact, lay in a Royal ban. But Beaumarchais's private readings so excited interest in his dangerous text —the eponymous *protagonist is a rebellious servant—that even the queen and the most defensively *ancien régime* nobles begged for a performance. The ban forgiven, the piece ran for some 76 performances, a record in the *repertory schedules of the day. The name "Beaumarchais," by the way, derives from the estate owned by Caron's wife.

THE BEAUTY PART

Satiric *farce by S. J. Perelman (1904–1979), prem. New York, 1962.

Perelman's loony picaresque takes a young innocent through the disillusioning maze of the American arts scene—disillusioning because everyone the boy meets is after "the beauty part": money. Perelman was a humorist rather than a playwright, and he filled his episodic show with the helter-skelter of his comic pieces—jarring shifts in tone, zany kennings, spoofs of jargon, and the characteristic Perelman nomenclature, including available beauty April Monkhood, sleazy womanizing actor Rob Roy Fruitwell, parvenu Seymour Krumgold, and dowager Mrs. Lafcadio Miflin. The real beauty part of the show is the star slot, five characters—suave plutocrat, sadistic magazine editrix, Hollywood producer, right-wing paranoid millionaire, television judge—to be played by one comedian. Bert Lahr, in the original Broadway production, was so brilliant that the work is virtually unthinkable without him, and thus is seldom revived. Lahr's unique voice and delivery haunt, for example, this exchange between the movie producer, Harry Hubris, and the actor, till recently a bus boy in Fort Wayne, Indiana. Readying his protégé for the lead in a movie bio of the painter John Singer Sargent, Lahr's Hubris leaped from con-man wheedling to mean-streets sarcasm, a Bowery Voltaire:

HUBRIS: (Whips open attaché case, produces smock and beret) Here, slip these on so you'll get used to the feel.
ROB ROY: What the hell are we making, a costume picture? You said I wear a sweatshirt and jeans.
HUBRIS: (dripping with sucrose) In the love scenes, pussycat. But when you're like sketching and dreaming up your different

masterpieces, we got to blueprint you're a artist. It establishes your identity.
ROB ROY: The way a sheriff puts on a tin star?
HUBRIS: Or a bus boy his white coat.

FRANCIS BEAUMONT (See Elizabethan Theatre)

JULIAN BECK (See The Living Theatre)

SAMUEL BECKETT (1906–   )

"I started writing for the theatre," he said, "because I hated it." From any other playwright, these would be strange words, but Beckett's steady progression into the anti-play, the nonevent without set, characters, or action, suggests that he continued to hate the theatre while becoming one of its most celebrated authors, even unto winning the Nobel Prize in 1969.

Beckett, an Irishman self-exiled in Paris, where he knew James Joyce, was a novelist of no renown whatsoever when he wrote *En Attendant Godot* (Waiting for Godot, 1953): in French, which he chose for all his works in this period specifically to subdue any accidental flights his native English might take. He wanted to write plain, short, empty. And he did. *Godot*'s tramps doing vaudeville while waiting for nothing to happen became the emblematic work of the postwar Western theatre. It is by far Beckett's most effective presentation of his world of confinement, stasis, babble, and fear. Yet in his very next play, *Fin de Partie* (Endgame, 1957), Beckett was already pulling back, reducing his world, muting his characters, denying his action even as he acted. He troubled to make his own English translations of the French originals, but he gave himself less to say. Two of *Endgame*'s four characters spend the play encased in garbage cans and do little more than cry. *Krapp's*

Last Tape (1958) goes further, with a single character who does nothing but play old tapes of himself talking, to reflect on them in bitter nostalgia. The ironically titled *Happy Days* (1961) gives us two characters, but the main one, Winnie, is buried in sand throughout the work, which consists largely of her monologue.

So it went, small plays getting ever smaller in a minimalism of composition: *Not I* (1973) shows us nothing but a woman's lips and a dim, robed figure, as an unseen actress speaks another Beckettian monologue; but *Breath* (1969) went yet further—a few moments of gasping: little to hear and nothing to see at all. It was written for *Oh! Calcutta!* and withdrawn when *Kenneth Tynan proposed to stage it with nude bodies copulating, a life-affirming betrayal of the sterile Beckettian scene.

But is it art? Or: it *is* art, but is it *theatre?* *Godot*'s comedy and surprises and *Krapp*'s at times affecting revelations hold the stage. But too much of the rest of Beckett does, as he warned, hate the theatre. Worse, Beckett hates life, rejecting its very possibilities with scatalogical ridicule and puns about nothing. Some of our greatest actors have paid their homage—Bert Lahr appeared in the first New York production of *Godot*, Peggy Ashcroft as well as Jessica Tandy and Hume Cronyn have played *Happy Days,* Tandy gave the world premiere of *Not I,* and Cronyn and *Albert Finney have given life to *Krapp*. Still, one wonders how much Beckett's nothing has to tell us about the complicated business of being alive.
(See also *Waiting for Godot*.)

BRENDAN BEHAN (1923-1964)

As boozy, eccentric, charming, and perverse as any stage Irishman of turn-of-the-century comedy, Behan wrote his plays to suit himself. He finished only two, *The Quare Fellow* (1954) and *An Giall* (The Hostage, 1958). (A third, *Richard's Cork Leg,* was still in composition at his death.) As *The Quare Fellow* and *The Hostage* were heavily revised for their first London productions at *Joan Littlewood's Theatre Workshop, and as the revisions somewhat shifted the originals into the recognizable macabre music hall style that Littlewood fancied, it has been said that Littlewood more or less "created"

Behan's theatre. She surely aided it; but Behan is Behan, and his two international successes bear his stamp in all major particulars, most notably in the deliberately off-kilter shape and tone of *The Hostage.* The subject is serious—a British soldier is held prisoner in pledge for an IRA man about to be hanged. There will be *no* executions . . . or *two.* But Behan, typically, locks his hostage not in some hugger-mugger IRA safe house prowled by square-jawed freedom fighters, but in a brothel peopled by a kind of grotesque version of *You Can't Take It with You*'s screwballs. Bawdy farce intrudes on moments of great tenderness; and at the end, when the hostage is accidentally shot, he immediately leaps up to lead the cast in a song. Behan called *The Hostage* "an uproarious tragedy." (See also *The Quare Fellow*.)

S. N. BEHRMAN (1893-1973)

Along with *Philip Barry, Behrman was America's major author of *comedies of manners in the years from the late 1920s through World War II. In his prime, the time of *The Second Man* (1927), *Brief Moment* (1931), *Biography* (1932), *Rain from Heaven* (1934), and *No Time for Comedy* (1939), Behrman was compared to Noël Coward. But Behrman lacked Coward's wit. Behrman was smooth and urbane but seldom sharp. He became politicized in the 1930s—*Rain from Heaven,* though set at an English house party, pictures the confrontation of German and American fascists and a refugee from Hitler, and *No Time for Comedy* worries over the usefulness of drawing room elegance in a world at war. Still, comedy was Behrman's forte, useful or not, especially comedy as played by Behrman's stars the *Lunts, Ina Claire, Jane Cowl, and *Katharine Cornell. Throughout his career, Behrman specialized in adaptations, both from fiction and foreign language plays, and by the 1940s he had become dependant on this secondary work.
(See also *Brief Moment*.)

DAVID BELASCO (1859-1931)

It is said that the actor George Arliss met with the playwright, producer, and director David Belasco in the latter's office in the old Belasco Theatre (now a movie house) on Forty-second Street between Seventh and Eighth Avenues. Arliss was up for a part in Belasco's *The Darling of the Gods* (1902), specifically that of the villain, Zakkuri. Arliss read for Belasco. After a long pause, barely moving at all, Belasco asked Arliss to return the next day and hear the Master's decree. Arliss returned as ordered. And there was Belasco sitting at his desk *precisely as Arliss had last seen him the day before*: "He had waited patiently and silently, perhaps without food or water, for my return." Or so Belasco made it seem.

Belasco hired Arliss for *The Darling of the Gods*; he always hired the best. To be a Belasco star had such cachet that Mary Pickford, who was to make uncountable millions in the movies and became perhaps the most famous person in the world, long looked upon her film work as a comedown after her exposure to Belasco in a small part in *The Warrens of Virginia* (1907).

However, Belasco's casting of actors was not as impressive as Belasco's casting of himself. Belasco's life and art were, together, a performance, whether in his PR manifestations in his minister's collar, in his temperamental management of his stars, in his evocative set and lighting effects. Everything in Belasco was absolute theatre. His working-class plays made a theatre of life with sets apparently (and sometimes literally) dragged in from the slums—a boardinghouse parlor, a tenement room, a pancake house. His romances tendered the scent of Japan, the ice of gold rush California. His public saw steam rising from coffee urns, shivered in his snow.

Some thought him a precursor of a new era of verisimilitude, but he more truly capped the nineteenth century movement toward honesty—at that, in a most dishonest way. Yes, Belasco's productions experimented with the atmospheric power of lighting and decor. But the plays he wrote (more often, co-authored) were largely pilfered from old fashion, especially the melodramas of *Victorien Sardou. Those who know opera will place George Arliss's role in *The Darling of the Gods* as a copy of Scarpia in Puccini's *Tosca*—from Sardou's play, while we're at it. Not surprisingly, Belasco similarly served Puccini, as the source of *Madama Butterfly*, from *Madame Butterfly* (1900),

and *La Fanciulla del West*, from *The Girl of the Golden West* (1905), yet another borrowing from Sardou: *Tosca* with sixguns and poker.

JACINTO BENAVENTE (See Federico García Lorca)

THE BERLINER ENSEMBLE

Retaining Austrian citizenship and a Swiss bank account, *Bertolt Brecht went to East Berlin in 1949 to found a company on Brechtian principles. Perhaps the Berliner Ensemble was less founded than merely permitted to happen. First, the troupe was nothing more permanent than a production of *Mother Courage*, mounted by Brecht at the invitation of the East German authorities and housed at the historic Deutsches Theater, one of *Max Reinhardt's old haunts. Then the show went on tour through the two Germanys, especially the Western one: for these same authorities of the East were uncomfortable with the "formalist" tendencies of the Brechtian style. As in Russia and all Soviet bloc nations. *"socialist realism" was the only acceptable form of theatre. Brecht the international celebrity was splendid prestige; but Brecht the thespian could be dangerous. Nevertheless, that first production of *Mother Courage* led to a full-fledged company, which moved in 1954 from the Deutsches Theater to the Theater am Schiffbauerdamm, where the original production of *Die Dreigroschenoper* (The Threepenny Opera) had played in 1928.

After Brecht's death in 1956, the Berliner Ensemble was run by his widow, Helene Weigel (1900–1971), famed for her exemplary performance (the word "portrayal" would be misleading, given the intellectual, nonorganic nature of Brechtian acting) of the heroines of *Mother Courage* and *St. Joan of the Stockyards*. Weigel's doughy figure and sodden demeanor were antithetical to what we normally expect in the word "actress," but then the entire Berliner Ensemble defeated stereotype in looks and behavior. They weren't actors, it appeared: they were people. The Ensemble has been accused of seeing itself as a nonstop Brecht festival, but this is like accusing the summer opera at Bayreuth of being a Wagner festival. It *is* a Wagner festival; and the Berliner Ensemble, less officially, is Brecht's troupe, though the company has also staged such politically appropriate dramatists as *Georg Büchner, *Frank Wedekind, and even *George Bernard Shaw.

JEAN-JACQUES BERNARD (See The Theatre of the Unexpressed)

SARAH BERNHARDT (1844–1923)

Bernhardt's life was so picturesque that a television bio, written by Suzanne Grossman for the brilliant Zoë Caldwell, was fabulous and bizarre and silly without exaggerating in the least. For here was a legend that really worked at being legendary, an actress of incomparable eccentricity who was also a tough businesswoman; a tragedienne of note in Racine, Hugo, and Shakespeare who paraded about in claptrap *vehicles by the hacks of her day; a woman known to fall obsessively in love with opportunists but who nevertheless braved the anti-Semites (Bernhardt was half-Jewish) to take the side of Alfred Dreyfus in France's great national scandal. "If there's anything more remarkable than watching Sarah act," remarked the playwright Victorien Sardou, "it's watching her live."

In historical details, Bernhardt emphasizes the contemporary transition from the company structure to the free-lancing, self-owned star. As befits a French actress, she was elected to the *Comédie-Française, but could not stomach that theatre's love of tradition, and broke away to join the less case-hardened troupe at the Odéon on the Left Bank. Though Bernhardt returned to the Comédie-Française at times, she vastly preferred the tour, assembling her own troupes for travels through Europe, to England, and even to America, where she was an immense success despite the language barrier (she gave everything, including Shakespeare, in French), her outspoken distaste for American mores, and resistance from the *Syndicate that drove her into skating rinks and circus tents.

Sarah had her great roles—*Racine's Phèdre, Marguerite Gauthier in *Dumas's *La Dame aux Camélias,* Sardou's Tosca, Napoleon's son in Rostand's *L'Aiglon.* But perhaps more than any other actor, Sarah was more than her roles. Sarah was an event. "What she cares about," complained Anton Chekhov, working as a theatre critic when Sarah swept into Russia in 1881, "is to be unusual. Her plan is to shock, astonish, amaze." She had a leg amputated and still wouldn't retire. "What's a leg?" she shrugged. On one of her American tours, someone remarked to her that she was getting more attention than Dom Pedro of Brazil, whose visit had preceded hers. "Yes," Sarah agreed. "But he was only an emperor."

THOMAS BETTERTON (?1635–1710)

The outstanding male actor of the *Restoration. Physically unprepossessing, Betterton held his public with a fine voice and a robust sense of character, sharp in comedy and grand in tragedy. His Hamlet remained a legend for generations, not least for its alleged authenticity: Betterton modeled his portrayal on that of Joseph Taylor, who in turn modeled his portrayal on that of Shakespeare's Hamlet himself, Richard Burbage.

MASTER BETTY (1791–1874)

At the age of thirteen, this child actor from Belfast, already seasoned on the provincial circuit, became a London sensation at *Covent Garden as Achmet in a tragedy called *Barbarossa.* Master Betty was "the Young *Roscius," handsome, soft, bright, quick. Most thespians thought him mechanical, a triumph of coaching rather than talent. But the public was infatuated and the critics, seizing the trend, intensified it. "Some vociferated that [*David] Garrick was returned to the stage," noted the novelist and playwright Elizabeth Inch-

"The Divine Sarah," as the age knew her, complete with autograph inscription. History trembles as we read, even if we can't make out her handwriting.

bald, who added, "I hate all *prodigies.*" Like so many, this one was shortlived, though Master Betty's stardom did last long enough for him to try not only Hamlet, Richard III, and Romeo but one of Mrs. Inchbald's comedies, *Lovers' Vows.* Just before young Betty began his second season, an even younger player, Miss Mudie, was hissed off the Covent Garden stage, not out of loyalty to Betty but in reaction against all child actors. Betty was able to prolong his career for a bit in the provinces, but his London stardom and history were over forever.

THE BIBIENA FAMILY (See The Galli-Bibiena Family)

BLACK COMEDY

A veritable prostitute of a term, so available that it changes according to the wishes of the user. Critics' efforts to describe twentieth century forms that seem to be some blend of the comic and the tragic, or something beyond them (as well as efforts to look into the past for possible sources) have thrown up such terms as "tragicomedy" and "dark comedy." Such playwrights as Anton Chekhov and Jean Anouilh in particular invoke such distinctions, the former because he described as "comedies" *The Seagull, Uncle Vanya,* and *The Cherry Orchard*—which, despite moments of humor, can scarcely be taken as comic constructions—and the latter because such works as *The Traveler Without Luggage* and *The Waltz of the Toreadors* yield bite as well as sweet wit. *Absurdism, too, often seems as funny as it is serious—ridiculous, even, on the world's direst topics. Samuel Beckett's very serious *Waiting for Godot,* for instance, *acts* like a comedy —much of Vladimir and Estragon's dialogue works best in the delivery of a vaudeville duo.

However, the very suggestion of a "theatre of the absurd," like tragicomedy and dark comedy, covers with majestic vagueness most of the possibilities in the twentieth century's unique invention of forms treating serious situations in a comic manner. Black comedy—as I take it—is a relatively recent development, in which the comic flavor is perverse, wicked, or morbid, in which the author deliberately teases his public by shocking them. *Joe Orton may be the most characteristic black humorist, for his slyly sensationalizing attitude toward his people; and Orton's *Entertaining Mr. Sloane* must be the essential black comedy, for the way Orton luxuriates in erotic gamesmanship while he denounces its moral vapidity—and especially in the way Orton arranges for a "happy ending" in a murderer's joint "marriage" with the brother and sister whose father he killed.

An odd footnote: Peter Shaffer's long one-actor *Black Comedy* (1965) is nothing of the kind. Pure *farce, it takes its title from a power mishap that plunges the characters into darkness. The play begins in absolute black. *They* can see; we cannot. Then their electricity goes, and the stage explodes in violently bright light as we watch them tripping and colliding.

(See also *Butley, The Cherry Orchard, The Quare Fellow, Rhinocéros,* and *Waiting for Godot.*)

EDWARD BOND (1934–   )

Ever since *John Osborne, English playwrights have lived on controversy. But this particular playwright may be the most controversial of all the post–World War II generation, not only for the hammering force of his leftism, but for the graphic violence he employs to push his points home. Violence in Bond is not a metaphor, a style. In Bond, violence is violence: war, personal aggression or self-defense, even the gratuitous violence of a gang of hoods killing a baby in its carriage for the sport of it. Bond says he turned out to be the kind of dramatist he is because of his army service, which forced him to look at the world in a new way: "The army's a sort of parodied version of civil society— it's without all the face-saving rituals and without all the social excuses and just the naked barbarism . . . an amalgam of sentimental sloppy reverence for dead idols combined with a real viciousness." Thus, "I write about violence as naturally as Jane Austen wrote about manners. Violence shapes and obsesses our society, and if we do not stop being violent we have no future." Bond, then, is not possessed by violence, as critics contended when he first arrived in the 1960s, at the *Royal Court Theatre. Bond is possessed by a need to purge the social contract of its violence.

In his first plays, *The Pope's Wedding* (1962) and *Saved* (1965), Bond wrote *naturalistically, contemporaneously. But *Narrow Road to the Deep North* (1968) explored nineteenth century Japanese history in a modified *Brechtian style, and *Early Morning,* earlier the same year, had delved into quasi-*absurdist fantasy with real-life figures of Victorian England. At one point, the Queen Herself rapes Florence Nightingale. The play was banned and the Royal Court warned of prosecution if it pursued *Early Morning,* even in the proposed semiprivate "club" setup. The theatre courageously went ahead with the production, precipitating the biggest scandal in the history of the Lord Chamberlain, Britain's theatre censor since 1737. In the end, *Early Morning* was closed by the police, and such was the air of establishment hostility that Bond's publishers feared even to print the text. (Another house brought *Early Morning* out.) This was the last play to be so honored in England. Later that same year, 1968, theatre censorship was abolished in Great Britain.

Meanwhile, Bond had expanded his canvas. Although his politics continued to drive him, he constantly shifted his compositional style, making him one of the richest entertainments (he may hate that word) in English theatre, as single-minded as any moralist yet far more imaginative, more surprising, than most of his contemporaries. Bond's rewriting of Shakespeare, *Lear* (1971), may seem arrogant to the old-fashioned, Brechtian to moderns. Did not Brecht rewrite plays by Christopher Marlowe, Carlo Gozzi, and, yes, Shakespeare, in *Coriolan?* Ironically, Bond's *Lear* is somewhat less violent than *King Lear* and is in any case not a rewriting but an adaptation, for political instead of poetic reasons. A grisly Bondian humor pervades even the Bondian violence, as in a soldier's torturing of Lear's lieutenant Warrington, for the pleasure of Lear's daughters:

FONTANELLE: Jump on his head!

SOLDIER: Lay off, lady, lay off! 'Oo's killin' him, me or you?

BODICE: (knitting) One plain, two purl, one plain.

FONTANELLE: Throw him up and drop him. I want to hear him drop.

SOLDIER: Thass a bit 'eavy, yer need proper gear t'drop 'em—

FONTANELLE: Do something! Don't let him get away with it. O Christ, why did I cut his tongue out? I want to hear him scream . . . Look at his hands! Look at them going! What's he, praying or clutching? Smash his hands! (The Soldier and Fontanelle jump on Warrington's hands.)

FONTANELLE: Kill his hands! Kill his feet! . . . Look at his hands like boiling crabs! Kill it! . . . Make him dead! Father! Father! I want to sit on his lungs!

BODICE: Plain, purl, plain. She was just the same at school.

Bond extended himself to examinations of American racism in *The Swing,* half an evening of one-acters called *A-A-America!* (1976); of homophobia in *Stone* (1976), written for Gay Sweatshop, a British fringe theatre group; of militarism in *The Woman* (1978). "What ought we to do?" Bond writes. "Live justly. But what is justice?" (See also *The Woman.*)

THE BOOTHS

Like most well-known American actors of the early nineteenth century, Junius Brutus Booth (1796–1852) was English. But he made his career in the United States, and sired a theatrical family. His greatest issue was Edwin Booth (1833–1893), an extraordinary tragedian, one of the few actors of his time to achieve a reputation extending beyond London, New York, and the English-speaking touring circuits. Edwin's home in New York's Gramercy Park became (and remains) housing for the famous Players' Club, the thespian equivalent of the typical men's social fraternity but a far livelier organization, with a co-ed membership and plenty of "amateur" theatricals (by pros). However, Junius Brutus's most famous son was not

Edwin but John Wilkes Booth (1839–1865), the man who shot Abraham Lincoln in Ford's theatre in Washington, DC, during a performance of the farce *Our American Cousin*.

DION BOUCICAULT (1820–1890)

This Irish actor and playwright is regarded almost as an American, for he spent much of his fifty-year career in the United States and strongly influenced its stage, in the humanizing of its *melodramas, in the introduction of the "road tour" of a single cast performing a single show (as opposed to the vagabond *stock company, weighed down with a revolving *repertory), and in agitating successfully for the passage of a copyright law to protect playwrights. Boucicault's plays still turn up from time to time, especially *London Assurance* (1841), his first hit, a satire on city sophistication; and *The Octoroon* (1859), a melodrama of love and bigotry in the American South with the added novelty of a camera, so new at the time that the villain of the play doesn't realize that it is taking his photograph in the act of murder. Versatile and prolific—he wrote well over two hundred plays, many of them adaptations from the French—Boucicault gave two children to the theatre, son Dot and daughter Nina, who created the lead in *Barrie's *Peter Pan*.

BOULEVARD THEATRE

The boulevard is Paris's Boulevard du Temple, a kind of *Broadway where stood a host of playhouses committed to popular fare. Thus, "boulevard theatre" is commercial—*farce and *melodrama rather than the classics one would see at the *Comédie-Française.

BOX SET (See Scenery)

ANNE BRACEGIRDLE (c. 1675–1748)

If *Nell Gwyn typifies the first generation of English actresses as charm for hire, "Bracey" (as her colleagues called her) typifies the next generation, as charm inviolable. Here was a Respectable Woman, "the Diana of the stage." She was a particular devotee of *William Congreve: Mrs. Bracegirdle (as her public called her) not only created all his heroines but played his personal heroine offstage. Or so they said.

THE BREASTS OF TIRÉSIAS

"*Surrealist drama" by *Guillaume Apollinaire, prem. Paris, 1917.

A delightful classic of the early avant-garde, successor to *Alfred Jarry's *Ubu Roi* and precursor of *absurdism. The bulk of this short piece was written in 1903, with a prologue and finale added in 1916. Yet unlike so much that was daring in the early 1900s, *Tirésias* remains fresh and crisp and, in its capering way, sensible. In fact, it has a theme, even as *Ibsen or *O'Neill do: a nation that wants to prosper must procreate vigorously. Apollinaire's *protagonist, Thérèse, turns feminist (in fact becomes a man, Tirésias) and leaves her husband, only to return at the end, once more woman and wife.

However, this is the work for which Apollinaire coined the term "surrealism," explaining in a preface that the realist, ideological, thematic theatre of Ibsen was exactly what Apollinaire had had enough of. Surrealism was better than realism: not as lucid, no, but more evocative, more profound, mining the reality hidden by the repressive patterns of society. So Thérèse not only changes sex but gives up her breasts, as balloons which she then explodes; the people of Zanzibar are played by one actor; an assortment of merry lunatics bicker, conspire, and prance about in non sequitur; and the abandoned husband carries on the work of childbearing alone, to a total of 40,049 babies. Apollinaire's fractious jesting, his atmosphere of a happy nightmare, reached ultimate completion as an opera, also called *Les Mamelles de Tirésias* (1947), by Francis Poulenc. This is not an adaptation: Poulenc simply set the text to music.

BERTOLT BRECHT (1898–1956)

Here is the ground zero of modern theatre *as theatre,* the performance that never lets one forget that it is a presentation of ideas. Brecht's theory of epic theatre overthrows everything his predecessors accepted as useful or pleasing in composition and performance. Epic theatre dismisses the pity and terror, the empathy, the catharsis of antecedent forms. Before Brecht, theatre drew its spectators into the action *emotionally.* Brecht holds his spectators at a remove, so they may comprehend the action *intellectually.* Brecht's is not a "feeling" stage; he strips the feelings away in order to demonstrate the processes of System. Thus he can denounce the prevailing church-and-capitalist ethic and urge on the revolutionary Marxist ethic.

Epic theatre is didactic theatre. Brecht himself preferred the latter description, at least partly because his rival, the director *Erwin Piscator, was already associated with the former term. The form, clearly, is not Brecht's invention. But he was the playwright and director who developed it to its very influential greatness. If he didn't invent it, certainly he perfected and individualized it, complete with the essential *Verfremdungseffekt* (*"Alienation" or, more literally, "distancing" Effect) that keeps the audience interested yet alert. The effect might comprise anything from the interpolation of an analytical song or the posting of headlines before each scene, warning us of what is about to happen (so we can interpret rather than experience it), to the chalking of soldiers' faces in a battle scene (to stylize the pallor of fear) or an actor's reading lines in a reportorial or explanatory rather than charac-

terological way. At times, the Brechtian style has the hieratic quality of a pageant, of an intellectualized ritual—but it has its naturalism, too. Staging the premiere of *Edward II,* Brecht became obsessed with a wartime hanging scene, forcing his uncomfortable players through it again and again till they could suggest the casual efficiency of soldiers stringing up a prisoner.

In 1931, Brecht published an essay on the epic theatre, specifically in regard to his and Kurt Weill's opera, *Aufstieg und Fall der Stadt Mahagonny.* What better way to test the ideology of the epic theatre than in the guise of the most unideological form in the West, opera? Brecht won the contest: *Mahagonny* is epic opera. He celebrated with a list outlining the differences between "dramatic theatre" and "epic theatre"—such as (the dramatic) "allows [the spectator] to feel" while (the epic) "forces him to decide": or "adventure" as opposed to "a view of the world"; or "suggestion" as opposed to "argument"; or "an unchanging humanity" as opposed to "changeable and changing humanity." In short, traditional theatre is entertainment that accepts the way of the world. Epic theatre is education that exposes the old way to argue for the new.

However, the didactic quality of the Brechtian stage never impinges on the qualities of flamboyance, screwy comedy, and the picturesque that also inform Brecht's art. This is why these plays are still very much in the *repertory. Often, they seem hard-headed, perversely cynical. But they are always cannily theatrical, inventive, absorbing. If some of Brecht's characters seem more like mouthpieces than characters, that is a facet of his approach, a function of epic dramaturgy.

Brecht was a bit slow in finding his form. His first three plays—*Baal* (written 1918, prem. 1923), *Trommeln in Der Nacht* (Drums in the Night, 1922), and *Im Dickicht der Städte* (In the Jungle of Cities, 1923)—are *expressionist in style. The seldom performed and utterly apolitical *Baal* surprises the Brecht veteran used to the ideological surveys of the more familiar plays; but *In the Jungle of Cities* gives us a taste of the mature Brecht who looked upon the great metropolises of the West as "jungles," cross sections of capitalism's class structure and rapaciousness. Brecht's fourth theatre piece, the *chronicle play *Leben Eduards des Zweiten von England (Life of Edward the Second of England, 1924), is, at least, an avidly political work, yet still not in full epic style. We get the "alienative" headlines describing each scene's action in advance, like the Major Causes and Key Effects of a history teacher. Yet Brecht details the energy of character as much as, if not more than, the energy of economic and social forces. Edward II is a complex work, imaginative, harassing, poetic, and absolutely fearless in its view of the human appetites for love and power that impel the sensual and ascetic, the public and private personalities, alike. Most of Brecht's plays are about history; this play, his most "historic," is about people. Most of Brecht's plays are comic educations; this play is a tragedy. An adaptation of Christopher Marlowe's Edward II, it is close yet not close, following the original's action quite faithfully while giving the characters a sharp edge of modern psychology in almost entirely rewritten or wholly new dialogue. The use of an older source is very Brechtian, as is the use of a collaborator, Lion Feuchtwanger, unbilled but credited in an epigram in the text. Brecht was to adapt quite a number of old plays, even versions of Sophocles's Antigone (1948) and Molière's Don Juan (1953), and he made extensive use of advisors, secretaries, research assistants, and, as here, an outright writing partner.

Edward II ends Brecht's first period, of youth in Augsburg and early maturity in Munich. In 1924 Brecht arrived in Berlin, where he helped bring High Weimar to a climax in—to Brecht—the utmost of city jungles, his German Chicago. "Mahagonny" he dubbed Berlin, relishing the sheer barbaric noise the word gives off in German. In this Berlin period, the epic theatre is fully developed both in composition and production style. Mann Ist Mann (Man Is Man, 1926) is entirely unlike the previous plays, more direct, distinctly comical, and punctuated by ceaseless application of the Alienation Effect. Better yet, Brecht's Berlin years ring in the collaborations with Kurt Weill (1900–1950), most notably Die Dreigroschenoper (The Threepenny Opera, 1928), Happy End (1929), and the aforementioned Aufstieg und Fall der Stadt Mahagonny (Rise and Fall of Mahagonny City, 1930), in which the music—songs and incidentals in the first two and full-scale operatic composition

in the third—bolsters the now resolutely, now playfully commentative nature of the epic theatre. In The Threepenny Opera especially, singing becomes not an expansion of the narrative, not an emotional opening out, but a dissection of its sociopolitical implications, an analytical closing in.

Unfortunately, the Berlin period ends as Weimar democracy did, with the Nazis' accession in 1933. Now Brecht launches his years of exile, cut off from his native culture and theatrical habitat, still writing but often lacking a stage, and seldom in a position to direct his plays in the appropriate style. Typically for this era, Die Heilige Johanna der Schlachthöfe (Saint Joan of the Stockyards), a "Joan of Arc" play set in Brecht's favorite American Mahagonny, Chicago, was written in 1930 but not staged till 1959.

At least Die Rundköpfe und die Spitzköpfe (The Roundheads and the Peakheads, 1936), Shakespeare's *Measure for Measure adapted to treat Nazi racism, and Mutter Courage und Ihre Kinder (Mother Courage and Her Children, 1941), episodes in the life of a profiteering peddler during the Thirty Years' War, reached the theatre within two years of their composition. Brecht was in his prime, however much in distress, turning from the possibly autobiographical confession piece Leben des Galilei (Life of Galileo, written 1939, prem. 1943) to the amusingly hard-headed Der Gute Mensch von Sezuan (The Good Person of Szechuan, written 1940, prem. 1943), thence to the almost loving Der Kaukasische Kreidekreis (The Caucasian Chalk Circle, written 1945, prem. 1948). All of these plays distinguish the epic theatre plan through emphasis of different aspects—Mother Courage's unflinching tragic grandeur within a punishing exposure of history; Galileo's incremental development of a monumental human figure; the Chalk Circle's strenuous use of spectacle and song.

It would be years before these plays could take an honorable place in the European *repertory. (They are still in the process of acclimatization in the United States, and seem to be making more progress in regional companies than on Broadway.) This is even more the case with Brecht's two "Nazi plays," so to say, Furcht und Elend des Dritten Reiches (Fear and Misery in the Third Reich, written 1938, prem. 1945, in English) and Der Aufhaltsame Aufstieg des Arturo Ui (The Resistible Rise of Arturo

Ui, written 1941, prem. 1958), the first a series of *naturalistic cameos (such as "Justice," "The Jewish Wife," and "The Informer"—a schoolboy denouncing his parents, by the way) quite out of the epic theatre line; and the second a kind of mock-Shakespearean *chronicle play that portrays Hitler as a gangster taking over Chicago.

Brecht's last period begins in 1949, when he at last assumed control of his own theatre company, the Berliner Ensemble, in East Berlin. These were interesting times—the rise of the garishly neon-lit, anything-for-money West Berlin, a Mahagonny beyond even Brecht's dreams; the Soviet blockade of the city and the Allies' airlift to feed its besieged citizens; the 1953 uprising of East German workers, ended when Soviet tanks shot down unarmed demonstrators. Yet Brecht managed to keep a foot in each world. He lived in the East, yet he retained a West German publisher, Suhrkamp (to protect himself from Soviet-bloc censorship), an Austrian passport (so he could travel to the West whenever he chose), and a Swiss bank account. This is questionable behavior from a lifelong Communist; we have to wonder how genuine Brecht's principles really were, how we should read the politics of the epic theatre. What might *Arturo Ui* have been like if the model for its world-devouring gangster had been not Hitler but Stalin? More to the point, why did Brecht, whose safety was virtually sacrosanct by that time, not denounce the oppressive government of East Germany in 1953? Brecht denounced the workers. It's a famous controversy, the more so because the authorities printed only a snippet of Brecht's letter to East Germany's honcho commissar Walter Ulbricht, flattering to themselves. Brecht apologists assure us that the letter as a whole showed a more sympathetic Brecht. In fact, the rest of the letter merely shows him temporizing. For all his free world citizenship, Brecht was just another bourgeois of the Gulag, happy as long as it is all the others who are the slaves. It may well be that what keeps his epic theatre fascinating is not its hypocritical lecture, but the style itself, the invigorating theatricality of a performance that keeps saying, Look, I'm a performance. Brecht is, above all, and whether he likes it or not, an entertainer. (See also *Baal, The Caucasian Chalk Circle, Man Is Man, Mother Courage,* and The Berliner Ensemble.)

HOWARD BRENTON (1942–   )

The futuristic fascist *black-comic horror play has become a genre of its own among today's leftist British playwrights, and Brenton gave us the outstanding example in *The Churchill Play* (1974)—"as it will be performed in the winter of 1984," the subtitle runs, "by the internees of Churchill Camp somewhere in England," Brenton has the gift of *going for it,* ending up outstanding through the simple act of not being able to hold back. Writing in a post-Brecht Brechtian manner, ruinously exposing Britain's heroes old and new yet avoiding the smug "I explain the world in two hours" dialectic that troubles some of Brecht's work, Brenton symbolizes the post-modernist radical, eager for a solution to the world's problems yet as cynical about the Party line as about establishment business-as-usual.

Brenton is as much an artistic as a political extremist. Even admitting that *The Romans in Britain* (1980) absurdly attempts to compare Caesar's imperialist invasion of England to the English-Irish Troubles, still the show itself is compellingly written, Brenton's typically questing analysis of human relationships outweighing his political interpretations. *The Romans in Britain* in fact became an act of politicized art when the government attempted a case against the premiere production at the National Theatre of Great Britain because of a scene in which Roman soldiers happen upon three Briton brothers, kill two of them and rape the third, not less shocking because the brothers, a few moments before, quite calmly murdered one of two stranger brothers who themselves had killed a stranger for his iron and his wine. "Didn't he squeal!" one of the culprits gloats. "Didn't he squeal!"

In the world that Brenton surveys—in almost all his plays, whether set in the past, the present, or, as with *The Romans in Britain,* in both—murder is a routine. One wonders if the failed legal harassment of *The Romans in Britain* was based simply on a wish to repress England's dangerous leftist playwrights, on squeamishness at the very frankly presented rape, or on Brenton's suggestion, in the writing of the scene, that male homosexuality is, despite fierce taboo deterrents, an appetite that will never go away. "Good shoulders," says one of the Roman soldiers, running his hand over his rape victim's back. Yet Brenton, curiously, is not really a proselytizer, not even politically. Willing or no, he must call his tales as he knows them, must confront reality, fix his public's eyes upon the truth. This will no doubt keep him in the repertory long after his more strictly political colleagues have been forgot, even after *The Churchill Play*'s 1984 has come and gone without seeing detention camps in Britain. Long art, long life.

BRIEF MOMENT

American *comedy of manners by *S. N. Behrman, prem. New York, 1931.

This is what became of *Restoration comedy in twentieth century America. Behrman's New Yorkers have money, looks, and various more or less pretty malaises, and Behrman is, as always, keen to praise the vigor of the "natural" personality as opposed to the well-bred gentleman or lady. But this tale of an aimless young dandy who marries a nightclub singer lacks wit. At least, it lacks the savor of true social comedy, the sense that nothing in life is too pure to deserve a satiric reproof. Stylistically typical is a character modeled on (and, on Broadway, actually played by) that elf of the Algonquin, Alexander Woollcott. As Harold Sigrift, Woollcott supplied the bulk of the evening's humor:

RODERICK: Well, Sig, how did you come out with your blonde?
SIGRIFT: She's one of those illiterate girls who expect a flowery approach. I didn't feel up to it, so I left her with a *Saturday Evening Post* reader whose success is inevitable.

A veritable town topic, the story was based, it was said, on the capers of the bandleader and "our crowd" scion, Roger Wolfe Kahn.

BROADWAY

Literally: a road that runs, in a cockeyed manner, up the length of Manhattan Island (and right on to Canada, counting highway extensions). Geographically: New York's theatre district. Artistically: a standard of thespian professionalism that in various genres at various eras—the 1920s and 1930s in *farce, the 1930s in working-class *naturalism, the late 1940s and the 1950s in sensationalist *melodrama, and timelessly in the musical—defined the American theatre style at its most intrepid.

Unlike the theatres of the great European cultural capitals, sedentary over the centuries in the city centers, New York's major playhouses have been on the move as a group since the eighteenth century, when plays were staged in the coffeehouses of John Street, way down in what was virtually an anglicized Nieuw Amsterdam. At the turn of the nineteenth century, "Broadway" had moved up Broadway to Park Row, the site of the first major American theatre building, the Park. In the late 1800s, the theatres clustered around Fourteenth Street, further north; but the city action continued to chug uptown, and by the early 1900s new theatres were being built in the Long Acre, the two facing isosceles triangles formed by the crossing of Broadway and Seventh Avenue. Most of today's "Broadway" theatres were erected in the 1920s in the West Forties, by which time the Long Acre had long been known as Times Square, after the New York *Times* building that commanded its southern boundary. (The Longacre Theatre, built in 1913 on West Forty-eighth Street, still stands under its original name as a reminder of Old Times.)

With Forty-second Street's facing lines of theatres almost entirely devoted to sleazy cinema and most outlying theatres razed, "Broadway" now runs from Forty-fourth to Fifty-third Streets within the single block between Broadway and Eighth Avenue, with a very few exceptions—one to the south, one to the west, and three to the east. One odd fact: the many theatres that faced directly onto Broadway some eighty years ago, their marquees feeding thespian data directly onto The Street, have almost all vanished—the Casino, the Empire, the Knickerbocker, the Standard, Weber and Fields's Music Hall, Hammerstein's Theatre (still standing, but given over to television since the 1930s and now named for Ed Sullivan)—leaving only the Broadway, the Winter Garden, and the Palace, plus the relatively new Minskoff and Marquis, to maintain entrances directly along the fabled way.

PETER BROOK (1925–   )

Brook was still in his twenties when he had established a reputation as England's *enfant terrible* of directors. In Shakespeare, at the Shakespeare Memorial Theatre (the home of what was to become the *Royal Shakespeare Company) in Stratford, the daring Brook was accused of classic-bashing. In opera, at *Covent Garden, Brook's vitality vastly startled, not least in his controversial *Salome* with decor by Salvador Dali. In the *West End, Brook impishly, perhaps perversely, staged not only *Jean-Paul Sartre's *No Exit* and *Jean Anouilh's *The Lark* but André Roussin's vapid sex comedy *La Petite Hutte* (The Little Hut) and even a musical, *Irma la Douce* (though here we see a flash of the *épatant* Brook, testing the bourgeoisie with a show whose cast consists of one prostitute and a troop of pimps and crooks).

Brook's major history began when he became codirector of the Royal Shakespeare Company in 1962, for with this company Brook put on his most influential productions: the post-*Godot *King Lear* in 1964, tragedy inverted into comic horror; the 1970 *Midsummer Night's Dream* on circus trapezes in an empty dazzling white box set; and, most notably, the 1964 *Marat/Sade,* which seemed to pull together elements of much that we call most modern in stagecraft, from the *Theatre of Cruelty to the improvisatory ensembles of *Jerzy Grotowski and *Joseph Chaikin.

Unfortunately, like Grotowski and Chaikin, Brook has increasingly deemphasized the communication of text. In 1970, in Paris, he founded the International Centre of Theatre Research, a workshop for the creation of arcane, even incoherent,

theatre pieces—a retelling of the Prometheus legend, for instance, performed on a mountain top in Iran in a newly made-up language called Orghast. It was fair to say, as Robert Brustein did, that Brook "wrestled with all the pressing theatrical issues of the day: the death of the word, the self-consciousness of modernism, the transaction between actors and audiences, the need to disarrange consciousness—all in an effort to make the theatre central once again to the modern sensibility." But this was the former Brook, the *adulte terrible.* The later Brook seems to be making his theatre as uncentral, even as useless, as possible.

GEORG BÜCHNER (1813–1837)

Büchner may be the most anomalous playwright who ever lived, so heedless of what his age considered practical in theatre that his plays waited generations before they were produced. One of them was not performed till three-quarters of a century after it was written. Büchner stands out, too, for his uncanny anticipation, in the early years of the nineteenth century, of methods of composition that are thought of as emblematically "modern"—*naturalism, *expressionism, and even the *absurd. And how many other dramatists maintain an important reputation for an output of only three titles?

These are *Dantons Tod* (Danton's Death, written 1835; prem. 1902), *Leonce und Lena* (written 1836, prem. 1885), and *Woyzeck* (written 1837, prem. 1913). The first is perhaps the most renegade of the trio, for it is at once most and least like the plays of Büchner's time, and thus especially heretical. A heroic tragedy using real-life figures of the French Revolution, *Danton's Death* rejects the very notion of heroism in its nihilistic philosophy. A hero chooses acts, must conquer or die; Büchner's Danton cannot find any meaning in life and thus makes no choice. His death at the guillotine is worthless: because his life is worthless, at least to him. Even more startling is Büchner's form, a montage of thirty-two scenes jumping from the intimate to the epic, some of them as short as a few lines. Nor did Büchner observe the poetic dialogue that was virtually essential in early Romantic tragedy. His characters speak in a shockingly earthy prose.

Leonce and Lena carries this to the scatological: he is Prince of Popo (German slang for "ass") and she the Princess of Pipi ("piss"). Otherwise, however, *Leonce and Lena* is a serene comedy, albeit one that develops Büchner's notion of mankind as puppets, helplessly jerked about on strings. This all-basic Büchnerian theme at length finds its climax in *Woyzeck,* adapted from a celebrated murder case in the city of Leipzig in the 1820s. An apparently psychotic man had murdered a prostitute and was beheaded (like Danton, note) despite the contention that he was insane and therefore unanswerable for his actions.

Woyzeck is the ultimate Büchnerian puppet. Danton, at least, had been (like Büchner himself) a political revolutionary. Danton took on a mission, despite his growing sense that all missions are ultimately absurd. But Woyzeck is an obscure haunted lunatic, no one, nothing. The play retrieves *Danton's Death*'s program of a series of irregularly shaped scenes—unfortunately left in a tangle of variants at Büchner's death at the age of twenty-three. (Even the play's title stands in confusion, for Karl Emil Franzos, who edited the first complete edition of Büchner in 1879, mistook Büchner's handwriting of "Woyzeck" for "Wozzeck." So the play was called for decades, which explains why Alban Berg's famous operatic setting of the text bears the incorrect title.) *Woyzeck* was the last of Büchner's plays to reach the stage, by chance at a time when its nightmarish images and social problem realism were very much in vogue. By the 1920s, *Woyzeck* had become the major test of the German stage director, and while the rise of Nazism made the work scarce—Berg's opera was entirely banned—it nonetheless has remained the most popular of Büchner's plays, more absorbing then the gladsome *Leonce and Lena* and less daunting to stage than the grandiose *Danton.* (See also *Danton's Death.*)

THE BURBAGES (See Elizabethan Theatre)

RICHARD BURTON (1925–1984)

The Welsh Burton is unique among British actors for having ruined his talent in film work. Where *Laurence Olivier, *John Gielgud, *Ralph Richardson, *Albert Finney, and Tom Courtenay maintained a professional equilibrium, balancing the career-stretching stage work with comparably intense movie roles (and the occasional money job), Burton went Hollywood. He did Shakespearean service at the *Old Vic in the early 1950s, played the Prince in *Jean Anouilh's *Léocadia* (as *Time Remembered*) on Broadway in 1957, and created King Arthur in Frederick Loewe and Alan Jay Lerner's musical *Camelot* in 1960: moving farther and farther yet from the source of thespian power. Burton gave New York an interesting *Hamlet* in rehearsal clothing under Gielgud's direction, and took over the lead in Peter Shaffer's *Equus,* arrestingly. But Burton's work was becoming erratic. In a 1980 revival of *Camelot* he was stiff, barely listening to himself, uncaring. It was a performance that deserved to be booed off the stage, but by then Burton was too famous to boo and too idle to worry about it.

BUSINESS

This term, an insistent stage direction in old scripts, refers to traditional or improvised byplay, pantomime, ad libs . . . shtick, in short. Charles Dickens's novel *Nicholas Nickleby* imagines "the port-wine business" in a trained horse's act with a clown. "He was clever in melodrama," we learn, "but too broad—too broad." In the port-wine business, "he was greedy, and one night bit off the bowl of the glass, and choked himself, so that his vulgarity was the death of him at last."

BUTLEY

*Black comedy by *Simon Gray, prem. London, 1971.

A day in the life of Ben Butley, a brilliant, acerbic, and reckless professor at London University whose romantic and professional lives have reached the final stages of disintegration just as Gray raises his curtain. Alan Bates's *tour de force in the title role in London and New York persuaded many that the script was his *vehicle. On the contrary, this is a superbly written character study, and not only Gray's best but most typical play: in the academic setting, the small cast and simple decor, the careful observation of homosexuality, and most of all in Ben Butley's glibly self-protecting thrusts and ripostes, as here discussing his ruined marriage with his very soon-to-be ex-lover:

JOEY: I can't help wondering whether you miss it.
BEN: Only the sex and violence. And these days one can get those anywhere.
JOEY: So there's absolutely no chance . . .
BEN: Chance of what?
JOEY: Of your marriage reviving. You don't want it to?
BEN: Reviving? It never died. I consider it inviolate. I'm a one-woman man and I've had mine, thank God.

• • •

JOEY: But supposing she wants to marry again?
BEN: Good God! Who would want to marry *her*?
JOEY: You did.
BEN: That was before she'd been through the mill.
JOEY: Listen, Ben, you could be making a mistake about Anne. If you really don't want to lose her—
BEN: Your conversation is beginning to sound as if it's been stitched together from song titles of the fifties.

LORD BYRON (1788–1824)

It is a commonplace that Byron's plays, all tragedies in blank verse, are unstageworthy. Byron himself anticipated the complaint in the preface to *Marino Faliero, Doge of Venice*. "I have had no view to the stage," Byron announces. "In its present state it is, perhaps, not a very exalted object of ambition." Worse yet was the prospect of holding one's self-esteem hostage to the whims of the theatregoing population. "The sneering reader, and the loud critic, and the tart review are scattered and distant calamities; but the trampling of an intelligent or of an ignorant audience on a production . . . is a palpable and immediate grievance." In short, let them *read* Byron's plays, not stage them.

Yet *Marino Faliero* was staged, at *Drury Lane in 1821, a year after its composition, and, after Byron's death, most of his other plays were marched into the playhouse—*Werner* (written 1822, prem. 1830), *Sardanapalus* (written 1821, prem. 1834), *Manfred* (written 1817, prem. 1834), and *The Two Foscari* (written 1821, prem. 1838). *Manfred* is probably the least theatrical, but it was the most influential, as its gloomy paragon of a Romantic hero cast a spell over European art for fifty years. (Robert Schumann wrote incidental music for it and Tchaikovsky wrote a *Manfred* Symphony.) Donizetti and Verdi got operas out of the two Venetian plays, respectively *Marino Faliero* and *The Two Foscari*, so they can't be all that untheatrical. (Verdi even went on to a second Byron opera, from the poem *The Corsair*.) But it is undeniable that Byron misjudges the rhythm of theatre storytelling. *Marino Faliero* is the best of his plays, yet we constantly feel the lack of good theatre sense—one scene gagging on its own poetry, another not paced out properly. The story is drawn from history: The fourteenth century Doge, Marino Faliero, turned against his fellow nobles to lead a popular conspiracy and was beheaded for treason. The hero's last speech, literally on the verge of the chopping block, should be a great moment. And yes, at first it is:

DOGE: I speak to Time and to Eternity,
  Of which I grow a portion, not to man.
  Ye elements! in which to be resolved
  I hasten, let my voice be as a spirit
  Upon you! Ye blue waves! which bore my banner,
  Ye winds! which flutter'd o'er as if you loved it,
  And fill'd my swelling sails as they were wafted
  To many a triumph! Thou, my native earth,
  Which I have bled for! and thou, foreign earth,
  Which drank this willing blood from many a wound!

The Doge may be forgiven for dragging out his last words on earth. Still, one can imagine the Drury Lane audience beginning to fidget and cough and call for the headsman to get on with it. At the climax, however, Byron rises to the moment, as Faliero curses his judges and homeland:

DOGE: Thou den of drunkards with the blood of princes!
    Gehenna of the waters! thou sea Sodom!
    Thus I devote thee to the infernal gods!
    Thee and thy serpent seed!
    (Here the Doge turns and addresses the Executioner.)
    Slave, do thine office!
    Strike as I struck the foe! Strike as I would
    Have struck those tyrants! Strike deep as my curse!
    Strike—and but once!
    (The Doge throws himself upon his knees, and as the Executioner raises his sword, the scene closes.)

CAFÉ THEATRE

Developed in New York in the 1960s, this extreme form of fringe theatre introduced such playwrights as Robert Patrick, John Guare, and Lanford Wilson in tiny "spaces" surrounded by drinkers and diners at their tables. Though the café movement, if it can be termed so, lasted only a few years, it marked the first of the major breakaways within *off-Broadway that led to the rise of the more independent and experimental off-off-Broadway scene.

PEDRO CALDERÓN DE LA BARCA

(1600–1681)

Calderón seems to be the favorite Spanish playwright of the Western theatre, exotically medieval in outlook yet, paradoxically with an edge of humanist clarity that renders him contemporary in any age. Calderón left some two hundred plays, nearly half of them *autos* ("acts")—religious pageants derived from *medieval forms—and many of the others allegorically doctrinaire or concerned with codes of honor and loyalty almost incomprehensible to audiences of today. Yet Calderón's imagination and energy hold the public far better than, say, the political *absurdist *Fernando Ar-

rabal, our own contemporary, yet somehow not as articulate as Calderón.

Perhaps such plays as *El Mágico Prodigioso* (The Wonder-Working Magician, 1637), on the thoughts and martyrdom of St. Cyprian, are too locked into Calderón's absolute Catholicism to go over well at present. But *El Mayor Encanto Amor* (Love, the Greatest Enchantment, 1635) relates the dalliance of Ulysses and Circe, and *La Vida Es Sueño* (Life Is a Dream, 1635), one of Calderón's most popular titles, asks which condition is more natural to man, civilization or savagery. The *protagonist, Segismundo, has been raised in stark captivity: what will he do if released? The premise is, like the best of Calderón, as basic to medieval thought as to the work of *Samuel Beckett and *Harold Pinter. However, how are we then to explain the endurance of the auto *El Gran Teatro del Mundo* (The Great Theatre of the World, 1675), one of the most antique of plays in its churchly analysis of the universe, from the Great Author Himself and His law of Grace to the Monk, the Worker, the Beggar? Many today must feel uncomfortable or even disgusted at Calderón's unqualified hymns to Christian dogma, to a God Who loves yet rejoices in a miserable world. However, such is Calderón's grasp of the event, his ability to locate its poetry, that we are disarmed. Shaking our heads at his benighted medievalism, we are nonetheless enlightened.

MRS. PATRICK CAMPBELL
(1865–1940)

The despair of her colleagues because of her lack of commitment, the actress who started out as Beatrice Stella Tanner nonetheless astonished the public the few times she rose to an important occasion —first as *Arthur Wing Pinero's Paula of *The Second Mrs. Tanqueray,* later as *Shaw's Eliza Doolittle in *Pygmalion.* Mrs. Pat also played *Maurice Maeterlinck's Mélisande and *Ibsen's Hedda Gabler; but she made her reputation as fallen women like Paula Tanqueray, perhaps because she ennobled them with her vitality. Anyway, as she said, "A good woman is a dramatic impossibility." Mrs. Pat was known for such sallies, and for the atrocious lap dogs she dragged about with her. By 1930, when she tried the Hollywood talkie, she was a cartoon of herself. Yet the legend of the brilliant, outrageous diva persists. Mrs. Pat had the luck to be recalled for her best rather than her most typical acts.

ALBERT CAMUS (1913–1960)

In his essay, "Le Mythe de Sisyphe" (1943), Camus extrapolates the Greek myth of Sisyphus as a paradigm of the "absurd sensibility." Forever pushing his rock up a hill only to see it tumble back down, Sisyphus—according to Camus—must realize that his life has no hope, and through this realization he becomes powerful, independent, self-willing. There is no God; the universe is man, each man unto himself.

"Le Mythe de Sisyphe" is central to Camus's work and to the French school of existentialism in general, though Camus officially broke relations with the other leading French existentialist, Jean-Paul Sartre, in the mid-1950s. However, Camus's use of the word *absurd* should not invite association with such French-speaking *absurdists as *Eugène Ionesco, *Samuel Beckett, *Arthur Adamov, or *Jean Genet. True, critic Martin Esslin doubtless referred back to Camus's Sisyphean absurd when Esslin coined the term *theatre of the absurd.* But

Camus's four original plays are far more realistic and rationalized than absurdist works tend to be; and in any case the quartet preceded the era of true absurdism. Camus's *Le Malentendu* (The Misunderstanding, 1944), *Caligula* (1945), and *Les Justes* (The Just, known as The Just Assassins, 1949), are absurd only in that the word figures importantly in Camus's worldview, most clearly in the Roman emperor Caligula, who becomes "senselessly" ruthless to prove that life itself is senseless. Closing the public granaries, Caligula briskly decrees famine for all, noting, "One is always free at someone else's expense. Absurd, perhaps, but so it is." However, Camus's fourth original play, *L'État de Siège* (State of Siege, 1948), in which the city of Cadiz suffers a plague, does in certain ways prefigure the picturesque anti-realism of absurd theatre, especially in Camus's merrily bizarre crowd scenes and the Plague itself, characterized as a uniformed official. Camus went on to adaptations of other writers, including William Faulkner, Dostoyevsky, *Calderón, and *Lope de Vega. Like *Joe Orton, Camus died as if in illustration of his art: the black comic satirist in a brutal murder, the spokesman of life's senseless absurdity in an automobile accident.

KAREL ČAPEK (1890–1938)

This Czechoslovakian man of letters, a frequent collaborator with his brother Josef (1887–1945), used the fantastic as a base from which to battle for humanist values. He excoriates the greedy, the bellicose, the hateful, but at a distance, through the form of parable. In his classic science fiction novel, *Válka s Mloky* (The War with the Newts, 1936), a despised species fights back at mankind by excavating the earth's land masses, drowning the world: a fable about racism. Čapek's theatre is the same, only more so. His and Josef's *Ze Života Hmyzu* (From the Life of the Insects, 1920) views the world in the behavior of butterflies, ants, and moths; and *R. U. R.* (1921), by Karel alone, takes a harrowing look at a future rebellion by the world's robots. Čapek coined the word, in fact, from *robota* (work). His robots are feelingless brutes created to slave for man; like the newts, they turn

The chilling third-act finale of Čapek's "fantastic melodrama" R. U. R., on Broadway in 1922. The titular initials stand for Rossum's Universal Robots, the firm whose technological perfection of the android leads nearly to the end of the world—at this very moment, in fact, as the human-hating robots take over. "Robots of the world! The power of man has fallen! A new world has arisen: the rule of the Robots!"

against the world's masters. But the robots cannot reproduce—until a doctor discovers a male and female robot couple who have somehow developed the ability to feel: to love. He sends them forth into the world as the second Adam and Eve.

A character's failure to feel compassion and understanding may be the greatest crime in Čapek's theatre. *Věc Makropulos* (The Makropulos Affair,

1922) affirms this belief in a humankind redeemable only through love, in the 347-year-old Elina Makropulos, daughter of an alchemist who discovered a formula for eternal life. It has one terrible side effect: a loss of emotion. At the final curtain, a young woman destroys the formula, and the heroine dies . . . in relief. Because *George Bernard Shaw's *Back to Methusaleh* had been published only a year before, *Věc Makropulos* has been taken as a rebuttal of Shaw's theory of "Creative Evolution." In fact, Čapek was unaware of *Methusaleh* and was simply restating a theme he had been concerned with throughout his life. The rise of Nazism led him to more realistic cautionary works, albeit in the *expressionistic mode, *Bílá Nemoc* (The White Plague, 1937) and *Matka* (The Mother, 1938). Čapek would certainly have been arrested had he not died three months before the Nazis entered Prague. His brother Josef died in Belsen concentration camp shortly before its liberation.

CAPOCOMICO

Italian for "head actor": the *actor-manager, or chief of a troupe.

THE CAUCASIAN CHALK CIRCLE

Parable on the rights of ownership by *Bertolt Brecht, prem. Northfield, Minnesota (in English), 1948.

This is Brecht's most delightful play, the closest he ever came to evoking the happy-ending sentimentality of the bourgeois theatre. Ironically, the play is also commonly cited as the most Brechtian of works, the one in which his theory of the epic theatre enjoys its densest implementation, what with the use of a prologue setting up a play-within-a-play, a narrator, song spots, masks (for the villains), and plenty of chances for the characteristic Brechtian *Alienation Effect. Yet the story deals with the triumph of a woman's love for her adopted child against murderous antagonists and includes a love plot—successfully resolved!

As so often with Brecht, the play itself is a borrowing, from a German version of a Chinese tale. (This is one reason why *The Caucasian Chalk Circle* is the ultimate example of epic theatre, for this form has much in common with those of the Eastern theatre.) The prologue, set in the war-ravaged Georgia of southern Russia, in the Caucasus (thus the "Caucasian" of the title), presents a dispute over who shall take charge of a fertile valley. Two groups contest rights to the land, one group

through legal ownership, the other because it defended the valley from the invading Nazis and intends to develop it as a collective farm. The false naiveté of the dispute—so peaceful, so rational—is shocking coming from a man as worldly as Brecht, and the atmosphere is hopelessly sappy. It's not propaganda; it's just silly. Luckily, the prologue is short and, once the play proper begins, the characters of the prologue are never seen again. What we do see is a defense of the notion that the one who can best use, or cultivate, or benefit from a thing is the rightful owner: an infant prince is abandoned by his selfish mother in the flurry of escaping a besieged city, a young peasant woman protects him, and now who shall claim him? The real mother wants the child for the fortune he will inherit; the adoptive mother wants the child for his own sake. The drunken, corrupt judge Azdak sets up the "chalk circle": each of the two mothers must grab an arm and pull. The winner is . . . the loser—for, to this bent Solomon of an Azdak, no "real" mother would hurt her child. So justice (love, really) wins out in this absurdly loving comedy. But if the hard-edged Brecht does let his edge down a bit for once, we note that the canny thespian gives no lines to the little boy. Better have him oddly (or perhaps "epically") silent than risk the problems inherent in the use of child actors.

CAVALCADE

Epic soap opera by *Noël Coward, prem. London, 1931.

This "upstairs, downstairs" spectacle views the fortunes of England in war and peace, from 1899 to 1930, in twenty-one scenes following the lives of the Marryots and their servants. Its very size and grandeur suggest a vastly different Coward—different, certainly, from the blasé gay dandy his legend recalls. But then it was this very spare, apolitical Coward who made a work like *Cavalcade* necessary. Coward was acting in his own *Private Lives* with Gertrude Lawrence—two simple sets, two stars, two (including Laurence Olivier) in support—when he "felt the urge to test my production powers on a large scale."

Cavalcade is as big as they come, then—but more than big: patriotic, tragic, sentimental, praising the received values of fatherland and family that the more usual Coward would ridicule. History merges with the personal, as when Mrs. Marryot wanders through a screaming Trafalgar Square on Armistice Day, trying to join the celebrants as the tears stream down her cheeks, thrilled for the peace but mourning for her son, who—she has just learned—was one of the war's last casualties. Or consider this scene, in which another Marryot son and his bride embark for a sea voyage on their honeymoon:

EDWARD: Look at father and mother; they're perfectly happy and devoted, and they always have been.

EDITH: They had a better chance at the beginning. Things weren't changing so swiftly; life wasn't so restless.

EDWARD: How long do you give us?

EDITH: I don't know—and Edward—(she turns to him) I don't care. This is our moment— complete and heavenly. I'm not afraid of anything. This is our own, for ever.
(Edward takes Edith in his arms and kisses her.)

EDWARD: Do you think a nice warming glass of sherry would make it any more heavenly?

EDITH: You have no soul, darling, but I'm very attached to you. Come on—
(Edith takes up her cloak which has been hanging on the rail, and they walk away. The cloak has been covering a lifebelt, and when it is withdrawn the words "S. S. Titanic" can be seen in black letters on the white. The lights fade into complete darkness, but the letters remain glowing as the orchestra plays very softly and tragically "Nearer My God to Thee.")

JOSEPH CHAIKIN (1936–   )

An actor with the *Living Theatre, Chaikin broke away to create the Open Theater, an experimental collective devoted to what might be termed "performance practice." The play was not the thing —that is, the writing of the play. Rather the *creation* of the play was the act that bore the art, the synthesis of individual players' instincts, communal interaction, directorial leadership of the resulting improvisations, and—last of all—the writer's imagination, or, more precisely, "structuring." So, indeed, runs the byline credit on the Open Theater's major work, *The Serpent* (1968): "words and structure" by Jean-Claude van Itallie (1932–   ), thus supervising, along with Chaikin, the rough draft, so to say, provided by the experimenting players.

Chaikin founded the Open Theater in 1963, perhaps in revolt against *Method naturalism and, again perhaps, in response to Antonin Artaud's *Theatre of Cruelty. Chaikin's troupe's style was glibly branded "eclectic," but knowledgeable theatregoers found Chaikin's players unique, all their own theatre insistently testing their own style. In *America Hurrah* and *Viet Rock,* both in 1966, the Open Theater burst out of the churches and garages of off-off-Broadway onto off-Broadway with highly critical views of American culture. *America Hurrah* was credited to van Itallie, *Viet Rock* to Megan Terry (1932–   ). But, as the critic Stanley Kauffmann pointed out, "Their scripts are by now as inseparable from the entity of the Open Theater as the hydrogen from the oxygen in water." *The Serpent,* an adaptation of the Old Testament with modern glosses, marked the Open Theater's culmination, the apex of the experiment. A vitiating fascination with improvisation over composition and audience relating over performing led to the company's dissolution in 1973. Still, it left its mark—*A Chorus Line* and *The Life and Adventures of Nicholas Nickleby* were "structured" out of company improvisations like those developed by the Open Theater. Chaikin himself went on as a free-lance director, ironically—in view of his emphasis on the visual over the verbal—suffering a stroke and the accompanying aphasia: a failure of speech. To cap the irony, Chaikin returned to the theatre with a production of *Eugène Ionesco's *The Bald Soprano on off-Broadway in 1987. (See also *The Serpent.*)

THE CHANGING ROOM

Absolute *naturalism by *David Storey, prem. London, 1971.

Another *Royal Court premiere (as with so

many unusual British plays of the day), *The Changing Room* looks in on a rugby team before a game, at half-time, and just after. In heavy northern factory town dialect, the men arrive, plan their strategy, trade observations on the news, local events, and each other, talk over their performance on the pitch (the playing field), and leave. The play's interest lies as much in how Storey reveals the feelings of life, the way we treat ourselves and each other, as in how expertly he duplicates the data of life.

ANTON CHEKHOV (1860–1904)

"It is necessary," he wrote, "that on the stage everything should be as complex and as simple as in life. People are having dinner, and while they're having it their future happiness may be decided or their lives may be about to be shattered." Yet at first, Chekhov was hard put to blend life's complexity and simplicity in a persuasive setting. *Ivanov* (1887), about a disillusioned, self-destructive landowner, and *Lyeshy* (The Wood Demon, 1889), about the disruptive visit of two city people to a country estate, typify Chekhov's early work in their melodramatic contrivances, their attempt to crowbar "life" into an old-fashioned format.

It was form that held Chekhov back, the *well-made play with its artificially ordered entrances, confrontations, and exits that had become an article of faith among thespians, critics, and theatre-goers. Thus, when Chekhov broke through to his own more loosely constructed and lifelike genre, in *Chaika* (The Seagull, 1896), the thespians failed to do the play justice and the critics savaged it. Even Tolstoy thought it "worthless" and gave it the ultimate derogation: "It reads like something by Ibsen." Yet *The Seagull* launches Chekhov's Big Four, the quartet of masterpieces generally regarded as a foundation in the development of the "modern" in theatre. Gone now were the "French scenes," as Chekhov called them, alluding to the well-made methods of *Scribe and *Sardou. Gone was the thundering curtain line, the ridiculous energy of *melodrama. Chekhov's stage is now—yes, as complex and simple as life: simple action, complex relationships. It is as if the "big scenes" were

all happening offstage, the rhetoric banned from our view as Chekhov lavishes his tremulous pauses upon his reticent, ambivalent characters. *The Seagull*'s principals are unusual for the day, mostly writers and actors of dubious gifts and humiliated ambitions. The anguished young playwright Konstantin Tryeplov has left his mother's house to chase after the unresponsive actress Nina Zaryechnaya, leaving the wretched Masha with Doctor Dorn:

DORN: (sighing) Youth, youth!
MASHA: When there is nothing more to say, they say, "Youth, youth." (She takes some snuff.)
DORN: (Grabbing the snuffbox from her and flinging it into the shrubbery) That's disgusting!
(Pause)
It seems they're making music in the house. We should go in.
MASHA: Wait.
DORN: What is it?
MASHA: I still want to tell you something. I have to talk . . . (She is upset.) I don't like my father . . . But you are very dear to me. Somehow, I have the feeling that we are close . . . Help me, then. Help me, or I'll do something stupid, destroy my life, ruin it . . . I can't go on . . .
DORN: What? How can I help?
MASHA: I'm suffering. No one, no one knows how I suffer! (She gently lays her head on his chest.) I love Konstantin.
DORN: How high-strung everyone is! How high-strung! And how loving . . . Oh, you sorcerer of a lake! (Tenderly) But what is there that I can do, my child? What? What?

And then the curtain falls.

It was in Petersburg that *The Seagull* suffered its disastrous premiere, at the Alyeksandrinsky (now the Pushkin) Theatre. So Vladimir Nyemirovich-Danchenko had to strive mightily with Chekhov for permission to stage *The Seagull* in Moscow with the new company he had formed with Konstantin Stanislavsky. Chekhov had decided to abandon the theatre altogether. But Nyemirovich won out, and here Chekhov's major history begins, for the new company was the *Moscow Art Theatre, their production of *The Seagull* (in 1898) enjoyed a triumph, and, with Stanislavsky directing and acting, Chekhov went on to complete his quartet of immortal plays with *Dyadya Vanya* (Uncle Vanya, written 1896, prem. 1899), a revision of *The Wood Demon; Tri Syostri* (The Three Sisters, 1901); and *Vishnyovy Sad* (The Cherry Orchard, 1904).

Chekhov's remarkable mixture of the complex and the simple, and Stanislavsky's revolutionarily realistic approach to acting are indisolubly linked in lore. Even in 1898, the Moscow Art Theatre saw its fortunes so closely bound to Chekhov's that the company adopted a seagull as its insigne. To do Chekhov properly, one had to be Stanislavskyan. Yet Chekhov himself complained that Stanislavsky *didn't* do Chekhov properly. Stanislavsky's ham-handed profundity made tragedies out of comedies. For so Chekhov labeled his plays. Of the Big Four, only *The Three Sisters* is termed a "drama." The other three are, Chekhov insisted, "comedies."

Almost no one but Chekhov sees them this way. Their intricate character relationships, unveiled in a series of dovetailed actions rather than a true plot, and their often very light but greyish tone, like the murmur of dejected party guests, certainly does not suggest the melodrama, problem play, or naturalism common to Western theatre in Chekhov's day, much less any form of tragedy. And there is the odd prankish touch here and there. Yet Chekhov's plays are not comedies in any of the many several modes in which the theatre implements comedy. They are funny at times; but they are, more consistently, touching and sad. They are, above all, honest, true to life. John Gielgud calls them "unique in the sense of reality which they create when one is acting in them. One seems to become part of the life of a group of people as well as an individual stage character."

Hence the all-important Stanislavskyan ensemble, the pervasive intimacy of the narration. What Chekhov achieved, at heart, was the substitution of an integrated dramatis personae to replace the star part, the *protagonistic hero or heroine that even *Ibsen never thought of retiring. The various personalities in these plays are wonderfully combined—so much so that the typical encyclopedia synopsis shorthand that might yield "Shakespeare's study of psychotic jealousy" for *Othello* or "farce

about a couple who can't live without each other —or with each other" for Noël Coward's *Private Lives* is virtually useless in the Chekhov of the four late masterpieces. How is one to make a comparable chicklet of *The Three Sisters*—"a tale of three women who want to go to Moscow"? True, but almost irrelevant. These are densely inhabited plays: beautifully attuned to the rhythms of reality, yes; deft in their ability to shift mood in a moment, yes. But in the main Chekhov is the novelist playwright, even admitting his "second" career as a master of the short story. On the stage, Chekhov commands not just a theme or a couple of characters, but the whole world.

(See also *The Cherry Orchard,* directly below.)

THE CHERRY ORCHARD

"Comedy" by *Anton Chekhov, prem. Moscow, 1904.

Of the four major plays that Chekhov wrote at the end of his life, this—the very last—is the least fraught, the most delightful. Even the sadness we may feel at the heroine's loss of her estate, and the handing over of her beautiful orchard of cherry trees to the real estate developer's axe, is mitigated by her extravagance, her silliness, her lack of concentration. She's the sort of person who deserves to lose her property.

As the play begins, she—Lyubov Andryeyevna Ranyevsky—returns to her estate after five years' high living in Paris; as the play ends, she leaves again, this time forever. The stage is crowded with odd characters—Lyubov's silly brother Gaev, who punctuates scenes by calling out billiard shots; the merchant Lopakhin, who begs Lyubov to *act* and save her holdings and, when she doesn't, buys it himself; a clerk who keeps falling over furniture; a governess who does parlor tricks; the eighty-seven-year-old butler, Firs, more *ancien régime* than his employers; and various others. There's a very slight feeling of *You Can't Take It With You*'s household of screwballs, which supports Chekhov's contention that *The Cherry Orchard* is a comedy. Few others find it so. Most directors (starting with Konstantin Stanislavsky, who staged the premiere and played the first Gaev) discover that a sensible reading of the text delivers a play far more moving

than comic. When a director does present *The Cherry Orchard* comically, as *Andrei Serban did for Joseph Papp's New York Shakespeare Festival in 1977, with Irene Worth as Lyubov Andryeyevna, the results are stylistically questionable. Serban's production itself was brilliant. However, if Chekhov had seen it, would he have cried, "Good! That's the way! A comedy at last! There's my *Cherry Orchard*!"?

Typical of the debate over whether the play is darkly lyrical or lightly vital is the final scene. Lyubov and her entourage have departed, the house is locked up, the dull whack of the axes sounds from the dying orchard . . . and the ancient and clearly ailing butler Firs appears:

FIRS: (tries the handles of the doors) Locked. They've gone . . . (Sits on the sofa) They forgot about me . . . never mind . . . I'll just sit here for a while . . . And I'm sure Leonid Andryevich [Gaev] didn't put on his fur coat and has gone off in the thin one . . . (sighs worriedly) I should have been watching him . . . These careless young people! (He mutters

Reader, brace yourself: we offer three shots of the original Moscow Art Theatre staging of The Cherry Orchard. *If Sarah Bernhardt a few pages ago was history, this is* epic. *See, top left, Act One, the arrival; bottom left, Act Two, the strollers in the park; and top right, Act Three, the soirée. Then, for Act Four (the departure), we drop in, bottom right, on a postmodernist production, Andrei Serban's 1976 staging at New York's Lincoln Center, with (left to right) Dwight Marfield, C. K. Alexander (at table), Priscilla Smith, Irene Worth, George Voskovec, Ben Masters (in background), and Michael Cristofer.*

something inaudibly.) Life has run by me, as if I hadn't lived. (He stretches out.) I'll lie down . . . All your strength is gone, nothing's left you, nothing . . . Oh, you . . . you good-for-nothing! (lies motionless).

After a sound like the sharp snapping of a string, and the continued chopping of the axes, the curtain falls. Now, is this finale meant comically: the cute old servant forgotten in the bustle of thoughtless aristocrats? Is it sad, pointing up the cruelty of their self-involvement, and the waste of a life spent

taking care of them? Commentators have noted that an ailing old man locked up in an unheated house during a Russian October will probably die of exposure before anyone finds him. (Or couldn't he simply break a window and hie himself to town?) Many productions make it explicit that Firs's "lies motionless" is in fact Firs's death. Surely this is not Chekhov's intention; it is certainly not his stage direction. But the oddly unresolved nature of the scene points up the rich ambiguity of Chekhov's dramaturgy. For life, too, is neither specifically sad or funny. Like Chekhov's plays, it varies, chilling and teasing and baffling us.

CHIKAMATSU MONZAEMON
(1653—1725)

The "Japanese Shakespeare." Though he was one of the pioneers of the puppet theatre style known as Jōruri, he is most celebrated for laying the foundation of the *Kabuki play repertory. Classic Kabuki virtually *is* Chikamatsu. However, because of Kabuki's uniquely detailed production system, Chikamatsu's texts are little more than blueprints. Thus his literature as such lies in his many Jōruri plays, not least those in which, unprecedentedly, Chikamatsu wrote of real-life contemporary events. One of his most famous works is *Hakata Kojoro Nami Makura* (Kojoro of Hakata and Her Pillow of Waves, 1718), about the doomed love of a courtesan and a smuggler. Both characters are based on figures that had become notorious in rumor that very year.

CHRISTOPHE COLOMB

Comic phantasmagoria by *Michel de Ghelderode, prem. Brussels, 1927.

"This play is spectacle and enchantment," the author warns us, "and plays . . . in the perspective of a dream." Of all de Ghelderode's plays, this one most prefigures the farcical side of the *absurd, in the wacky platoon of archetypal characters that assist or hinder Columbus's voyage to the New World—L'Homme-foule ("The one-man crowd"), for instance, who cries out, "Stupendous! Stupid! Right! Wrong!" as Columbus prepares to embark, and, when Columbus returns, takes him for Lindbergh. Montezuma and Buffalo Bill are in it, too. It's one of the most crowded *small* plays ever devised.

CHRONICLE PLAY

Where *documentary drama *seizes* a historical subject, dramatizes it in order to stimulate a particular reaction from the public, the chronicle play simply dramatizes history, presents it. Authors of chronicle plays are not without an opinion, a slant, true. But the chronicle play is usually about character, while documentary drama is usually about history. Another difference: documentary drama treats recent events while the character play can reach centuries into the past.

The chronicle play is by far the older form, counting roughly a third of Shakespeare's output and such works as *Friedrich Schiller's *Don Carlos* and *Johann Wolfgang von Goethe's *Egmont*. All three of these writers tend to put history at the service of their personal feelings, but not till the latter half of the twentieth century did the frankly partisan interpretation of history—documentary drama—become popular.
(See also *The Crucible* and *The Deputy*.)

COLLEY CIBBER (1671—1757)

One of the most popular of English *actor-managers, yet vastly disliked: popular with the audience and disliked by the elite. Cibber apparently had a certain low dash in comic parts, especially as that basic ingredient of *Restoration comedy, the fop. But as playwright, Cibber was deemed a hack, and the intelligentsia was scandalized when Cibber was made Poet Laureate. Alexander Pope, infuriated at some anti-Pope jests that Cibber had thrown into a perfomance, wrote:

> Cibber! write all thy Verses upon Glasses,
> The only way to save 'em from our Arses.

This being the day of pamphlet feuds, Cibber replied with an open letter to Pope, recalling a night of carousal at "a certain house of carnal recreation, near the Haymarket":

His lordship's frolic proposed was, to *slip his little Homer,* as he called him, at a girl of the game . . . in which he so far succeeded, that the smirking damsel who served us tea, happened to have charms sufficient to tempt the little-tiny manhood of Mr. Pope into the next room with her.

Cibber, mindful of Pope's health, interferes:

Shakespeare wrote chronicle plays, but so does our contemporary Rolf Hochhuth. Here's his extraordinarily controversial The Deputy. Professional Catholics cringe and shriek at Hochhuth's honesty, but our photo catches Pope Pius XII suddenly suffering an attack of fog when a priest reminds him that God's minister owes protection to Jews as well as to those in the official parish. Here we have the 1964 New York staging, with Emlyn Williams as the Pope, Carl Low as Count Fontana, and Jeremy Brett as his Jesuit son, who flaunts the Jewish star to wear on his cassock "until Your Holiness proclaims before the world a curse upon the man who slaughters Jews like cattle."

I . . . threw open the door upon him, when I found this little hasty hero, like a terrible *Tom-tit,* pertly perching upon the mount of love! But such was my surprize that I fairly laid hold of his heels, and actually drew him down safe from danger.

They played rough in those days.

LE CID

"Tragi-comédie" by *Pierre Corneille, prem. Paris, winter, 1636–1637.

The first masterpiece of French theatre, still unsurpassed as an expression of Classical *noblesse.* Don Gomès insults Don Diègue, who, too old to defend himself, sends his son Don Rodrigue in his place. Rodrigue kills Gomès; but Rodrigue loves Gomès's daughter Chimène, who must now beg the King of Castille to punish her lover. One more complication—the Moors are on the attack, and there is only one knight capable of defending Seville: Rodrigue.

All ends well. But the plot is of no importance. What matters is Corneille's opulent evocation of the honor-above-all mindset that impels his characters, his ability to make chivalry comprehensible, persuasive, poetic. An immediate popular success, *Le Cid* set off that unique French invention, the art-is-politics controversy, here known as the *querelle du Cid.* Corneille was accused of treating a worthless subject, cheating on the accepted format for drama, blundering in his verses, and stealing from others what little beauty there was. Only the second charge is true—Corneille veers all over Seville instead of holding to one location, and, in order to honor the idiotic "unity of time," had to cram an unbelievable density of event into a twenty-four-hour span, thereby mocking the required *vraisemblance*. No matter. *Le Cid* quickly became so absolute in the French repertory that it gave birth to the phrase, "beau comme *Le Cid*": as fine as *Le Cid*—still in use today.

CIRCLE REPERTORY COMPANY

One of the essential *off-Broadway organizations in its commitment to new authors and uncelebrated actors, even in its eventual location, smack in the middle of Greenwich Village, at the Sheridan Square Playhouse. When the company opened shop in 1969, however, it occupied a loft at Eighty-third Street and Broadway, on a lease from The Council for International Recreation, Culture, and Lifelong Education: thus, in acronym, the CIRCLE Rep. Founding members included most notably, director Marshall W. Mason (1940–   ) and playwright Lanford Wilson (1937–   ), whose collaboration has run right through the group's history, Mason heading the organization until mid-1987. Mason's approach is direct: clarify the action, enlighten the players, engage the public. Wilson's charm is intimacy, getting his audience acquainted with his characters. Thus, directness of intimacy has been the Circle's salient theme, and one reason why it has outlasted so many of New York's companies, from the *New Theatre in the 1910s through the *Group in the 1930s up to the *Open Theater in the 1960s. Another reason for the Circle's staying power is the high quotient of holdovers, works it sent on to the commercial theatre: Wilson's microcosm-in-a-lobby, *The Hot l Baltimore* (1972)—note the burned out "e" in the street sign of the hotel, due to be razed, its denizens doomed to be liberated; Mark Medoff's hood-holds-cross-section-of-population-at-bay thriller *When You Comin' Back, Red Ryder?* (1973); Edward J. Moore's enchanting two-character working-class romance *The Sea Horse*

(1974), with Moore himself as the sailor who tames —disarms, maybe—Conchata Ferrell's touchy *cabaretière*; cartoonist Jules Feiffer's Americanized *Beckett, *Knock Knock* (1976); Albert Innaurato's South Philadelphia comedy of manners, *Gemini* (1977); Wilson's Chekovian *Fifth of July* (1978); William M. Hoffman's study of an AIDS victim, *As Is* (1985); and a Broadway original, Wilson's *Burn This* (1987).

CIVIC REPERTORY COMPANY

In 1926, actress Eva Le Gallienne (1899–   ) took over a downtown theatre, left behind when *Broadway moved from Fourteenth to Forty-second Streets. It was a kind of *off-Broadway, *little theatre in a big house. Le Gallienne pulled out the classics—Shakespeare, Ibsen, Molière—and such novelties as her own adaptation of Lewis Carroll's *Alice in Wonderland* (1932), not to mention *Alla Nazimova, thrown out of Hollywood and a matchless Madame Ranyevsky in Chekhov's *The Cherry Orchard*. The smart money, mindful of the precarious welcome that repertory theatres enjoy in the commercial arena, gave Le Gallienne three years at most. But the Civic lasted nearly a decade, till 1935, when Depression blues imploded it.

CLAQUE

A group of (usually) penniless aficionados, paid to supply applause. In the claque's heyday, the nineteenth century, its duties varied from swelling the public's reception to directing it, virtually forcing an unmoved audience to what would sound like a series of ovations. As the claques were inexpensive —many stars or playwrights simply paid for their confederates' seats—they became a fixture in most European cities, more so in Italy, Spain, and France, less so to the north. Occasionally a claque was ordered to create a fiasco, but generally its job was to create excitement. In a letter to the actress *Rachel, the *chef de claque* reviews the performance of his troops: "At the first night, I led the attack myself thirty-three times. We developed three acclamations, four hysterias, two portions of *frisson,* four encores of applause, and two interminable explosions."

PAUL CLAUDEL (1868–1955)

Claudel, a French Catholic, was the most religious of playwrights, folding all his subjects, whether historical or contemporary, into parables on the richness of the life of the soul, the absolutism of destiny, the innocence of God. Claudel's theatre has an allegorical and epic atmosphere reminiscent of the medieval theatre. He wrote as if human striving—history itself—had proved itself useless and must now learn from the clarity of religion and rebuild Western civilization into a City of God. As the critic Jacques Guicharnaud saw it, "Claudel was the poet of the end of the world."

Claudel termed his best-known play, *L'Annonce Faite à Marie* (The Tidings Brought to Mary, 1912), a "mystery" in the medieval manner. And lo, a medieval mystery play it virtually is, though Claudel's poetry is more sophisticated, more insistently metaphorical, than that of the middle ages, and his saintly heroine, who brings a dead infant back to life, would have been thought a heretical creation. *Partage de Midi* (Break of Noon, written 1906, prem. 1916) is much smaller and contemporary in setting, though just as redolent of spiritual teaching. These two works were Claudel's first important contributions to the repertory, even if he had begun his playwrighting in the 1890s, when he launched his tour of the world in high-ranking diplomatic posts.

It was in the early 1920s, while serving as France's ambassador to Japan, that Claudel started work on his most momentous play, *Le Soulier de Satin* (The Satin Slipper), not performed till 1943, in *Jean-Louis Barrault's extraordinarily eclectic production for the *Comédie-Française). This immense pageant of sixteenth century Spain has been likened to *Goethe's *Faust,* even to Dante. But it seems more like an ultra-Catholic *Racine, perhaps an ultra-Raciniste *Calderón. Claudel set *The Satin Slipper* during the Counter-Reformation, the war between rationalism and faith and the time, as well, of the discovery and colonization of non-European continents. (Claudel's hero, in fact, is a conquistador headed for the Americas.) As Guicharnaud points out, "The whole surface of the globe was either fighting Rome or working for Rome's triumph." Thus Claudel reaches out to, even surrounds, every member of his public, for we are all descendants of one side or the other. It is a fascinating work, written to be read but (with cuts) quite stageable, and the French regard it as a cornerstone in the modern repertory, flocking to the Avignon Festival in the summer of 1987 for the first uncut performance—some twelve hours of theatre. Claudel is arcane but Claudel is a classic. However, it is hard to resist the feeling that, had Claudel lived in the Middle Ages, he would have been burning nonconformists instead of entertaining them.

HAROLD CLURMAN (1901–1980)

His ex-wife Stella Adler worried in 1982 that Clurman's "legacy to the theatre . . . may be lost because he didn't create an heir." But Clurman did leave an important sense of his times, and his place in them, in *The Fervent Years* (1945), a glance backward at the *Group Theatre and Broadway's 1930s. As theoretician-becoming-director, Clurman was one of the Group's founders, and he became as well a critic while pursuing a director's career on Broadway after the Group disbanded in 1941, handling such special assignments as Carson McCuller's *The Member of the Wedding* (1950) with *Julie Harris and Ethel Waters; Dorothy Parker and Armand d'Usseau's *The Ladies of the Corridor* (1953); *Jean Anouilh's sorrowful backstager *Mademoiselle Colomb* (1954), again with Harris; *Jean Giraudoux's *Tiger at the Gates* (1955); Rodgers and Hammerstein's would-be Steinbeckian musical *Pipe Dream* (1955); and the 1959 revival of *George Bernard Shaw's *Heartbreak House,* with Maurice Evans, Pamela Brown, Diana Wynyard, Dennis Price, and Sam Levene; along with *Eugene O'Neill and *Tennessee Williams.

This much suggests the connoisseur thespian. But Clurman also found room for such projects as Arthur Laurents's *The Time of the Cuckoo* (1952), with Shirley Booth; *William Inge's *Bus Stop*

(1955), a courtship comedy (cowboy ropes dance-hall "chantoosie") made intense by Kim Stanley's Chérie; and Harry Kurnitz's comedy-thriller *A Shot in the Dark* (1961), an adaptation from the French, yet again with Julie Harris. Clurman, then, is one of the few of Broadway's idealists who made his peace with its commercial aspects, treating Kurnitz with the same respect he gave to *Clifford Odets back when the Group, and American social problem theatre, were young. "Some people," says Adler, "will perhaps recognize what they have inherited" from Clurman. Perhaps.

JEAN COCTEAU (1889—1963)

Has any other playwright devised, produced, and expounded from so central a position in the arts world? Novelist, ballet scenarist, and filmmaker as well as thespian, Cocteau was one of the key Parisians when Paris was still Europe's cultural capital, the friend and collaborator of such composers as Igor Stravinsky, Francis Poulenc, Darius Milhaud; such artists as Pablo Picasso, Juan Gris, and Georges Braque, as well as Misia Sert and Syergyey Diaghilyev. "Astound me!" Diaghilyev ordered Cocteau. Cocteau astounded Paris, all France, the world. "This sickness, to express oneself," he asked. "What is it?" His plays are often opaque parables, especially *Orphée* (1926) and *La Machine Infernale* (1934), both drawn from Greek myth (*La Machine* deals with Oedipus), and *Les Chevaliers de la Table Ronde* (The Knights of the Round Table 1937), on the Arthur legend. *Les Parents Terribles* (1938), on the other hand, is *fourth-wall *naturalism intended to reach a wide public and fan controversy, both of which it did. Some critics scorn Cocteau's theatre as aimless experimentation, writing on a dare, so to speak. But his first play, the short *Les Mariés de la Tour Eiffel* (The Wedding on the Eiffel Tower, 1921), is a key event in the *surrealist avant-garde that led to *absurdism: dancers mime the many characters while two actors costumed as phonographs declaim the lines for them. Cocteau intellectualized show biz. Under the childlike love of games, the teasing delight in shocking the town, and the worship of *monstres sacrés* ("great stars"), his was a restlessly venturesome mind and a fearlessly individual vision.

COME BLOW YOUR HORN

Domestic *farce by *Neil Simon, prem. New York, 1961.

Though this was Simon's first play, written some twenty years before he developed from a technician of gags into a writer of character comedy, it demonstrates a telling gift for social observation under the clichés of plot reversal and an irritatingly sentimental resolution. The play's premise has classic possibilities: worldly older son neglects the family business for partying; naive younger son runs away from home, moves in with brother, and becomes a party boy himself just as his older brother starts to reform. Simon gives little more than an outline of these characters, and of their bossy father and deliriously woebegone mother. (She feels faint; she needs water; younger son fetches it. "Do you feel any better?" he asks. She groans, "When did I ever feel better?") What Simon does capture, however, in loving burlesque, is the patriarchal conservatism of Jewish middle-class society. The family is named Baker, but we cannot mistake the ethnic derivation in point of view and accent in this confrontation of father and older son:

FATHER: Do *I* wander in at eleven o'clock in the morning? Do *I* take three hours for lunch . . . in night clubs? When are you there? . . . You take off legal holidays, Jewish holidays, Catholic holidays . . . Last year you took off Hallowe'en.

ALAN: I was sick.

FATHER: When you came back to work you were sick. When you were sick you were dancing.

• • •

ALAN: You don't give me the same respect you give the night watchman.

FATHER: At least I know where he is at night.

ALAN: . . . I think what I do at night should be my business.

FATHER: Not when it's nighttime four days in a row. Listen, what do I care? Do whatever you want. Go ahead and live like a bum.

ALAN: Why am I a bum?

FATHER: Are you married?

ALAN: No.

FATHER: Then you're a bum!

The Comédie-Française, facade and foyer.

THE COMÉDIE-FRANÇAISE

The French *national theatre, formed in 1680, when King Louis XIV merged two troupes, one of which contained survivors of the company that had worked under *Molière. The Comédie-Française is the oldest national theatre in the West, but the most conservative, as opposed to the audacious National Theatre of Great Britain. The British balance classics with new work—the newest, absolutely contemporary in tone and attitude. The Comédie observes a museum-like poise, with a repertory that is for the most part several centuries old. Privileges of seniority and the lure of a pension encouraged a roster of actors unusually "settled in" for the volatile world of the theatre, though ambition and envy are aggravated by the concentration of talent, and *greenroom intrigue runs at a high temperature. An old company joke claims, "We're just one big happy family—the Atridae." (This refers to the doings of the house of Atreus, celebrated in Aeschylus's *Oresteia*: adultery, blood murder, and cannibalism.) The Comédie *is* a family in its strong sense of tradition, passed from generation to generation. It is said that, even today,

three hundred years later, a certain line reading in Corneille or piece of business in Racine dates back to the original productions. Not for nothing is the Comédie-Française referred to as "the house of Molière"—but for centuries the French have also been calling it the "théâtre français," virtually "our theatre."

COMÉDIE-ITALIENNE (See Pierre de Marivaux)

THE COMEDY OF ERRORS

*Farce by William Shakespeare, prem. unknown, probably London, 1591.

A man and his servant arrive in Ephesus, unaware that their identical twins live in that city; each twin is mistaken for the other, and the confusions multiply. A classic starting point for farce, even Classical: for Shakespeare based his play on two by Plautus, *Menaechmi* (which has only one set of twins) and *Amphitruo* (on the Amphitryon myth, in which Jupiter and Mercury take the forms of a man and his servant, Jupiter to dally with Amphitryon's wife while her real husband fumes in the street). One of Shakespeare's earliest plays, *The Comedy of Errors* is perhaps his most sheerly amusing one, though modern directors often seek to emend the fun with revisionist productions. John Pasquin's *Comedy of Errors* at the New York Shakespeare Festival's 1975 Central Park summer season set the action in a sweltering Italian town of the early twentieth century, delightfully centralized in June Gable's mafiosa gun moll of an Adriana, a Chicagoesque Anna Magnani. Speaking of Chicago, in 1983 the Goodman Arts Center presented a crazy-gang, anything-for-a-laugh, free-for-all *Comedy of Errors* with the Flying Karamazov Brothers, a production filled with juggling, acrobatics, contemporary references (including in latter performances note of the Iran-Contra scandal), bizarre costumes (including a drag queen), ad lib asides to the audience, ditsy crossovers, rope tricks, roller skates, puppets, and, of all things, William Shakespeare himself. He seemed bewildered.

COMEDY OF MANNERS

Worldly, satiric, and dealing with life in the cultural capital (or with city influences on country ways), the comedy of manners (also called social comedy) exposes the follies of the day. The form begins in the *Restoration, with the work of William Wycherley, George Etherege, and William Congreve: the setting is the London they know and the topics take in courtship rituals, hypocrisy, vanity, pedantry, such fads as astrology, the conflict of parents and children, and the fashionable substitution of style for substance. All of this is still timely, and the best social comedies are in fact agelessly applicable to the social condition. They are as well, above all, comedies of wit, though this is more salient in the Restoration and the succeeding era of *Richard Brinsley Sheridan than in later times. The form was virtually witless by the nineteenth century; such writers as *T. W. Robertson, and the American Anna Cora Mowatt (1819–1870), celebrated for *Fashion* (1845), are more impressive for their moral point of view than for brilliance of language. However, at the century's end *Oscar Wilde revived the vigor of wit in social comedy. In *The Importance of Being Earnest,* the setting moves from London to the country, but this is the "weekend country," so to say, a rustic London for vacationing townsfolk. Courtship rituals and the fashionable style still provision the action, but the devious Wilde introduces a unique topic in "Bunburying," essentially the homosexual escapades of the closeted gay male.

The twentieth century's comedy of manners, again, lacks wit. W. Somerset Maugham (1874–1965) and *Noël Coward practiced in this form, the latter most successfully in *Private Lives,* less witty than colorful and so chicly self-absorbed in its worldview that it appears that style is actually becoming substance at the author's own contrivance. The Americans *Philip Barry and *S. N. Behrman similarly found a high society "look" more useful than a grip of classic wit. As for the setting, they routinely prefer the suburban house party to the dense brilliance of urban characters in their urban haunts, making their plays stodgy in comparison with the ribald tang of Wycherley and Congreve. Today, perhaps only *Tom Stoppard and *Simon Gray command language sharp and comely enough to revive the comedy of manners, though *Alan Ayckbourn's middle-class characters function in a milieu reminiscent of the satiric boulevard and salon of the Restoration masters.
(See also *Brief Moment, The Importance of Being Earnest, The School for Scandal,* and *The Way of the World.*)

COMIC RELIEF

A scene of light or sportive nature, used in tragedy to relax the tension. The comic Gravedigger's scene in *Hamlet,* so out of kilter with the haunted, questing nature of the rest of the play, is a classic example.

COMMEDIA DELL'ARTE

Literally "skilled theatre." This improvisational art, uniquely Italian, developed in the late Renaissance. It was funny, fast, and physical, delivered in the popular tongue by experts in fanciful costumes and leather masks around the eyes, each actor bearing a traditional name and representing a stereotyped figure—the foolish old father Pantalone, the stuttering lawyer known as the Dottore, the scheming servants Arlecchino (Harlequin) and Colombina, the braggart soldier called the Capitano, and so on. These characters were known as *le maschere,* "the masks"—a term of almost mythical reverberation in Italy even today.

At *commedia*'s height, in the late 1600s, such troupes were the delight of kings and workers throughout Europe, and proved highly influential, impressing many playwrights (including *Molière and *Marivaux, most notably) to incorporate elements of the *commedia* style. By the 1700s, however, the style was moribund even in Italy, and enjoyed a last fling in the comedies of the Venetians *Carlo Gozzi (who elaborated pure *commedia* into a fairy-tale blend of the romantic and the grotesque) and *Carlo Goldoni (who tamed and reformed it).

(For details of the *commedia* style, see also Lazzi, Slapstick, and Zanni.)

WILLIAM CONGREVE (See Restoration Theatre)

JACQUES COPEAU (1879–1949)

This director, actor, and teacher was France's impresario of twentieth century style: sound psychological ensemble acting, uncluttered productions, art stripped to its clarity. Copeau also believed in playhouses stripped of traditional decorations and pretenses. When in 1913 he took over the Athénée Saint-Germain, on Paris's Left Bank, he simplified a fancy, public-friendly auditorium into a stark, almost monastic hall. Even the *proscenium had been ripped away, till there was nothing but seats and a raised platform. (The *wings, too, had vanished; Copeau's actors had to make their exits literally into adjacent buildings.) Renamed the Vieux-Colombier, the house presented a bill of fare ranging from the medieval to the contemporary, emphasizing unknown playwrights or even unknown works by known playwrights and barring star turns absolutely. Wags dubbed it all "the Calvin Follies." However, as a purifying influence, Copeau is one of the essential French thespians. War emergencies led him to take his company to New York for two years in 1917, so Copeau had the chance to leave his mark on the American stage as well. However, the language barrier compromised his effect on the Broadway scene, whereas at home his protégés included virtually all of his contemporaries who were not sworn conservatives—and his disciples passed *le Copeauisme* on to the next generation. From *Louis Jouvet to *Jean-Louis Barrault, Copeau spread his instruction among the idealists of the French theatre, and he even assumed directorship of the *Comédie-Française, a sign that the old guard had accepted the probity of Copeau's genius.

CONSTANT-BENOÎT COQUELIN (1841–1909)

Known as Coquelin *aîné* (the elder) to distinguish him from Coquelin *cadet* (the younger), his brother Ernest (1848–1909), also an actor. Coquelin *aîné* is generally called the greatest French actor of his time, especially for his strutting grandeur in comic parts. From 1860 to 1886, he was at the Comédie-Française, taking over important roles in Molière and as Beaumarchais's Figaro. Coquelin's outstanding part was contemporary, though written in the grand manner of the old days, as the hero of Edmond Rostand's *Cyrano de Bergerac.*

PIERRE CORNEILLE (1606–1684)

Alexandre Hardy (?1575–1631) was France's first playwright of Classical tragedy and comedy (that is, discounting the authors of the *medieval pageants and fairgrounds vaudevilles). When Hardy died, the French theatre was just coming into its early prime, and Corneille is the first of the two reasons why. (The other reason, of course, is Corneille's successor Jean Racine.) The form that Corneille inherited was strictly governed by state officials (not least, Cardinal Richelieu) and critics, who insisted on adherence to *la vraisemblance* (likelihood of plot action), *la bienséance* (propriety of behavior), the poetic line called the *alexandrine, and, above all, *les règles* ("the rules"), or, as we term them, "the *unities." In the famous words of Nicolas Boileau, in *L'Art Poétique* (1674): "Qu'en un lieu, qu'en un jour, un seul fait accompli": Execute a single action in a single place in a single day. This hampered French playwrights as it had not their *Elizabethan cousins two generations earlier. Elizabethan theatre was free, direct, poetically naturalistic on all matters from love to death. French theatre was grandiloquent, truculently "noble" and effortfully comely. Shakespeare could dart across the map in a couplet; Corneille and his colleagues had to force all events into one spot, usually by crowbar. And how much can believably happen in a single day? Given all this, it is surprising that Corneille's plays have such vitality, especially in his heroes, types of an ideal and touchingly ingenuous honesty that far outrank Corneille's often interesting but almost invariably underpowered heroines.

Corneille ran up against the rules—all of them —in his ninth (and first great) play, *Le Cid* (1637), at least partly because its tremendous popular success excited a jealous cabal. Then too, the state regarded its theatre as something of a secular arm, a moral demonstration of authoritarian beliefs. Dramatic subjects, characterizations, and language were all held to account for the improvement of the intellect and the initiation of the spirit. *Le Cid* was made an example *pour encourager les autres,* and it certainly "encouraged" Corneille. His later work observed the strictures more acutely: *Horace* (1640), *Cinna* (1640), *Polyeucte* (1643), and *Nicomède* (1651), all drawn from "respectable" Roman sources (*Le Cid* derived from a contemporary Spanish play), are considered, with *Le Cid,* Corneille's masterpieces. And we note that Corneille settled the *querelle* ("controversy") *du Cid* by dedicating *Horace* to Richelieu.

(See also Jean Racine and *Le Cid*.)

KATHARINE CORNELL

(1893–1974)

This American actress, one of Broadway's outstanding leading ladies in the 1930s and 1940s, created roles later filmed by Katharine Hepburn (Clemence Dane's *A Bill of Divorcement,* 1921), Dorothy McGuire (*Arthur Wing Pinero's *The Enchanted Cottage,* 1923), Greta Garbo (Michael Arlen's *The Green Hat,* 1926), Jeanne Eagels and Bette Davis (W. Somerset Maugham's *The Letter,* 1927), Joan Crawford (*Dishonored Lady,* 1930— which its authors *Edward Sheldon and Margaret Ayer Brown proved in court was the unacknowledged source of MGM's *Letty Lynton*), Norma Shearer (Rudolf Besier's *The Barretts of Wimpole Street,* 1931; not to mention Cornell's 1934 production of *Romeo and Juliet,* which may have inspired Irving Thalberg's rendition for wife Shearer), and Rosalind Russell (*S. N. Behrman's *No Time for Comedy,* 1939). The aggregation of personalities thus conjured out of Cornell's roles suggests an actress of notable versatility, but Cornell was in fact a somewhat limited technician. Rather, she won her following for grace, concentration, and an incredible set of cheekbones. With her husband, producer and director Guthrie McClintic (1893–1961), Cornell rose from workmanlike *vehicles to George Bernard Shaw, Maxwell Anderson, Jean Anouilh, and Christopher Fry. The Cornell-McClintic production of Anton Chekhov's *The Three Sisters* in 1942 (with Judith Anderson, Gertrude Musgrove; and Ruth Gordon as Natasha) was a rare Broadway hit for the Russian playwright, and Cornell's wryly loving portrayal of Shaw's Candida was so successful that she mounted five different stagings over the years, the last one, in 1946, to the very young Marlon Brando's Marchbanks.

CORRAL THEATRE

These corrals, or courtyards, closed in by the backs of neighboring houses, offered a space for players and their public in sixteenth and seventeenth cen-

Katharine Cornell in one of her greatest roles, G. B. Shaw's Saint Joan, in 1936.

tury Spain. The effect was rather like that of the *Elizabethan playhouse, with the high-ranking spectators seated in the balconies and windows of the corral houses, the *groundlings in the pit, and the actors on a long, narrow stage at one end of the corral. The same setup could be found in the patios of Spanish inns, and not till the eighteenth century did the Spanish begin to build actual theatres, on the Italian model.

COUP DE THÉÂTRE

This virtually untranslatable French term (*coup* means, among other things, "blow," "stroke," or "act") refers to an inspired moment of theatricality —a sudden surprise in the action, for instance, or a mesmerizing pictorial display. The term isolates one of the theatre's unique qualities, shared by no other art—that flash of communication between presentation and public, glowing for a second or two, then extinguished, over, irretrievable. The first act curtain line of Friedrich Dürrenmatt's *The Visit* is a good example. The billionairess Claire Zachanassian, feted by her bankrupt native village, calmly offers her former neighbors an unholy fortune if they kill her former sweetheart, who is present in the room. The people, of course, are horrified and offended. They refuse her offer. Never would they even consider such an uncivilized act. *Never.*

The billionairess is calm. "Ich warte," she tells them: I'll wait.

Curtain.

COVENT GARDEN

Three Theatres Royal by this name have stood on this site on Bow Street around the corner from London's famous flower market. The first playhouse, built in 1732 and managed by John Rich, saw performances by *Peg Woffington and David Garrick. The second playhouse, built in 1809 after a fire destroyed the first, played host to a challenging rivalry with London's other important Theatre Royal, Drury Lane; this was the Covent Garden of John Philip Kemble and Sarah Siddons, of the Old

Prices Riots, and *William Macready. The third building, dating from 1858 after another fire, became the home of Great Britain's major opera company, a Covent Garden of Adelina Patti, the de Reszke brothers, Nellie Melba, and Fyodor Shalyapin. Today, Covent Garden is the home of the Royal Opera and the Royal Ballet.
(See also Master Betty, Drury Lane, David Garrick, and The Kembles.)

NOËL COWARD (1899–1973)

Lying in bed in Tokyo's Imperial Hotel in 1929, Coward had a vision: "Gertie [Lawrence] appeared in a white Molyneux dress on a terrace in the South of France and refused to go away again until four in the morning, by which time *Private Lives,* title and all, had constructed itself." A bit later, bedridden with influenza in Shanghai's Cathay Hotel, Coward wrote it all out in four days, in longhand.

Private Lives (1930) is the ultimate Coward piece: tautly fey, bright, chic, and apparently amoral and apolitical. It looks bony and contrived on paper, but it plays beautifully and nearly rivals *Hamlet* for number of famous lines: "Moonlight is cruelly deceptive"; "Strange how potent cheap music is"; "Very flat, Norfolk"; "Women should be struck regularly, like gongs." It's very frivolous. Even Coward's vision of Gertrude Lawrence in a white Molyneux dress on a terrace in France is frivolous. But, as the critic John Lahr reminds us, "Only when Coward is frivolous does he become in any sense profound."

Coward's shallow appearance is his way of defeating humiliation and despair—so he himself reminds us, again and again, in his scripts. Style in Coward is not snobbery, but a form of disguise, of balance in a vertiginous existence. Coward could shock, as in his first success, *The Vortex* (1924), about a drug addict more or less in love with his mother. Coward could be honest, as in *A Song at Twilight*—one of three one-acters played in London as *Suite in Three Keys* (1966) and in New York in 1974, minus one play, as *Noël Coward in Two Keys* —which exposes the lifelong heterosexual pose of a gay writer. (The writer was generally thought to have been based on W. Somerset Maugham, who had died just the year before. But Coward's own experience must have had some bearing on the case.) Most telling of all is *Blithe Spirit* (1941), ostensibly about a man caught between his present wife and the ghost of his former wife, but in fact the most potent metaphor for the homosexual closet triangle—man, wife, and secret lover—since *Oscar Wilde first aired the notion of "Bunburying" in *The Importance of Being Earnest.*

In the main, the public Coward coolly preened, saying nothing. However he himself played the telltale leads in *The Vortex, A Song at Twilight,* and *Blithe Spirit.* He could be that shocking, that honest. He was an all-around thespian, not only playwright, actor, and director in the old style, but a composer and lyricist as well—of such Cowardesque songs as "Mad Dogs and Englishmen" and "I Travel Alone," but also of full-scale musicals, operettas, and revues: *This Year of Grace* (1928), *Bitter Sweet* (1929), *Conversation Piece* (1934), *Sail Away* (1961). Perhaps Coward made it look too easy—writing *Private Lives* in four days and *Blithe Spirit* in eight, clipping out satiric commentary on everything in sight in impeccably creased trousers and a dandy's mask of a face, and lasting out era after era. By the end of World War II, the London critics were gunning for him and savaged everything he produced. It took two decades for him to jump back into favor, in the National Theatre of Great Britain's 1964 revival of *Hay Fever* (1925). Ironically, this is one of Coward's most perfunctory plays, a gruesome farce about some innocents trapped into a country weekend with an eccentrically selfish family. (It had happened to Coward himself, staying with *Laurette Taylor and her husband J. Hartley Manners.)

No matter. Suddenly Coward was a classic. The Master of the "talent to amuse." He was knighted. Few modern actors control the brittle throwaway delivery his lines need, yet his best plays endure. So does his wisdom, often encoded in "cover" procedures. Every so often, however, a passage strikes unmissably home, such as this one, from *Design for Living* (1933), apparently about the sensual union of one woman and two men but really about . . . well, listen:

OTTO: We're not doing any harm to anyone else.
We're not peppering the world with illegitimate children. The only people we could possibly mess up are ourselves, and that's our lookout.

(See also Sacha Guitry, *Cavalcade,* and *To-night at 8:30.*)

GORDON CRAIG (1872–1966)

Of all the key figures of the transition from the old theatre-as-usual to the daring modern stage, Edward Gordon Craig became the most famous for doing the least. As the (illegitimate) son of actress *Ellen Terry and architect Edward Godwin, he combined theatre and fine arts, first as an actor, then designer and director, but primarily as theoretician, in *The Art of the Theatre* (1905). Craig proclaimed that the theatre must blend and reblend the elements of "action," "words," "line and colour," and "rhythm" under the stewardship of the super-director. "He enjoyed becoming a legend," recalled Craig's first cousin once removed, *John Gielgud, "but he was too suspicious to let anybody manage him or help him to carry out his ideas."

A professional eccentric. Thus Craig became known more for the theories he advanced (even if most if not all of his ideas were drawn from Richard Wagner's concept of the *Gesamtkunstwerk,* the "fusion of the arts") than for his implementation of them. Indeed, despite a long life spent in voluntary exile in Italy and France, Craig did very little actual work—Ibsen's *Rosmersholm* for *Eleonora Duse in Florence in 1906, a *Hamlet* for the *Moscow Art Theatre in 1912. The *Hamlet* tells us why a *Max Reinhardt, a *Lugné-Poë—and not Craig—would be the directors of the age. For in Moscow, Craig as designer was reckless, impractical; and Craig as director treated actors as puppets. The *Hamlet* production was undeniably brilliant, planned around a construction of huge screens to be moved, as the scenes changed, before the audience's eyes. One hour before the curtain was to rise on the first night, the whole kaboodle crashed to the floor.

But then this too fed into Craig's legend: the impractical became him. He lived on into his nine-

Two extraordinary Britons: (left) Noël Coward and (above) Gordon Craig. Let us admire as well a historic site, the entrance to Craig's villa at Genoa. Coward, too, ended his life an expatriate, mainly in Jamaica. Craig fled English culture; Coward fled English tax laws.

ties, into the age of the *absurd, the "happening," the "angry young men" of London's *Royal Court Theatre: into a bold modern stage that somehow had heard of Craig while having forgot him and his glorious puppet productions. "When I knew him," says Gielgud, "he was a very old man but still in wonderful spirits. He had no teeth but ate enormous meals and chattered away, looking picturesquely sly and coy and nodding, like an old raven, with his head on one side."

RACHEL CROTHERS (1878–1958)

The outstanding American woman playwright in the years between the world wars dealt with the social problems of the middle class—the generational gap, weak vocational motivation, repressive manners, and, especially, women's rights. Crothers's greatest success was *Susan and God* (1937), about a wife and mother so caught up in born-again religious fervor that she almost loses her family. This is typical Crothers, testing controversies of the day only—sometimes—to pull back at the finale for a happy ending. At other times, Crothers maintains her bite. Her best such play is *Mary the 3d* (1923), a strongly feminist piece that suggests that women's encompassing love of men and marriage oppresses her as much as legal prejudice and the double standard do.

THE CRUCIBLE

Timely *chronicle play by *Arthur Miller, prem. New York, 1953.

Boldly unveiled at the height of the McCarthy purge of liberals, Communists, and other nonconformists, this look at a purge of "witches" in old Salem, Massachusetts makes a vivid case against trial by character assassination. Careful research of the 1692 hearings revealed to Miller a town rent by politics and ruled by hypocrites, a fair parallel for the postwar American nation. Still, Miller felt the socialist Good versus Evil of the history needed a personal, sensual element, and built his narrative around the scheme of a vicious adulteress to kill off

her lover's wife and—when he resists—to kill her lover. *The Crucible* seems to have overtaken *Death of a Salesman* as Miller's most performed work, less for its relevant exhortations than for its compelling picture of remorseless bigots overwhelming reason. Critics, then and now, are uncomfortable with the play, perhaps because they see themselves in Miller's high-handed, ignorant judges of witchcraft.

THEATRE OF CRUELTY

The theory, developed by Antonin Artaud (1896–1948) and expounded in his book, *Le Théâtre et Son Double* (The Theatre and Its Double, 1938), that the stage must free itself of its literary foundation to become a more physicalized, primitive experience, a ritual more sensed than understood. Artaud's use of the word "cruelty" is misleading. "Theatre of exorcism" suits his program better, though his manifestos are anything but lucid in the first place. In his own words, "The Theatre of Cruelty was created to restore to the stage a passionate and convulsive conception of life." (A few of Artaud's stage directions, from his short play *Le Jet de Sang* [Jet of Blood, 1927]: "Two stars crash into each other"; "They eat each other's eyes"; "An army of scorpions enters.") Where theatre before Artaud generally sought out images of nobility or an ordering of naturalistic experiences with which to enlighten the spectator, the Theatre of Cruelty forces the spectator to face the basic, barbaric drives within himself. Artaud's stage, then, is savagely cathartic. His influence is far-reaching, touching *Jerzy Grotowski's Polish Laboratory Theatre, the *Living Theatre, *Joseph Chaikin's Open Theater, and, by his own admiring admission, *Peter Brook.

CURSE OF THE STARVING CLASS

Domestic drama by *Sam Shepard, prem. London, 1977.

Arguably Shepard's finest play. Critic Ruby Cohn has noted "Shepard's attempts at Greek tragedy," his use of the family scene to analyze monumental problems in human relations: as if the family were the world. We sense this especially in this play, not least in the dense images that drunken, unreliable father Weston, alienated wife Ella, and children Wesley and Emma give voice to —images of escape, exploitation, hunger, cheating, battle, of a doom passed genetically from generation to generation:

WESTON: Look at my outlook. You don't envy it, right?

WESLEY: No.

WESTON: That's because it's full of poison. Infected. And you recognize poison, right? You recognize it when you see it?

WESLEY: Yes.

WESTON: Yes, you do. I can see that you do. My poison scares you.

WESLEY: Doesn't scare me.

WESTON: No?

WESLEY: No.

WESTON: Good. You're growing up. I never saw my old man's poison until I was much older than you. Much older. And then you know how I recognized it?

WESLEY: How?

WESTON: Because I saw myself infected with it. That's how. I saw me carrying it around. His poison in my body.

Some of the play's images are visual, as in the principals' obsession with the refrigerator, which they constantly open and stare into (and even talk to), whether it's empty or full. The most arresting image is introduced by Weston at the start of the third and final act, recalling a day when he was castrating the spring rams, a seasonal routine. Weston tells us that an eagle swooped down like a mad pilot to gorge on the discarded testes, "those fresh little remnants of manlihood." At the end of the act, with Emma dead and Weston on the run to Mexico, Ella takes up the story: a tomcat is attracted by the gore, and now the eagle carries *him* off:

ELLA: And they fight. They fight like crazy in the middle of the sky. The cat's tearing his chest out, and the eagle's trying to drop him, but the cat won't let go because he knows if he falls he'll die.

WESLEY: And the eagle's being torn apart in midair. The eagle's trying to free himself from the cat, and the cat won't let go.

ELLA: And they come crashing down to the earth. Both of them come crashing down. Like one whole thing.

And there Shepard pulls his curtain.

CURTAIN-RAISER

A short piece, usually comic, musical, or otherwise light, used to launch an evening of theatre in the nineteenth century, when performances lasted well over three hours. The practice survives today, fitfully, in the preceding of a shortish main piece by a one-acter. Technically, any one-acter may apply; but the ideal curtain-raiser is short and sweet, merely initiating the audience into the theatre experience in order to bank the performance's success on the major title. Audiences at the original West End and New York stagings of *Tom Stoppard's The Real Inspector Hound* (1968) got a demonstration-level taste of this approach in London's *The Audition* and New York's *After Magritte, Hound's* curtain-raisers. Each is a delightfully silly piece. Sean Patrick Vincent and Andrew Lawson-Johnston's *The Audition* offers a pathetically awful run-through of a grotesque musical; Stoppard's own *After Magritte* presents a logical explanation for the odd costumes and positions of the figures in avant-garde painting. Each play thus promoted an air of the naturalistically bizarre that prepared the public for *Hound's* spoof-surrounding-spoof play-within-a-play. On the other hand, the 1967 Broadway staging of Peter Shaffer's *Black Comedy,* a very thin farce, was overshadowed by its curtain-raiser, Shaffer's *White Lies,* a one-acter about a fortune-teller suddenly driven, at a climactic moment in her life, to tell the truth. This upended the structure of the event, especially as the great Geraldine Page made a fine fortune-teller but was wasted as the vapid vamp heroine, Clea, of *Black Comedy.*

CURTAIN SPEECH

The rhymed epilogue of *Restoration Theatre, spoken "before the curtain" by the lead actor or actress (see Prologue for an example), led audiences to anticipate that last little address from the edge of the stage at the close of an evening. When the epilogue died out, important actors kept the practice alive on noteworthy occasions—a premiere, a season's closing, and so on. Absolutely Guaranteed Last Farewell Performances of course demanded a ceremonial speech, even when an actor was planning to make a decade of Them, and the growing importance of the author in the late 1800s brought him into the picture as well, on opening nights. American audiences loved this personal touch more than those of other nationalities, but even on Broadway the curtain speech was moribund by the 1920s, except for very special situations. Perhaps the most famous recent curtain speech was *David Merrick's opening night address after the musical *42nd Street*—announcing the death of the show's director, Gower Champion.

CYCLORAMA (See Scenery)

CYRANO DE BERGERAC

"A heroic comedy" by Edmond Rostand (1868–1918), prem. Paris, 1897.

Rostand's generic classification is informative: this is an amusing play with a serious hero, the brilliant poet and soldier whose physical appearance humiliates his beauty of soul. In technical detail, Rostand gives us the agony of the ugly man forced out of generosity of heart to play agent for his own rival. In overall atmosphere, however, the play laments the passing of the old fashions in playwrighting, the death of style and delight and the picturesque in favor of realism, political moralizing, and dreary decor. This is, for 1897, a very ancient play, in its period magnificence, its poetic spirit, and its devotion to the star actor—for all *Cyrano*s stand on the powers of the title player.

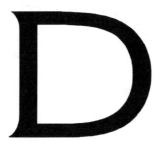

DADA

Never say "dadaism": dada's founders were too impetuous, improvisational, and anarchic to support the ism of an active movement. Eventually, especially in Germany in the 1920s, dada did take on some sense of structure, some aim, even some politics. But in 1916, when dada "came about" (that's the closest one can get) in Zurich's Cabaret Voltaire, it was far more an atmosphere and inspiration than an attempt to create anything. Indeed, dada was anti-creative, a response to the insanity of World War I. Life no longer made sense, decided dada's founders, Tristan Tzara (1896–1963) and Roger Vitrac (1899–1952): therefore art must be senseless, uncivilized, anything that pops into the mind. Pure dada was too bizarre and narrow to enjoy anything like an era of stage history, but its elements fed into *surrealism and the *absurd; and Tristan Tzara remains with us, spouting aesthetic, as one of the characters in *Tom Stoppard's *Travesties.

GABRIELE D'ANNUNZIO

(1863–1938)

D'Annunzio's love affairs and wartime escapades (he led an expedition to capture the port city of Fiume, or Rijeka, disputed between Italy and Yugoslavia, in 1919) were as famous as his flamboyant medieval tragedies; and he combined romance, war, and the theatre in the scripts he wrote for his lover *Eleonora Duse, often as bellicose as they are passionate. Ardently Italian—not only as patriot but as cultural ideologue and historicist—D'Annunzio held the stage so surely that every actress had to test her mettle in his roles, every Italian composer had to turn at least one D'Annunzio text into an opera. Riccardo Zandonai set *Francesca da Rimini* (1901), Alberto Franchetti and, later, Ildebrando Pizzetti claimed *La Figlia di Jorio* (Jorio's Daughter, 1904), Italo Montemezzi took *La Nave* (The Ship, 1908), and Pietro Mascagni got *Parisina* (1913). *Francesca,* on the classic love triangle mentioned in Dante's Inferno, was by general agreement D'Annunzio's loveliest piece and one of Duse's greatest triumphs. However, the savage *La Nave* gives us a truer D'Annunzio. He lays the scene in the Venetian lagoon, more or less at the moment of the founding of the Venetian Republic —the eponymous ship, the Totus Mundus, sets off at the play's end to conquer and loot and thus inaugurate the Republic's merchant empire. D'Annunzio's theme, in almost everything he wrote, applauds the taker, the egotist, the superman. At *La Nave*'s curtain, the hero ties his lover to the ship's prow to give her "a beautiful death." Next to this, Tristan and Isolde are Hänsel and Gretel.

DANTON'S DEATH

Nihilistic *chronicle play by *Georg Büchner, prem. Berlin, 1902.

Büchner wrote *Dantons Tod* in 1835, but—like all Büchner—it was hopelessly ahead of its time. This look at revolutionaries devouring each other during Paris's Reign of Terror pits the aimless voluptuary Danton (of the moderate party) against the frigidly ascetic Robespierre (of the radicals). "Vice must be punished and virtue must rule through Terror," Robespierre insists, hopes, purrs. "You," says Danton, "and your virtue, Robespierre!" Robespierre wins. But—Büchner implies—only for a time. No man *can* win, for there is nothing to win, no choice to be made, no destiny to cultivate. Birth is a kind of death. "Life's a whore," says Danton. "She fornicates with the whole world." The play emphasizes an anti-existentialist despair, an almost *Godot*-like emptiness. It's a colorful work, poetic, brutal, witty, furious; at the climax it opens up to take in the extermination of Danton and his friends ("I'm going to have a wig made from your lovely hair," a woman in the crowd tells one of them) in the Place de la Révolution. Yet we are meant to feel not the loss of a hero but the hollowness of his and every life. A masterpiece—however, like *Thornton Wilder's *Our Town,* it's very hard to take.

THOMAS DEKKER (See

Elizabethan Theatre)

DÉNOUEMENT

Literally, in French, "untying": the unraveling of the plot strands at a play's end.

THE DEPUTY

*Chronicle play in free verse by *Rolf Hochhuth, prem. Berlin, 1963.

This may be the most important play in history. It is notorious rather than popular, discussed more than admired. But the storm of controversy it inspired on its tour through the West (London, Paris, Vienna, Stockholm, Basel, Copenhagen, and Athens mounted it within months of the premiere) made it that rare item, a play every intellectual must know about. For Hochhuth tackled the century's most imposing issue, Hitler's attempted extermination of the Jewish people; and he built his eight-hour pageant around one momentous and unarguable historical fact: that Pope Pius XII stood by and did nothing, even as Jewish Romans were being rounded up virtually outside his windows.

Such explosive material was bound to inspire passionate reactions—so much so that it was difficult to separate the play itself from the furor it engendered. Let us do so now. First, the play. Hochhuth researched his subject exhaustingly and kept strictly to fact. The events he treats actually occurred; his characters, where not real-life figures (Adolf Eichmann, Kurt Gerstein, the Pope), are modeled on them, such as his *protagonist, an Italian Jesuit who pins a yellow star to his soutane and assumes a Jewish destiny; and the protagonist's opposite, a German doctor based on the demonically sadistic Joseph Mengele, still at large and laughing when Hochhuth wrote *The Deputy* from 1959 to 1961. The director of the Berlin premiere, *Erwin Piscator, likened Hochhuth's approach to *Schiller's historical dramas; but Schiller romanticized. Hochhuth reports. He was criticized for writing a play too long to stage except in some compromised version, but he clearly meant his text to be read as well as seen, for he comments on the action between the lines of dialogue. The Broadway mounting of 1964 may have discouraged the public from reading the script, for the universally denounced production was an inadequate staging of a butchered text, "bare, crude, and shockingly listless in places," as Alfred Kazin saw it. "Much if it is an anti-Nazi movie of the John Garfield period." Only Emlyn Williams's fastidiously oily Pope centered the historical gravity of Hochhuth's indictment.

Now, the controversy. Catholics of course attacked the play, along with the American Nazi Party, which picketed the Broadway production.

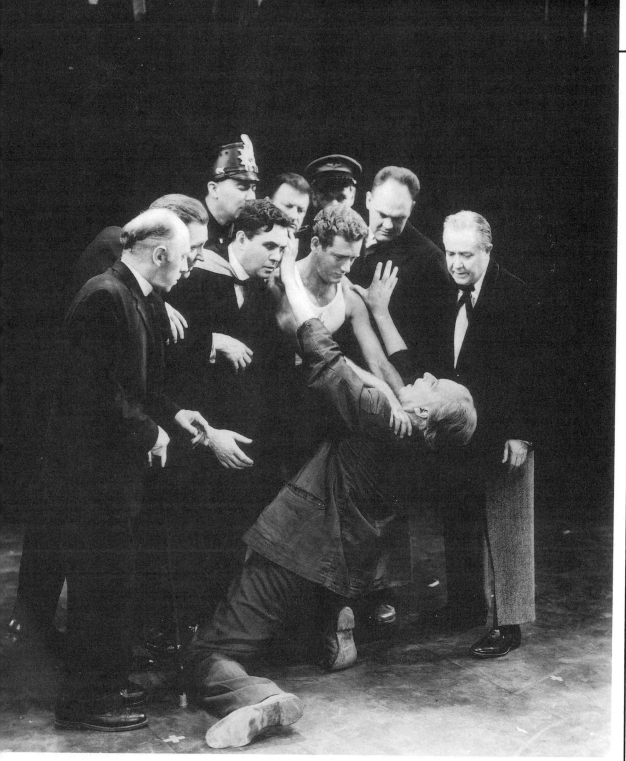

Protagonist: *the richest woman in the world.* Problem: *she offers an unspeakable fortune to her penniless hometown if it kills the man who seduced and abandoned her years before.* Conflict: *the town's conscience versus the woman's money.* Dénouement: *above, the townspeople make their deal. The play is* *Friedrich Dürrenmatt's The Visit, *in its American premiere in 1958, on the occasion of the farewell of Alfred Lunt (on floor) and Lynn Fontanne.*

The intelligentsia generally discussed the issues rather than the work. Professional apologists argued that the whole world was responsible for Hitler—why single out the Pope? What could he have done? *Everything,* says Hochhuth: Hitler greatly feared the power of the Church. But Hitler would keep Stalin from the gates of the Vatican. So the Pope made his bargain with hell—which Hochhuth is at pains to show us. *The Deputy's* final act is set at Auschwitz.

DEUS EX MACHINA

"The god [brought in] by machine": the problem-solving deity of *Greek theatre, dropped in at the climax on a crane to resolve an otherwise adamant conflict, popularized by *Euripides (though the term itself is Latin, not Greek). Many centuries after, the term covered the positive interference of any character—an emperor dispensing clemency, a sage counseling wisdom. Eventually the term became a derogation, suggesting that the playwright "fixed" his plot by contrivance rather than ingenuity.

COLLEEN DEWHURST (1926–   )

Most stage actors aspire to the great roles of their type: as a Laurence Olivier seeks out Hamlet and Sophocles's Oedipus, a Peggy Ashcroft works toward Lady Teazle (in *The School for Scandal) or Hedda Gabler, Dewhurst is distinctive in defeating the notion of type—in being wrong for virtually every great role in the repertory. Large, deep, gala, as dense as a Babylonian fertility goddess, Dewhurst has played some odd Shakespeare and Brecht, but found a niche in O'Neill—especially for a stunning Josie Hogan in *A Moon for the Misbegotten* on Broadway in 1973 and in Barbara Gelb's one-woman reminiscence, *My Gene* (1987), on the life and work of Carlotta Monterey O'Neill—and in Albee, as the picturesque heroine of *The Ballad of the Sad Café,* which climaxed in a grease-and-grope public wrestling contest with her redneck husband, and in the 1976 revival of *Who's Afraid of Virginia Woolf?* with Ben Gazzara, directed by the author.

JOHN DEXTER (1925–   )

British director especially noted for his collaborations with imaginative designers, as in the bleakly class-conscious barracks walls swinging open and closed in *Arnold Wesker's *Chips with Everything* (1962), the evocative Incan ritualism of Peter Shaffer's *The Royal Hunt of the Sun* (1964), or the centaurs-in-the-boxing-ring psychiatric duel of *Equus* (1973). Faced with a small cast and nondescript decor—as for instance in the 1985 Broadway revival of *Tennessee William's *The Glass Menagerie* with Jessica Tandy—Dexter seems to have little to say.

DENIS DIDEROT (1713–1784)

The great French encyclopedist took an interest in the theatre as a place of practical moral instruction. Opposed to the Classically elevated character of heroic drama, Diderot urged playwrights to deal with the persons and situations of everyday life, and actors to develop a natural, lifelike, style. Diderot's own plays, most notably *Le Père de Famille* (The Father, 1761) and *Le Fils Naturel* (The Natural Son, 1771) were more read than performed; *Le Fils Naturel* was published and discussed for fourteen years before it gained the stage. But Diderot's theories, disseminated throughout continental Europe, were influential and led directly to the reforms of *Gotthold Lessing.

DIONYSIA

The annual spring theatre festival held by the ancient *Greeks.

THE DIRECTOR

There are two essential figures in theatre: the playwright and the actor(s). For centuries, production

—the performing functions that regulate the actors and bring the playwright's words to life—was traditional, conventional, self-organizing. Who designed and lit the *Greek theatre? Dionysus and the sun. Who "produced" *Elizabethan theatre? The actors. Who staged *Molière? Molière himself. As late as the middle 1800s, there was no such thing as a "director"—meaning the person who stands apart from the actors to instruct and integrate their portrayals, who coordinates the efforts of the various technicians, even edits the author's text. Someone had to officiate, of course: but this was invariably an *actor-manager or the playwright (who was often an actor himself). Still, from the early-middle 1800s on, certain actor-managers began to take a greater interest in the placement of actors, the delivery of text, the balance of the ensemble. The first notable director per se—perhaps the first director ever—was George II, Duke of Saxe-Meiningen, a true *amateur* who in the late 1800s ran a troupe of actors and technicians under close personal supervision. The *Meiningers, as they were called, overthrew the *star system for a close-knit interaction of character, even drilling bit players and chorus into the entity. On other stages, the star came first. With the Meiningers, the play came first; and their many European tours promoted this new approach.

Increasingly, actor-managers and playwrights sought to implement this integrity of craft. Also increasingly, leading figures explored the responsibility of directing. The playwright and manager *David Belasco emphasized both naturalistic and impressionistic spectacle as a factor of stagecraft; the actor and coach *Konstantin Stanislavsky instilled a revolutionary verisimilitude of portrayal in his casts. Note that, still, these were not "directors," per se; they held other posts, and directed only additionally. Not till the 1920s did many thespians with a bent for artistic organization renounce acting or playwrighting to become, exclusively, the director (the English term is "producer") of one production after another. Perhaps the outstanding example is *Max Reinhardt, truly the "author" of his productions. The *Theatre Guild, the self-appointed bastion of art on Broadway, pioneered the employment of the all-powerful, really all-encompassing, director; as did its rebellious offshoot, the *Group Theatre. At the

same time, in Broadway's more commercial precincts, such playwights as *Rachel Crothers, *Elmer Rice, George Kelly, *George S. Kaufman, Howard Lindsay; and such actor-managers as Mae West, *Eva Le Gallienne; and such producers (in the American usage) as Gilbert Miller, *Jed Harris, Arthur Hopkins, Winthrop Ames, Brock Pemberton, and Guthrie McClintic; and such all-arounders as George M. Cohan, Frank Craven (the original Stage Manager in *Our Town*), and *George Abbott upheld tradition by directing their properties for clarity and pleasure rather than for Art.

The star director, whose personality more or less envelops all his projects, whether new or classic work, emerged after World War II in such figures as *Peter Brook and *Joan Littlewood in England, *Elia Kazan and Tom O'Horgan in America, Luchino Visconti and *Giorgio Strehler in Italy. Not that the director comes first, exactly: but that the work and the director's unique conception of it become indivisible. Shakespeare wrote *A Midsummer Night's Dream*—but Peter Brook's 1970 staging for the *Royal Shakespeare Company in a white-walled space hung with trapezes offered a reading of the text so special that Brook became perforce Shakespeare's collaborator. This is the emancipation—and idolatry—of the theatre's youngest element, Production.

DITHYRAMBOS (See Greek Theatre)

DOCUMENTARY DRAMA

A recent phenomenon in theatre history, the adapting of recent historical events, ideally with great realism of detail but often with a political bias that selects the details. As Pontius Pilate asked, "What is truth?" Does Donald Freed's *Inquest* (1970), on the trial of the Rosenbergs for espionage, report the case or dramatize it; defend the innocent, or exculpate the guilty? Does Eric Bentley's *Are You Now or Have You Ever Been* (1972) comprehend the inhumanity of the McCarthy era

—the ignorance and opportunism of the aggressors, the confusion, heroism, and treachery of the victims—or does it reduce the period to transcripts of a few hearings?

(See also *Juristen*.)

DON JUAN

Existentialist comedy *avant la lettre* by *Molière, prem. Paris, 1665.

Molière seems to have written *Don Juan* in response to the banning of *Tartuffe* by religious reactionaries. For while *Don Juan* appears to damn the hero's libertine solipsism, it fails to offer any reply to his challenges to conventional morality. And, like *Tartuffe,* it affirms Molière's sardonic salute to hypocrisy as the fashionable vice. *Don Juan* is a rich play, a cross section of class (from nobles through the bourgeoisie down to the peasants), manners, and even language—the nobles appear at times to echo the grandiose Corneille but the peasants speak in an invented rustic patois. Most taking of all is Molière's realistic ambiguity of tone: is this a farce or a romance? It has elements of both. Surely the last line is the ultimate comic gesture, for a stone statue representing heavenly justice drags Don Juan to hell and his servant Sganarelle cries *"Mes gages!"* (My wages!). Yet Antoine Bourseiller's 1967 staging at the *Comédie-Française presented the play as a tragedy, Georges Descrières's Juan a gloomy *étranger* in the *Albert Camus mode and Jacques Charon's Sganarelle fervently battening on his master's glamour. Charon's *"Mes gages!"* was a keen of agony as he flung himself over his hero's corpse.

DOWNSTAGE

Toward the audience: a reference to the raked stages of the eighteenth and nineteenth centuries, slanted downward to favor the public.

DOYEN

French for "senior," referring to the oldest member of the company of the *Comédie-Française. (A woman would be *doyenne*.) In times past, the *doyen* headed the troupe, in some eras actively and in others more metaphorically. The tradition-loving Comédie still observes this distinction, but it is a perfunctory honor, as the troupe is now led by a director hired from outside.

DRAMATURG

German for the person in charge of the literary side of a theatre company's activities: the one who reads the new scripts, recommends titles for revival, edits the program book, and adapts recalcitrant texts. In England the term is *literary manager.*

THE DREWS AND THE BARRYMORES

America's greatest acting dynasty, now in its fifth generation. Louisa Lane (1820–1897), the *actor-manager who founded the family, claimed English thespian ancestry back to Shakespeare's day. She put some Celtic blood into the line when she married John Drew, a typical blood-and-thunder Irish "character," and as Mrs. John Drew set up headquarters in Philadelphia at the Arch Street Theatre. Two children, John and Georgiana Drew, went on the stage, and "Georgie" married a British actor, the dashing Maurice Barrymore. Thus Lionel (1878–1954), Ethel (1879–1959), and John (1882–1942) had the unique advantage of growing up as the grandchildren of one of the theatre institutions of the English-speaking world.

Grandmother Drew was, as they used to put it, a "caution": she once wrote a tender note to young Lionel, musing on his lack of ability in a small part and firing him from the company. Her fire passed to the three young Barrymores, who were bright, adventurous, and charismatic—just the sort of people who thrived on the American stage in the early 1900s, when the acting professional's requirements were rather those of a debating club president. Presence. Voice. Wit. A certain "way." Lionel tended to melodrama and Ethel had charm, but John, they say, was the genius of the trio, possibly the greatest American actor of his day.

The interior of Theatre Royal, Drury Lane in 1804, the third of four theatre buildings that have occupied this site.

His outstanding turn was as Hamlet in 1922–1923, first in New York, then in London, a celebrated performance that, in New York, broke by one performance *Edwin Booth's long-standing record of 100 consecutive Hamlets. (John E. Kellerd had played 102 Hamlets in New York a mere decade earlier, but perhaps Kellerd wasn't famous enough to set a precedent.) John Barrymore unfortunately abandoned the theatre for Hollywood. Alcoholism slowed him up. He left a few performances on film in which he is clearly sopping wet, staggering and mumbling, and he made hay of his intemperance in a last theatrical fling, *My Dear Children* (1940). For different views on Bar-

rymore, compare the titles of the two standard biographies. Barrymore's drinking buddy Gene Fowler called his *Good Night, Sweet Prince*. John Kobler's is entitled *Damned in Paradise*.

Note the charming dynastic obeisance in the name of the latest of the family, Drew Barrymore.

DRURY LANE

The essential London playhouse, Theatre Royal, and host to an amazing history, from *Thomas Betterton, Anne Oldfield, and *David Garrick through *Sheridan, *Mrs. Siddons, and the other

*Kembles, on past *Edmund Kean, *Henry Irving, and *Ellen Terry, to the still-current cycle of musicals—American operettas in the 1920s, Ivor Novello's spectacles in the 1930s, then back to the Americans with Rodgers and Hammerstein, *My Fair Lady* and *Camelot,* then *A Chorus Line, Sweeney Todd,* and—still on at the present writing—*42nd Street.*

Four buildings have borne the name "Drury Lane," the present one a lovely monster of a place seating 2,283, opened in 1812. There have been other Theatres Royal. But *Covent Garden has been an opera house for well over a century and the Haymarket's history is even more chequered by miscalculations, neglect, and closings. One odd note: "Old Drury" is barely on Drury Lane at all. The building's back wall is—but the facade and public right-of-way lie on Catherine Street.

JOHN DRYDEN (See Restoration Theatre)

ALEXANDRE DUMAS, PÈRE (1802–1870) AND FILS (1824–1895)

Taken together—rather, taken consecutively—*les Dumas,* father and son, spanned a volatile era of French cultural history, from the Romantics' overthrow of the rigid traditions of Classicism to the rise of *naturalism. The French Romantic theatre, a place of costume dramas inspired as much by Shakespeare as by a native need to reinvigorate the tired emulation of *Corneille and *Racine, is generally dated from the notorious premiere of *Victor Hugo's *Hernani*. But the elder Dumas's *Henri III et Sa Cour* (Henry III and His Court) came along in 1829, a year before *Hernani. Henri III*'s fire and color and activity dazzled, though the Classicists thought it an affront, especially as it was given at the Comédie-Française, the national theatre, sacred to tradition, the very "house of Molière." But Molière himself had offended conservatives in his day.

Worst of all was the rumor that a gang of Romantics, waiting till the audience had filed out of *Henri III*'s premiere, invaded the foyer to dance a lurid gavotte around the bust of Racine, shouting, "Racine is dead! Bury Racine!"

Historical dramas remained Dumas's interest, though he dared a very contemporary subject in *Kean* (1836), about—and produced but three years after the death of—England's most fascinating actor, *Edmund Kean. Dumas was prolific, but he left his most enduring work in such novels as *The Three Musketeers* and *The Count of Monte Cristo,* both of which did service on the stage, in Dumas's own adaptations. "There are neither long nor short plays," Dumas observed, "only amusing plays or boring plays." But *Monte Cristo* (1848) was so long it took two nights to perform; and no one was amused. Oddly, the play outlived all the rest of Dumas, even his masterpiece, *La Tour de Nesle* (1832), for an adaptation of *Monte Cristo* by Charles Fechter (1870) became the lifelong vehicle of *James O'Neill, father of Eugene.

Just as the young O'Neill broke entirely with his father's theatre, so did Dumas *fils* help lead the French stage into a new era. Like his coeval Émile Augier (1820–1889), Dumas emphasized modern dress realism; but where Augier retained the poetic composition of the Romantics, the younger Dumas naturalized his subjects in prose. Dumas was especially notable for the *pièce à thèse*: the problem play. "I realize," he said, "that the prime requisites of a play are laughter, tears, passion, emotion, interest, curiosity—to leave life in the cloakroom." This was the theatre of the elder Dumas. "But I maintain," quoth *le fils,* "that if by means of all these ingredients . . . I can exercise some influence over society . . . if, for example, while I satirize and describe and dramatize adultery I can find means to force people to discuss the problem, and the lawmakers to revise the law, I shall have done more than my part as a poet: I shall have done my duty as a man."

Among the problems Dumas engaged was his own, the social and legal humiliation of the illegitimate child, in *Le Fils Naturel* (1858). He treated capitalist speculation in *La Question d'Argent* (The Question of Money, 1857), sexual dissipation in *La Femme de Claude* (Claude's Wife, 1873), and other themes that one might call contemporary but for the fact that they became so only because Dumas introduced them to the theatre. His one enduring play, ironically, is almost purely a *romance sans thèse,* theatre for its own sake, *La Dame aux Camélias* (1852), roughly meaning "The Lady of the Camellias" but generally called *Camille.* It was a mainstay in the repertory for fifty years as vehicle for, among others, *Sarah Bernhardt, *Eleonora Duse, Gabrielle Réjane, Olga Nethersole, *Helena Modjeska, Edwige Feuillière, Greta Garbo (on film), and, in *Franco Zeffirelli's 1963 Broadway disaster, Susan Strasberg. The play has never quite disappeared, though it has been overshadowed by Verdi's operatic adaptation, *La Traviata.*

(See also *Kean.*)

THE DUMB WAITER

One-act *black comedy by *Harold Pinter, prem. Frankfurt, 1959.

The play's humor derives from the turnabout of watching two bullies bullied. The pair are hit men, awaiting orders for their next job, who find themselves answering increasingly bizarre *food* orders mysteriously coming in through the dumb waiter in the wall of their room, apparently a former kitchen. From "Two braised steak and chips" the requests mount to "Macaroni Pastitsio" and "Char Siu and Beansprouts." The two men never learn who is sending these orders, but they finally get the instructions for their hit: one of them is to kill the other. The situation, in outline, recalls *Samuel Beckett's *Waiting for Godot*—two men expecting something that is never clearly defined, grousing and joking as they pass the time, and encountering the fantastical (*Godot*'s Pozzo and Lucky; the dumb waiter's orders) along the way. This may well mark the strongest link between classical French *absurdism and the otherwise naturalistic Pinter.

CHRISTOPHER DURANG (1950—   )

Durang is America's playwright-as-scamp, a preppy Till Eulenspiegel making facetious references to high lit and low pop as he outruns a pack of exasperated nuns. If there were a school of New York wits in contemporary theatre, Durang would lead it; but wit is rare today, especially the high-tech wit that demands a highly cultured public simply to get the jokes and a casually self-mocking public to be able to laugh at them. This is Durang's wit. It eludes those who have not read or seen a great deal, as when he writes a role in *The Idiots Karamazov* (1974) for Constance Garnett, a name known to several generations of students and literati because she made the first popular translations of classic Russian novels. Those who have strived through the Modern Library *War and Peace* are amused to touch base with this known yet unknowable character. Others, to whom the joke must be explained, become irritated.

This is a problem the class-track satirist has today. Durang's *A History of American Film* (1978) closed after a very short run on Broadway despite an extremely funny retrospective of the conventions, characters, and famous moments of the movies: idiot critics, missing the jokes, blasted it. A double bill of *Sister Mary Ignatius Explains It All for You* (1979) and *The Actor's Nightmare* (1981), on the other hand, enjoyed a long run on off-Broadway. The two plays turn a telling key into Durang's art. *The Actor's Nightmare,* though regaling, is a one-joke piece: a man finds himself more or less forced to go on stage as an understudy, having absolutely no idea of his lines or *business. From Noël Coward through Shakespeare to *Samuel Beckett he flounders till, as Sir Thomas More in Robert Bolt's *A Man for all Seasons,* he is executed —apparently for real. Much of the fun depends on one's recognizing key lines, such as "Women should be struck regularly, like gongs," from Coward's *Private Lives,* and enjoying the way the epigram falls to pieces on repetition. However, the play never gets anywhere, never quite tallies out. It serves nicely, though, as a *curtain-raiser for *Sister Mary Ignatius,* for this charmingly ghoulish lecture on Catholicism by a parochial school teacher is of substance. On the page, Sister reads as a bigoted tyrant; in performance, she plays as attractive and even kind, and one begins to see how insidiously the Church spreads its dogma. The play also takes on a wider audience than most of Durang, addressing themes of compassion and individuality rather than quoting from the chronicles of camp. *The Actor's Nightmare* is very amusing—but *Sister Mary* is greatly disturbing.

FRIEDRICH DÜRRENMATT

(1921–   )

As dramatist, the Swiss Dürrenmatt is very much of his time and place, middle Europe in the age of Godot. His comedy is *black, his technique is *absurdist, and his subjects are existential, ontological. However, as novelist and short story writer, Dürrenmatt deals in wry parables, and some of the fable-like tone of his fiction colors his theatre. *Romulus der Grosse* (Romulus the Great, 1949) finds the last of the Roman emperors merrily presiding over the fall of the empire as he awaits the dreaded barbarians: but the Teutons come not to bury Romulus but to . . . pension him off. The text bears an almost Shavian lilt, a feeling that a crucial historical encounter is being toyed with to illustrate a thesis. The dialogue is clever, satiric, timely. But the action, in outline, suggests the universals of parable—the last emperor, the first barbarian, the shifting of epochs. *Die Ehe des Herrn Mississippi* (The Marriage of Mr. Mississippi, 1952) and *Ein Engel Kommt nach Babylon* (An Angel Comes to Babylon, 1953) emphasize the "illuminating tale" aspect of Dürrenmatt. But his first international success, *Die Besuch der Alten Dame* (The Old Lady's Visit, 1956), known as *The Visit,* brought in Dürrenmatt's macabre side; as did his second major hit, *Die Physiker* (The Physicists, 1962). This pair deal with very post–World War II topics, respectively communal guilt and menacing technology. Thus, though Dürrenmatt's parables have grown more frightening, his messages have become more relevant to the Western audience.

(See also *The Visit.*)

ELEONORA DUSE (1858–1924)

A favorite anecdote finds some buff at his first Duse performance. She enters: does not Make an Entrance, just comes onto the stage. She avoids maj-

Eleonora Duse at thirty-five: beauty, clarity, simplicity.

esty, declamation, posing. She does not present. She *is.* Finally, after ten minutes of this complete lack of thespian advertisement, the spectator turns to his companion and asks, "When is she going to *act?*"

Duse was one of the key artists who turned *acting* into acting: lifelike portrayal. *George Bernard Shaw found in Duse a beneficial opposition to her contemporary *Sarah Bernhardt. The Divine Sarah was always on parade, while Duse thrust herself into her characters—*Dumas's Marguerite Gauthier in *La Dame aux Camélias,* Shakespeare's Cleopatra, most of the important *Ibsen leads, *Goldoni's innkeeper Mirandolina (Duse's sole comic role) in *La Locandiera,* and even some *Sardou and *Pinero's *The Second Mrs. Tanqueray.* Her romantic liaison with the dramatist *Gabriele D'Annunzio led her into a different repertory, calling for extravagance instead of her customary delicacy. *Luigi Pirandello, who adored Duse, thought that D'Annunzio "distorted" her. "Here is a shy and retiring art," Pirandello wrote, "which . . . she suddenly put by for the least shy and most assertive poet who ever lived." Nevertheless, the heroine of D'Annunzio's *Francesca da Rimini* became one of Duse's most famous roles.

THE DYBBUK

Supernatural *folk play by Sholem Ansky, prem. Moscow, 1922.

Exploring the mystical side of Jewish culture, the play tells of a young woman possessed by the spirit of her dead fiancé, whom her father shoved aside when a richer suitor declared an interest. The work's history is bound up in the problems of a culture in exile: Ansky wrote *The Dybbuk* in Russian in 1914 for the *Moscow Art Theatre, but the anti-Semitic state forbade production of a play with so positive a view of minority folk life. Ansky then translated *The Dybbuk* into Yiddish as *Tsvishn Tsvey Veltn* (Between Two Worlds). Finally it was translated into Hebrew for production by *Habimah as *Bney Schney Olamot: Hadibuk,* incorporating both titles. Texturing Ansky's ethnicity yet further, Lodovico Rocca made it an Italian opera in 1934, as *Il Dibuk.*

EKKYKLEMA (See Greek Theatre)

T. S. ELIOT (1888–1965)

Born in St. Louis and educated at Harvard University but a naturalized Englishman who declared himself "an Anglo-Catholic in religion, a classicist in literature, and a royalist in politics," Eliot had already achieved his reputation as the poet of "The Love Song of J. Alfred Prufrock" (1917), *The Waste Land* (1922), and "The Hollow Men" (1925) when he decided to bring verse back to the stage. His first full-length play, *Murder in the Cathedral* (1935), in fact, jumps back and forth between prose and poetry, and *The Family Reunion* (1939) is rather heavily laden with its author's sense of artistic mission. But the comedies *The Cocktail Party* (1949), *The Confidential Clerk* (1953), and *The Elder Statesman* (1958) developed a kind of drawing room comedy dialogue that looks like verse on the page but speaks easily—one might almost say prosaically—on the stage.

Murder in the Cathedral, on the martyrdom of Thomas à Becket, seems to be Eliot's most enduring play, not least for its use of the Women of Canterbury as an *Aeschylean chorus and for the pleasant jolt of hearing Becket's four murderers suddenly rationalize their act to the audience in playfully earnest vernacular. The play's investigation of the saint's attitude toward his own willing doom—"the greatest treason: To do the right deed for the wrong reason"—underlines Eliot's insistently religious temperament. Though the following four plays were all drawn from Greek originals (*The Elder Statesman* most clearly: from *Sophocles's *Oedipus at Colonus*), they deal with man's spiritual journey in highly Christian times.

Oddly, Eliot's first essay in the verse play, *Wanna Go Home, Baby?,* is not as much in verse as in jazz rap, and even includes two lyrics to be set as popular songs in minstrel show style, "Under the Bamboo Tree" and "My Little Island Girl." The play was left incomplete. Eliot published two fragments in 1926 and 1927 and later retitled the whole *Sweeney Agonistes*. First given at Vassar College in 1933 under Hallie Flanagan (who later headed the *Federal Theatre program), *Sweeney Agonistes* is seldom staged. But it's a compelling piece, echoing *The Waste Land* and anticipating the theatre of the *absurd, especially *Waiting for Godot. Sweeney* suggests what wonders Eliot might have wrought in the theatre if he had followed this path instead of concocting pseudo-Greek drawing room morality comedies. Dangerous Sweeney offers to take pretty Doris to a cannibal isle: and he'll be her cannibal. "That's all the facts when you come to brass tacks," he tells her. "Birth, copulation, and death."

(See also *The Oresteia.*)

ELIZABETHAN THEATRE

A city with a population of about 220,000 (in the year 1600 or so) supported seven public playhouses, some of them holding between two and three thousand people. In a good week, then, something like seven percent of the citizenry attended the theatre. This was London at the height of the Elizabethan era, in the late 1500s and early 1600s, the London of Christopher Marlowe, Ben Jonson, and William Shakespeare.

This extraordinary flowering of theatre, this opulent profusion of vital texts and popular enthusiasm, has no parallel anywhere else in history, not even in coeval France, Italy, or Spain. Yet all this grew, with relative suddenness, out of England's *medieval theatre of mystery and morality plays, with some stylistic infusion from educated men's common reading of the *Roman playwrights— Terence and especially Plautus for comedy and Seneca for tragedy. On this somewhat slender operational base, the English derived an entirely new system of composition and performance, completely free of direction by the Church and participation by amateurs, as the medieval spectacles never were.

The transition occurs a little after the middle of the sixteenth century. We note the appearance, for instance, of what appears to be the first of the Elizabethan tragedies, *Gorboduc; or, Ferrex and Porrex* (1561), written by lawyers named Thomas Norton (1532–1584) and Thomas Sackville (1536–1608) and performed at the Inner Temple by their colleagues. Clearly, the authors had read their Seneca. However, their subject was not Classical but historical, drawn from Geoffrey of Monmouth. *Gorboduc* in fact introduces that very Elizabethan staple the *chronicle play (though its chronicle seems more imaginary than reportorial), detailing the breakdown of civil order when a weak king allows his two sons to battle over the succession and plunge the nation into vendetta, then rebellion, then total war. (Shakespeare used some of this in the planning of *King Lear:* King Gorboduc and sons Ferrex and Porrex surely advised the relationship of Gloucester and sons Edmund and Edgar.) *Gorboduc* is a cautionary tale, like the old morality plays. Most important, it offered an alternative to the officious meter of classical poetry in adopting blank verse, ideally elastic for the structuring of a dramatic English.

Even more influential was the rise of the public stage. *Gorboduc* was heard privately, at a lawyers' Christmas revel, and most of the early Elizabethan stages were similarly the survey of the professional or court elite. But in 1576, James Burbage (1530–1597) erected The Theatre (how choice but inevitable a name: what else to call the only one?) outside the London city limits, well beyond Bishopsgate, to the north in Shoreditch. A year later, the nearby Curtain joined The Theatre. ("Curtain" derives not from the familiar theatrical enclosure, as there was none at the time, but after the street of its address, variously spelled at the time but surviving as Curtain Road today. A tablet at number 86 honors the site of Burbage's Theatre.) Ten years later, the Rose settled another location, now not north but south of the city, across the Thames in Southwark. The Rose in turn was joined by the Swan and, in 1599, the Globe, Shakespeare's haunt.

Building these playhouses beyond the city's legal boundaries was not a chance matter. The city authorities would have loved to ban the theatre. These gatherings of all sorts of rabble encouraged crime. The necessarily daytime performances discouraged folk from work. This unbridled outpouring of poetry disseminated potentially subversive views. And the packing in of the population dared the spread of plague, a particular danger in Elizabethan London. But Queen Elizabeth I enjoyed the theatre and gave it her protection. Despite periodic skirmishing between her Privy Council and the city satraps, the theatre could not be altogether closed down. Therefore, as a compromise, the thespians soothed the outrage of civic jurisdiction by setting up shop beyond its borders.

Centuries later, when the recreational "midtown" of London had shifted to the west in the megalopolitan jointure of London and Westminster, the theatre district would stand considerably distant from these preserves to the north and south. At that, it is difficult to imagine such an extensive fraction of the population marching out at midday far afield to Shoreditch to the Theatre and the Curtain, or across London Bridge to the

Rose or the Globe for their matinée. Yet so they did, in great numbers, to stand in the pit or sit in the galleries (at a higher entrance fee) from something like two o'clock to five in outdoor theatres, encircled but open to the sun. Eventually, the actors established indoor winter quarters. Still, our image of Elizabethan theatre focuses upon the great "wooden O," with its thrust stage tossing each piece virtually into the public's lap. The Greeks took their playgoing in vast amphitheatres stretching away from the stage on the incline of a hillside; the Elizabethans stood or sat but a few feet from the actors. There was no scenery and little in the way of props, but the players were often elaborately costumed. Plays were presented in repertory, the bill changing from day to day; and the performing forces were real companies, with playwright-actors providing scripts cut to fit the resident talents—as Shakespeare, for example, wrote for James Burbage's troupe, bestowing his great male lead roles on Burbage's son Richard (c. 1567–1619). There were no women actors. Teenage boys played women characters. Yet we wonder how a stripling could have managed Shakespeare's Regan, Goneril, Lady Macbeth—even Cleopatra, a youthful character, yes, but one who must command highly sophisticated poetry. We wonder, too, about the audience, often attacked in Elizabethan texts as scoundrels and fools, yet receptive of what is surely the most expansive vocabulary and most finely factored metaphorical mathematics in all theatre.

The authors, of course, especially locate the spirit of the age for us, the uniquely Elizabethan "all the world's a stage" aesthetic that made the theatre not only essential to London life but almost a religious duty, a chance to comprehend the universe. This may explain why Elizabethan London was more or less mad wild for the stage: in an extraordinarily sectarian society just coming out of the oppressively limited middle ages into the modern world, theatre opened up one's personal horizons, presented the range of social class, of philosophical doctrine, of adventurous possibility, sectioned up the universe for public investigation. All the world veritably *was* a stage.

The earliest of the major Elizabethan writers was Christopher Marlowe (1564–1593), author, most notably, of the two parts of *Tamburlaine the Great* (?1588, ?1589), *The Jew of Malta* (?1589), *The*

Tragical History of Doctor Faustus (?1592), and *The Troublesome Reign of Edward II* (1592). Marlowe fascinates for the outrageous outpourings of personality his plays roughly contain; and academics note his unusual lack of support for the typically noble tragic hero. Tamburlaine, emperor by force of arms, begins as a shepherd, and of Marlowe's other great *protagonists, only Edward II is by lineage a natural "hero." Already, Elizabethan tragedy is varying its possibilities, gambling with elements that in other countries (see Corneille, Racine, and The Unities on the strict French form of tragedy) were made short, tight, and absolute. What life breathes in Marlowe! We have no trouble envisioning an Elizabethan actor, after the trumpet summons draws the crowd into the theatre, sweeping out onto the stage to launch *Edward II,* his lines tumbling out as the audience reckons the place, time, and action.

GAVESTON: "My father is deceased! Come, Gaveston,
And share the kingdom with thy dearest friend."
Ah! words that make me surfeit with delight!
What greater bliss can hap to Gaveston
Than live and be the favourite of a king!

We can imagine as well the zest with which the Elizabethans greeted tales of stupendous sadism, the violence especially appealing, it seems, when visited upon the most innocent and most beautiful characters. *Edward II,* at least, reserves its harshest treatment for those who have taken dangerous choices upon themselves—Edward for flouting the aristocracy with his favorite, "that base and obscure Gaveston"; Gaveston himself, for encouraging Edward's mockery of the brutal niceties of class; Young Mortimer for attempting to usurp the throne; and Queen Isabella for abetting Mortimer.

It is a dangerous world that Elizabethan drama stages, one of endless conspiracy, revenge, and terror. John Webster (c. 1575–?1635) marks a high point of the blood lust in *The White Devil* (?1612) and *The Duchess of Malfi* (?1614), both set in Italy among courtiers as passionate in murder as in romance. The white devil is a woman who uses death and love as instruments of power, and the blame-

Shakespeare then and now: one very traditional and one very avant-garde production of A Midsummer Night's Dream *give us a fix on changing styles. First (left), the *Old Vic in 1953, in the grand old manner, with ballet dancers as the fairies, rough comics as the "rude mechanicals," and romantic heroes as the lovers. Here's Moira Shearer as Queen Titania, Robert Helpmann as King Oberon, the two and their respective bands in confrontation—"Tarry, rash wanton; am I not thy lord?"—then Stanley Holloway (as Bottom) and his fellow buffoons, and finally the pretty sets and lighting of the *Henry Irving era for the first scene, as the four youngsters kneel before Duke Theseus and the outraged father, Egeus. He is outraged because he cannot order his daughter's heart; but love, Shakespeare shows us in every scene of the play, is disorderly. Now (right) to 1970 and the *Royal Shakespeare Company's staging under Peter Brook in Sally Jacobs's famous white box set. See what a different Titania Sara Kestelman presents compared with Shearer's. Marvel at her four attendants on trapezes. Oberon (Alan Howard) and Puck (John Kane) mount the trapezes, too, as Kestelman dallies with Bottom (David Waller) in this eerily sterile, sneakily vital forest. Admire the stilt work as well. A* Midsummer Night's Dream *by . . . *Samuel Beckett?*

less Duchess of Malfi is destroyed by her own brothers. So intent were the authors and public on plays dealing with the methodical elimination of most of the principals that an entire genre flowered in this ferocious garden, *revenge tragedy. An extremist psychology inflates many if not all of these works. Were their playwrights truly discovering the world on their stage or exaggerating, even debasing it? At around the end of the sixteenth and the start of the seventeenth centuries, the beauty of the poetry mitigated the horror of the action in tragedy. But the later style of the Jacobean (named after King James I) and Carolinian (after Charles I) eras, upon Elizabeth's death in 1603, tended more and more toward rhetoric rather than poetry, and seemed to want to paint the world in prettier colors than Marlowe and Webster would have done. Francis Beaumont (1584–1616) and John Fletcher (1579–1625) typify this later epoch rather neatly, as they were tireless collaborators, partnering many of their colleagues but especially, around 1610, each other—so consistently that one can scarcely mention one without the other.

Elizabethan and post-Elizabethan comedy is especially associated with Ben Jonson (1572–1637). True, comedy thrived in the work of such writers as the romantic yet realistic Thomas Dekker (c. 1572–c.1632) and the glowering moralist Philip Massinger (1583–1640). But Jonson towers above his contemporaries for the bite with which he rendered his satires. Tragedy did not suit Jonson—as Sejanus (1603) and Catiline (1611) prove. But his comedy, Jonson proposed, would "show an image of the times"—however agelessly—"and sport with human follies, not with crimes." Jonson's "comedy of humours" refers back to the personified symbolist figures of the medieval morality play: in a healthy man, the "humours" act in balance, but when one quality overshadows all the others we get a fool, a hypocrite, a villain. Jonson, whose colorful life and fierce opinions were a theatre in themselves (he was in prison several times, once for murder) suffers almost no one gladly, whatever his humours. This exchange of two scholars in Every Man in His Humour (1598):

MATTHEW: Why, I pray you, sir, make use of my study, it's at your service.
STEPHEN: I thank you, sir, I shall be bold, I warrant you; have you a stool there to be melancholy upon?

recalls the scathing cut of *Aristophanes as he tilts at the—to him—self-reverent majesty of *Euripides.

A number of Jonson's titles have outlasted all those of his colleagues, especially Epicoene; or, The Silent Woman (1609), the source of Richard Strauss's opera Die Schweigsame Frau; The Alchemist (1610), whose character names anticipate *Restoration nomenclature with Sir Epicure Mammon, Tribulation Wholesome, Mr. Face, Mr. Subtle, and the prostitute Dol Common; and Bartholomew Fair (1614). But these are overshadowed by Jonson's Volpone; or, The Fox (1606), a savage exposé of the humour of greed. Here Jonson bends the Elizabethan "all the world's a stage" syndrome into a spectacle of thieves gulling knaves, as Volpone fakes a deathbed passing in order to lure gifts from would-be beneficiaries. The worship of gold in Volpone is a religion, worthy of pageants in which all the participants are actors: phoneys. Though the play is generally regarded as a classic of farce, it is in fact a bitter work, closing with terrifying punishments of all concerned. Volpone, the greatest actor of the lot, is sentenced to live his role in full true. All his wealth is confiscated:

FIRST AVOCATORE: And, since the most was gotten by imposture,
By feigning lame, gout, palsy, and such diseases,
Thou art to lie in prison, cramped with irons,
Till thou be'st sick and lame indeed.

Of course, William Shakespeare (1564–1616) overwhelms any citation of Elizabethan playwrights, of playwrights at all. Shakespeare more than anyone demonstrates the vitality, the dazzle and the point, of Elizabethan dramatic poetry. Even Christopher Marlowe, Shakespeare's nearest rival, falls far short of a true comparison. Moreover, Marlowe, born the same year as Shakespeare, died before he was thirty, while Shakespeare passed fifty, giving his prolific output far more seasoning time than Marlowe's got. Indeed, it is not Shakespeare's poetry alone but his experimental approach to the forms of his time that make him virtually the first Western dramatist, most agelessly and omnipresently active in the Classic repertory.

Shakespeare was an innovator, at least an innovative developer of stock forms. His first reformation reclaimed the chronicle play, a favorite genre in the late 1500s for its ability to present history with vast immediacy to a public that often knew little more of its past than the names of the principal characters. Shakespeare's chronicle plays *impersonated* history, creating for such works as *Richard II* (1595), *Richard III* (?1593), and the two parts of *King Henry IV* (c. 1598) figures not merely out of the annals but out of life itself. If the world's a stage, the Elizabethan stage might also be a world, putting its public directly in touch with the events that shape civilization, much as the Greek festivals did. These Elizabethan pageants retold a mythology of life, so—as with the Greeks—it mattered not at all that most if not all the plots and characters were borrowed, retreaded. Originality of action was of no moment; originality of insight was. Note, too, Shakespeare's dexterity in mixing his elements, as when the buffoonish Sir John Falstaff of *King Henry IV* Part One and *The Merry Wives of Windsor* (1597) becomes something of a tragic hero in *King Henry IV* Part Two, when his old buddy the Prince of Wales becomes King and thrusts him away. "Banish plump Jack," Falstaff has warned him early in Part One when he is still Prince Hal, "and banish all the world." We laugh then, so far from their minds—and ours—is coronation or banishment. Yet so it transpires, and Falstaff dies of a broken heart.

It is with *A Midsummer Night's Dream* (?1594) that the unique Shakespeare emerges. After the early farces in the manner of Plautus (see Roman Theatre), *The Comedy of Errors* (?1591) and *The Taming of the Shrew* (?1593), here, in the *Dream*, is something entirely new in the history of theatre, a comedy with farcical elements (especially in the capers of the "rude mechanicals" putting on *Pyramus and Thisbe* and in the volatile allegiances of the four young lovers) but so rich in enchantment of language, so mysterious of mood, and so elegiacal of theme that Shakespeare has abandoned simple comedy for "romance." Similarly, *Love's Labour's Lost,* which used to be thought an early work, is now regarded as contemporary with the *Dream*, comparably sophisticated in its delight in and won-

der at the human condition. If *A Midsummer Night's Dream* was indeed first staged in 1594, we can understand what a loss was the death of Christopher Marlowe but a year before: for what would we have thought of Shakespeare if he had put down his pen having left only the tragedy *Titus Andronicus* (?1593) and the comedy *The Two Gentlemen of Verona* (1593), along with *The Comedy of Errors, The Taming of the Shrew,* and some chronicle plays?

In fact, the post-*Dream* Shakespeare is astonishingly masterly in his absorption and revision of the formalities of Elizabethan drama. Even the *Dream,* for all its profound music on the subject of love, does not truly sing of character (except perhaps in Bottom). But the later romances, as able thematically, are more expert psychologically, especially *The Merchant of Venice* (?1595), the densely characterized *Twelfth Night; or What You Will* (?1602) and *Measure for Measure* (1604), and the magical but oddly disenchanted *The Tempest* (1611), in some ways an austere correction of *A Midsummer Night's Dream.* More glorious yet is Shakespeare's intensity in tragedy—all the great ones date from after the turning point of the *Dream.* There is, on one hand, the terse rapture of the writing in *Antony and Cleopatra* (?1607):

CLEOPATRA: O Charmian,
  Where think'st thou he is now? Stands he or
    sits he?
  Or does he walk? or is he on his horse?
  O happy horse, to bear the weight of Antony!
  Do bravely, horse; for wot'st thou whom thou
    mov'st?
  The demi-Atlas of this earth, the arm
  And burgonet of men. He's speaking now,
  Or murmuring "Where's my serpent of old
    Nile?"
  For so he calls me. Now I feed myself
  With most delicious poison. Think on me,
  That am with Phoebus' amorous pinches black,
  And wrinkled deep in time? Broad-fronted
    Caesar,
  When thou wast here above the ground, I was
  A morsel for a monarch; and great Pompey
  Would stand and make his eyes grow in my
    brow;
  There would he anchor his aspect and die
  With looking on his life.

and on the other hand, the breadth of grasp yet intimacy of projection of *King Lear* (?1606), arguably the greatest—or, let us say, the most absolute —tragedy ever written:

LEAR: Howl, howl, howl, howl! O, you are men
    of stones!
  Had I your tongues and eyes, I'd use them so
  That heaven's vault should crack. She's gone for
    ever.
  I know when one is dead and when one lives;
  She's dead as earth . . . No, no, no life!
  Why should a dog, a horse, a rat have life,
  And thou no breath at all? Thou'lt come no
    more,
  Never, never, never, never, never.
  Pray you undo this button. Thank you, sir.
  Do you see this? Look on her. Look, her lips.
  Look there, look there!

As William Hazlitt put it, "All that we can say must fall far short of the subject, or even what we ourselves conceive of it."

The increasingly court-centered theatre of the early 1600s drew many writers into the alternate theatre of the masque (see Scenery), and the elite system of private theatres—the troupe approach that, for instance, built the Globe Theatre and gave Shakespeare his precinct—became more and more unavailable to the public. Finally, when the theatre-hating Puritans seized control of the state, the public stages were closed down, in 1642. English theatre as such went underground till after the Restoration of the Stuarts in 1660.
(See also *The Comedy of Errors, Measure for Measure, Tamburlaine the Great,* and *Troilus and Cressida.*)

ENTR'ACTE

Literally, "between the acts": usually a musical piece played before the next rise of the curtain. In *Broadway and *West End theatres of the early 1900s, pit orchestras played entr'actes of atmospheric music right through the intermission.

EPIC THEATRE (See Bertolt Brecht)

EPILOGUE (See Prologue)

GEORGE ETHEREGE (See Restoration Theatre)

EURIPIDES (484–406 B.C.)

His predecessor *Aeschylus was revered and his contemporary *Sophocles was greatly admired; but Euripides was too revolutionary to be even liked. Sophocles won the Athenian Dionysia, the annual play contest, over twenty times. Euripides won only four times. Yet for all their appreciation of Aeschylus and Sophocles, many commentators find Euripides the most absorbing and timeless of the trio, the most individual. "The modern mind is never popular in its own day," writes Edith Hamilton. "People hate being made to think, above all upon fundamental problems . . . Euripides was the arch-heretic, miserably disturbing, never willing to leave a man comfortably ensconced in his favorite convictions and prejudices."

Euripides was modern enough to write, in the time of Athens's aggressive war making, one of the most terrifying views of the destructive rigidity of war, *The Trojan Women.* He was modern enough to make an alien woman—to the Greek mind, a person without any legal or social rights—into the ferocious *protagonist of *Medea.* Democracy was crumbling as he wrote, yet he insisted on the dramatist's duty to lecture his audience with extreme prejudice. He was an unstoppable realist. According to *Aristotle, Sophocles said, "I make men as they should be—Euripides makes them as they are." Oddly, the realist was also a comic—Euripides's *Cyclops* is the only *satyr play that has survived, and his *Helen* is notable for its mockingly romantic flavor.

Euripides was also something of a formal innovator. The singing and dancing chorus, the oldest element in Greek theatre, was too old for Euripides's modern mind, and he often deemphasized it to spend the time among his principals—far more characters per play than we find in Aeschylus or Sophocles. (Be it said that when Euripides decides to deploy his chorus decisively, as in *The Trojan Women* or *The Bacchae,* he is second only to Aeschylus.) Euripides also seems to have used the machinery of the Greek stage a great deal, insistently swinging in a peacemaking deity or sending off a disruptive character on the *mechane* (the crane) and constantly rolling out the *ekkyklema* (the wheeled platform) with its heap of corpses. *Aristophanes delighted in savaging Euripides's unique dramaturgy—by name—in his satires. *The Acharnians* finds an Athenian Citizen calling on Euripides:

EURIPIDES: (offstage) I'm too busy to come down there.
CITIZEN: Well, can't you have yourself rolled out?

Euripides was also known for the rags he put his characters in, and the dingy little props he allotted them. The Citizen begs for a gift:

CITIZEN: Dear, sweet Euripides—nothing more than a little pot stoppered with a sponge?
EURIPIDES: You villain! I could get through an entire tragedy with that!

(See also Greek Theatre, *The Bacchae,* and *The Trojan Women.*)

EDITH EVANS (1888–1976)

We often hear of actresses whose beauty invigorated a modest talent, or who conquered through force of personality rather than finesse of portrayal. Edith Evans, on the other hand, was unattractive and emotionally somewhat introverted. She was the kind of actress who can hope for greatness only eventually, in the "old lady" roles such as Lady Wishfort in William Congreve's *The Way of the World,* Mrs. Malaprop in *Richard Brinsley Sheridan's *The Rivals,* or Lady Bracknell in Oscar Wilde's *The Importance of Being Earnest*—all of which Evans did indeed play. She even suffered the humiliation of being rejected on her first audition for the *Old Vic strictly because of her looks.

However, from the first, Evans displayed a remarkable gift for creating character, so persuasively that *managers helplessly cast her in heroine parts—Shakespeare's Portia and Cleopatra, *Henrik Ibsen's Rebecca West in *Rosmersholm,* even that cynosure of *Restoration vivacity and glamour, Millamant in *The Way of the World.* It was perhaps Evans's great role of her late youth. "She purred and challenged, mocked and melted," recalled *John Gielgud, "showing her changing moods by subtly shifting the angles of her head, neck, and shoulders. Poised and cool, like a porcelain figure in a vitrine, she used her fan—which she never opened—in [the marriage contract scene] as an instrument for attack or defense, now coquettishly pointing it upwards beneath her chin, now resting it languidly on her cheek."

How did a plain woman suggest the lavish charms of a prima donna? Someone was once ungallant enough to ask, and Evans replied that when she played a beautiful woman, she simply went onstage believing that she was beautiful, and doing what beauty does. "I would love a photograph of Edith Evans," Gielgud concludes. "I never know what she looks like; she always looks like the part."

Like most of the stars of her generation, Evans switched off classic and new roles. She played Shaw and Chekhov, but also Florence Nightingale and (mildly disguised) Nellie Melba in biographical plays, even *Kaufman and Hart. In her seniority, her great role was Lady Bracknell, so decisive a portrayal that it shadowed everything Evans did later. She filmed the part in 1952 and taped it for records (with John Gielgud and Pamela Brown) shortly after, and her reverberations in such lines as "A *handbag*?" held strong in 1982, when Judi Dench played Lady Bracknell at the National Theatre of Great Britain. When the action neared the "handbag" line, one could sense the audience ready to audition Dench against the memory of Evans. Rather than try to outdo Evans's elephant's trumpet of a reading, Dench played it with a pensive sense of affront. Interesting; but Evans still holds the patent on the line.

MAURICE EVANS (1901–)

Evans, slim and elegant, is ready to play Shakespeare's Falstaff for director Margaret Webster. "Are you fat and lusty?" Webster asks. "I can act," replies Evans. Especially Shakespeare, who, with George Bernard Shaw, provisioned the bulk of Evans's repertory—seldom did he venture into the contemporary. Yet Evans was a popularizer of the classics, breaking John Barrymore's famous record of 101 consecutive performances in *Hamlet* and missing, by one performance, the chance to equal John Gielgud's, the Broadway precedent till *Richard Burton's 137. Evans even revised *Hamlet* to emphasize the hero's strength of character, deleting evasive "intellectual" passages when playing the show to troops overseas during World War II, as the *G. I. Hamlet*.

A naturalized American, Evans became Broadway's resident Shakespearean. In the 1950s, he gravitated to television to popularize the good old plays to an even wider audience on the *Hallmark Hall of Fame*. Some critics thought him the greatest actor of his generation; but his lack of interest in moviemaking has now eclipsed him in history, while his contemporaries Gielgud and Olivier flicker for posterity.

EXPOSITION

The "protasis" of the Greek theatre: the set up. The exposition, following the curtain's rise, defines the setting, introduces the essential situation, programs the tone of a work, and delivers whatever else is necessary for the audience's immediate understanding—background plot material, for instance. The exposition of *Aeschylus's *Agamemnon,* the first part of the *Oresteia,* goes to great lengths to explain what happened in the past that will pay

out fatal consequences in the ensuing scenes. First, a night watchman of Argos explains that he is searching for signal fires announcing the fall of Troy, incidentally giving us a preview of the forceful nature of Clytemnestra and an announcement that day is breaking. Then the chorus of the town ancients enters to give a detailed explanation of events leading up to the Trojan War, and how it directly affected the royal family of Argos, thus preparing for *Agamemnon*'s single act, Clytemnestra's murder of her husband for sacrificing their daughter to Artemis. The old men's scene is no mere recounting, but a highly colored discussion blending reportage with thematic points that Aeschylus will develop throughout the *Oresteia.* Meanwhile, the serenely terrifying Clytemnestra has obliviously been tending her altar fire. The chorus asks her for news of the war. Clytemnestra replies that the Greeks have won—and the exposition is over. The play is on.

Later eras favored much less stately expositions. Shakespeare's *Romeo and Juliet* opens with a *prologue just long enough to warn us of the Capulet-Montague feud ("new mutiny, where civil blood makes civil hands unclean"), the location ("fair Verona"), the central principals ("star-cross'd lovers"), and even the outcome (the lovers "doth with their death bury their parents' strife"). Immediately, Act One opens in a plaza in the city: two Capulets incite a quarrel with some Montagues, and the action is in motion.

The *"well-made play" of the nineteenth century favored expositions more fully delineated than those of the Elizabethans but without the grandeur of the Greek style. The theatre of the *absurd, in part a revolt against nineteenth century art, dispensed entirely with the exposition—*Samuel Beckett's *Waiting for Godot* begins, so to say, in its middle, without explanatory preamble. (It virtually ends in its middle, too.) However, most theatre today still honors the beginning-middle-end structure, and thus observes some sort of exposition, though the more gifted writers prefer to filter the introductory material into the body of the action itself. One of the last instances of the full-scale, old-fashioned expositions may be found in *Eugene O'Neill's *The Iceman Cometh,* written in 1939, exactly ten years before Beckett finished *Waiting for Godot.* Slowly, in paragraphs broken by interjections, O'Neill explores the setting and characters of the "No Chance Saloon" of losers, his basic concept of the delusional "pipe dream" that allows the losers to accept their wasted lives. At great length, and only through other characters' allusions, O'Neill introduces his *protagonist, the good-time, drinks-for-everybody, have-you-heard-this-one? universal pal, Hickey. Seventy-six pages into the printed text, Hickey himself finally arrives —"Hello, gang!" Not till that moment is O'Neill's exposition officially consummated.

EXPRESSIONISM

Forms of composition and stagecraft through which the wishes, fears, and obsessions of the human psyche are made audible and visible. I say *forms* because there is no one expressionism. Nor was expressionism a unified movement. The term came into use in the early 1900s to describe the use of distortion, repetition, symbolism, and nightmarish fantasy that was marking the Continental arts scene with increasing vigor. Such disparate sources as the blindingly bright-hued French painters known as *les fauves* ("the wild ones") or the Viennese composers grouped around Arnold Schönberg and his grotesquely disjunct "twelve-tone technique," or even the writings of Sigmund Freud . . . all this contributed to the feeling that some new program had taken hold in the arts, something that we of today might, from our vantage of hindsight, see embodied in Edvard Munch's famous painting, *The Scream.*

Expressionist theatre developed in allied but various ways. We note the style, for instance, in the fantastical and lurid action of *Die Menschen* (Humanity, 1918) by Walter Hasenclever (1890–1940). The play opens in a cemetery. A corpse rises up. A murderer carries in a head in a sack. The corpse takes the sack and the murderer jumps into a grave. A young couple notice the corpse. The girl faints. The boy gives his coat to the corpse. The corpse leaves. The girl awakens and the youth embraces her. "I have deceived you!" she screams.

We note the style in the pictorial exaggerations of *Eugene O'Neill's *The Hairy Ape* (1922), when an ocean liner's forecastle, crowded with coal men, is designed and staged to resemble a cage of neanderthal beast-men; or when a prison appears to be a very world of cells, "as if they ran on numberless, into infinity."

We note the style in the vague scene plot of *Bertolt Brecht's *Baal* (1923), suggestive of dreams, even of ideas for paintings: "Brightly lit room with table," "Whitewashed houses and brown tree trunks," "A cabin," or "Trees. Evening." We note as well Brecht's very oblique dialogue, made of non sequiturs, contradictions, outbursts of poetry, chance revelations, and wrenching shifts of mood, as if the characters were literally speaking their minds.

In short, expressionism is—in tone, look, and feeling—a symbolist dream world. It was highly influential in all the arts, and affected theatre most strongly in Germany, where it especially attracted designers and leftist ideologues. Germany's two most famous expressionist playwrights were Ernst Toller (1893–1939) and Georg Kaiser (1878–1945). One senses a universalistic scope in their very titles: Toller's *Die Wandlung* (Transubstantiation, 1919), *Masse Mensch* (Man as the Masses, 1921), or *Hoppla, Wir Leben!* (Hey, We're Alive!, 1927); Kaiser's *Von Morgens bis Mitternachts* (From Morn to Midnight, 1916) or *Gas* (in two parts, 1918 and 1920).

Actually, the prolific Kaiser wrote a great variety of stage works, including *chronicle plays, sex comedies, and musical works with, among others, Kurt Weill, most notably *Der Silbersee* (The Silver Lake, 1933). At that, Kaiser's best known play, *Alkibiades Gerettet* (Alcibiades Saved, 1920), a look at love, politics, and male rivalry in Socrates's Athens, is scarcely expressionistic at all. It was Toller, rather, who epitomized German expressionism, in his stirring attempts to reform the world through a theatre made of epic considerations of the human condition. *Masse Mensch* is typical, even archetypal, in its alternation of depictive scenes with dream interludes; its allegorical confrontations of the bourgeois heroine (who seeks a peaceful solution in a workers' strike) and The Nameless One (who urges on a bloody revolution); and, in the original production at Berlin's Volksbühne, its stark segregation of the principals from antagonistic groupings of fascist soldiers and agonized, huddling

Sophie Treadwell's *Machinal, *one of Broadway's most persuasive experiments in expressionism. Convicted of murder, the Young Woman (Zita Johann) is confessed by the insensitive, dreary Priest (Charles Kennedy) moments before her electrocution. "Am I never to be let alone?" she cries. "Never to have peace? When I'm dead, won't I have peace?" "Ye shall indeed drink of my cup," drones the Priest.*

masses ranged along a stage-wide flight of steps. Not surprisingly, Toller wrote *Masse Mensch* in prison, serving time for his part in Munich's Soviet uprising of 1918–1919. Toller was the kind of artist who is on stage, in jail, or on the run for his life—as, indeed, he was after Hitler's takeover in 1933. In *Hoppla, Wir Leben!,* Toller pictured an idealistic reformer hanging himself in despair of changing the world. Sad to say, Toller was predicting his own end, in New York's Mayflower Hotel in 1939.

(See also *The Adding Machine, Baal,* and *Machinal.*)

THE FAMILY REUNION (See *The Oresteia*)

FARCE

This comic form developed on plot contrivances and horseplay rather than on verbal wit or character painting. There are farcical elements in Aristophanes and Shakespeare—but the one is a satirist, the other a poet. Not till *Georges Feydeau do we find farce in its modern form, in three acts: Act One setting up the plot, Act Two playing up the fun, and Act Three rounding out the plot, with plenty of sneaking around, blundering in and out, mistaken identity, eavesdropping, dithering, and denouncing. Modern farce tends to expand the fun into the first and last acts, thus avoiding the perfunctory quality of Feydeau's first acts, the anticlimactic dip of his third acts. Consider Ben Hecht and Charles MacArthur's *The Front Page* (1928), a brawl from curtain rise to curtain fall, or the postwar *West End farces of *actor-manager Brian Rix. *Joe Orton created a leaner, slyer farce in *What the Butler Saw* (1969), formally correct but thematically subversive; but Michael Frayn's *Noises Off* (1982) retrieved Feydeau's worldly innocence in its look at the inter-company relationships of a touring troupe in a tired farce, the action played both "onstage" and off.
(See also *Come Blow Your Horn, The Matchmaker,* and *The Comedy of Errors.*)

GEORGE FARQUHAR (1678–1707)

Along with *John Vanbrugh, Farquhar may be regarded as either the last of the major *Restoration playwrights, or a transitional figure into the less licentious and more humanistic theatre of the eighteenth century. In Farquhar's most famous plays, *The Recruiting Officer* (1706) and *The Beaux' Strategem* (1707), we desert the swells of the town for the provincial bourgeoisie; and Farquhar's best characters are more personable revisions of Restoration stereotypes. *The Beaux' Strategem*'s Mrs. Sullen, for instance, unhappily married to a drunken grouch, is not the amorously grasping gin-widow we might expect from *William Congreve, but a woman who attempts to improve her condition with virtue and wit. An Irishman, Farquhar began as an actor but turned to playwrighting after tackling a dueling scene with a sword instead of a foil, very nearly killing his colleague. Sadly, Farquhar did little better as a writer, and died penniless at the age of twenty-nine, begging his best friend, actor Robert Wilks, to look after Farquhar's two little girls.

FAUST

The cosmos in two nights by *Johann Wolfgang Goethe, Part One published 1808, Part Two published posthumously 1833, prem. (of both parts together) Weimar, 1876.

The curtain rises on a "Prelude in the Theatre": the Director presses for a hit, the Poet refuses to pander to the mob, and the Comic offers a compromise—let the Poet write a work of art of such vitality, of such "full humanlife," that it *cannot* fail. The Director concurs:

> So encompass on the narrow stage
> The whole circle of Creation;
> And rove, with contemplative speed
> From heaven through the world to hell!

Goethe worked on this monumental verse play (mostly in iambic pentameter) for most of his life. He followed his own instructions, filling *Faust* with humanlife of vast variety (not to mention the spirit world), and roving not only from heaven to hell but into the past and the imagination. However, Goethe moved with more contemplation than speed, and the complete *Faust* is longer than *George Bernard Shaw's *Back to Methusaleh,* or *Eugene O'Neill's *Strange Interlude,* and just about ties with the *Royal Shakespeare's *Nicholas Nickleby.* *Faust* is almost never given complete—most companies give Part One cut down, or the so-called *Urfaust* ("the original *Faust*"), an early draft that Goethe abandoned as being unworthy of his majestic conception. Essentially the tale of a philosopher and scientist who bargains with the devil, *Faust* marks a great sage's reflections upon reason, beauty, and nobility as they may be found in the world.

There apparently was a real Johann Faust, a university professor with an inclination toward the black arts. Goethe alludes by *hommage* to certain aspects of *Christopher Marlowe's *The Tragical History of Doctor Faustus,* but he may have been more strongly influenced by a German tradition of puppet plays on the *Faust* theme, exploiting the comic and grotesque side of the tale. Most educated people today know of Goethe's hero from the most popular operatic adaptation, Charles Gounod's *Faust.* Arrigo Boito's less familiar *Mefistofele* makes the devil the *protagonist, but otherwise it adheres more closely to Goethe. Gounod's version so emphasizes Faust's ruinous romance with the village girl Margarethe that German opera houses traditionally retitle it with *her* name—to avoid "confusion" with the humiliated Goethe.

THE FEDERAL THEATRE

During the first term of President Franklin Roosevelt's regime, the Works Progress (later Projects) Administration mandated four programs of government-sponsored employment: one each for musicians, painters and sculptors, writers, and thespians. The Federal Theatre, organized in 1935 under the direction of the idealistic Hallie Flanagan, was designed to support every kind of theatre from Aeschylus and Shaw to *Uncle Tom's Cabin* and children's shows. The intention was to keep theatre available at nominal admission prices to an impoverished populace while aiding the theatre community itself with artificially created opportunities for playwrights, directors, actors, and techies.

Many of the Federal Theatre's presentations were extremely daring. A series of black shows included not only *The Swing Mikado* (1938), a jive version of Gilbert and Sullivan introduced by the Chicago Federal Theatre, but Shakespeare removed to Haiti, directed by *Orson Welles for the New York outfit as *The Voodoo Macbeth.* (Some genuine voodoo was involved. When the fastidious critic Percy Hammond questioned the validity of a Caribbean Macbeth, some of the cast held a *soirée noire* in Hammond's honor. He immediately caught pneumonia and died.) Flanagan was careful to keep the project *nationally* imposing, with extensive regional offices and, for a bit of PR eclat, the simultaneous premiere of *It Can't Happen Here* (1936), from Sinclair Lewis's novel, in seventeen cities. However, Lewis's picture of a fascist takeover of

The Federal Theatre's Living Newspaper: these views of Triple-A Plowed Under *give us a taste of the fantastic and intense quality of this unique American form, unfortunately neglected since the collapse of the Depression's political stage.*

America—a homegrown fascism, not an alien invasion—chilled many people and outraged others. This proved to be the Federal Theatre's fatal flaw: its gift for raising controversy.

The bulk of the Federal Theatre's controversial material originated in the New York office, headed by the playwright Elmer Rice, who had abandoned the commercial theatre in despair at its hit-or-flop mindset. Faced with the necessity of employing a host of people at once, Rice developed a unique spectacle, the "Living Newspaper." A series of timely documentaries, the Living Newspaper gathered up a veritable flash of forms and approaches in great, whirling pageants: mask, dance, sitcom, film clips, pantomime, loudspeaker harangues, bizarre lighting effects, *agitprop, crowd scenes, monologues, parody, cameo tragedies, choral chanting—all this to dramatize the news of the day. Rice resigned in fury when the government closed *Ethiopia* (1936) after the dress rehearsal, but

such other Living Newspapers as the class-conscious *Injunction Granted* (1936) or the Marxist view of agriculture, *Triple-A Plowed Under* (1936), brought heat down on the Federal Theatre from Washington, DC. Conservative congressmen, many of them professional anti-intellectuals, had never cottoned to the idea of a subsidized stage, anyway. The Federal Theatre's leftist bias gave them something to bite on, and in 1939 the project was disbanded.

GEORGES FEYDEAU (1862–1921)

The father of modern farce. Restructuring the classic form of French farce laid down by *Molière and developed by *Eugène Labiche, the *boulevardier Feydeau ordered everything around what he took to be farce's salient feature—adultery. Almost all

Two shots of Feydeau's Hotel Paradiso *in New York in 1957 give us an elemental sense of the Feydeauvien construction: Bert Lahr is married to Vera Pearce (left) but lusts after Angela Lansbury (right). Adultery plus complications equals farce.*

Feydeau's works are innocently salacious sex comedies: the libidinous urge is genuine, but, in the Feydeau second act of nonstop hurlyburly, seldom consummated. It is a tribute to Feydeau's naturalism that his plays need considerable adaptation to go over outside France. Outstanding modern English-language versions of Feydeau include Peter Glenville's *Hotel Paradiso,* from *L' Hôtel du Libre Échange* (1899), seen in London with Alec Guinness and in New York with Bert Lahr and Angela Lansbury; Noël Coward's *Look After Lulu,* from *Occupe-toi d' Amélie* (1908), starring the established Vivien Leigh in London and the just star-born Tammy Grimes in New York (in a Cyril Ritchard–Cecil Beaton production); and adaptor Barnett Shaw's (but really director Gower Champion's) *A Flea in Her Ear,* from *Une Puce à l' Oreille* (1907), a staging for the American Conservatory Theatre of San Francisco, one that least honored Feydeau's boulevardier style but best served his extravagant comic

energy. As so often with Feydeau, Champion's first act was bearable and his third act a little tiresome. But the second act was stupendously funny.

EDUARDO DE FILIPPO (1900–   )

One of Italy's greatest thespians, though so resonant of native language and culture that his fame abroad is spotty. As playwright and actor (in partnership with brother Peppino and sister Titina), De Filippo revels in traditional *commedia dell' arte, or replaces its characters in modern-day Naples, pulling Italian theatre history into the age of neorealism, of De Sica and Rossellini. De Filippo once claimed that "the conflict between individual and society" is his key theme, but he is best known for the simple humanity of his family studies, the conflict *among* individuals *within* a minature society, as in *Sabato, Domenica, e Lunedì* (Saturday, Sunday,

Monday, 1959), seen both in London and New York in Franco Zeffirelli's production. Still, De Filippo does not translate well. His best known work, *Filumena Marturano* (1946), about the marriage of a prostitute and a businessman after a twenty-five-year affair, was done *twice* in New York, first as *The Best House in Naples* in 1956, then as *Filumena* in 1960. Both tries failed (the second even with Joan Plowright repeating her London success in the title role). Yet this is regarded as De Filippo's masterpiece.

ALBERT FINNEY (1936–   )

Trained at the Royal Academy of Dramatic Art and seasoned at the Birmingham Repertory Company, Finney hit the *West End at just the right time, the late 1950s. The era of the "angry young man," in full revolt against the well mannered salon stage of *Terence Rattigan and *Noël Coward, was still young; Finney's roughhewn proletarian-voiced approach was of moment. Not, perhaps, in his first stabs at Shakespeare. But as the dashing Yorkshire loser in *Billy Liar* (1960) and the impulsive prelate in *John Osborne's *Luther* (1961), Finney took London. Aging into wisdom and perspective, he refined his Shakespeare, rounded out his contemporary portrayals. He has left some of his best work on film—the irresistibly good-natured hero of *Tom Jones* (1963), in John Osborne's screenplay, or the fastidiously eccentric detective Hercule Poirot in *Murder on the Orient Express* (1974). The two roles suggest Finney's extraordinary range. Yet a third and unfortunately obscure film, *Alpha Beta,* with Rachel Roberts, based on the E. A. Whitehead play about a sagging marriage that Finney and Roberts played in 1972 at the *Royal Court Theatre, preserves the highly physicalized, working-class Finney of *Billy Liar* and *Luther,* a very center of the man's career.

MINNIE MADDERN FISKE
(1865–1932)

She was an old-fashioned actress in many ways, billing herself as "Mrs. Fiske" and resisting the formation of *Actor's Equity because acting was an honor, not a trade. She was new-fangled, too, an insistent proselyte of the then all but taboo *Henrik Ibsen and a champion of a number of causes thought zany, including animal rights. (Spotting a man whipping his horse, she called a policeman and pressed charges.) She was fearless, the most defiant opponent of the *Syndicate theatre cartel, though their power drove her shows into the most remote and neglected houses. After all this, it seems almost incidental to add that she was by all accounts the greatest American actress of her day.

Her talent is hard to pin down. She was versatile, a comic and a tragedienne, adept in classics as well as ephemeral commercial fare. Most agree that, besides the charm and presence that contemporary audiences demanded, Mrs. Fiske had a natural quality, an honesty that made her outstanding in a time of posing and suggesting. Some have said that technique was everything to Mrs. Fiske, that she planned her performances to the most minute touches, then locked it all in and played it *just* so till the play had run its course. Others swore to her spontaneity, her ability to imply that the spectator was attending, that day, her only perfect reading on the tour. Her great roles included the heroines of *Tess of the D'Urbervilles;* Langdon Mitchell's *Becky Sharp* (one of the several adaptations of Thackeray's *Vanity Fair* then in use); *Edward Sheldon's *Salvation Nell;* and Ibsen's Nora (in *A Doll's House*), Hedda Gabler, Mrs. Alving (in *Ghosts*), and Rebecca West (in *Rosmersholm*). She kept them in trim even into late middle age, and finally added Mrs. Malaprop (in *Sheridan's *The Rivals*), still tantalizing in the calculation of her . . . improvisation.

CLYDE FITCH (1865–1909)

This prolific playwright was the king of *Broadway at the turn of the century, especially in comic works of light social critique written around the charisma of an established woman star or promising newcomer. The unknown Ethel *Barrymore made stardom as an opera singer taming a debonair firefighter in Fitch's *Captain Jinks of the Horse Marines* (1901); the brilliant Clara Bloodgood played the last role of her tragic life (she died a suicide) as the compulsive liar of *The Truth* (1906). Fitch cut his ware to fit popular taste so well that he went into eclipse almost immediately after his death. Still, for all his manufacturing, he had a gift for repartee and real thespian's craft. *The Truth* is very playable, as is Fitch's satire on the craze for divorce among the jeweled classes, *The New York Idea* (1906).

HALLIE FLANAGAN (See The Federal Theatre)

FLAT (See Scenery)

FLIES (See Scenery)

JOHN FLETCHER (See Elizabethan Theatre)

DARIO FO (1926–   )

Italy's jester of the left, gadfly and baiter of the forces of reaction and compromise. Fo is an all-around thespian, not only as *actor-manager (as chief of the troupes La Nuova Scena and, more successfully, La Commune) but as a practitioner of the moribund art of *mime, in his solo show, *Mistero Buffo* (1969), adapted from *medieval material and meaning roughly, *Comic Mystery Play.* However, Fo is best known for his political defiance,

and not only in Italy: The U.S. State Department's refusal to grant Fo entry in 1980 made international headlines.

Fo works in comedy, but of a gritty sort that veers from farcical *naturalism to pointed *absurdism. He favors bizarre, super-*Pirandellian titles, such as *Settimo: Ruba un Po' Meno* (Seventh Commandment: Thou Shalt Steal a Little Less, 1964) or *Tutti Uniti! Tutti Insieme! Ma Scusa, Quello non È il Padrone?* (All United! All Together! Uh-oh, Here Comes the Boss!, 1971). His most popular play is *Non si Paga! Non si Paga!* (We Won't Pay!, 1974), comic *agitprop inviting the audience to fight inflation by stealing necessities—the *autoriduzione,* or "do-it-yourself price reduction," as such civil-disobedience theft is known in Italy. However, Fo's admirers prefer *Morte Accidentale di un Anarchisto* (Accidental Death of an Anarchist, 1970), a macabre lampoon of the Pinelli case, in which an anarchist suspected of terrorism fell out of a four-story window during police interrogation. This is typical Fo, sardonically sparking an extremely incendiary topic, and keeping the show dangerous by adding lines during the run to reflect the findings of the real-life investigation of the case. At one point, a police chief warns that he has spies planted in the audience. At his signal, voices in the auditorium respond, "Yes, sir! What are your orders?" The public giggles at this—our Fo's at it again. But then the character called The Maniac (Fo himself, of course: prophets are mad) turns to them with a smile. "Not to worry," he says. "They're only actors. The real ones won't give themselves away *that* easy!"

FOLIO

Latin for "leaf," designating a page size of $8\frac{1}{2}$ by $13\frac{1}{2}$ and referring to the proportions of the first collection of Shakespeare's plays—the famous First Folio—published in 1623, seven years after Shakespeare's death. In his lifetime, some of his plays were brought out separately in quarto size, the pages trimming at $6\frac{3}{4}$ by $8\frac{1}{2}$. Some of these were hastily brought out by unscrupulous printers—these are the so-called "bad quartos." Some were put forth by Shakespeare himself, apparently in self-defense—the "good quartos." However, even these contain inaccuracies, most of which were retained in the First Folio, edited by two members of Shakespeare's company, John Heminge and Henry Condell. Later folios came out in 1632, 1663, and 1685. The quartos sold at sixpence each, the folios at a pound.

FOLK PLAY

This term, popular in America in the 1920s and 1930s, denotes theatre depicting racial or cultural systems, not only in setting and characters but in language and even song—Hatcher Hughes's melodrama *Hell-Bent fer Heaven* (1924), on life in the Carolina hills; or Lynn Riggs's *Green Grow the Lilacs* (1931), chivalry out west punctuated by such ditties as "Get Along, Little Dogies," "Home on the Range," and "Come a Ty Yi Yippy." The black folk play, almost invariably by white writers, tended toward pageant-like tragedy, especially in DuBose and Dorothy Heyward's *Porgy* (1927), from Heyward's novel and the source of George Gershwin's opera *Porgy and Bess;* or in Marc Connelly's *The Green Pastures* (1930), a view of Bible stories seen through the eyes of a Sunday school class as a kind of Dixie Goshen.

The folk play era ended in the late 1930s. The whites' black plays were finally seen as exploitative —not least when Paul Green smoothed over the political vigor of Richard Wright's novel in their joint adaptation of *Native Son* (1941)—and the white plays worked better as musicals, as in *Oklahoma!* Richard Rodgers and Oscar Hammerstein's adaptation of *Green Grow the Lilacs.*

LYNN FONTANNE (See Alfred Lunt)

EDWIN FORREST (1806–1872)

This great shouting beast of an actor was one of America's first native stars in an era that worshiped only British players. Forrest specialized in mon-

Edwin Forrest: a characteristic pose. Even calm, Forrest is anything but collected.

strous tragic heroes—Shakespeare's Lear and Othello and title roles in two plays written at Forrest's commission, Spartacus in *The Gladiator* (1831) and the Indian chief in *Metamora* (1829), subtitled *The Last of the Wampanoags.* Temperamental to a vast fault, Forrest tested his reputation in a feud with the reigning English favorite, *William Macready. The hostilities became politicized, and climaxed in the terrible *Astor Place Riot.

FOURTH WALL

In the *naturalistic theatre of the late 1800s and early 1900s, the public was virtually invited to witness "real life." A few actors in a set were reality: as if the rising curtain made transparent a room's "fourth wall" through which spectators might glimpse life as it is lived. "I knock down the wall of an apartment," explained *Ibsen, "then observe what's taking place inside." The term, prideful in its day, became derogatory in the experimental, anti-naturalistic years, from about 1905 in Europe and 1920 in America.

MAX FRISCH (1911–   )

Another of the German-speaking "national guilt" playwrights, though Frisch is Swiss, nationally guilty of nothing worse than the cuckoo clock. Frisch's most typical work is *Andorra* (1961), a parable of Nazi racial policies. But his most successful work is *Biedermann und die Brandstifter* (Mr. Babbitt and the Arsonists, 1958), translated as *The Fire Raisers* (in England) and *The Firebugs* (in America). This *absurdist look at a city gradually burned down tells us that giving in to the enemy only makes him stronger. It might be viewed as a companion piece to *Eugène Ionesco's *Rhinoceros,* in which the population of a town literally *becomes* the enemy, dehumanized from friends and neighbors into a mob of marauding beasts. Both plays are fantastical comedies. But where Ionesco sees the collapse of civil order as overwhelming, Frisch, a determined moralist, urges us to reason and resist.

CHARLES FROHMAN (1860–1915)

Frohman was a progenitor of the modern day producer, as the only notable American *manager who neither acted in nor staged his attractions. He played the establishment honcho, disdaining the avant-garde, snubbing unknown playwrights, sternly upholding the *star system, and lending his prestige to the rapacious monopoly of theatre owners known as the *Syndicate. Yet Frohman had charm, disarming his associates by his refusal to write out a contract, preferring verbal agreements —and Frohman held to them. His older brothers Daniel and Gustave were also managers, but Charles was the outstanding one, especially for his high rate of success, guaranteed by his sound instinct for the finer brand of popular theatre, including the plays of *James Barrie and the Gaiety

musicals, named for the London theatre in which they were developed. A confirmed Anglophile, Frohman was active in the *West End, and shuttled back and forth across the Atlantic. Thus he died: a passenger on the Lusitania when the Germans torpedoed it, Frohman urbanely watched the others filling the lifeboats, whimsically quoted a line from Barrie, and settled into a deckchair to go down in style.

CHRISTOPHER FRY (1907–   )

With *Maxwell Anderson and *T. S. Eliot, Fry forms the great modern triangle of verse playwrights. But Fry's almost playful lyricism contrasts with Anderson's striving grandeur and Eliot's deadpan ironies. "I repeat myself unendurably, like the Creation," is typical Fry; or "I have my father mapped so that I know which way to travel." Both are from *The Firstborn* (1948), Fry's retelling of events leading up to the Jewish Exodus from Egypt. Playful, too, is Fry's invention of a plot that might have served the young Shakespeare in *The Lady's Not For Burning* (1948), or the premise that an aging rake might hold a golden apple contest to select a wife from among his three mistresses—his son to choose—in *Venus Observed* (1950). A healthy complement of acting talent contributed to Fry's prominence in the *West End —John Gielgud, Laurence Olivier, Edith Evans; and Katharine Cornell and Anthony Quayle played *The Firstborn* on Broadway in 1958, under Quayle's direction. But Fry's late prime coincided with the era of "angry young man" realism, and Fry's pacifism and antique subjects—not to mention his poetry—put him out of favor. Ironically, he may be recalled better for his adaptations—for instance of *Giraudoux's *The Trojan War Will Not Take Place* (under the title *Tiger at the Gates*) and *Anouilh's *The Lark*—than for his own work.

ATHOL FUGARD (1932–   )

As a South African who writes with honesty and clarity of race relations, Fugard is more often performed abroad than at home. Yet as playwright, director, and actor, he is not overtly political in the manner of, say, *Rolf Hochhuth or *John Arden. Fugard calls his work "theatre of defiance," mounting a personal protest "against the conspiracy of silence about how the next man lives." Still, the essential Fugard situation treats a few people of conflicted feelings about their ties of blood, loyalty, or affection—"the bond between brothers," to quote a line from one of his best known plays, *The Blood Knot,* first performed privately in 1961 in a much longer version than is currently in use. A low-key naturalism marked his first titles; later Fugard took on an experimental flavor and more political themes, as in *Sizwe Banzi* [later *Bansi*] *Is Dead* (1972) and *The Island,* first given as *Die Hodoshe Span* (1973).

Still, one cannot separate Fugard's humanism from his social report, for his sense of character is overpowering. Thus, *"Master Harold"* . . . *and the Boys* (1982), for all its polemical bite, remains most vital as a study in human relationships—here, among a young white man and two black servants. Probing this "bond between brothers" of two races in a racialist state, Fugard reaches a climax in which one of the servants responds to the master's racist joke by showing his ass. Immediately contrite, the servant touches the boy's shoulder . . . and the boy turns and spits in his face. It is one of the most arresting moments in postwar English language theatre, all the more so because Fugard has denoted the play's autobiographical nature. His given name, in fact, is Harold.

G

THE GALLI-BIBIENA FAMILY

Italian architects and designers who developed and popularized (but seem not to have introduced) the famous *scena per angolo,* the scenery of receding perspective, in which a vaulting castle hallway or intersection of streets appears to extend indefinitely into the unseen distance. Galli is the family name, Bibiena (also Bibbiena) the birthplace of the founder of the line, Giovanni Maria Galli (1625–1665). Giovanni's sons Ferdinando and Francesco brought greater honor to the name, and established the family tradition of traveling throughout Europe from post to post. The Gallis's influence was thus firmly set; as late as the 1870s, Giovanni's descendants were working on the construction of Richard Wagner's opera house of the future at Bayreuth.

JOHN GALSWORTHY (1867–1933)

Though today the major part of his fame rests on his cycle of novels, *The Forsyte Saga,* Galsworthy was one of England's most eminent and prolific dramatists. He worked in a *naturalistic and carefully dispassionate style, probing such social problems as legal favoritism by class, in *The Silver Box* (1906); labor relations, in *Strife* (1909); penal re-

form, in *Justice* (1910); nationalistic militarism in *The Mob* (1914); and the sensationalism of the press, in *The Show* (1925).
(See also *Justice.*)

FEDERICO GARCÍA LORCA (1898–1936)

García Lorca was one of Spain's most cultured talents, a musician, painter, and poet who turned to playwrighting to express profound theories on the politics of sex. He was an accomplished thespian as well as writer, sharpening his instincts in work with a university theatre group, *La Barraca* (The Shack), that toured classic Spanish theatre in the provinces. However respectful of stage tradition, as a playwright Lorca was a revolutionary. In his most famous plays, the trilogy of "rural tragedies" *Bodas de Sangre* (Blood Wedding, 1933), *Yerma* (1934), and *La Casa de Bernarda Alba* (The House of Bernarda Alba, written 1936, prem. 1945), Lorca opposes the personal to the public, feelings to customs, love to honor. One cannot, he says, have both halves of each pair; the latter devours the former. The social code, whether that of national law or of township institutions, enervates and destroys.

As an artist and a homosexual in one of Europe's

most brutally repressive nations, Lorca challenged the reigning native dramatist, the urbane Jacinto Benavente (1866–1954), with a poetic anthropology of the Spanish soul. In Lorca, love is defiance and vengeance is inexorable. Thus, the marital ritual in *Blood Wedding* is overwhelmed by the ritual of family vendetta, and the barren wife Yerma strangles her husband in despair—better a widow than a childless wife. Even in the farcical *La Zapatera Prodigiosa* (The Shoemaker's Prodigious Wife, 1930), which views life as a series of unconsummated flirtations, suggests that the heroine is too spirited to survive happily as anyone's wife.

García Lorca looked to be one of Spain's greatest playwrights, and, despite the growing civil turmoil of the 1930s, had projected truly adventurous plays—*La Destrucción de Sodoma* (The Destruction of Sodom) and *La Bola Negra* (The Black Ball), on the alienation of the homosexual in straight society. But the apolitical Lorca was mysteriously caught up in the hostilities between left and right, and was executed by a Facist firing squad at the age of thirty-eight.
(See also *The House of Bernarda Alba*.)

DAVID GARRICK (1717–1779)

Of all the historic English actors, from *Richard Burbage to *Edmund Kean, Garrick is thought the greatest—the *Laurence Olivier, so to suggest, of the years that connect Shakespeare to the *Old Vic. This renown is based partly on Garrick's intensity of portrayal, but perhaps even more on his management of *Drury Lane, at the time even more central to London life than its only rival, *Covent Garden. (A third house, the Haymarket, was permitted activity during the warm months, when the two official patent theatres were closed.) Garrick, who ran Drury Lane from 1747 to 1776, not only made the playhouse the talk of the town —from the intelligentsia to *hoi polloi*—but instituted essential reforms: in the staging of productions, in the development of lighting technology, and in banning *bons vivants* from their accustomed seats on the stage. It seems unthinkable to us today that such a practice ever held sway; it was unacceptable to the gentry that Garrick should oust them. Yet he did, symbolically defending the in-

tegrity of theatre against the self-interest of the theatregoer. Garrick also celebrated his country's outstanding dramatist more than any of his co-evals. They called him "David Shakespeare." His epitaph, in Westminster Abbey, concludes:

Shakespeare and Garrick like twin stars shall shine,
And earth irradiate with a beam divine.

Ironically enough, Garrick was almost as fond of bedraggling the Bard as his colleagues were. Though Garrick did produce a more or less pure *Antony and Cleopatra*, he shredded *The Taming of the Shrew* into an *afterpiece, dropped out lumps of *The Tempest* to fill in with ballet and song in the form known as semi-opera, and upheld the era's soothing of *King Lear*—not as boldly as others, no: but still dropping the Fool and retaining Nahum Tate's revisionist happy ending.

David Shakespeare.

THE GATE THEATRE, DUBLIN

An alternative to Dublin's *Abbey Theatre, founded in 1928 by Hilton Edwards (1903–1982) and Micheál MacLiammóir (1899–1978), Edwards directing most of the productions and MacLiammóir designing them. (Both also acted.) The alternative lay in the two men's emphasis on production. The Abbey, though established as Ireland's *national theatre, tended to rely on the gifts of the dramatist and the resolution of the players. Abbey direction concentrated on little more than a clear presentation of the text; and the decor was very erratic, often slapdash. Then, too, the Gate's reputation ranged far more widely than the Abbey's, taking in Eugene O'Neill, Karel Čapek, Johann Wolfgang von Goethe, Aeschylus, and Elmer Rice, as well as troubling to develop such new Irish writers as Denis Johnston (1901–   ), Maura Laverty (1907–1966), and Mary Manning (1910–   ).

GENERAL UTILITY

This term denotes the bottom rung of the actors in a *stock company, the ones who played the small-

A visit to America's ever-burgeoning regional theatre, here the Hartford Stage Company, yields a key moment in Genet, from The Balcony. *All of Genet deals with performance, presentation, style as character. Thus, though we see the Judge (Charles Kimbrough, right) urging the Executioner (Edward J. Moore) to punish the Thief (Jane McLeod), all three are phonies. The Judge is the client of a bordello selling wish-fulfillment, the Executioner and Thief, bordello employees. Veteran theatregoers will recognize Moore as the author of* The Sea Horse *(1974), a wonderful two-character piece about an amiable sailor and a feisty bar owner that Moore and Conchata Ferrell played for the *Circle Rep.*

est speaking parts—anything from a Restoration servant to an Elizabethan conspirator. An English term borrowed by Americans in the heyday of the Anglophile stock companies in the nineteenth century, the term is of strictly nostalgic reference in Britain today and is totally obsolete in America.

JEAN GENET (1910—1988)

It is perhaps more Genet himself than his work that has linked his name with the *absurdists, for as a criminal and homosexual he has made himself into a kind of living icon of bourgeois-loathing rebellion. The very nature of his life renders society "absurd" by contrast: if this thief and lover of thieves is serious—and Genet is nothing but serious—then what is the rest of the population but a bunch of silly puppets, incapable of a self-assertion comparable to the absolute independence of Genet's Nietzschean underworld?

However, Genet's five plays are the least "absurd" of the absurdist repertory. They are bizarre, and the later ones at moments touch base with the gamboling lunacy of *Eugène Ionesco, the driving action of Arthur Adamov, or the isolation of *Samuel Beckett. But, in all, Genet's theatre is very strongly motivated both personally and politically—something true absurdism never can be. Absurdism reflects life as a hollow rigamarole, a masquerade. Genet is obsessed with the masquerade not as a theatrical metaphor but as a revolutionary tic, a constant reminder that authority is a sham to be exposed, unmasked. Although Genet's career just precedes and runs right through the 1950s, the high time of the absurd, he is more a fellow traveler than a member of the group, a poet trained on patterns of power and deception as they may be unraveled . . . yet, as Genet unravels, he reweaves, as entranced as he is disgusted.

Genet's first play, *Haute Surveillance* (Maximum Security, known in English as *Deathwatch*), was written in 1946, but it had not been staged when his second play, *Les Bonnes* (The Maids, 1947), was mounted in Paris by *Louis Jouvet. Both works strongly reflect Genet's outlaw background, the first in its loving view of macho rites among prisoners, the second in its adaptation of a real-life case in which two maids, sisters, brutally murdered their mistress and her daughter. The symbolism of the powerful and the miserable comes through so intently that it creates a fantastical naturalism, mimetic yet ecstatic. A year after the premiere of *The Maids,* a petition to the President of the Republic from notable literati (including Paul Claudel, Jean Cocteau, André Gide, and Genet's most exhaustive critic, Jean-Paul Sartre) freed Genet from a sentence of life imprisonment, and in 1949 *Deathwatch* was produced.

Genet's third and perhaps most characteristic play, *Le Balcon* (The Balcony, 1957), inaugurated a new era for him, one of flamboyant theatricality. The plays are now overtly political and imposingly detailed, often with important textual variants from one version to another, as if Genet were becoming impatient with the vagaries of stage production and wants to write his plays to be read. He is, after all, a novelist as well as a playwright, a man of letters. Yet the theatre continues to intrigue him as a place of ritual, atonement, exhortation. *Les Nègres* (The Blacks, 1959) deals with race relations in an extraordinarily confrontational manner, and *Les Paravants* (The Screens, 1964), on the Algerian War, was not performed in France for two years after its English and Swedish premieres, and then only under police protection.
(See also *The Balcony*.)

GESAMTKUNSTWERK

German for "work made of all the arts." Richard Wagner (1813–1883) introduced the term describing his later, artistically revolutionary operas, so technically this is a concept of the musical theatre. However, Wagner was influential in theatre generally, and his notion that the most absorbing theatre must be written and staged to encompass poetry, music, dance, and design in a harmonious blend inspired much of the avant-garde in the twentieth century. Ironically, Wagner's most notable spin-off, the epic theatre pioneered by *Erwin Piscator and *Bertolt Brecht, used "all" the arts (Piscator more than Brecht) not in fusion but in a calculated separation of elements. Wagner sought to give his public a religious experience. The epic theatre demands intellectual distance.

MICHEL DE GHELDERODE
(1898—1962)

This Belgian playwright was anything but a thespian. He wrote some fifty plays (in French and Flemish) but had little to do with the day-to-day of the theatre world. There was no Reading of the

Play to the Assembled Company for De Ghelderode, no rehearsal escapades, no star divas, no first night *greenrooming. A recluse in his seventeenth century Brussels townhouse filled with archival folklore, puppets, and masks, De Ghelderode wrote apparently for his own pleasure, and never got used to his championship by the Parisian avant-garde in the early days of *absurdism. Yet in his quiet, even arcane way, De Ghelderode turned the key into the freakish whimsy that unites the earlier *Jarry and *Apollinaire with the later *Ionesco, *Adamov, and *Beckett. De Ghelderode enjoys the carnival, picturesque aspects of absurd anti-realism—some of his plays reminded critics of Breughel. But at other times, De Ghelderode naturalized the bizarre, rooted it in a profound and terrifying view of human drives, especially in an emphasis on the sensuality of sadism that anticipates William Burroughs. As the executioner says, in *Hop, Signor!* (written 1935, prem. 1949), "On the evenings after executions, women become pregnant."

De Ghelderode's plays, the best of which date from the late 1920s through the early 1940s, tend to be short and small-scaled. A few of them, however, call for huge, whirling casts and complex productions—like *La Mort du Docteur Faust* (The Death of Doctor Faust, 1926), "a tragedy for the music hall" that takes the familiar legend through a series of plays-within-the-play, or *Christophe Colomb* (1928), a helter-skelter farce on the discovery of America. "Masqueraders, grotesque figures, living corpses, gluttonous and lustful men and women frantically move about in a decor of purple shadows, full of strong smells," writes critic Jacques Guicharnaud, "and throw violent, foul, or mysterious phrases at each other in highly-colored language filled with Belgian idioms, archaisms, and shrieks." This is less true of some of De Ghelderode, such as *Trois Acteurs, Un Drame* (Three Actors and a Play, 1929), a takeoff on *Luigi Pirandello's *Six Characters in Search of an Author;* or *Barabbas* (1929), replete with the expected Gospel figures (including a mute Jesus); or *Pantagleize* (1939), a madcap, contemporary piece (the setting is "a city of Europe, on the morrow of one war and the eve of another") about an innocent caught up in political intrigue. But Guicharnaud's description of the De Ghelderode landscape certainly applies to the medieval *Hop, Signor!,* with its bamboozling dwarfs, bawdy nobles, and rowdy populace that dotes on tossing unpopular figures in a sheet, higher and higher, till they break like puppets on the stones of the street; or *Sire Halewijn* (Lord Halewyn, 1936), even more medieval, with its castles, knights, and peasants, and its patrician hero whose pleasure it is to go hunting for pretty women to hang; or *Fastes d' Enfer* (Ceremonies of Hell, written 1919, prem. 1949), a "tragedy bouffe" known in English as *Chronicles of Hell,* an almost indescribably perverse Church-hating farrago. *Fastes d' Enfer* had enormous impact on the theatre scene in Paris, where it was first staged (and was withdrawn because of conservative protest), and much of the avant-garde in the 1950s drew energy from it. However, De Ghelderode's relation to absurdism is a matter of form and tone, not of philosophy. He does not see life as meaningless, action as futile. On the contrary, De Ghelderode's theatre is filled with vitally appetitive figures getting more or less what they want. What they want, however, is often ugly or depraved—and De Ghelderode, looking on, pensively poetic, suppresses a thrill.

(See also *Christophe Colomb.*)

GHOSTS

*Naturalistic Greek tragedy by *Henrik Ibsen, prem. Chicago, 1882.

The epic of theatre history regards us in this work, for here Ibsen looks back to Aeschylus and forward to Eugene O'Neill: in structure, theme, and atmosphere. The past (the title's symbolical ghosts) decides the present, the family is essential yet unbearable, and life involves the making of terrible choices. Is this not Aeschylean? O'Neillian? Because *Ghosts* too deeply explored a mother-son relationship and treated the unmentionable taboo of syphilis, it raised up the prime controversy of Ibsen's life, and prompted him to write the tragically ironic *An Enemy of the People.* Note the venue of the premiere—Chicago, in Norwegian, by a touring Norwegian troupe, for an audience of Norwegian-Americans. No proper Scandinavian theatre would touch the piece.

JOHN GIELGUD (1904–   )

"The finest actor on earth," *Kenneth Tynan called him, "from the neck up." Not for Gielgud, then, *Laurence Olivier's feat, at Stratford-upon-Avon in 1959, of falling from a precipice as the murdered Coriolanus, a body tumbling from the heights of power to the gutter of exhausted glory, to be caught by the ankles by two terrified supers. All London talked of Olivier's Coriolanus in a way they were never to talk of any of Gielgud's portrayals. "Now and then," wrote Tynan of Gielgud, "he takes a step or two to right or left and permits his hands, which spend much of the evening protectively clasping each other, to fly up in gestures that claw the air." To which, at lunch with the lawyer and playwright John Mortimer, Gielgud replied, "What did he want me to do, bring out my prick?"

Indeed, from the neck up, Gielgud maintained a career as outstanding as that of any British actor of his time, for, if he could not rival Olivier's physical showboating, he was, alone among even the most distinguished company, as fine a director as he was an actor. And one wonders how many Jack Worthings (in *Oscar Wilde's *The Importance of Being Earnest), Leonteses (in Shakespeare's The Winter Tale), Prosperos (in The Tempest), Hamlets, and Joseph Surfaces (in *Sheridan's *The School for Scandal) were as finely judged as Gielgud's. It is too easily forgot that he varied this very upright, classical fare of Great Roles with the unusual— *Noël Coward, *Edward Albee, *David Storey, *Harold Pinter, *Edward Bond, even Raskolnikov in Rodney Ackland's adaptation of Dostoyevsky's Crime and Punishment (1946). Gielgud is surprising in comedy—surprisingly good, considering his essentially sober cast of feature and grand-manner baritone. In comedy, Gielgud was especially memorable as the retiring headmaster in Alan Bennett's Forty Years On (1968), forever searching the perspective for schoolboys' infringements of the proprieties ("You may regard this as a heaven-sent opportunity to draw with your fountain pen on that boy's neck . . ."). Similarly, while Gielgud left some of his Shakespeare on film, it may be his sternly whimsical Mr. Ryder in the British video adaptation of Evelyn Waugh's Brideshead Revisited that best shows Gielgud's extraordinarily apt sense of character.

JEAN GIRAUDOUX (1882–1944)

As playwright, Giraudoux benefited from his association with the *actor-manager *Louis Jouvet, for Jouvet was not only an impeccable Giraudoux stylist but a devotee of the eye-filling production. Just as well: for Giraudoux believed in theatre as pageant, as a poetic communion of writer and public. "The theatre," he wrote, "is like a Catholic Mass of language." Enchantment plays a part in it, and wit, and luxury. Though Giraudoux grew up during the climax of the *naturalistic revolution that led the stage toward absolute realism or, through counter-revolutionary reply, toward the deliberately fantastical, Giraudoux practiced his Mass of language in a loving semi-realistic milieu that as easily pictured water sprites or gods as it did peasants or Parisian street trash.

Yet if Giraudoux wrote with a delicate hand, he treated subjects of weight and moment. "There are no great people," he observed. "There are only great topics." There are great people in Giraudoux's plays—the mythological heroines of Judith (1931) and Electre (1937), the Trojan Prince Hector in La Guerre de Troie n'Aura pas Lieu (The Trojan War Will Not Take Place, known in English in *Christopher Fry's translation as Tiger at the Gates, 1935). Still, the topics are indeed greater. At times in Giraudoux, everything appears to hang upon the purity of modest boy-girl romance. But he also deals with French Germanophilia in Siegfried (1928), his first play, from his novel Siegfried et le Limousin (1922); with the mindless irresistibility of the war machine in La Guerre de Troie; and with the terrifying virtuousness of blood revenge in Electre.

All the same, Giraudoux never loses his sense of the playful, the paradox, the quirky. This gives his serious theatre a startling grace, his comedy a shimmer. Ondine (1939), on the fatal mating of a fairy and a mortal, is delightful despite a depressing story line; and La Folle de Chaillot (The Madwoman of Chaillot, 1945) melds whimsy and lyricism in a plot to destroy the world's profiteers, scavengers, and agents. Giraudoux calls them "mecs" (pimps), and may be referring to the honchos of Paris's thriving black market, or to the occupying German Army, which treated Vichy Paris as its feudal playground. The play is filled

Giraudoux's Amphitryon 38 *(1929), so entitled because the playwright counted it as the thirty-eighth setting of the legend of Zeus's seduction of Alcmene while disguised as her husband Amphitryon. Giraudoux's predecessors most frequently saw the tale as the basis for a phenomenological disquisition. Giraudoux saw it as a sex comedy. *S. N. Behrman adapted it for the *Lunts in 1937. Here, in the Prologue, Zeus (Lunt) looks down upon earth in the company of Mercury (Richard Whorf). Set designer Lee Simonson concocted their, uh, costumes.*

not only with madwomen (there are four; apparently each *arrondissement* in Paris has one) and human bizarrerie, but with silly fun. Still, Giraudoux is serious about getting rid of the bad guys, driving them through a tunnel into a pit of no return. "Well, there we are," says the titular heroine, "Countess" Aurélie. "The world is saved . . . There is nothing so wrong in the world that a reasonable woman cannot correct in the course of a day." Charming. Fantastic. But Giraudoux means his fantasy intently. He has great people *and* great topics.

(See also *Intermezzo*.)

JOHANN WOLFGANG VON GOETHE (1749–1832)

The great summoner and exorcist of his day. A post-Enlightenment Romantic become post-Romantic Classicist, Goethe was the exponent of all that art and philosophy had developed before him as well as the instigator of much that followed, a one-man Great Books shelf. Goethe is Germany's outstanding literary personage as poet and novelist. But he was as well a philosopher, a statesman, a scientist . . . and an *actor-manager and dramatist, which brings him, most importantly, into this book.

Goethe's first play, *Götz von Berlichingen mit der Eisernen Hand* (written 1771, prem. 1774), mixed the theories of *Gotthold Lessing into the tangy structure of Shakespeare and the atmosphere of political insurgency, all this concurring with the *Sturm und Drang movement that was getting underway virtually that moment: Goethe as follower but mainly leader. His hero, an idealistic petty noble caught between oligarchic church and state and unscrupulously rebellious peasantry, struck a nerve throughout Europe—as did the freedom-fighter *protagonist of Goethe's *Egmont* (written 1787, prem. 1789), a less intense hero in a slightly better organized formal entity.

Meanwhile, the twenty-six-year-old Goethe had come to one of Germany's most important cultural capitals, Weimar in Thuringia, where his duties as courtier of Duke Karl August included running the ducal theatre. There Goethe presented the premiere of his *Iphigenie auf Tauris* (1779), a very slightly *Racinian view of the same play that Racine himself had adapted from *Euripides. The effect of Goethe's love affairs on his art is considered so telling that German university students are required to memorize the women's names and the years of contact—and Charlotte von Stein, the presumed inspiration for Goethe's Iphigenia, may well be the most evocative name on the list. Goethe devoted many a line to her powers as a goddess of healing transcendence, the very image of the bringer of love and peace and self-esteem to the turbulent heart of man. This image, combining grace and eroticism, was to run through Goethe's work in considerable variation. Ironically enough, Frau von Stein seems to have been literally *von Stein* (made of stone), prudish, even ascetic, and melancholy and unattractive to boot. There is no doubt, however, that Goethe's imagination built her into an all-basic female figure to complement Goethe's all-basic male, passionate, brilliant, and venturesome—the poet hero, say, of *Torquato Tasso* (1807), at war with a philistine environment, endlessly striving toward self-knowledge in the perfection of his art. *Torquato Tasso* marks the evolution of the more Classically attuned Goethe, writing his plays in verse as if to "correct" the jumbly, now here, now there prose *melodrama of *Götz von Berlichingen*. Indeed, Goethe had already recast *Iphigenie auf Tauris* from prose into verse. The revision, completed in 1787 and first staged in 1802, is almost invariably the one seen today, as if moderns prefer the smoother, transcendant sage to the resolutely exhilarated youth.

The Classical Goethe is not a reformed Romantic, however, as much as an enhanced one, structuring his emotional turmoils, seeking out the perennial mysteries—not to enjoy the engulfment but to reason it out, spanning the eras from Romantic excess to Classical balance, attempting to reconcile the nature of man with the nature of the world. This apparent paradox finds its highest and most complete statement in Goethe's epic *Faust,* his life's work in that he began it when young and worked on it throughout his long life—fifty years, in all, of composition. Again we have the striving hero whom Goethe built his theatre on, a wise ancient who pacts with the devil to seek out a moment of pure happiness. Goethe scholars warn us against seeing in Faust the author's self-characterization, but the temptation is irresistible—and is there not a touch of Goethe as well in the alter ego of the devil as showman, raising up the visions for Faust (humanity) to contemplate? Goethe's *Ewig-Weibliche* ("the eternal woman") checks in in several forms, now innocent, now sensual. Altogether, it is as if Goethe were divvying up the elements of his Weltanschauung in order to reintegrate them into a whole. Thus the fifty years of labor on *Faust:* the final statement of this amazing mind would necessarily occupy a lifetime. (See also *Faust* and *Götz von Berlichingen.*)

NICOLAI GOGOL (See *The Government Inspector*)

CARLO GOLDONI (1709—1793)

Voltaire called Goldoni "the Italian Molière," pointing up the two latter playwrights' use of *commedia dell'arte*. But where Molière simply borrowed from a foreign form, Goldoni regarded *commedia* as his national inheritance, and himself as its reformer. *Commedia* had become jaded, sloppy, moribund. The vitalilty of the style was worth saving, but the prancing improvisations must be taken over by a playwright, to be fully written out rather than left to the players to devise. In *Il Servitore di Due Padroni* (The Servant of Two Masters, 1743), Goldoni constructed a full-scale *farce using commedia*'s traditional situations and characters—Brighella, Clarice, Smeraldina—but leaving the spontaneous *business only to the servant hero, Truffaldino. Play by play through over 150 titles, Goldoni increasingly abandoned the remnants of *commedia,* absorbing its best features into his own art. Thus, while he banned *commedia*'s leather masks and fanciful costumes, he retained *commedia*'s "vulgar" tongue—in fact, Goldoni made the use of the dialect of his native Venice an important

quality of his texts, prefiguring by a century *naturalism's attempt to fill the theatre with life as lived.

Goldoni's rival *Carlo Gozzi dubbed Goldoni a *"scrittore da fogna"* (an author of the sewer), and conservatives were irritated, too, by Goldoni's broad social canvas, centered on the middle class (Goldoni's favorite people) but taking in the aristocracy (Goldoni's favorite target), the working class (Goldoni's favorite buffoons, though they came off far better than his selfish, idiotic nobles), and the typical *commedia* servants, smarter than their masters. In Goldoni's most enduring titles, such as *La Vedova Scaltra* (The Wily Widow, 1748), *Il Campiello* (The Square, 1756), *Il Ventaglio* (The Fan, 1763), *Le Barufe Chiozzotte* (Squabbles in Chioggia, 1770), and *I Rusteghi* (The Babbitts, 1760), we find a tintype, a Goldonian model: some eight or nine principals wrangling over a macguffin of a plot from morning to evening of a single day (capped, usually, by multiple conjugal engagements) as Goldoni lets events take care of themselves so he can observe and comment on the human condition.

Thus, while the title article of *The Fan* passes from hand to hand throughout the cast, the play is not about a fan but about the people roiling about it; and the Chioggian squabbles, stemming from nothing at all, set off a lively look at the society in a fishing town in the Venetian lagoon. Goldoni's most famous play, *La Locandiera* (The Hostess of the Inn, 1751), is simpler, essentially the wooing of the heroine Mirandolina by two worthless nobles, one of old money and one of new. A third noble, sympathetic but fearful of marriage, also falls for Mirandolina. But at the end of the Goldonian day, she chooses . . . her virile, resourceful servant, Fabrizio. Comes then her famous understated line to the other two scoundrelly nobles: "Please be good enough to find other lodgings."

Goldoni is still performed today, especially in Italy, where Mirandolina is regarded as an important test of greatness in an actress. (It was one of *Eleonora Duse's famous parts, and her only comic one.) In the post–World War II years, Luchino Visconti and *Giorgio Strehler mounted major Goldoni revivals, and the scripts live on in faithful operatic settings by Ermanno Wolf-Ferrari (1876–1948), a fellow Venetian.

MAXIM GORKY (1868–1936)

Alyeksei Maksimovich Pyeshkov adopted the pen name Gorky ("bitter") in an outrage at the inequality of life in tsarist Russia. Today, a theatre in Moscow and even a city (Gorky's birthplace, formerly Nizhni-Novgorod) bear his name, in testament to his unswerving faith in the Revolution. However, Gorky's plays, both before and after the passing of the Romanov autocracy, are not remotely the simplistic essays in *"socialist realism" that this might suggest. On the contrary, Gorky seems to have been the only major Russian artist (in any form) who worked free, or relatively free, of authoritarian restraint.

Like Anton Chekhov, Gorky wrote for the *Moscow Art Theatre. It was Chekhov, in fact, who brought Gorky to Stanislavsky and Nyemirovich-Danchenko. Gorky's first play, *Myeshchananye* (The Philistine Bourgeoisie, 1902), led directly to Gorky's masterpiece, *Na Dnye* (On the Bottom, 1902, generally known in English as *The Lower Depths*). The dense naturalism of this look at a group of derelicts, visited by a mystically enlightened old man, carries tremendous power. As many commentators have pointed out, it bears a fetching resemblance to Eugene O'Neill's *The Iceman Cometh,* not least in Gorky's examination of the benefits of truth telling in an atmosphere of hopeless cultural disinheritance.

The bulk of Gorky's plays follow up on the social critique of *Myeshchananye*—*Dachniki* (The Vacationers, 1904) indicting the materialism of the intelligentsia, *Varvari* (Barbarians, 1906) worrying over the gap between the educated and the peasantry, *Vragi* (Enemies, 1906) monitoring official intolerance of workers' grievances. Gorky continued to produce right up to his death—a mysterious one, like the deaths of so many other Russians who had the misfortune to live under *Stalinshchina,* the rule of Josef Stalin.

Mit der Eisernen Hand, the original title goes on: "With the Iron Hand." The real-life Götz lost his right hand in battle and wore a rude metal glove. Caught between forces of conservatism and upheaval during the Protestant Reformation, the freebooting knight Götz tries to survive by *Faustrecht* (literally "fist right," meaning "might is morally right": if you win, you deserved to). This being a tragedy, Götz dies, but Goethe, defying convention much as Götz does, laid his text down in prose rather than the poetry expected of a hero's tragedy, and set his scenes to race through time and space in the manner of the *Elizabethan stage, without regard for the *unities and other amenities. "Shakespeare has utterly ruined you," said Johann Friedrich Herder, Goethe's mentor, upon reading the manuscript. Shakespeare "ruined" many a playwright in the Romantic nineteenth century, the first era—after his own—when his genius began to be appreciated in the full intensity of its survey. *Götz von Berlichingen* is, in fact, no masterpiece, and it produced, by imitation, a troop of cheap *Ritterdramen* ("knight plays") of noble brigands martyred by *Faustrecht* in the *Sturm und Drang ("storm and stress") of a nation breaking out of the Middle Ages into the Romantic era with scarcely a taste of the Enlightenment to serve as a transition. If Shakespeare helped foster the young Goethe, Goethe helped foster the Sturm und Drang movement in art, especially with this play and, later the same year, the novel *Die Leiden des Jungen Werthers* (The Sorrows of Young Werther). In our own time, *Götz von Berlichingen* served as the source of another of *John Arden's fascinating *Brechtian history plays, in *Ironhand* (1963). This is in fact a very faithful adaptation of Goethe's text—yet very different. What Goethe implies, Arden forcefully presents. When Goethe lags, Arden efficiently hastens. Where Goethe tries to transcend, Arden demands to experience and react. A rare case of an authentic modern adaptation of a classic, the same only more so.

GÖTZ VON BERLICHINGEN

*Chronicle play by *Johann Wolfgang von Goethe, prem. Berlin, 1774.

THE GOVERNMENT INSPECTOR

Social *satire by Nicolai Gogol (1809–1852), prem. Petersburg, 1836.

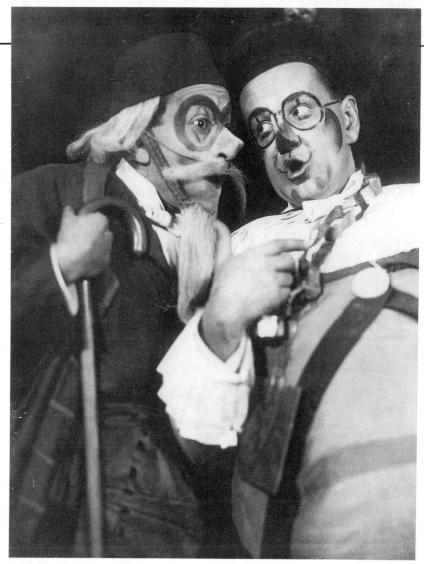

Gozzi's Turandot *at Moscow's Vakhtangov Theatre. Notice the stylized* commedia *costuming, absolute Gozzi.*

Also known as *The Inspector General,* though the original Russian title, *Ryevizor,* simply means *The Inspector.* The plot premise is a classic: the corrupt officials of a provincial town mistake an obscure clerk for an all-powerful state inspector. They fête and bribe the imposter, even affiance him to the mayor's daughter. Just before the boom falls, the clerk makes a run for it.

The play is famous not only for its universal appeal as entertainment and insight, but because, for reasons unknown, the censor passed it and Tsar Nicholas I loved it, though it pictures the Russian bureaucracy as pompous, dishonest, and stupid. "Everyone got what he deserved," the Tsar supposedly declared after the premiere, "and I most of all."

CARLO GOZZI (1720–1806)

Gozzi was a Venetian, a reactionary, a patrician, a snob, and a playwright, in something like that order. He was disgusted by his contemporary *Carlo Goldoni's reformation of *commedia dell'arte* in dialect comedies with bourgeois and even servant heroes, so Gozzi decided to reform *commedia* in the opposite direction. Correcting Goldoni's *naturalism, Gozzi emphasized the marvelous, the bizarre. Hating Goldoni's broad social purview, Gozzi reveled in royalty, with prince heroes in love with princess heroines. Despising Goldoni's Venetian vulgate, Gozzi wrote in Tuscan dialect, the poet's Italian. Finally, reproaching Goldoni's humanization of *commedia*'s archetypal figures, Gozzi brought them back in their original stereotyped form, acrobatics, masks, and all, even allowing them room for the old improvisational routines that Goldoni banned.

Gozzi termed his plays *"fiabe"* (fables), emphasizing the storybook nature of his plots. Wizardry and terror abound. In *L'Amore dei Tre Melarance* (The Love for Three Oranges, 1761), a prince is cursed with an obsessive desire for magic oranges, each containing an enchanted princess. *Il Re Cervo* (The King-Stag, 1762) finds a young king metamorphosed into a stag on a sojourn in the forest. In *La Donna Serpente* (The Serpent Woman, 1762), a princess turns into a snake when her husband fails his test of fidelity. *Turandot* (1765) gives us an Oriental princess who puts three riddles to her suitors; those who cannot answer correctly are executed. Gozzi's flamboyant pieces have served many opera composers, most notably in Prokofyev's *The Love for Three Oranges,* Busoni's more (and Puccini's less) faithful versions of *Turandot,* and Hans Werner Henze's *The King-Stag.*

GRACIOSO

The comic servant in Spanish theatre, an essential character from the days of *Lope de Vega and *Calderón.

GRAND GUIGNOL

The *guignol* is a French one-act form devoted to macabre violence. The genre is usually referred to outside France as "grand guignol" after Paris's Théâtre du Grand Guignol, which specialized in full evenings of such fare.

HARLEY GRANVILLE-BARKER

(1877–1946)

As playwright, *actor-manager, and polemicist, Granville-Barker was the outstanding elitist figure of late-Victorian and Edwardian England. Running the *Royal Court Theatre with J. E. Vedrenne (1867–1930), Granville-Barker sought out bold contemporary writing, especially George Bernard Shaw, some of whose greatest plays were introduced at the Royal Court in experimental matinées for the cognoscenti. Staging Shakespeare in an unconventional modernist style, Granville-Barker broke the stranglehold that *Henry Irving's postcard pageantry had put on England's greatest playwright. Directing actors, "he was like a masseur"—so recalls *John Gielgud, who worked on *King Lear* with him in 1940—"who forces you to discover and use muscles you never knew you possessed." And, as a dramatist himself, Granville-Barker threw open a stage of ideas, a revolutionary stage interested in women's rights, corruption in the political and business worlds, and bourgeois hypocrisy. They are "difficult" plays, somewhat like Shaw's but less glib, less neatly structured. Still, *The Marrying of Ann Leete* (1902) and *The Voysey Inheritance* (1905) heartened progressive elements in the theatre, and *Waste* (1907) became a cause célèbre when it was banned after two performances. Sadly, Granville-Barker became increasingly disenchanted with the making of the theatre, and by the end of World War I had virtually retired to concentrate on scholarship and lecturing. Only now is Britain coming to terms with this remarkable talent in important revivals—*The Madras House* (1910), for instance, at the National Theatre in 1977 with *Paul Scofield, Paul Rogers, and Ronald Pickup.

SIMON GRAY (1936–   )

Gray is a *West End hitter in the batting style of *Noël Coward and *Terence Rattigan, along with *Alan Ayckbourn one of the few British playwrights of today who feel as comfortable in the commercial theatre as in the subsidized *repertory stage. Typically, neither Gray nor Ayckbourn is overtly political, as virtually all of their colleagues are. But neither is as versatile as Rattigan or the musical, comic, and serious Coward. Where Ayckbourn treats the suburban middle class, Gray deals with literary and academic life, especially with those whose education led them to aspire to greater things than they personally feel themselves capable of, or those who suffer from an almost pre-schizoid isolation from their environment. As someone says to the *protagonist of Gray's *Quartermaine's Terms,* "You have an amazing ability not to let the world impinge on you." Gray likes witty failures and not just cool but cold customers, the also-rans and the self-destructive charmers.

The blackly comic *Wise Child* (1967) and the murder-thriller (with a theatrical background) *Stage Struck* (1979) expanded Gray's terrain. Still, he is at his best on his own turf—looking in on a sequence of interruptions that keep an apparently agreeable man from listening to a recording of Wagner's *Parsifal* in *Otherwise Engaged* (1975); following the marital calamities of a book editor in *Dog Days* (1976); sympathizing with a lonely, repressed language teacher, as likeably dim as an old bulldog, in *Quartermaine's Terms* (1981); or charting twenty years in the very shared lives of six Cambridge graduates in *The Common Pursuit* (1984).

(See also *Butley.*)

GREEK THEATRE

It is said that Western theatre began in the sixth century B.C., when one Thespis introduced an actor to engage in dialogue with the traditional choral *dithyrambos,* a narrative poem, sung and danced. Whether Thespis was a poet who instituted the solo actor or that first actor himself (hence "thespian": a person of the theatre) is not known. But the masked and costumed actor, with his high-soled shoes *(kothurnos)* and high-topped wig or hair-dressing *(onkos),* clearly established the sense of conflict (or *agon:* "contest") that true theatre turns on. The actor was not limited to one role. By changing masks he could change characters, and thus fill out the sections of a given story. (As in the classic Japanese *Kabuki and *Nō styles, all characters, male and female, were played by men.)

By the fifth century B.C., the performance of plays had become an essential civic event in Athens, where play contests were held every spring in honor of Dionysus, whose rites had originated the dithyramb. (Other cities held similar festivals, but Athens remained the Greek theatre capital; and all the texts that have survived were written for the Athenian Dionysia.) In the open air, successively larger amphitheatres nearly surrounded the orchestra, the chorus's circular dancing area, backed by the *skene,* a simple building corresponding roughly to the modern backdrop (hence, "scene") and extending through its "wings," the *paraskenia,* to enclose the acting areas. There was no scenery as such, just indications of generic locations on the revolving *periaktoi.* But the *skene* contained the *mechane,* a crane used to transport characters portraying gods; and the *ekkyklema,* a wheeled platform drawn out of the *skene* to display, usually, the bodies of dead characters.

Most of the texts are lost. But of surviving dramatists, Aeschylus was the grandest, Sophocles the most dramatic, and Euripides the most fiercely nuanced. Aeschylus added a second actor, freeing the action considerably. Sophocles added a third actor, Euripides a fourth. With doubling and tripling of roles (and the mute extras, able to emote but not speak), the narratives became considerably populous. Euripides's *The Bacchae numbers eight parts (for these same four actors) besides the chorus.

The annual Dionysia included an invocational procession and other festivities, but it centered on the performances of tetralogies, three tragedies and a comic *satyr play, all related by plot or theme. Three poets were chosen, each to present his quartet of plays on one day, each production backed financially by the *choregos,* the forerunner of the modern-day producer, and the "best" tetralogy acclaimed the winner of the contest. (In thanks for his community service, the *choregos* was forgiven that year's taxes; but as his expenses outweighed his savings, the post was honorary rather than remunerative.) The stories of the plays were drawn from familiar events in history and mythology. Thus the productions drew their power not from surprise of event but from the poetry and insight the author could develop from his subject and, we presume, from the vitality of the acting, singing, and dancing—for such evidence as we have suggests that Greek tragedy was more like opera than like spoken theatre.

Perhaps never since the days of the Dionysia has

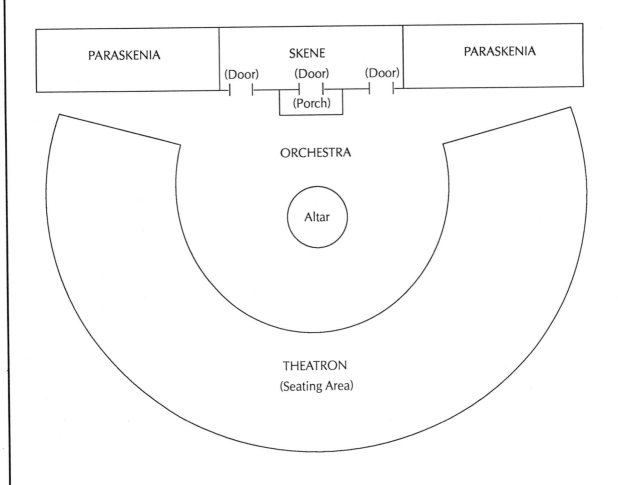

PARASKENIA	SKENE	PARASKENIA

(Door)   (Door)   (Door)

(Porch)

ORCHESTRA

Altar

THEATRON
(Seating Area)

A diagram of the Greek theatre.

drama been held so crucial a clause in the social contract. Audiences at these performances were swept up indivisibly in art and polemic, and it was one of the several paradoxes of Athenian democracy that the theatre will be—at least occasionally must be—subversive, questioning and even attacking state policy. However ancient their subject matter, these plays dealt with such universal questions that the fascist colonels of the *coup d'état* of April, 1967, banned classic works from Greek theatres.

Greek comedy, performed in a modification of the visual trappings of tragedy, is personified in the work of Aristophanes, bawdy and irreverant and eager to lampoon living persons—Socrates, we hear, rose from his seat in the audience to acknowledge, in good humor, a particularly brutal caricature. Aristophanes's Old Comedy gave way to the little-known Middle Comedy and the influential New Comedy (see Roman Theatre), whose chief exponent was Menander (c. 340–293 B.C.), apolitical, tidy, prim.

(See also Aeschylus, Aristophanes, Euripides, Sophocles, *The Bacchae, Lysistrata, The Oresteia,* and *The Trojan Women.*)

Douglas Campbell as Sophocles's Oedipus at Stratford, Ontario, directed by *Tyrone Guthrie in 1955 —not that far removed from what the original production might have been like, in this friezelike moment of *protagonist and chorus in *agon.

GREENROOM

The traditional backstage area where, during a performance, actors can sit, grouch, and gossip while waiting for their cues and where, after the performance, the public may congregate to offer their congratulations. The greenroom is more a European than an American custom; American actors usually receive their guests in their dressing rooms.

LADY AUGUSTA GREGORY (See The Abbey Theatre)

JERZY GROTOWSKI (1933–   )

This Polish director is the master of theatre as arcane rite, limiting the home audience for his Polish Laboratory Theatre to the citizens of Wroclaw —not unlike taking the *Comédie-Française to Shaker Heights—and, on tour in the Western cultural capitals, admitting absurdly elite groups of one hundred or so; placing utmost importance on the actor as a physical rather than intellectual or emotional presence; and keeping as far from the standard *repertory as possible. Grotowski's ensemble did offer one (neglected) classic, *Calderón's *El Principe Constante* (The Constant Prince), the script shredded to its visual essentials. But more typical of Grotowski's theatre was *Apocalypsis cum Figuris,* improvised, in the style of *Joseph Chaikin's Open Theater, by Grotowski and his actors out of snippets of the Bible, *The Brothers Karamazov,* *T. S. Eliot, and Simone Weil. Grotowski's theatre is evocative rather than representational, imagistic rather than textual. Some commentators think Grotowski has broken too conclusively with the verbal component of theatre. Others praise his fresh vision and the virtuosity of his executions. Certainly, the Polish Lab Theatre's tours greatly impressed the Western theatre scene, even admitting that most people learned of Grotowski's work through description instead of *in situ* as spectators. Founded in 1965, the Polish Lab was dissolved in 1976, and Grotowski moved to California.

GROUNDLING

*Elizabethan theatre architecture set the fancier people in seats in the enclosing galleries and the mob, at cheaper admission prices, on their feet on the ground—hence, groundlings. The word carries a nuance of derogation, presuming the groundlings to be coarse and impatient, unlike the aficionados in the seats of rank. Thus Hamlet, in his advice to the players:

HAMLET: Oh, it offends me to the soul to hear a
    robustious periwig-pated fellow tear a passion
    to tatters, to very rags, to split the ears of the
    groundlings, who, for the most part, are
    capable of [i.e., able to respond to] nothing but
    inexplicable dumb shows and noise.

After the *Restoration revamped theatre buildings, bringing them closer to the rectangular, *proscenium-style auditoriums common today, the term *groundling* hung on to denote the lower form of theatregoer, though by the 1800s the cheaper seats were in fact *up*stairs, in the galleries.

THE GROUP THEATRE

"I had been impelled by the feeling," wrote *Harold Clurman, "that if one's will is strong enough, if one's desire is sufficiently hot, these alone can mold events." Clurman's desire was to assist in the raising up of a theatre company *on* Broadway but not *of* it, "an art of direct communication grounded on shared social and moral values." Not a sheer business, not a confectionary, not a cheap escapism: an intercourse on important public matters, in the spirit that made the ancient *Greek theatre an absorbing civic function.

The time was 1931, early in the Depression, and Clurman was a play reader and minor actor for the *Theatre Guild. Now, the Guild had been founded by thespians of strong will and ardent desire back before World War I, and had prospered in the 1920s by cultivating what might be called the middle-class intelligentsia. But Clurman thought the Guild's principles self-serving and innocuous, a midcult art of no stylistic focus. With two other Guild employees, casting director Cheryl Crawford (1902–1987) and fellow minor actor Lee Strasberg (1901–1982), Clurman launched his company, at first as a Guild fledgling, soon enough independent. Clurman, Crawford, and Strasberg's group —*the* Group, why not?; for it would be unique— would concentrate on social problem theatre with an acting troupe trained to breathe real life into their roles. Too much of Broadway acting was helter-skelter, artificial, uninflected. The Group would revitalize the scene with a naturalistic ensemble.

There was considerable excitement among the company when they began work, a powerful sense of shared mission. The Group was an enclave within the free-lance milieu of Broadway, banding together in commune style for summer talk and training sessions, even camping out en masse in cheap housing back in town when times were hard. Unfortunately, this was almost always the case with the Group: hard times. Only passionate dedication kept Lee J. Cobb, Stella Adler, Morris Carnovsky, and other Group actors from signing up with more munificent organizations, not to mention Hollywood. Moreover, low funds necessitated many a compromise, brought on by lost opportunities. Though the Group eventually grew famous for Strasberg's *Method training of the ensemble, the productions were weak in design, seldom counting on the artistic imagination and telling concepts that *Robert Edmond Jones and the Guild's Lee Simonson introduced in the 1920s— though Jones, at least, designed a production for the Group's first season.

Then, too, the Group's concentration on social problem theatre limited its audience and, too often, irritated establishment critics. Nevertheless, some of the Group's offerings made significant American arts history—their first entry, Paul Green's *The House of Connelly* (1931), a study of idealistic youth fighting ingrained ignorance in the American South; *Maxwell Anderson's *Night Over Taos* (1932); *Sidney Kingsley's *Men in White* (1933); Green's musical *Johnny Johnson* (1936), a pacifist parable with a *Brechtian score by Green and Kurt Weill; Irwin Shaw's *The Gentle People* (1939), in which the people, none too gently, murder a gangster, Shaw's cure for the rise of fascism; and *William Saroyan's *My Heart's in the Highlands* (1939).

By far the essential Group playwright was *Clifford Odets, whose *Waiting for Lefty* and *Awake and Sing!*, both in 1935, affirmed the four-year-old Group's importance as a brilliant interpretive medium and a sponsor of highly individual new voices. But just as actors Franchot Tone, J. Edward Bromberg, and John Garfield abandoned the Group for Hollywood, so did Odets, underlining the overwhelming problem any noncommercial organization faces on Broadway: how long can you keep on bucking those hard times?

In 1941, after ten years, the Group dissolved. It did not disband—did not formally cease production. But step by step in that last year, it lost the integrity of its ensemble, the intensity of a continuing presence. Attempts by some Group members to reorganize failed, and the Group more or less faded away. Nevertheless, it left an impression on the American theatre, as business and art. In 1940, Morris Carnovsky finally lucked into a hit in the farce *My Sister Eileen* (which was to run over two years) as the eccentric landlord Mr. Appopolous. Someone asked Carnovsky how it felt to be in a success. Carnovsky replied, "I've been in a success for ten years."

(See also The Method and *Awake and Sing!*)

ALEC GUINNESS (1914–   )

Of the English actors prominent in the second half of the century, Guinness stands out for his odd blend of "character parts," comic roles, and more or less heroic leads. He has checked in with the inevitable Shakespeare, Chekhov, and Sheridan, but he really made his name in offbeat roles— Garcin in Jean-Paul Sartre's *No Exit,* the harried would-be adulteror in Feydeau's *Hotel Paradiso,* T. E. Lawrence in Terence Rattigan's *Ross,* even a drag role in Simon Gray's *Wise Child.* Offbeat, too, was Guinness's apparently simple delivery of parts that *Laurence Olivier and *John Gielgud would have rendered more elaborately. "I like," Guinness has said, "a line drawing." He will probably be best remembered for his many and very varied movie roles—the unbearably resolute English colonel in *The Bridge on the River Kwai,* Ben Kenobi in *Star Wars,* and, most notably, the eight Ascoyne D'Ascoynes whom Dennis Price kills off, one by one, in the *black comedy *Kind Hearts and Coronets.*

SACHA GUITRY (1885–1957)

Lucien Guitry (1860–1925) was a noted French actor, and his son, christened Alexandre Georges Pierre and nicknamed Sacha, went the father one better as actor *and* writer. As James Harding notes in the very title of his biography of Guitry, Sacha was "the last *boulevardier": the man who rounded off an era of elegance and sensuality that drew its inspiration as much from the salons and cafés as from the chic of the comedies and operettas of the boulevard playhouses. This was Sacha's theatre: the clever charm of the beautiful, the joy of their wit.

Guitry is often compared to *Noël Coward, and the two do come together in that both wrote operettas for Yvonne Printemps, though only Guitry married her. But Coward was far more versatile than Guitry, composing the scores for his musical shows himself, writing fiction as well as play-scripts, and leaping, in his subject matter, from the historical epic of *Cavalcade to the nine formally very varied one-acters of *To-night at 8:30, from the doleful society scandal sheet melodrama of The Vortex to the vivacious Private Lives. Guitry, too, claims shifts of approach, running as far afield as the all-male Pasteur (1919), with father Lucien as the pioneering biologist. And unlike Coward, Guitry specialized in filmmaking as well as theatre. Still, Coward left so diverse an output that he is continually in the process of rediscovery. Guitry's carefree seductions of the boulevardier, his 120-odd wispy confections that filled the Bouffes-Parisiens, the Théâtre Édouard VII, the Théâtre de la Madeleine, and even the *Comédie-Française, are things of a virtually irretrievable past: Nono (1905), Le Scandale de Monte Carlo (1908), La Jalousie (1915), Faisons un Rêve (Let's Dream, 1916), Le Grand Duc (The Grand Duke, 1921), On ne Joue pas pour s'Amuser (One Doesn't Play to Have a Good Time, 1925), Mozart (1925), Mariette (1928), Tout Commence par des Chansons (Everything Starts With a Song, 1931), Adam et Ève (1933), Quand Jouons-Nous la Comédie? (When Do We Start the Show?, 1935). They are not unrevivable. But—unlike Coward's oeuvre—they are so bound up in the personality of the author that one can scarcely think of giving them without him.

TYRONE GUTHRIE (1900—1971)

Brilliant, unpredictable, and brusquely loving, Guthrie is one of the most fondly remembered directors of the English stage. Yet his approach was far more production-oriented than actor-friendly, concentrating on the decor, the fetching bits of inspired *"business," the jumbly vivacity of the crowd scenes, while the actors were left relatively free to triumph or fall on the rightness (or misjudgment) of their portrayals. "Very often he saw somehow the finished production," recalled Hume Cronyn. "It was all in his mind, and he worked toward that. And if you happened to be clued in . . . and you were running on the same route or, at least, a parallel one, things were liable to happen very well. But if your concept was different and he hadn't checked it, caught it, changed it early on, the marriage was never really satisfactory."

Be it said, however, that Guthrie's best stagings stood among the most imaginative and compelling of their day—his 1945 *Old Vic *Peer Gynt with *Ralph Richardson; his two Tamburlaine the Greats, first with *Donald Wolfit, then with Anthony Quayle; *The Matchmaker at the Edinburgh Festival, in London, then on Broadway, with Ruth Gordon; the Old Vic's 1956 *Troilus and Cressida, Greek and Trojan characters speaking Elizabethan English in Edwardian dress. Even the original Broadway Candide that same year, though commercially unsuccessful, began to look much better in the face of its merrily shallow revisions and revivals.

Guthrie worked over a wide span, not only from the West End to Broadway, from the Old Vic to Dublin's *Gate, but at Stratford, Ontario and Minneapolis, both of whose festivals Guthrie helped organize. (The Minneapolis auditorium bears his name.) Everywhere Guthrie went, from his first stagings in Cambridge in 1929 to his last, of Rossini's opera Il Barbiere di Siviglia (The Barber of Seville) in Brighton in 1971, he astonished his public. Even his failures were interesting. He had absolute command of the spectator's eye—as when, in Pirandello's Six Characters in Search of an Author at New York's Phoenix Theatre in 1955, he had the six principals not enter, but materialize. "Stagehands" were dragging equipment back and forth across the empty stage, and just as the audience had grown used to them and blacked them out, one of them came on pushing a flat. Guthrie then befuddled the house with some business in the corner, and when everyone had turned back, there stood the six characters—they had sneaked in behind the moving flat.

All who worked with Guthrie—and this takes in Laurence Olivier, Paul Rogers, Sybil Thorndike, Stella Adler, John Gielgud, Margaret Leighton, Robert Morley, and Alec Guinness among others —recall how amusingly shocking were his personal habits. Six feet six and married to a woman six feet tall herself, "Tony" Guthrie lived contentedly in tiny rooms in an atmosphere of avid squalor. For a time, the Guthrie domicile was a boat on the Thames; Judy Guthrie would dip a pitcher into the river and call out, "Tea, anyone?" There are enough Guthrie stories to fill a book. Here's one: in London, casting a play for Broadway, Guthrie and the author considered an actress whose husband, also an actor, was already having a great success on the stage and a wild affair on the side. The author thought the actress in question "would be delighted to go to New York because her husband has a hit there."

Said Guthrie, "She'll be delighted to go to New York because her husband has a Miss there."

GUY DOMVILLE

Legendary disaster by Henry James (1843–1916), prem. London, 1895.

James was so nervous at the prospect of attending his own *first* first night—*Guy Domville* being his first production in a lifetime of passionate theatregoing—that he spent the evening at the Haymarket seeing Oscar Wilde's *An Ideal Husband,* which he loathed. Alas, he then marched the few blocks of *West End real estate over to the St. James's, where *actor-manager George Alexander had produced *Guy Domville.* James, backstage, heard an audience filled with notables (and a gallery packed with louts) applaud the players. James heard cries of "Author Author!" James nervously allowed Alexander to lead him out. The notables welcomed James; but the gallery treated him to one of the loudest and longest vocal attacks recorded in British theatre annals. Shattered beyond perhaps even his own minute description, James returned to the less immediately exposed world of fiction.

In fact, *Guy Domville* was not a flop. It ran its set course of four weeks and a short tour of Brighton and got sympathetic notices. George Bernard Shaw, in the *Saturday Review,* thought the play "no worse than that it is out of fashion"—rather forgiving praise from the man who didn't like what was fashionable in theatre. James's problems lay in too much zest for antique costume—the play takes place in 1780—and a second act in which the contrivances of melodrama disfigured his portrait of a Roman Catholic postulant drawn back from the cloister into the world because his noble lineage needs an infusion of biology. "I'm the last, my lord, of the Domvilles," he explained at one point —at which, on opening night, an oik in the balcony called out, "It's a bloody good thing y'are!"

NELL GWYN (1650–1687)

What other legendary actress counted a career but six years long? And how much of her biography is fact, how much pure legend? She was (supposedly) the daughter of a brothel madam and (possibly) a prostitute herself, at the age of (so it's said) thirteen. Certainly she was what she is best known to have been, an orange seller at *Drury Lane whose beauty and high spirits gained her the celebrated stage when she was fourteen. She played courtesans, mad maidens, and *trouser role pages. She was praised in comedy, not tragedy. But she was praised. King Charles II took her for his mistress and she left the theatre to enjoy a lucrative retirement. On his deathbed, Charles (it was rumored) cautioned his brother James, next in line to the throne, "Don't let poor Nelly starve." She didn't. At her death, she was worth one hundred thousand pounds, the equivalent today of something like four million dollars.

HABIMAH

Hebrew for "The Stage." Formed in Moscow in the early 1900s, this Jewish troupe played in classical Hebrew rather than the vernacular of the Jewish exile, Yiddish. Setting an exact date for the founding of the company is difficult, as the authorities persecuted it, and some of its early history was spent underground. Apparently it was assembled by Noam Zemach, about a decade before the Revolution of 1917. After the Revolution, Habimah thrust itself forth publicly under the protection of Stanislavsky and Gorky. In 1922, it presented the premiere of what was to prove its signature production, Sholem Ansky's *The Dybbuk,* directed by Yevgyeny Vakhtangov; when Habimah began a period of world touring and artistic reorganization in the mid-1920s, *The Dybbuk* made the company's reputation. Habimah settled down in 1932 in Tel Aviv in what was then called Palestine, took over its own theatre at the end of World War II, and became Israel's *national theatre in 1958. (See also *The Dybbuk*.)

JAMES HENRY HACKETT (1800–1871)

In an America totally dominated by British thespians, Hackett emerged as the first absolutely American star *actor-manager. A specialist in "Yankee" roles, he built his career on the character of Colonel Nimrod Wildfire, a tintype of Davey Crockett, in James Kirke Paulding's *The Lion of the West* (1831).

PETER HALL (1930–   .)

Hall must be the only director to have run two different *national theatres in the same country, first the *Royal Shakespeare Company, from 1960, then the officially entitled National Theatre of Great Britain, from 1973. Both regimes saw the respective companies through artistically triumphant eras, though Hall's own productions tend more to the competent (as in Peter Shaffer's *Amadeus* and Alan Ayckbourn's *Bedroom Farce*) than the brilliant (as in Harold Pinter's *The Homecoming* and *No Man's Land*). In 1983, Hall published excerpts from his diaries, from 1972 to 1980, a rich read for anyone who wants a taste of the theatre world that lies behind the stage and *greenroom. Hall reveals harrowing difficulties with the stagehands' union, a furor of calumny from the press on the opening of the National Theatre complex, and expert revelations on how plays are commissioned, written, staged, reviewed. However, Hall's dismissal of Stephen Sondheim's *Sweeney Todd* as "a derivative procession of tonic and dominant with camp rhythms" is astonishingly ignorant for someone who has staged opera at Glyndebourne, the Met, and Bayreuth. And what is "camp rhythms" supposed to mean? If you want to use the word "faggot," Hall, come out and use it like a man.

CHRISTOPHER HAMPTON (See *Total Eclipse*)

HANAMICHI

Japanese for "flower path," referring to the walkway running from the back of the playhouse to the stage, in *Kabuki theatre.

HANSWURST

German for "Jack Sausage," a low comic figure performing in the vernacular and something of an equivalent to the Arlecchino (Harlequin) of *commedia dell'arte*. Hanswurst counted many variants, but the most typical was a servant character getting in and out of tight spots through luck and insouciance more than wit. Hanswurst died out when improvised comedy did, in the early 1800s,

though he had already been immortalized as Papageno in Mozart's opera *Die Zauberflöte* (The Magic Flute).

HARLEQUIN (See *Commedia dell'arte*)

JED HARRIS (1900—1980)

Few theatre encyclopedias list Harris, though in his day he was Broadway's brash genius, the producer-director with a demon's gift. "The horridest man I've ever worked with," *Laurence Olivier said, explaining why he based his lurid, pinch-toned Richard III on Harris. *Alfred Lunt, too, modeled an unattractive character on Harris, in *S. N. Behrman's *Dynamo*. Still, Harris left his mark on The Street, most legendarily perhaps in his production of *Anton Chekhov's *Uncle Vanya* with Lillian Gish, Osgood Perkins, and Walter Connolly in 1930. In a business known for difficult personalities, Harris was so difficult that finally no one would work with him at all. His direction of *Arthur Miller's *The Crucible* in 1953 virtually rescued Harris from anonymity, but only temporarily. "Jed Harris," someone once said, "is his own worst enemy." And *George S. Kaufman shot back, "Not while I'm alive."

JULIE HARRIS (1925—   )

Is there another great actress who played almost nothing but hackwork and garbage? Yes, the gossamer Harris became known for Carson McCullers's touching *The Member of the Wedding* (1950), acted *Jean Anouilh's St. Joan in *The

Lark, and has done a little Shakespeare. But the Sally Bowles of John van Druten's *I Am a Camera* (1951) that finally put Harris over was trapped in a barely competent adaptation from Christopher Isherwood's Berlin stories, and seldom (if ever) after did Harris play in the work of a distinguished playwright, sinking into such pieces as the who-dunit *A Shot in the Dark* (1961), the sex comedies *Ready When You Are, C. B.!* (1964) and *Forty Carats* (1968), and one of Broadway's most atrocious musicals, *Skyscraper* (1965). Like Zoë Caldwell and Colleen Dewhurst, Harris found a worthy niche for her talents in a one-woman show based on a real-life figure. Caldwell did Lillian Hellman, Dewhurst the widow of Eugene O'Neill. Harris, as Emily Dickinson in *The Belle of Amherst* (1976), retrieved some of her lost prestige in, for once, material of poetry and wit.

MOSS HART (See George S. Kaufman)

GERHART HAUPTMANN

(1862–1946)

Hauptmann is a curious figure. One of Germany's outstanding playwrights and a key entry in the rise of *naturalism, Hauptmann is little more than a historical "name" in England and America, his forty-five full-length plays (there are also short plays, novels, and volumes of memoirs) seldom read and almost never performed. Moreover, Hauptmann, of artistic bent but without calling, seems to have *willed* himself into the theatre, apparently under the spell of the plays of *Henrik Ibsen. Hauptmann's first work, *Vor Sonnenaufgang* (Before Sunrise, 1889), on a peasant family's descent into decadence through sudden wealth, announced an Ibsenite dramatist with a wider scope than the Norwegian, a playwright eager to fill his stage with color and detail. The year 1893 saw Hauptmann at the center of a naturalist furore with three major works, *Die Weber* (The Weavers), the comic *Der Biberpelz* (The Beaver Skin), and *Hanneles Himmelfahrt* (Hannels's Journey to Heaven). *The Weavers* especially made Hauptmann's name. A look at the unsuccessful 1844 uprising, in Hauptmann's native Silesia, of artisans forced out of work by industrialization, it merged the naturalist's documentary with the tragedian's lyricism, giving naturalism a kind of poetic license. Hauptmann continued in this vein, finishing off his naturalistic era with *Die Ratten* (The Rats, 1911), an urban melodrama using a multitude of characters and stories as the backdrop for an argument between an advocate of romantic melodrama and an advocate of social-polemic naturalism. It is Hauptmann's implied argument that the two together are preferable to either alone.

Ironically enough, Hauptmann himself had begun long before to abandon naturalism for *symbolist tragedy. His most notable such entry is *Der Versunkene Glocke* (The Sunken Bell, 1896), about a man torn between loves for a mortal woman and a fairy. (Hauptmann, who divorced an adored wife for a younger, more vivacious woman, would return to the triangle theme often.) By the 1920s, in the face of Germany's burgeoning avant-garde, Hauptmann retained his reputation as the national master playwright but lost his hold on the opinion makers. His epoch seemed to have passed, yet he continued to produce, and prolifically. There is something ominously telling in the title of *Vor Sonnenuntergang* (Before Sunset, 1932), a reversal of the titular image of Hauptmann's very earliest play and presented a year before Hitler took power. Hauptmann remained in Germany under the Nazis, exploring myth, history, and fantasy— *Hamlet in Wittenberg* (1935), which gives us more on the capers of Rosenkrantz and Guildenstern; *Die Tochter der Kathedrale* (The Daughter of the Cathedral, 1939); *Die Atriden-Tetralogie,* a retelling of Aeschylus's *Oresteia,* written during the war years. But by then Hauptmann was old news outside his homeland. Even today, but for sporadic revivals of *The Weavers* and *The Sunken Bell,* he is a playwright without a stage.

(See also *The Oresteia.*)

Among Helen Hayes's important roles, this one is nearly forgot: Amanda Wingfield in the London premiere of Tennessee Williams's The Glass Menagerie *at the Haymarket in 1948.*

HELEN HAYES (1900–   )

Of all American actresses, Hayes bears perhaps the most disputed legend. Scarcely anyone writing on theatre today has anything good to say about her, yet from about 1935, when she played Queen Victoria in Laurence Housman's *Victoria Regina*, aging from fluttering maiden to redoubtable monarch, she was a peer of Ethel Barrymore, Katharine Cornell, and Jane Cowl, a Queen of Broadway. (Lynn Fontanne, the unique partner of the unique Alfred Lunt, was *hors de concours* in all such sweepstakes.) Marriage to the newsworthy playwright and *bon vivant* Charles MacArthur and a spell in Hollywood in the first talkie years (variously, opposite Ronald Colman, Gary Cooper, and Clark Gable) added to her fame. Hayes chose her roles well, trading off the charm parts in *James M. Barrie and *Ferenc Molnár (*The Good Fairy,* 1931) with sterner material, including *Maxwell Anderson's verse tragedy *Mary of Scotland* (1933) and *Anton Chekhov's *The Cherry Orchard*, reset in the American South as *The Wisteria Trees* (1950). Over the years, Hayes had the public more than the critics. But by the 1950s she had become an institution, fit for the masters, and played not only *Jean Anouilh's *Léocadia* (as *Time Remembered,* 1957) and *Eugene O'Neill's *A Touch of the Poet* (1958) but full-dress *repertory with the APA–Phoenix in the mid-1960s: *Sheridan, *Pirandello, and the termagant Mrs. Fisher in George Kelly's *The Show Off*. Her public admired her dedication; the critics thought her out of her league, unstylish, a show off herself. Nonetheless, Hayes made her farewell in one of America's few heroic roles, Mary Tyrone in O'Neill's *Long Day's Journey into Night*.

HEARTBREAK HOUSE

"A fantasia in the Russian manner on English themes" by *George Bernard Shaw, prem. New York, 1920.

As the subtitle suggests, and as Shaw explains in the typical Shavian preface, the "Russian fantasia" denotes a *Chekovian format, conversations rather than a plot, character as theme. But note that, contrary to cliché "criticism," Shaw creates very different characters of his cast. There is no *protagonist. But the doings are superintended by the eighty-eight-year-old Captain Shotover, so much like Shaw in attitude and tone that tradition demands he be played in Shavian makeup, beard and all. Who's running England, the West, the world? Shaw asks. "Navigation," he recommends, through Shotover's mouth just before the climax. "Learn it and live; or leave it and be damned." Shotover's boat-like abode is the scene of a day-long house party, one of flirtations and confrontations, that ends in an air raid. Two people die, yet the others are fascinated by the beauty of the fireworks. Says one, "I hope they'll come again tomorrow night." Leave it and be damned.

LILLIAN HELLMAN (1905–1986)

Some dramatists put so much of their lives into their plays that criticism must take in biography. Eugene O'Neill is an example. One steers the analysis through his points of being: the waterfronts, the lying, the family. O'Neill, and his past, and the people he knew. The work is the biography.

On the other hand, some playwrights are so famous for what they represent—more than what they did—that the biography is the work. Here's an instance. Hellman is much better known for her leftist politics, her nearly lifelong affair with the mystery writer Dashiel Hammett, her defiance of the House Un-American Activities Committee during the McCarthy era, her canonization in the "biographical" film *Julia* (Hellman "is" Jane Fonda; but Hellman isn't, as we shall see), and her lawsuit attacking Mary McCarthy for calling Hellman a liar. Hellman was not a leftist; Hellman was a Stalinist who would answer questions about the 1930s show trials, the cult of Stalin, the murder of millions, with "Prove it!" Hellman's affair with Hellman was punctuated by adulteries with not only Hammett but numerous other men: she was not attractive, but she was aggressive. That sometimes works. She *did* defy the HUAC; that is her one great moment. As for her *Julia* heroism: McCarthy called it correctly.

There were worse aspects to Hellman—read William Wright's biography for the details. What of Hellman the playwright—and who even cares any more, with so much biography to deal with? As dramatist, Hellman started political and ended humanist, began in form and fame and reached that uniquely American eclipse wherein one's latest play is heralded in advertising and seriously reviewed: but no one comes. Hellman's major plays are *The Children's Hour* (1934), *The Little Foxes* (1939), *Watch on the Rhine* (1941), the book of the original version of Leonard Bernstein's *Candide* (1956), and *Toys in the Attic* (1960). *The Children's Hour* is almost supernaturally prescient, treating the character assassination that the later McCarthy years thrived on. But *The Little Foxes* is the best of Hellman, a *melodrama on the power of greed, on the uncurbed hunger of capitalists for total control. Personally, Hellman was a creep. But this one play will outlive her "biography," and it will outlive her friends, and her enemies. And all of them are in it.

HENRY IV

Tragic comedy by *Luigi Pirandello, prem. Milan, 1922.

Enrico IV may have been the first costume drama set in the present. The nameless *protagonist, decades before, had taken part in a pageant dressed as the German emperor Henry IV when Baron Belcredi, his rival in love, spooked his horse and caused a fall. Struck mad, the victim now "is" Henry IV, and all around him must play his court in ancient clothes. When a doctor exorcises Henry's madness, he runs his sword through Belcredi. Was he sane all along? Is he mad *now*? Pirandello leaves us—of course—guessing. However, it is in all particulars a conventional script—linear, credible, mimetic. Lifelike. This is the straightforward Pirandello, experimental in ideas but *"well-made" in form.

HERNANI

Romantic verse tragedy by *Victor Hugo, prem. Paris, 1830.

Oh, to have been at the *Comédie-Française on *Hernani*'s first night! All intellectual Paris had been seething with the war of the establishment against the avant-garde, of traditionalists against innovators, of the Racinistes against the Shakespériens, of the critics against the artists—and it was decided by general consent to fight it out at *Hernani*. Victor Hugo, one of the chiefs of the avant-garde, wrote his tale of a brigand, an aged noble, and a king, all in love with a woman (who of course loves the brigand) explicitly to demonstrate the fire and freedom of Romanticism. Hugo's henchmen filled over a quarter of the theatre's seats. The players marshaled their separate *claques. The reactionaries were there in force. The traditional three knocks of French custom were sounded. The curtain rose. The heroine's black-clad servant spoke, not in the customary end-stopped *alexandrines of Corneille and Racine but in enjambed alexandrines, one line, with the Romantic's reckless passion, storming into the next.

And the riot began.

The Hugoistes cheered, the reactionaries booed—not only that night, but right through the play's forty-five performance run (an astonishing record for the day, by the way). The Hugoistes won, partly through Hugo's talent and partly because the Romantics fought with every weapon available. Suavely turning to a woman who dared to laugh at the play, one Hugoiste told her, "You shouldn't laugh, Madame—not with teeth like yours."

That was crummy of him; but she shouldn't have been laughing.

JOHN HEYWOOD (See Interlude)

AL HIRSCHFELD (1903–   )

Cartoonist Hirschfeld's renderings of Broadway shows became emblematic through exposure in the Arts and Leisure section of the Sunday *New York Times* over the last four decades. Besides his impressionistic revelations of what was heading into town (usually caught during the tryout period),

Hirschfeld gave his public a puzzle, lacing his daughter Nina's name into the drawings and giving the total of "Ninas" next to his signature. Once, Hirschfeld substituted "Lisa" (for critic Louis Kronenberger's daughter) and woke up Monday morning to a hoard of congratulations on the new arrival.

ROLF HOCHHUTH (1931–   )

The German Hochhuth became the playwright of the hour with his first work, *Der Stellvertreter* (The Deputy; known in England as *The Representative, 1963*). It was the age of the *chronicle play and *documentary theatre, and Hochhuth's indictment of Pope Pius XII for his silence during the Nazi war on the Jewish race seemed to fulfill the promise of these forms, in impact if not in art. Hochhuth went on to *Soldaten* (Soldiers, 1970), a virulent portrait of Winston Churchill, and *Guerillas* (1970), on a United States Senator's attempt at a bloodless revolution. Neither work held the stage as *The Deputy* had, and later works diminished Hochhuth's reputation, till *Juristen* (Judges, 1980), on postwar Germany's failure to punish Nazi judges, put him back in the international headlines.
(See also *The Deputy* and *Juristen*.)

THE HOUSE OF BERNARDA ALBA

"A drama of the women in the villages of Spain" by *Federico García Lorca, prem. Buenos Aires, 1945.

This was the last of García Lorca's plays, finished (though perhaps lacking a last revision) just before the author's execution by the Fascists in 1936. As the consummation of his trilogy of rural tragedies, it is fierce, earthy, and shocking. *Blood Wedding* is *symbolistic and *Yerma* sympathetically tragic, but here Lorca deals in cold-blooded naturalism, insisting that his all-woman cast represents "a photographic document." In the matriarch Bernarda Alba, we meet a ruthless exponent of the social code. Señora Alba knows no law but folk tradition, no virtue but female chastity, no act but absolute

obedience. At the end of Act Two, Lorca catches his terrifying heroine in an essence of tyranny, crowing over the impending punishment of a village girl who, unmarried and pregnant, killed her baby in shame. It is not the infant's murder that outrages Señora Alba, but the mother's sensuality. "Let whoever loses her decency pay for it!" cries Bernarda Alba, as the villagers drag the screaming girl away. "Hot coals in the place where she sinned!" Señora Alba advises, adding, as the curtain falls, "Kill her! *Kill her!*" And there's another act yet to play.

HROSWITHA (See Medieval Theatre)

VICTOR HUGO (1802–1885)

Hugo combined the insights of the man of letters with the attack of the politician, for he was both: writer and senator. Everything in his monumental output—which includes the novels *Notre-Dame de Paris* and *Les Misérables* and many volumes of poetry—tends toward a Republican ideal of legalized equality, not to chasten individual initiative but to check the advantages of the villainous. In Hugo's world, to be a hero is to "suffer" from a nobility of character that makes one prey to a conscience, a compassion, unknown to one's enemies. Thus *Les Misérables*'s Jean Valjean at times seems to bear the whole world upon his shoulders; thus Hernani is a bandit, Ruy Blas a lackey, both superior in nature to those around them; and thus Hugo himself, a political exile after the *coup d'état* of 1851, replied, when offered full amnesty, "Quand la liberté rentrera, je rentrerai": When liberty comes home, I will come home.

It was partly a yearning for liberty that led Hugo to the theatre. Just as inequality enslaved the lower half of the population, Classicism enslaved the theatre, with its veneration of dead names, its obsession with tradition, its fetish for *les règles* ("the rules," meaning the *unities) and the *alexandrine. The Romantic movement was in flower, but Classicist reactionaries were cutting it off, bud by bud—even unto disdaining and decrying a visit in 1827 by Charles *Kemble and his troupe in a season of authentic Shakespeare that had the Parisian Romantics in awe. Hugo, looked on as the leader of the movement, identified Shakespeare as everyone's master, not least for his quality of "the grotesque": that combination of irony, absurdity, brutality, beauty, and comedy that seemed to Hugo and the Romantics to duplicate the richness of the world on stage. *Alexandre Dumas *père* underlined this in calling Shakespeare "the greatest creator after God Himself." Hugo followed suit—all too well—with the unperformably sizable *Cromwell,* published in 1827 with a preface meant to rally the Romantic troops. Came then the battle itself, at the premiere (and throughout the run) of Hugo's *Hernani* (1830), designed to re-tailor Classical verse tragedy on the very stage of the *national theatre, the *Comédie-Française. *Hernani*'s success led to *Le Roi S'Amuse* (roughly The King Steps Out, 1832), so political in its view of a licentious king that it was banned after a single performance, though all Paris read it and Verdi, a generation later, reintroduced it to the theatre as the opera *Rigoletto.*

It is unfortunate that Hugo's next plays dropped the versification, because it was the fire and lilt of his poetry that energized his theatre, not his extravagant plotting. *Lucrèce Borgia* (1833), *Marie Tudor* (1833), and *Angelo, Tyran de Padoue* (1835) are considered laughable *melodramas today. Hugo returned to verse in *Ruy Blas* (1838), often called his dramatic masterpiece. But it is not as much his plays themselves as their inspiration and influence that matter. Hugo really did his best work in other forms. But he above all others reclaimed the stultified French stage, broke up the Classicist monoply and taught that important writers deal with important problems, sociopolitical ones if the times demand it.

Liberty presumably returned to France, because Hugo did, to find himself a legend. His funeral was nothing less than apotheosis: the corpse lay in torchlit state all night under the Arc de Triomphe, then was taken—in a pauper's coffin, at Hugo's demand—to the Panthéon for burial. It was said that the entire city took part in the cortège. (See also *Hernani.*)

HURLYBURLY

Conversation piece by David Rabe (1940–   ), prem. Chicago, 1984.

Rabe became prominent for two plays on the Vietnam War, produced in 1971, *The Basic Training of Pavlo Hummel* and, on a blinded veteran's homecoming, *Sticks and Bones. Streamers* (1976), also on the military life, developed Rabe's use of dialogue as an expression of character and image. But here in *Hurlyburly,* Rabe joined *David Mamet in the absolute naturalism of dialogue. *Hurlyburly*'s characters, like most people, are inarticulate. They leave out more than they convey:

PHIL: This guy, what a fuckin' guy.
ARTIE: You shoulda seen him. He was unbelievable.
EDDIE: So what happened?
PHIL: I decked him; he deserved it.
EDDIE: So what happened?
PHIL: He made me mad.
ARTIE: He was a jerk.
EDDIE: So you decked this guy.
ARTIE: You shoulda seen it. The guy went across the room. He looked like he was on wheels.
EDDIE: So what'd he do?
PHIL: He got up.
ARTIE: The dumb fuck.
EDDIE: I mean, why'd you hit him?
PHIL: He got up!
EDDIE: I mean, before he got knocked down—the first time you hit him, why'd you hit him?

Why? Because he was "sayin' this unbelievable dumb stuff " to "this genuinely repulsive broad."

PHIL: And he's talkin' to her like she's somethin' gorgeous. *This dog!* It was offensive. Who'd he think he was with, you know? This was nobody of any even remotely dynamite qualities, you

Hurlyburly: *You want movie stars? We got movie stars. Above, left to right, neatly posed for the camera out of stage action but still in character for their roles: debonair Christopher Walken, saturnine Harvey Keitel, smooth William Hurt, dashing Sigourney Weaver, hi-ho Jerry Stiller, lavish Judith Ivey, and dear Cynthia Nixon. Overleaf: the show itself, all PR neatness set aside for some good old one-on-one confrontation.*

know what I mean? You don't talk to some dog in the manner he's talking. It's disgusting!

ARTIE: Very irritating guy.

Phil hits women, too. He's one of the most atrociously dislikable characters in modern theatre, but then *Hurlyburly* is made of unattractive people, four men and three women in present-day Hollywood who are good for nothing but exploiting other people, or being exploited. Interestingly, it was the "Hollywood" in the casting of the original Goodman Theatre production (immediately brought from Chicago to New York) that made *Hurlyburly* a hit: William Hurt, Sigourney Weaver, Harvey Keitel, and Christopher Walken, all gifted thespians who do some of their best work on screen.

HYBRIS

Also *hubris*: "arrogance." In *Greek theatre, too much pride is a favorite tragic flaw, especially when the prideful character ignores a divine warning. Consider *Euripides's Pentheus in *The Bacchae*. This young king puts more faith in his own rule than in Dionysus's attraction to the disorderly human race. The term *hybris* (more correct Greek, by the way, than the more commonly used corruption *hubris*) is still in use because the concept has remained theatrically vital. Shakespeare's Macbeth, Lear, and Julius Caesar all share the flaw, and one may trace its fascination through the centuries, though the political, *absurd, and *black comic writers view a world without enough nobility to deserve a tragic hero. Perhaps Simon Gray's *Butley?

I

HENRIK IBSEN (1828–1906)

The Beethoven of modern drama. As the history of modern symphony starts with Beethoven's expansion of the performing forces, interrogation of thematic material, and grandeur of reach, the history of the stage looks upon Ibsen as the playwright who obliterated flattery of the public, instituted consideration in place of diversion, and insisted that realism of topic was the essential energy. (Ibsen did *not* expand the performing forces—in his prime he was notorious for his tiny casts.) However, just as Beethoven built his symphony upon the structures of his predecessor Haydn, Ibsen based much of his output upon the formulations of the *well-made play. Ibsen gave it integrity of theme, true. Still, like virtually all his contemporaries, he took it for granted as the basis of good theatre.

After early tries in the verse play, Ibsen switched to prose, embarking on the series of "problem plays" that would urge the nineteenth century into the twentieth: *Et Dukkehjem* (A Doll's House, 1879), *Gengangere* (Ghosts, 1882), *En Folkefunde* (An Enemy of the People, 1883), *Vildanden* (The Wild Duck, 1885), *Rosmersholm* (1887), *Hedda Ga-bler* (1891). The oppression of the individual by bourgeois society is a constant theme in these plays, written by an expatriate. (The relentlessly middle-class Norwegian culture strangled Ibsen.) This may be the key factor in Ibsen's worldview: the grim, set faces roused against the truth teller, the "enemy of the people." *Jean Cocteau was threatened by matinée matrons, who offered to blind him with pins for his offenses; but at least Cocteau was chic and bizarre. Ibsen was "heavy." His blunt dramaturgy, for a time, excited thespians far more than the public. What, no staircase entrances? But even most theatre professionals were daunted by Ibsen's mystical last plays, *Lille Eyolf* (Little Eyolf, 1895), *John Gabriel Borkman* (1896), and *Nar Vi Døde Vågner* (When We Dead Awaken, 1900), written when Ibsen had at last returned to his homeland to steep himself in atmospheric, reflective poetry, putting aside social problems for humanist universals.

Of course the critics savaged Ibsen; such individuality was truly threatening: an enemy of the people. An enemy, really, of enraged schmucks. America's most influential critic, William Winter, bellowed in castrated rage at Ibsen's aggressive subject matter, even at the "class" of folk who

The Henrik Ibsen Memorial in Oslo, Norway, as it looked in 1930.

attended Ibsen's plays. But Ibsen had his champions, especially certain star actors, like America's *Mrs. Fiske, who found his strong women characters irresistible. Where such comparable iconoclasts as *Eugene O'Neill and *Harold Pinter won their attention on, respectively, the energy of the post–World War I art movement in American culture and the novelty of discovering a native British *absurdist, Ibsen became popular because imposing talents insisted on performing him.

Once the dust cleared, it was evident that ideological vitality was the essential "fact" of Ibsen, not just his ability to stimulate actors. The William Winters went down screaming, but their theatre—soft, moist, innocuously thrilling—was doomed: if not to pass away, then to move to the side. When Ibsen was young, the important playwrights were trendy entertainers. By Ibsen's death in 1906, one had to *be important* to be important. One had to be an enemy of the people: of the hypocrisy and insensitivity that rule societies. Yet Ibsen was more than a transitional figure. Like Beethoven, he is still around, universal, precise, inspiring. Good theatre.

(See also *Ghosts, Peer Gynt,* and *When We Dead Awaken.*)

THE ICEMAN COMETH

Naturalistic parable by *Eugene O'Neill, prem. New York, 1946.

A waterfront bar's worth of life's losers look forward to the arrival of Hickey, the good-guy salesman who'll buy the drinks, tell the jokes, and pass the time. But Hickey proposes to disabuse his pals of their "pipe dreams": the delusions with which they have made their adjustment to life. Disturbed, Hickey's friends go along with him till they learn that he freed himself of his own delusion of married happiness by killing his wife. Death of a salesman. As the police take Hickey away, the bar settles back into its misty bliss of lies and denials.

Parables treat the life of the spirit, and O'Neill regarded the spirit as his subject. His theme was human life, its despairs, fulfillment, salvations. O'Neill's salvations, throughout his career, are compromised by the fulfillment of a false salvation —the pipe dream delusion that stalls despair. But what happens when we face the truth, when Hickey makes us align with reality? No good, all bad. Too much truth. Truth is poison. Lies are medicine.

O'Neill came to terms with truth in the later *Long Day's Journey into Night.* But that play is autobiographical: the author as confessor. *The Iceman Cometh* makes the most complete statement of a theme O'Neill had worked from his first scripts in the late 1910s right through *Strange Interlude* and *Mourning Becomes Electra*: the author as observer, and the world of men and women as pathetic deluded souls, seeking a place beyond the conflicts that crippled them. "It's the No Chance Saloon," says one of *Iceman*'s characters:

LARRY: It's the Bedrock Bar, The End of the Line Café, The Bottom of the Sea Rathskeller! Don't you notice the beautiful calm in the atmosphere? That's because it's the last harbor. No one here has to worry about where they're going next, because there is no farther they can go.

There's an echo of *Maxim Gorky's *The Lower Depths* in the setting and characters. But this was terrain O'Neill had been mining for decades. *The Iceman Cometh* marked O'Neill's return to Broadway after twelve years' absence, yet it seemed like the most basic of O'Neill's plays. Like those of his prolific 1920s, when the distance between O'Neill premieres was often a matter of days, *Iceman* was a *Theatre Guild production. Legend tells us that the staging failed the text, not affirmed till *José Quintero's 1956 *off-Broadway revival with Jason Robards, Jr. emphasized not the play's flaws but its critics'. As so often, oafs who weren't bright enough to get it the first time blamed the original production. Suddenly they see it. No: important art, like an elite courtesan, does not necessarily expose all its secrets upon first encounter.

THE IMPORTANCE OF BEING EARNEST

*Comedy of manners by *Oscar Wilde ("a trivial comedy," he warns, "for serious people"), prem. London, 1895.

One of the few immortal English comedies between *Sheridan and *Shaw, and perhaps the most quotable of all. (Author's choice: Lady Bracknell's "Come, dear, we have already missed five, if not six, trains. To miss any more might expose us to comment on the platform.") Nothing else in Wilde is remotely as funny. The cleverness courses so furiously that the play is a virtual babble of wit

"Who was your father? . . . Was he born in what the Radical papers call the purple of commerce, or did he rise from the ranks of the aristocracy?" Lady Bracknell (Mabel Terry-Lewis) interrogates Jack Worthing (John Gielgud) in Act One of The Importance of Being Earnest. *Of course, the real importance lies in being* facetious: *to humiliate the authorities with sedition disguised as impudence.*

—the triviality Wilde spoke of. But below the noise, for the serious spectator, Wilde reveals a gruesome society built entirely of vanities.

IMPROVISATION

Literally: any impromptu delivery—a scene played on wit and traditional *business in *commedia dell'arte, a "variations on a theme" suggested by the audience in *café theatre. Since the 1960s the term most often refers to rehearsal or preperformance exercises designed to loosen up and stimulate the actors. The musical A Chorus Line (1975) bitterly burlesqued the improv in the song "Nothing," the confessions of a Puerto Rican acting student alienated by the ersatz dedication of kids pretending to play tables and ice-cream cones. However, at the height of the off-off-Broadway commune-troupe in the late 1960s and early 1970s, improvisation proved a potent element in composition: company experiments stimulated the "shaper" of the proposed "text," and the author in turn re-stimulated the company to further improvisation. The *Open Theater's *The Serpent is a prime example. But so is A Chorus Line, developed (by writers James Kirkwood and Nicholas Dante and songwriters Marvin Hamlisch and Edward Kleban under Michael Bennett's supervision) out of autobiographical improvs.

WILLIAM INGE (1913—1973)

Of famous American playwrights, Inge is the most questionable. In his heyday, the 1950s, Inge racked up four consecutive Broadway hits, all on the sexual psychology of midwestern life: Come Back, Little Sheba (1950), a very *O'Neillian title; Picnic (1953), which won the Pulitzer Prize; Bus Stop (1955), the only comedy in the set; and The Dark at the Top of the Stairs (1957), another O'Neillian title and Inge's most detailed play. Throughout these years, Inge benefited from strong leads (Shirley Booth, Kim Stanley, Eileen Heckart) and strong directors (Joshua Logan and Elia Kazan). This was strong theatre, then—but of course, as the critics assured us, this was strong composition

in the first place. Suddenly, they tired of Inge. They savaged plays as good as the first four. Comparing him with his coevals, they said he lacked *Arthur Miller's moral code, *Tennessee Williams's poetry. The plays failed disastrously—A Loss of Roses (1959) ran 25 performances, Natural Affection (1963) 36—and Inge died a suicide.

INTERLUDE

This term loosely includes various forms of short plays popular all over Europe in the late Renaissance: the French jeu ("game"), sottie ("foolery"), and intermède; the German Fastnachtsspiel ("Shrovetide Carnival Play"); the Italian intermedio; and others such. More strictly, the interlude was the English variety, at first an allegorical dialogue but later a plotted farce. John Heywood (?1497–1580) holds his place in the indexes for his development of the English interlude from an outgrowth of the *medieval morality play into *Elizabethan comedy.

INTERMEZZO

Comic fantasy by *Jean Giraudoux, prem. Paris, 1933.

The play is known in English in Maurice Valency's translation as The Enchanted, but Giraudoux's title (literally, "interlude") works better, descriptive of the fairy-light tone of the piece but also of the plot—for a small French town is suffering an "interlude." A terrifying, even subversive rationality has taken over. Suddenly, life makes sense. The town is haunted by a ghost and bedeviled by a witch. In fact, the ghost is a mortal man and the witch an imaginative young woman who believes herself his sweetheart. This is very Giraudoux. But when the authorities shoot the "ghost," they create a real one—extra very Giraudoux—and now the town is truly haunted and the heroine falls into a coma. It all turns out well, in Giraudoux's unique vein of affectionate satire and delicate whimsy, aided, in *Louis Jouvet's original production, by Francis Poulenc's mock-*melodramatic harpsichord accompaniment. Note that, where in *The Madwoman of Chaillot* Giraudoux disposes of the pompous and powerful, here he treats them sweetly, even lets them off without a warning. Giraudoux at his gentlest.

EUGÈNE IONESCO (1912–   )

"Ionesco's is a world of isolated robots conversing in comic-strip balloons of dialogue that are sometimes hilarious, sometimes evocative, and quite often neither . . . M. Ionesco certainly offers an 'escape from realism,' but an escape into what?" So critic *Kenneth Tynan, in 1958, launched one of the great controversies in modern theatre, in which Ionesco himself took part—not, as one might assume, with the impish gusto of the *absurdist anti-theatre thespian, but seriously: because Ionesco *is* serious, however funny, even silly.

Today audiences take *La Cantatrice Chauve* (The Bald Soprano, 1950) as a dizzy tour through the passionless precincts of bourgeois life. But Ionesco intended it as a lamentation, a despairing. Almost no one attended the original Paris production; at times the three or four spectators who showed up were given their money back and sent home. But as the 1950s wore on, Ionesco and absurdism became, if not the rule, the chic exception. Later Ionesco plays not only succeeded in Paris, but roved the world: *La Leçon* (The Lesson, 1951), *Les Chaises* (The Chairs, 1952), like *The Bald Soprano*, one-acters; *Amédée, ou Comment s'en Débarasser* (Amédée, or How to Get Rid of It, 1954), *Tueur sans Gages* (Killer for the Fun of It, 1959), *Rhinocéros* (1959), *Le Roi se Meurt* (Exit the King, 1962), all full-length evenings. However, Ionesco was not chic, but an oracle; not satiric, but profound; not absurd, but desperate; not exceptional but standard modern theatre; and, incidentally, not Rumanian (though he is by birth) but French (because he is by practice).

In fact, Ionesco is all of the above, on both sides of the buts. *Surrealism led to absurdism, but Ionesco founded absurdism—to the extent that anyone founded it. His implausibly (and, we learn, insistently) murderous teacher in *The Lesson,* his momentous lecture given, it turns out, by a mute in *The Chairs,* his costume-play king defying his own stage instructions in *Exit the King:* these are among absurdism's most basic images. Ionesco also gave absurdism a basic character, Bérenger, the all-purpose *protagonist: bourgeois in *Rhinocéros,* royal in *Exit the King,* and—most authoritatively—foolish compromiser in *Tueur sans Gages.* In Ionesco, the style of life is apocalypse and the characters either conform or rebel—either way, to their doom.

(See also *The Bald Soprano,* and *Rhinocéros.*)

HENRY IRVING (1838–1905)

This English actor-manager so dominated his age —the late Victorian era—that he was known simply as The Old Man for two generations after his death. At a time when actors were generally regarded as trash, he won a knighthood—England's first for an actor. At a time when most *actor-managers thrust themselves forward and let the rest of the show carry on unobtrusively, Irving made his management of the Lyceum Theatre famous for its detail of ensemble and nuance of decor. However, at a time when the boldest actors were taking up Ibsen and other archons of the avant-garde, Irving stuck to Shakespeare and cheap melodrama. It was the latter that gave Irving his fame and his most constant role, that of Mathias the Burgomaster in *The Bells* (1871). The (sleigh) bells of the title haunt Mathias with the memory of a robbery and murder he committed long before; in a trial scene, a hypnotist tricks him into reenacting the crime. The writing was pure rubbish; no doubt Irving's intense commitment to his thud-and-blunder leads transcended their innate silliness —and the grace of his longtime partnership with *Ellen Terry (1847–1928) must have given the Lyceum's bills a startling finesse. The reverberation of "Sir Henry Irving" struck the average theatre-goer of his day much as "the challenge of the Old Man" struck the young *Laurence Olivier. "I determined to become the Old Man myself," Olivier wrote. "Let them impersonate me fifty years after my death." For Olivier to have felt so challenged bespeaks a legend of true greatness. Irving must have been something.

(See also Lighting.)

ALFRED JARRY (1873–1907)

Jarry is a central figure in the rise of the "modern" in theatre, though only one of his several plays was actually staged, at that for a very brief run after the scandalous premiere: *Ubu Roi* (King Ubu, 1896), a scampy, lurid piece of nonsense. Novelist, journalist, artist, and publisher as well as playwright, Jarry ultimately became famous not for what he did as much as for what he inspired: some of the major isms of the twentieth century stage, particularly the theatre of the *absurd.
(See also *Ubu Roi*.)

HENRY ARTHUR JONES
(1851–1929)

Like his contemporary *Arthur Wing Pinero, Jones was a transitional playwright, standing between Victorian sweetshop theatre and the age of *George Bernard Shaw. Yet where Pinero was an able *West End entertainer and Shaw ideologically shocking, Jones was a serious moralist—but a conservative, an accommodator. Thus today he is a name out of a virtually useless history, not as colorful as Pinero and not as absorbing as Shaw. At least Jones had the good sense to apologize, at some years' length, for *Breaking a Butterfly* (1884), an adaptation of *Ibsen's *A Doll's House* in which Nora is reconciled with her selfish husband. Duty calls, woman! But it is unlikely that few if any of Jones's eighty-odd other plays would impress us any more than his castrated Ibsen.

JAMES EARL JONES (1931–   )

In the past, black American actors had to steer their careers around the currents of white racism. *Ira Aldridge, of the nineteenth century, went to Europe to play Shakespeare's heroes. Two generations ago, Paul Robeson (1898–1976) and Canada Lee (1907–1952) could play very limited Shakespeare—Robeson's Othello and Lee's Caliban (though Lee did play Bosola in John Webster's *The Duchess of Malfi* on Broadway in 1946, with Elisabeth Bergner), otherwise depending on contemporary black roles. But Jones, today, is the senior of a generation of black American Shakespeareans, not least through the color-blind casting policies of *Joseph Papp's New York Shakespeare festival, for whom Jones has played Macbeth, Ajax (in *Troilus and Cressida*) and Oberon, as well as Othello and Caliban, nicely tying into history in Robeson's and Lee's parts. Jones's rolling bass voice and bravura style take him from the classics through *Eugene O'Neill's Brutus (*The Emperor*) Jones to *Athol Fugard and even, in a controversial one-man show, *Paul Robeson* (1978), despicably denounced by a crowd of Names who hadn't seen the piece. Jones added to his standing as an actor of contemporary naturalistic portraiture in 1987 in the domestic drama *Fences.* But his greatest part, significantly, drew on the turbulent saga of American race relations. This was Jack Jefferson, the hero of Howard Sackler's verse tragedy *The Great White Hope* (1967), based on Jack Johnson, the boxing champ of early twentieth century America.

LEROI JONES (See Amiri Baraka)

ROBERT EDMOND JONES
(1887—1954)

It's hard to know what to term Jones, professionally. He was primarily known as a designer, especially attuned to the needs of the playwright, the director, the actors, the very sense of production itself—a column of purple light representing the Ghost in John Barrymore's 1922 *Hamlet,* the Greek portico and endless dark of the doorway in the exterior of the Mannon house in Eugene O'Neill's *Mourning Becomes Electra,* thus to underline the work's derivation from Aeschylus's *Oresteia.* But this is only a piece of Jones. He was also a theatre historian, a director, and, as one of the founders of the *Provincetown Players, a leader in the *little theatre movement that opened up the potential for an artistic as opposed to a commercial theatre. In short, Jones was the compleat backstage personality.

BEN JONSON (See Elizabethan Theatre)

JOURNEY'S END

Antiwar war play by R. C. Sherriff (1896—1975), prem. London, 1928.

Sherriff's look in at the British trenches at Saint-Quentin, France in 1918 is more atmospheric than documentary. Where America's outstanding World War I play, *What Price Glory?,* is obscene (for its time), jocular, and impenitent, *Journey's End* is reserved and manful. *What Price Glory?* revels in the advantages of the furlough; *Journey's End* gets on with the war. *What Price Glory?* treats male bonding as a Dionysian excess forgivable in times of emergency; *Journey's End* thinks hero worship is acceptable only if kept within strict bounds. British classicism versus American naturalism. (See also *What Price Glory?*)

LOUIS JOUVET (1887—1951)

This French actor and director is primarily known for his virtually career-long partnership with the playwright *Jean Giraudoux. Jouvet learned his trade as *Jacques Copeau's man Friday, thus linking the early avant-garde with the dawn of *absurdism. He left with us the very French observation, "One works in the theatre because one senses that one has never been oneself, that one cannot be oneself—that, at last, one has found the way to *become* oneself."

JURISTEN

*Documentary drama by *Rolf Hochhuth, prem. (simultaneously) Hamburg, Heidelberg, and Göttingen, 1980.

Like Hochhuth's *The Deputy, Juristen* (Judges) deals with Nazism. But where *The Deputy* is a grandly measured out tragedy set during World War II, *Juristen* is tighter, contemporary, and far more opinionated. *The Deputy* is chronicle, the known historical record adapted for the stage. *Juristen* is *fiction* based on historical events, with an authorial voice keenly guiding our moral judgment. Why, asks Hochhuth, were the judges of Hitler's courts allowed to sit on the bench in a supposedly de-Nazified Germany? To shock us, Hochhuth brings the past to life in film made with the same actors who play his modern-day characters, thus merging the nature of documentary with the processes of imagination. Certainly, the Prime Minister of Baden-Württemberg was shocked. Hochhuth mentioned him by name as having been one of Hitler's judges. The politician—at the time thought to be a likely candidate as President of West Germany—sued Hochhuth and lost his case, his post, and his political hopes. Good riddance.

JUSTICE

Social problem tragedy by *John Galsworthy, prem. London, 1910.

The carefully dispassionate Galsworthy seldom argued for one side or another in his plays, letting the audience do the work of empathizing. However, in *Justice,* Galsworthy unbent a little in the story of a law clerk who steals to help an abused wife. Tried fairly, the clerk is sent to prison and, in the brutal rigors of punishment, is destroyed. At the time, three months' solitary confinement was a routine initiation for all prisoners, regardless of their crimes or character, and the scene in which the helpless *protagonist is thrust into his black cage so impressed the public that reform measures in both England and America (where John Barrymore played the hero) were immediately instituted.

The Art of Kabuki: a scene from Renjishi showing Kabuki's typical Lion Dance, a choreographic stylization of manly nobility. Buffs of the American musical might recall use of the Lion Dance in Stephen Sondheim's Pacific Overtures, closing Act One in an ironically ritualistic rendering of Commodore Perry's celebration of victory in forcing Japan to receive emissaries from the West.

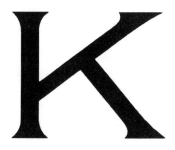

KABUKI

The classic Japanese theatre, flamboyant and intense, virtually a recited opera. Introduced in the seventeenth century, Kabuki has so guarded its traditions (even while developing them) that performances today are replicas of those in the 1600s. Kabuki is especially notable for its emphasis on elaborate production: decor, costume, use of narrator, visible but unnoticed (because dressed in black) stagehands, climactic poses (the *mie*), music, dance, female impersonation (the *onegata* or *ōyama*), and the runway connecting the back of the theatre to the stage (the *hanamichi,* or "flower path"). For centuries, when Western theatre was centered on star acting in come-as-you-are productions, Kabuki reveled in style of presentation as well as stars. However, the performers are so essential to the form that the names of the founders of the various habitual characters are passed on from expert to expert, more or less by popular acclaim.

Kabuki regards its public as an intrinsic element, not docile witnesses. The virtually daylong entertainment often saw its audience chatting and eating (this is now discouraged, in response to Japan's modified Westernization), and aficionados would call out, "Yes, like that!" or "I was expect-

ing it!" at a particularly effective *mie.* Typically, the very word Kabuki claims a derivation as complex as the art itself, owing to the combination of two terms, *kabuku* ("to swank around") and *kabusu* ("to sing and dance"), each with antagonistic nuances: *kabuku* implies a louche attitude, while *kabusu* is matter-of-fact. Kabuki essentially means "the skill of performing an intricate musical play with as much extrapolation as physique and declamation can command." That about says it all.

GEORG KAISER (See

Expressionism)

GEORGE S. KAUFMAN
(1889—1961)

Kaufman typifies Broadway: urbane, adaptable, confident, smart, impatient. *Broadway.* As director, Kaufman worked in all fields, emphasizing comedy and musicals; as playwright, Kaufman almost invariably collaborated, especially with Marc Connelly (1890–1980), Edna Ferber (1887–1968), and Moss Hart (1904–1961); and Kaufman even acted, playing a sardonic playwright waiting for Godot in a Hollywood producer's office in his and Hart's *Once in a Lifetime* (1930), a spoof of the talkies. The Connelly collaborations are gentle comedies, except for their savage satire of American commercialism, *Beggar on Horseback* (1924). The Ferber series injects a farcical note, especially in *The Royal Family* (1927), apparently a look at the offstage lives of Georgiana *Drew and Ethel and John Barrymore. With Hart, Kaufman redoubled the pace of plotting in epitomes of American *farce, yielding two classics, *You Can't Take It with You* (1936) and *The Man Who Came to Dinner* (1939).

A wit but a cynic—again, typical Broadway—Kaufman left one of the theatre's ace quotations: "Satire is what closes Saturday night." He also left a kind of heir in Hart. A stagestruck kid when he first teamed with Kaufman, Hart became a master himself, like Kaufman, versatile of genre and a director as well as writer. However, unlike Kaufman, Hart enjoyed writing scripts on his own—Kaufman only produced one full-length play under his own byline, *The Butter and Egg Man* (1925), a show biz spoof.

By the way, it's pronounced *Cough-man*.
(See also *The Man Who Came to Dinner* and *You Can't Take It with You*.)

ELIA KAZAN (1909–   )

Kazan began as an actor with the *Group Theatre in the mid-1930s, but quickly turned to directing. At first, Kazan roamed: from *Thornton Wilder's pre-*absurdist *The Skin of Our Teeth* (1942) to Kurt Weill's musical *One Touch of Venus* (1943), and on to *S. N. Behrman's comedy *Jacobowsky and the Colonel* (1944). History, sensuality, racism, a broad palette for an artist. But Kazan soon found his metier in what might be called American poetic melodrama. A partial list: *Deep Are the Roots* (1945), *Arthur Miller's *All My Sons* (1947),

*Tennessee Williams's *A Streetcar Named Desire* (1947), Robert Anderson's *Tea and Sympathy* (1953), *William Inge's *The Dark at the Top of the Stairs* (1957), opening up the scene to sexual frustration, marital inertia, working-class truculence, miscegenation, bourgeois guilt . . . and this is not to mention Archibald MacLeish's verse drama *J. B.* (1958), the Book of Job reset in a circus tent. Williams, Miller, Inge: these were the names of the day. And Kazan was not merely their henchman, but their initiator, famed for his extrapolation of personality, his demand for a new third act, his ability to walk the line between *melodrama and poetry. Kazan became the director who rejected more scripts than any other director on Broadway. His name itself was a box office lure, a promise of opulent enactment, now intellectual, now "depraved." Affirming his ties to the Group, Kazan was active in the Actor's Studio (see The Method), enhancing his prominence as an expert in American psychotheatrics. He may be the only major Broadway director to have been born in Constantinople.

EDMUND KEAN (1789–1833)

In his prime as the king of *Drury Lane from 1814 to 1825, Kean was the prototype of the shockingly villainous hero the Romantic era adored. But Kean was as well the unstable, self-destructive high liver who complicates his popularity with acts of arrogance. Even at his best he was controversial. One theatregoer, Miss Mary Russell Mitford, thought him "a little insignificant man, slightly deformed, strongly ungraceful . . . with a voice between grunting and croaking . . . and a vulgarity of manner which his admirers are pleased to call nature." Nevertheless, in a second opinion, that of the poet Coleridge, we learn that "To see him act is like reading Shakespeare by flashes of lightning." Kean was a lurid Shylock, virtually a demented butcher, and even Macbeth, so often the bane of stars that it's considered bad luck in the profession (bad luck even to mention it—traditionalists refer to it as "the Scottish play"), gave Kean a main chance. But halfhearted, or drunken, or even

Edmund Kean as Shakespeare's Richard III. "Richard is a man," said Lord Byron, who had despaired of seeing anything natural on the stage, "and Kean is Richard." One of the first "true to life" actors.

wholly canceled performances enraged the public, and a successful suit against Kean for adultery with an alderman's wife caught the hero up, emphasized the villain.

(See also *Kean,* directly following.)

KEAN

Backstage *melodrama by *Alexandre Dumas *père,* prem. Paris, 1836.

The flamboyant actor Frédérick Lemaître, too undisciplined for the *Comédie-Française, was king of the *boulevard theatres. It was for Lemaître that Dumas wrote this intimate glimpse of the work and loves of the English tragedian *Edmund Kean. Assignations and intrigues abound; nobles patronize and proles adore the rascally hero; and Dumas cleverly set his key scene on the stage of *Drury Lane, with the characters placed in the auditorium boxes, visibly reacting as Kean throws off Shakespeare's Romeo, the role of the evening, to rant at his personal enemies.

A touch of existential alienation—is Kean a man or a medley of characters?—attracted *Jean-Paul

Sartre, who presented an adaptation of Dumas's play in 1953 (again, for a flamboyant actor, Pierre Brasseur). Keeping to Dumas's story, characters, and construction, Sartre tightened the action, polished the lines, and, especially, developed the concept of "Kean the actor, acting the part of Kean the man." Dumas ends Act III, the tavern scene, with a brawl. When it's over, Kean says, "Let us return to finish our wonderful supper!" and the curtain falls. Sartre ends the same scene with Kean's "What a magnificent ending to the act!" He also makes much more of Kean's onstage mad scene, changing the play-within-the-play from sweet *Romeo and Juliet* to the more dangerous *Othello,* and bringing the offended audience into the action. One may fairly say that Dumas has been perfected; but then Sartre was, too, in a quasi-operatic Broadway musical version under the same title (1961), yet again for a flamboyant actor, Alfred Drake.

THE KEMBLES

This English acting dynasty dates to the eighteenth century. Its greatest days were those of John Philip Kemble (1757–1823); his sister Sarah (1755–1831), known by her married name as Mrs. Siddons; their brother Charles (1775–1854); and his daughter Fanny (1809–1893). The Kembles's London was a city crazed for theatre, gentry and common folk alike crowding into the Theatres Royal, *Drury Lane, and *Covent Garden, making these playhouses focal points of town life. This was London one generation after *David Garrick and one generation before the erratically brilliant *Edmund Kean, a stimulated and vociferously aficionado London. John Philip Kemble, as manager of both Theatres Royal, took this public head on, especially in his reforms of thespian and theatregoing practices alike. At times, it must have seemed to Kemble as if everyone needed better manners but he; but the public thought Kemble needed more fire in his acting.

Kemble's most famous battle with the audience stemmed from the raising of admission prices when Covent Garden, devastated by fire in 1808, reopened the following year. The so-called "Old Prices Riots" totally disrupted performances for three months—only partly because of the higher tariff. This was a battle of the class war, too, in resentment of a new tier of private boxes for the rich. Even spectators sympathetic to Kemble's problems (as manager, he was out of pocket for the cost of rebuilding the theatre) were said to have enjoyed putting on nightly performances of their own. The very letters "OP" became a city fetish. The "OP Dance," in which the audience stamped and clapped rhythmically—*during* the show—became a regular feature, and town bloods sought to distinguish their contributions with whistles, bells, toy drums, and other noisemakers. One night, someone even brought in a live pig. Fistfights would break out, parades surged through the aisles—anything to show Kemble that the public could, at will, overwhelm his art. Kemble's resolution might have seen him through, but the riots had simply become too enjoyable for the rioters, an essential social event. So Kemble gave in, reducing the number of private boxes, reinstating the old prices for admission to the *pit (the ground floor), and indulging the public in sundry other humiliations.

Speaking of Kemble himself, the history grows less colorful. He pursued, in a small way, Garrick's reforms in purifying Shakespearean texts. Still, he lacked Garrick's brilliance. Mrs. Siddons was by far her brother's superior; Garrick himself had introduced her to London, though her first season did not go well. In time, however, she became an awesome figure, her dignity majestic, her insinuation chilling. Her whisper filled the largest houses; her fury scourged them. Siddons was the kind of actress who plays an amazing Lady Macbeth—as Siddons reputedly did. Everyone of her day who wrote of theatre, it seems, wrote of Siddons in this role, and wrote mesmerized. When she bade farewell to the stage, in 1812, it was of course as Lady Macbeth; and the public rendered her stunned homage by demanding that the show end after the sleepwalking scene. Siddons dwarfed her relatives, though her niece Fanny achieved a certain fame by hating the family profession and retiring at the age of twenty-five to marry an American southerner, a plantation slaveholder.

KENNEDY'S CHILDREN

Monologues by Robert Patrick (1937–), prem. New York, 1973.

Five characters in an American bar, each oblivious of the others, take turns delivering the monologues, cut up into paragraphs to intersect over the course of the evening. These are John Fitzgerald Kennedy's children: a Vietnam veteran, a Marilyn Monroe cutout, a wryly gay off-Broadway actor, a professional leftist, and an aging social worker deeply committed to Kennedy and the cult of the Assassination. The voices of missed chances, wasted opportunism, and betrayed dedication thus commingle and fade away. A unique and very touching work, it traveled from off-Broadway to London before trying Broadway in 1975.

SEAN KENNY (1932–1973)

This Irish architect made his fame as a *West End set designer of high-tech productions, especially musicals—the Dickensian *Oliver!* (1960) and *Pickwick* (1963); the smoky *Blitz!* (1962), a Jewish *Romeo and Juliet*; the *Drury Lane spectacle *The Four Musketeers* (1968), with the erstwhile Pickwick Harry Secombe—all electrified constructions of wooden bridges and towers. Kenny's sets looked complex, but were so simple technologically that —supposedly—a single stagehand could run them by pulling switches. Kenny's work at the Mermaid Theatre, *Joan Littlewood's "Stratford East," and the *Old Vic, all on a smaller scale, strongly influenced London's theatre scene, though *Kenneth Tynan, for one, could not shake the impression that Kenny on any scale overshadowed the actors, the text, the very idea of theatre as we know it. After *Blitz!,* Tynan wrote, "I have a fearful premonition of the next show Mr. Kenny designs. As soon as the curtain rises, the sets will advance in a phalanx on the audience and summarily expel it from the theatre. After that, the next step is clear: Mr. Kenny will invent sets that applaud."

SIDNEY KINGSLEY (1906–   )

Something like a middle man between *Ned Sheldon and *Arthur Miller, Kingsley worked the arena of social problem melodrama—the slums abutting the world of plenty on the eastern end of Manhattan's East Fifty-Third Street, for instance, in *Dead End* (1935). *Detective Story* (1949), one day's worth of microcosmic feelings in a New York precinct house, similarly typifies Kingsley's driving style—though in *Lunatics and Lovers* (1954) he stepped out in a farce as near to *absurdism as the Broadway of his time could get. Notably, Kingsley was probably the last major playwright to direct his own plays, as had been common in the early 1900s.

"KITCHEN-SINK" THEATRE

A label pasted on British "angry young man" and social problem plays in the late-1950s and 1960s, because so many of them took place in rundown one-room apartments. The term was used by approvers and detractors alike, the former neutrally, as a useful shorthand denoting productions following the trend begun by *John Osborne's *Look Back in Anger*; and the latter reprovingly, as if theatre must be beautiful rather than honest. Note the demotion from the Victorian *T. W. Robertson's "cup-and-saucer" drama: the naturalistic focus has moved from the bourgeoisie to the working class.

HEINRICH VON KLEIST (1777–1811)

An atmosphere of exaltation hounded by pessimism, a field of play in which authoritarian forces must bring the errant genius to heel, and a belief that free choice does not exist yet must be cultivated . . . all this makes von Kleist a model Romantic. He had no influence in his lifetime, for those few of his plays that were produced were failures, leading von Kleist to kill himself in despair. But such works as the comic *Der Zerbrochene Krug* (The Broken Jug, 1808); *Die Hermannsschlacht* (written 1808, prem. 1871), on a medieval hero's battle with the Romans; *Penthesilea* (1808, 1876), about an Amazon destroyed through love for the unconquerable Achilles; and *Prinz Friedrich von Homburg* (1811, 1821) are regarded as seminally important in the rise of modern German drama. If von Kleist was too "difficult" for his contemporaries, he spoke profoundly to later generations. *The Prince of Homburg* (as it is called in English) is particularly noteworthy. Its hero is a soldier trained to obey, but who disobeys, and who is both "allowed" to die and "sentenced" to live. The piece is so rich in thematic paradox that it became a mainstay of the German repertory, first as a Romantic "dream play," next as a pre-*absurdist tragicomedy, later as an existentialist work.

ARTHUR KOPIT (1937—   )

Kopit was still a student at Harvard when the play that was to make his reputation was produced there. This was *Oh Dad, Poor Dad, Mamma's Hung You in the Closet and I'm Feelin' So Sad* (1960), a *black comedy spoofing the vicious mother, the wormy son, and the aggressive girlfriend of Freudian paradigms. Rather than build on this, Kopit explored the possibilities of form to create an entirely different kind of theatre in each work. *Indians* (1968) tackles American history through the device of Buffalo Bill's Wild West Show, framing scenes both historical and personal and taking in Sitting Bull, Ned Buntline, Annie Oakley, Jesse James, Billy the Kid, and the President, First Lady, and U. S. Senators. *Wings* (1979) treats a stroke victim's therapy by viewing the action through the patient's own shattered senses. *End of the World* (1984) uses the conventions of the detective story to discuss nuclear disarmament. Throughout his career, Kopit has emphasized state-of-the-art stagecraft and somewhat avoided the Broadway scene—*Oh Dad* was mounted on off-Broadway and, despite its great success, never moved to a big house; *Indians* received its premiere in London (by the *Royal Shakespeare Company) a year before trying Washington, DC's Arena Stage and, only then, the Brooks Atkinson Theatre on Manhattan's West Forty-seventh Street. Like a very few major American playwrights—Maxwell Anderson and Edward Albee come to mind—Kopit tried collaborating on the major American form, the big Broadway musical, writing the book to Maury Yeston's *Nine* (1982), based on Federico Fellini's film 8½.

JAN KOTT (1914—   )

This Polish critic earned international fame for his book *Szkice o Szekpirze* (1964), translated as *Shakespeare, Our Contemporary.* This sizable work analyzes Shakespeare's major plays in detail, title by title, to develop Kott's thesis that Shakespeare's timelessness makes him contemporary in any age. Thus, Kott likens Hamlet to "a young rebel who has about him something of the charm of James Dean," and the references span from the Bible, *commedia dell'arte,* Jonathan Swift, Victor Hugo, and Friedrich Nietzsche to Stanislavsky, Brecht, and, especially, Samuel Beckett. Kott's discussion of *King Lear* in fact compares the tragedy to Beckett's *Endgame,* and the book came out in America with an authenticating introduction by Martin Esslin, author of *The Theatre of the Absurd.* Kott's theory is derived in part from *Peter Brook's production of Shakespeare's *Titus Andronicus,* which Kott saw in Warsaw in 1957; and Brook in turn applied Kott to Brook's later stagings of *King Lear* and *A Midsummer Night's Dream.*

THOMAS KYD (See Revenge Tragedy)

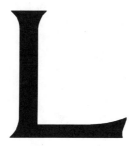

EUGÈNE LABICHE (1815–1888)

Ancient French *farce found its last master in Labiche, whose plays resemble *Molière's comedies more than those of Labiche's successor in the form, *Georges Feydeau. Where Molière is an acknowledged genius and Feydeau no more than an entertainer, Labiche's talent is arguable. He often seems a charming hack, but at times delves into character persuasively enough to hearten his admirers into comparing him to Molière. Labiche habitually collaborated rather than wrote solo; as with *George S. Kaufman, this compromises his reputation. Labiche produced one classic, however, *Le Chapeau de Paille d'Italie* (The Italian Straw Hat, 1851), an evening-long misadventure that begins when a horse eats a hat.

THE LARK

*Chronicle play by Jean Anouilh, prem. Paris, 1953

In French, *L'Alouette*. Within the framework, Joan of Arc's trial for heresy and witchcraft, Anouilh presents a fluid retrospective of the events leading up to her martyrdom. Switching from the court to Joan's past, back and forth, Anouilh avoids the episodic nature of *Shaw's *Saint Joan*; and by his own nature the Frenchman would not match the Irishman's terse ironies. Anouilh's lark is a dear child rather than a warrior, wistful where Shaw's heroine is weighty. Typically, the Broadway mounting of 1955 (adapted by *Lillian Hellman) gave *Julie Harris one of her greatest parts. *Gentille alouette*.

LAZZO

Italian for "joke," referring to the traditional jests and *business of the *commedia dell'arte*. The plural is *lazzi*.

EVA LE GALLIENNE (See Civic Repertory Company)

Nicholas Nickleby: *Dicken's humanist agenda led him to expose and attack Victorian England's social evils, including the Yorkshire boarding schools for unwanted boys, often the bastard progeny of "reputable" men. The schools were an open secret; Dickens made them a scandal. Here, Nicholas (Roger Rees) extends his arms to protect the broken youths of Dotheboys Hall, Wackford Squeers, proprietor. (Note David Threlfall, as the pitiful Smike, just behind Rees's right hand.)*

GOTTHOLD LESSING (1729—1781)

As playwright (and critic), Lessing was more a seminal figure than a builder of important repertory. His most famous play, *Nathan der Weise* (Na-than the Wise, produced posthumously in 1783), a reasoning out of the humanistic beauty of religious and racial tolerance, is admirable but not enjoyable. Like, one might add, all of Lessing: a sound thinker, an earnest man, but always the theorist and seldom the thespian. His major contribution lay in questioning the German convention that great drama must be historical in setting and majestic of character. Why not, Lessing asked, depict all kinds of characters, from the low to the grand, in heroic and comic genres? Lessing's suggestion, thus prompting *Goethe and *Schiller, strongly encouraged the developing German stage. Is not Goethe's *Faust something of a Lessing project in its mixture of the chivalric and the bourgeois, the natural and the fabulous? Lessing himself had planned a Faust play but never began it. It needed the talent of a master, not a critic.

THE LIFE AND ADVENTURES OF NICHOLAS NICKLEBY

Epic adaptation by David Edgar, prem. London, 1980.

"There once lived in a sequestered part of the county of Devonshire . . ." So begins Charles Dickens's novel, and so begins the play that the *Royal Shakespeare Company made of it. The show is unique in theatre history, partly for its length (eight-and-a-half hours of playing time, not counting intermissions) partly for its mass authorship (the actors' sociohistorical research inspired improvisations, developed by co-directors Trevor Nunn and John Caird, then edited and rewritten by dramatist David Edgar), and partly because it seemed to unite contemporary stagecraft with the old-fashioned pseudo-*naturalism that delighted our grandparents. Thus, while the forty-two actors played the one hundred twenty-three parts in a realistic manner, any of them might group together to present, impressionistically, the London poor staring at the gorging rich, the sounds of Portsmouth harbor, or even, in one of the play's most enthralling moments, a coach bumping off to Yorkshire.

The transformation from novel to play was so stylish and faithful to Dickens that few noticed that Edgar and the actors had slipped in bits here and there to rather than from the novel, most notably a spoof of Victorian theatre in the doctored Romeo and Juliet, as performed by the Vincent Crummles troupe, that closed Part One. However, virtually every commentator hailed the players' versatility, as when Lila Kaye's snarling Mrs. Squeers turned into the campy tragedienne Mrs. Crummles; or when Bob Peck's roughhewn good guy John Browdie slithered into the elegantly loathsome Sir Mulberry Hawk. There are many villains and a number of good guys in Nicholas Nickleby, but Roger Rees's *protagonist centered the action with hesitant and naive but ultimately assertive good will. Rees was direly missed when the 1986 revival brought the work back to New York, still in trim as a production but with nearly all the principals replaced by second stringers. Even the resourceful Jane Carr, taking over Suzanne Bertish's parts, justified only the spiteful Fanny Squeers, missing out the near-miss heroine attitudes of Miss Snevillicci the actress, and not even attempting the cockeyed physique that Bertish brought to Peg Sliderskew. Above all, it was Rees's moral outrage that the revival needed, the authenticity of his Dickensian righteousness. Luckily, the original production has been preserved on videotape.

Nunn and Caird started out with the notion of adapting Dickens, but with no certain novel in mind. They very nearly pitched on Our Mutual Friend—which has even more plot than Nicholas Nickleby—and only backed out because it would have been too difficult to capture the brooding weight of the River Thames, so essential to Our Mutual Friend's atmosphere. However, there is a special justice in the adapting of Nicholas Nickleby. Dickens was a lifelong theatre buff, and the sequence on- and offstage with Crummles's troupe honors the author's great love. Indeed, the novel was turned into a play several times in the 1800s, and in 1927 *actor-manager Nigel Playfair revived George Lillo's forgotten melodrama George Barnwell; or, The London Merchant as it might have been performed by the Crummleses in the good old days, complete with Nicholas and Smike, Miss Snevillicci, and the Infant Phenomenon, Crummles's superannuated child. The evening, denoted as When Crummles Played, flopped in New York, a sad prevision of the 1986 Royal Shakespeare revival. One last thing: the novel is dedicated to the Victorian actor "*W. C. Macready, Esquire."

LIGHTING

Illumination was a simple matter for the Greeks and Romans, for the practitioners of the mystery and miracle plays, for the Elizabethans and the Spaniards of the *corrales*. One emphasized the matinée and thanked the sun. Not till the wholly enclosed theatres of the 1600s did the science of theatre lighting begin, developing from candle to oil, then gas, at first hung overhead, then in the *wings and down at the front of the stage (the "footlights").

All this was simply to enable the audience to see. The matter of effects, of emphasis and suggestion, became important in the late 1800s, when, at long last, auditoriums were darkened as a rule, following the innovation of Richard Wagner at his opera house in Bayreuth, Germany, opened in 1876. Electric light, far more flexible than its predecessors, also became standard. Primitive lighting had been basically a matter of on or off; now there were possibilities in dimming, shaping, spotting, masking, focus, and coloration that even the adaptable gas lamp could not equal (though *Henry Irving abandoned electricity for gas, which lay a denser atmosphere upon his pageants at London's Lyceum). Lighting became a strategy in stagecraft, a crucial discipline all its own, by the early 1900s, and has become increasingly sophisticated. One mark of contemporary lighting, however, recalls the early days of the candle chandeliers: the public gets to see the apparatus. The exposed, mounted spot lamps are a convention of today's theatre, as much a facet of the scene as was the Greek mask or the Victorian *melodrama curtain tableau.

THE LINCOLN CENTER
REPERTORY COMPANY

This was to have been, for once and all, an alternative to the crass New York show markets, a permanent home for important theatre, on Broadway but never of it. While waiting out the construction of the new Lincoln Center house, exterior designed by Eero Saarinen and auditorium by *Jo Mielziner, the company took charge of a provisional home in Washington Square in 1964. That first season gave warning of the direction the company would take in three productions—one new play by a current celebrated playwright, one old play by a bygone celebrated playwright, and one new play by a bygone second-rank playwright in decline. The first play was *Arthur Miller's autobiographical *After the Fall,* which could easily have been done on Broadway. The second play was *Eugene O'Neill's comedy *Marco Millions,* which could almost as easily have been revived on Broadway. The third play was *S. N. Behrman's *But For Whom Charlie,* which possibly should not have been done anywhere.

Perhaps there was too much flavor of Broadway "doing" prestige—in the choice of plays (what could be more prestigious than forgotten O'Neill?), the choice of artistic directors (Robert Whitehead and *Elia Kazan, of the commercial stage), and the production styles. Some good actors were caught up in the deal and lost in the shuffle—Barbara Loden, Hal Holbrook, David Wayne, Faye Dunaway. But the very names bespeak a narrow range; what they are good for is contemporary American stuff. The second season, combining another new Miller play *(Incident at Vichy)* with an Elizabethan *revenge tragedy and Molière's *Tartuffe,* was a disaster. The company moved uptown to its proudly *thrust stage and changed administrations. The new team hired a new ensemble and pulled out the Brecht and the Shaw and the Shakespeare, the ineffable *William Saroyan, the hip *Sam Shepard. Yet work at the Vivian Beaumont was never serious theatre, only serious Broadway: Lee J. Cobb's Lear, an all-star *Camino Real* (what could be more prestigious than forgotten *Tennessee Williams, especially as it is his Most Difficult Play?), a *Saint Joan* for black Diana Sands. In 1973, *Joseph Papp took over the Beaumont, reinstating action at the neglected "second" stage in the basement, the Newhouse (formerly the Forum). Yet this was still no alternative, just a downtown Papp moved uptown. This administration, too, failed. Fitful reorganization in the 1980s has done nothing to affirm the notion of a Lincoln Center theatre company to complement the opera, symphony, and dance organizations.

We get a sense of the low-budget vivacity of the little theatre movement in this shot of Vera Tompkins, a quaintly charming Millamant in William Congreve's *The Way of the World *in the late 1920s at New York's Cherry Lane Theatre, way downtown in the West Village on Commerce Street. Unlike the big houses of Broadway, but like the little houses of what was to become known as off-Broadway, the Cherry Lane's auditorium was cut into an already existing structure. It was not originally a theatre; it had theatre thrust into it. Also typical of the little theatre approach was the Cherry Lane's fondness for idealistic companies, which banded up and dissolved with disheartening regularity, beaten by public indifference. The building still stands and the companies still play. In the off-Broadway era, such instructive playwrights as* *Samuel Beckett, *Edward Albee, Gertrude Stein, *Harold Pinter, Jean-Claude van Itallie, and *Edward Bond *have taken stage at the Cherry Lane.*

THE LITTLE THEATRE MOVEMENT

America, circa 1910. A few rebels declare the established theatre—from Broadway through the touring circuits right down to the shabbiest local "opera house"—artistically bankrupt. Playwrights and *managers cater to stars, stars play the same old roles, and the stage knows neither reality, nor psychology, nor social awareness. The rebels theorize, commission avant-garde scripts, gather disciples, and put on new art any old place.

This was the "little" theatre, so termed because most of them were small, not to say makeshift. But the term was ironical, for the "little" alternative was big in spirit, in ambition. The movement was based in the northeastern United States, almost invariably in cities, and especially in New York, breaking the ground for what would eventually become *off-Broadway. The *Provincetown Playhouse, where Eugene O'Neill got his start, was the site not only of influential little theatre productions, but of important off-Broadway entries in the post–World War II years. However, another little theatre group, the Washington Square Players, went on to become an essential feature of establishment Broadway: the *Theatre Guild.
(See also The Provincetown Players.)

JOAN LITTLEWOOD (1914–   )

A prototype of the modern director, collaborating with the author, the actors, the techies. An auteur: to the grouching of some critics (and playwrights) that Littlewood had usurped the author's authority. Yet Littlewood's regime in a battered old theatre in London's slummy East End revealed a number of new playwrights. Most notable of these were *Brendan Behan and Shelagh Delaney; and neither complained of administrative interference. Littlewood's atelier, the Theatre Royal, Stratford, in fact became a center of the British avant-garde, drawing a *West End crowd to its remote hostel —and, given the nature of its working-class neighborhood, "hostel" is a pun. Ironically, Littlewood

disdained the bourgeois theatregoer to cultivate a working-class public. Yet her successes kept getting transferred to the big-time houses in the *West End.

Littlewood herself stayed put. From 1953 to 1961, she resolutely housed her company, Theatre Workshop, at "Stratford East," blending elements of the music hall, melodrama, and spoof with the thrust of dead-on naturalism. Still, the question of authorship dogs her chronicle. When, in 1963, Littlewood returned to Stratford East to stage *Oh, What a Lovely War,* a reconstitution of the English Pierrot-troupe musical variety show along the lines of *Brechtian *epic theatre—all this on the subject of World War I—the published text listed, in the byline, "Theatre Workshop, Charles Chilton, and members of the original cast."

LIVING NEWSPAPER (See The Federal Theatre)

THE LIVING THEATRE

A typical *off-Broadway troupe: neglected in its prime and destined for legend in posterity. Founded in 1951 by Julian Beck and his wife Judith Malina, the Living Theatre staged *Pirandello and *Brecht but won notice for newly iconoclastic subjects in avant-garde stagecraft. Jack Gelber's *The Connection* (1959) presented a group of drug addicts awaiting their dealer to the accompaniment of a jazz combo as show biz exploiters hung around on the fringes, looking for a sensation to tap into. Like the music, the performance had a chillingly improvisational air, an honorary reality that shocked New York, sending the midcult critics into hysterics of disgust and convening the daredevil intelligentsia in full congress. Kenneth H. Brown's harrowing *The Brig* (1963), on life in a Marine Corps prison, was less a play than a cautionary nightmare.

Still, the Living Theatre did not win international attention till it took up the countercultural fads of the late 1960s with a helter-skelter "acting" company given to physical stunts, nudity, and spontaneous screamings of such aperçus as "I want to take off all my clothes." *Frankenstein* (1965) was the Living Theatre's idea of the new wave babbitt, artificial American man, but the gang promised— or threatened—*Paradise Now* (1968) if everyone smoked pot, screwed, and didn't read. Acclaimed abroad on a wave of anti-American sentimentality, the Becks were harassed and even jailed at home. They are authentic revolutionaries of art. But they might have made a more telling revolution with (their earlier) work of art than with (their later) work of trend.

CHARLES LUDLAM (See The Ridiculous Theatrical Company)

AURÉLIAN-FRANÇOIS LUGNÉ-POË (1869–1940)

In Paris, in the last days of the nineteenth century and the first of the twentieth, conservatives, revolutionary realists, and anti-realistic mannerist revolutionaries waged a war of the arts. Lugné-Poë, an all-around thespian, was a mannerist. Though he staged such realists as *Ibsen and *Strindberg at his company, the Théâtre de l'Oeuvre, Lugné-Poë was the particular champion of the dreamy *Maeterlinck, the erotically chevaleresque *D'Annunzio, the blatantly bizarre *Jarry, the lubricious *Salomé* of *Oscar Wilde.

Lugné-Poë's repertory, clearly, had impact. But his productions often held to the absolute minimum, street clothes against stock sets dimly lit. There was so little money for wardrobe that the actors effected costume changes by wearing their overcoats inside out or changing the tilt of their hats. All the same, Edvard Munch was invited to design Lugné-Poë's production of Ibsen's *John Ga-*

briel Borkman—and, on a Scandinavian tour, Lugné-Poë's *The Master Builder* impressed the Master himself: Ibsen had the King of Norway decorate Lugné-Poë in gold.

ALFRED LUNT (1892–1977) AND LYNN FONTANNE (1887–1983)

It was Lunt's idea that the two should team up— that playing as a duo would distinguish charismatic qualities they might lose playing separately. This charisma seemed most potent in erotic situations—rendezvous, seductions, adulteries. Though they played Shakespeare, Shaw, Chekhov, Giraudoux, and Dürrenmatt, the Lunts are remembered as having dallied, deftly effervescent, in sex comedies by second-rate writers.

They did play a lot of sex comedy, some even by first-rate writers—the Giraudoux, adapted by S. N. Behrman, was *Amphitryon 38,* on Zeus's seduction of Alcmene, and the Shakespeare was *The Taming of the Shrew,* a celebrated production— Lunt's own—with an air of carnival elation. However, the Lunts made their mark not in the parts they played but in how they played them. Lunt had been right: being so magnificently bonded and having a permanent access to each other gave their performances an interrelational subtlety beyond the reach of other players. Technically, the Lunts were the equals of anyone; spiritually, they were everyone's superiors. Their habit of interlacing their lines—painstakingly developed when they began regular joint appearances for the *Theatre Guild in the mid-1920s—was so naturalistic that it proved controversial amid the artificial melody that passed for dialogue in other actors' scenes. The pure *coherence* of Lunt-and-Fontanne seemed too sophisticated even for these sophisticates, too nuanced, strenuously dazzling. By the time such other disciples of naturalistic delivery as the *Group Theatre caught up with the Lunts in the mid-1930s, however, Broadway was acclimatized and the urbane comedians of sex were reigning stylists of the American stage.

One may lament the great plays they never got to try—Arthur Miller's *Death of a Salesman,* for instance. But long memories treasure their part-

These shots of the Lunts' 1935 The Taming of the Shrew *demonstrate the pictorial spirit of the staging. Direction was credited to Harry Wagstaff Gribble, sets to Carolyn Hancock, and costumes to Claggett Wilson, but Lunt was the auteur: refashioning the text, overseeing all aspects of the crafting, alarming critics with his earthy, bum-slapping Petruchio, and calling a full dress rehearsal the morning of the very last Saturday of the run because Friday night had gone a bit ragged. Sydney Greenstreet, later the favorite villainous fat man at Warner Brothers (especially in* The Maltese Falcon *and* Casablanca*), played Baptista, and may be seen directly left of Fontanne in the curtain call above.*

nership with *Noël Coward in Coward's *Design for Living* (1933), written so the three could thumb their noses at bourgeois convention, as bohemians all more or less in love with each other and to hell with the world; or their stint as shabby nightclub song-and-dance man and bogus Russian countess watching the world actually go to hell in a world war in *Robert E. Sherwood's *Idiot's Delight* (1936); or their textured masquerade as a progressively aging couple in *Behrman's *I Know My Love* (1949), twenty-one years after they had launched their regime in exclusive duet. By far the most distinguished work of their last decade was their farewell in *Dürrenmatt's *The Visit* on Broadway in 1958, nationally in 1959, and in London in 1960.

MACHINAL

*Expressionist tragedy by Sophie Treadwell (1890–1970), prem. New York, 1928.

Apparently based on the Ruth Snyder–Judd Gray murder case, *Machinal* uses machine-age alienation as the background for a young woman's unhappy marriage to a shmoo, her temporary adultery with a hunk, her murder of her husband, and her execution. Typically expressionist (and supporting Treadwell's view of modern civilization as dehumanizing) is the large cast of characters, listed by profession or type rather than by name. Even the *protagonist is called simply "Young Woman." Zita Johann played the lead, but the most famous member of the cast was Clark Gable, who played the hunk shortly before departing for Hollywood.

STEELE MACKAYE (1842–1894)

This American actor, playwright, and *manager was an innovator in production techniques, anticipating the better known *David Belasco in experimental lighting and set design. Regarded as a seminal rather than an achieving figure, MacKaye did write one extremely popular play, *Hazel Kirke* (1880). His playwright son, Percy MacKaye (1875–1956), was less distinguished, specializing in *masques and pageants, especially for outdoor festivals.

MICHEÁL MACLIAMMÓIR (See The Gate Theatre)

WILLIAM MACREADY (1793–1873)

One of the great English tragedians of the transatlantic theatre circuits of the mid-nineteenth century. Macready's great contribution was to return Shakespearean production to the original texts, despising the heavily adulterated versions introduced during the *Restoration and still more popular than pure Shakespeare. (Nahum Tate's *King Lear,* for instance: shorn of the Fool, beribboned with a Cordelia-Edgar love plot, and wrapped up in a happy ending.) Macready's most famous gift to theatre history was his feud with the actor *Edwin Forrest that climaxed in the bloody *Astor Place Riot.

See someone familiar? Look again. This is Sophie Treadwell's Machinal, *with Zita Johann (far right) as the Young Woman and . . . Clark Gable, facing us, to her right. Note the center couple's emptiness of rapport and the odd look on the waiter's face: Treadwell's play, like many expressionist works, accepted as a given humans' inability to communicate even on the most basic level.*

MAURICE MAETERLINCK

(1862–1949)

The Belgian playwright's heyday was the turn of the century—the era of *symbolism, art nouveau, and Debussy. Maeterlinck lived most of his life in France and wrote in French; he was a Parisian when Paris was still the cultural capital of the Western world. Yet as the arts moved into modernism, as Stravinsky, Proust, and *Cocteau strode onto the world stage, Maeterlinck held to his fin-de-siècle aesthetic, his legends and romances of indecision and wonderment. A typical Maeterlinck drama is set in a medieval castle. In the first act, someone arrives; in the middle acts, nothing happens; in the last act, someone leaves, or at least dies. Maeterlinck's dialogue is freighted with a feverish poetry, yet his characters seldom truly interact. The *Theatre of the Unexpressed, in which the silence is more eloquent than the spoken lines, was Maeterlinck's invention. He was the world's last (perhaps only) *vrai-naif.* His plays were so chaste that he recommended them for puppet troupes. The ones that have survived did so in adaptation: *Pelléas et Mélisande* (1893) and *Ariane et Barbe-Bleue* (1901) as operas, and *L'Oiseau Bleu* (The Blue Bird, 1908) as a Shirley Temple movie. Before you laugh, consider that *The Blue Bird* had its premiere at the *Moscow Art Theatre, directed by Konstantin Stanislavsky.

JUDITH MALINA (See The Living Theatre)

DAVID MAMET (1947–   )

First, some samples of Mamet's astonishing ear for American speech, whether brutish working-class:

TEACH: Ahh, shit. We're sitting down, how many times do I pick up the check? But—No! —because I never go and make a big *thing* out of it—it's no big thing—and flaunt like "This one's on me" like some bust-out asshole, but I naturally assume that I'm with friends, and don't forget who's who when someone gets *behind* a half a yard or needs some help with— huh?—some fucking rent, or drops enormous piles of money at the track, or someone's *sick* or something . . .

or affected show biz gamesmanship, as when aging actor Robert tells younger actor John that the critics may have overpraised him:

JOHN: I thought they were rather to the point.
ROBERT: You did.
JOHN: Yes.
ROBERT: Your reviews.
JOHN: Yes.
ROBERT: All false modesty aside.
JOHN: Yes.
ROBERT: Oh, the Young, the Young, the Young, the Young.
JOHN: The Farmer in the Dell.
ROBERT: Oh, I see.
JOHN: Would you hand me my scarf, please?
(Pause)
ROBERT: You fucking TWIT.

or even post-yuppie loner rap:

EDMOND: And I think, in our soul, *we, we* feel, we sense there is going to be . . . a cataclysm. But we cannot flee. We're fearful. All the time. Because we can't trust what we know.

The first excerpt is from *American Buffalo,* the second from *A Life in the Theatre,* the third from *Edmond;* and already we have a problem—or, rather, Mamet does, with the critics. Three such different plays make him difficult to type, which unnerves the typers. Worse yet, Mamet's belief in an honest theatre—a reportorial, which means at times a confrontational theatre—threatens them. Mamet's range is too broad, his passion too truthful, for a professional turd to encompass. The first rule of the critic is: What you don't comprehend, you attack.

Yet despite "mixed" (very mixed) reviews, Mamet has gradually set himself forth as one of the reigning American playwrights. His early work revealed a dialectician, happiest in short forms based entirely or mostly on two-character conversations, such as *Duck Variations* (1972), with its pair of old men schmoozing on a park bench; or *Sexual Perversity in Chicago* (1974), on courtship rituals. However, *The Water Engine* (1977) introduced a dramatist, not only a sound plotter of action but an ingenious developer of thematic motifs within the motion of the dialogue. Mamet also branched into the monologue play—an American obsession from *Eugene O'Neill to *Sam Shepard—in *Mr. Happiness* (1978), written to accompany the shortish *Water Engine* in its Broadway mounting. Absorbingly played by Charles Kimbrough, *Mr. Happiness* complemented the wary optimism of *The Water Engine*'s Depression setting with a Mr. Fixit radio personality who answers personal problem letters on the air, delving and wondering and disquieting us.

In such an output, *A Life in the Theatre* (1977) was a setback, another two-person charade about very little, in which the veteran and the neophyte talk of this and that while treating us, "onstage," to spoofs of genre. Yet here was a New York success for the Chicago-based Mamet, an act of acceptance by the Metropolis, even if the play was produced on *off-Broadway. So was *Edmond*

(1982), but this dark adventure, the picaresque self-degradation of an alienated man, didn't succeed commercially. It was as if critics and public want only Mamet's ear, not his mind. Yet the reviewers love to slam him for having only the ear, for lacking plot, even a theme.

On the contrary, in these years Mamet delivered himself of the two plays that will sustain his reputation and that illustrate his major theme. In *American Buffalo* (1975), crime is a business; in *Glengarry Glen Ross* (1983), business is a crime. This is Mamet's view of American capitalism, of Corporation politics, of money as the religion of a culture. *American Buffalo* concerns mean streets no-accounts in a heist that never comes off. *Glengarry Glen Ross* deals with a competition among real estate salesmen. Yet the pair—and *The Water Engine*—hit upon an essential Mamet belief, that in American business, in American life, any act that turns a profit is the "right" act, the true and even the fair act. The critics, with their usual acumen, ran screaming like banshees from *American Buffalo* (note the punning title, denoting both a coin and "national scam") because the characters use "shit" and "fuck" all the time. But this is how such people talk—and Mamet is as fascinated with the inarticulate argot that defines character and influences action as he is with the simple reconstruction of real-life colloquialism. The language of the streets, and of the board rooms, is an element in Mamet's aesthetic. American theatre "criticism" stands on such a low level that reviewers judge a work not by its quality but by its quota of *New York Times* no-no words. Yet the 1981 Long Wharf revival of *American Buffalo,* brought to Broadway, had the same writers suddenly hailing it as a modern classic. As Teach says in this same play, "What am I doing demeaning myself standing here pleading with you to protect your best interests?"

(See also *The Water Engine.*)

MANAGER

This word has largely disappeared from usage. In its prime, it denoted the essential thespian. In brief: the manager was the one in charge. In the nineteenth century, his great era, the manager not only ran the troupe but played the leads and staged (sometimes even wrote) the plays. This was the *actor-manager, his own boss. The rise of the producer in the American theatre empires of the late nineteenth century separated some star actors from management, as when manager *Charles Frohman presented Ethel Barrymore, Maude Adams, and others such; while actor-managers Mrs. Fiske or George M. Cohan continued to run their own concerns. By the 1920s, the very word manager was falling out of fashion, replaced by "producer" (although *Harold Clurman used "manager" in his book *The Fervent Years,* published in 1945).

In England, "manager" has lasted virtually to the present, as "producer," in British use, refers to the *director of the show, not the person who capitalizes it, rents the theatre, and tries to make the playwright rewrite the third act. Again, in brief: in America a manager would be, say, *David Merrick called by another name (producer). In England, a manager would be David Merrick.

MAN IS MAN

Didactic *farce by *Bertolt Brecht, prem. (simultaneously) Darmstadt and Düsseldorf, 1926.

Also known as *A Man's a Man:* meaning that variables of personality and religious or social belief are powerless to distinguish an individual when the System puts its claim on him, whether as worker, farmer, or, as here, soldier. Subtitled "The Transformation of the Dockworker Galy Gay in the Army barracks of Kilkoa in the year 1925," *Mann Ist Mann* takes us into the world of Kiplingesque imperialism, a Brechtian haunt. The piece is heavily plotted and full of the mischance and overturn of farce, as three soldiers "dismantle" and then reconstruct Galy Gay into a replacement for one of their comrades. No—not a replacement. Galy Gay is turned into the missing fourth soldier, virtually becomes this other fellow. What's the difference? Man is man, and each warm body is as exploitable as the next.

THE MAN WHO CAME TO DINNER

*Farce by *George S. Kaufman and Moss Hart, prem. New York, 1939.

A classic comic premise: sophisticated New Yorker and his eccentric friends bouncing off the mid-American bourgeoisie. The title role of Sheridan Whiteside, modeled on the unbearably precious critic and radio commentator Alexander Woollcott and played on both stage and screen by the pungently nasty Monty Woolley, is a rare thing in farce: the whole play. Whiteside isn't just the *protagonist, but almost the exclusive source of the evening's fun. The middle-class household that Whiteside occupies (after a mishap on the icy front steps) doesn't offer farce's usual complement of screwballs—as we find, for example, in Kaufman and Hart's *You Can't Take It with You. This play does have one dotty aunt who turns out to be a former ax murderer. But otherwise the midwesterners are simply straight men for Whiteside's attacks and ripostes, though he gets some help from sidekicks based on Harpo Marx and Gertrude Lawrence.

MARAT/SADE

*Brechtian *absurdist *Theatre of Cruelty by *Peter Weiss, prem. Berlin, 1964.

How can there be a Brechtian Theatre of Cruelty? Brecht's art is centered on intellectual reception—the famous *Alienation effect. Antonin Artaud's Theatre of Cruelty is meant to intoxicate, stimulate, terrify. Nonetheless, Weiss has combined these two approaches, at that in a work based on a debate between an intoxicated individualist (the Marquis de Sade) and an intellectual of the Revolution (Jean-Paul Marat). As Weiss's complete title reveals (see the Weiss entry for more on this), the play is set in an asylum for the insane— actually the socially "difficult" as well as the demonstrably mad—where de Sade "stages" the assassination of Marat in a roomful of outcasts, zanies, and gibbering lunatics. Brechtian songs and Artaudian shocks abound, especially in the final cataclysm in which the inmates riot and the head of the institution helplessly signals for the close of the curtain. *Peter Brook's brilliant staging for the *Royal Shakespeare Company in 1965 made Marat/Sade internationally notorious, a signet of what is "modern" in theatre as surely as

*Pierre Corneille's *Le Cid essentializes the Classical French stage or *Eugène Ionesco's *The Bald Soprano typifies the theatre of the absurd. And note that Weiss leaves his confrontation of the libertarian and the socialist unresolved. "He searches for meaning instead of defining one," says Brook, "and puts the responsibility of finding the answers back where it properly belongs. Off the dramatist and onto ourselves."

PIERRE CARLET DE CHAMBLAIN DE MARIVAUX (1688–1763)

The outstanding French playwright of the eighteenth century. Marivaux left thirty-five plays, about half one-acters and half full-length, almost all in prose, all but one comedies and most of those written for the Comédie-Italienne, the Parisian home of *commedia dell'arte. Though originally the Italian players communicated in their own language and mime, lines in French were added bit by bit to appeal more directly to the Parisian public. Finally the Comédie-Italienne took to commissioning whole scripts in French from French playwrights, more or less tailored to the company's talents. Here was where Marivaux built the bulk of his career, for his sole tragedy, Annibal (1720), was a failure; anyway, Marivaux was uncomfortable working with the ultra-conservative *Comédie-Française even in comedy. At the Comédie-Française, *Molière was the onlie begetter of comedy, to be imitated by his unworthy descendants. Marivaux preferred to write in an entirely different form of his own devising, one based entirely on "la surprise de l'amour" (the tender awakening of the love urge in young people), played out in conversations of the most delicate romantic nuances and philosophical overtones and often ignoring the bienséance (decorum) and vraisemblance (believability) of the Classical French stage—as in Marivaux's beloved transvestissement, in which two characters, often master and servant, change costumes to impersonate each other and test the powers of love.

Marivaux was not much appreciated in his lifetime. He was a model for many who followed him, however, and the celebrated marivaudage, the brilliant Marivaux dialogue, degenerated in less gifted hands till the term turned derogatory, meaning "pretentious and artificial writing." All the same, twentieth century revivals have reimposed Marivaux's genius, and among writers of comedy he is now second only to Molière in number of performances at the Comédie-Française, the Comédie-Italienne having been absorbed into the Opéra-Comique nearly two hundred years ago.

As time goes on, more of Marivaux's plays will be rediscovered, but for the present the official masterpieces are: the one-acter *Arlequin Poli par l'Amour* (Harlequin Tamed by Love, 1720); *Le Jeu de l'Amour et du Hasard* (The Game of Love and Chance, 1730), in which two young fiancés who have never met undergo the *transvestissement* with their servants in order to scout each other out; and *Les Fausses Confidences* (The Misleading Revelations, 1737), a romance delightfully replete with plot twists. Unlike Molière, Marivaux does not translate well, and is seldom performed beyond French-speaking borders. One problem is the intellectualized *tendresse* of the *marivaudage,* too finely spun to go well in other languages. However, Marivaux's background with the spirited players of the Comédie-Italienne inspired a more immediate, even primitive sense of humor that slips in now and then. In *Arlequin Poli par l'Amour,* a selfish fairy has kidnapped the droll Harlequin in a mad passion. Harlequin loves the sweet shepherdess Silvia, and resists the fairy's blandishments. Finally, she orders up a program of romantic music to stimulate him:

THE FAIRY: Dear Harlequin, don't these tender songs inspire anything in you? What do you feel?

HARLEQUIN: Hungry for dinner.

CHRISTOPHER MARLOWE (See Elizabethan Theatre)

MARSHALL W. MASON (See Circle Repertory Theatre)

MASQUE (See Scenery)

THE MATCHMAKER

*Farce in the classic manner by *Thornton Wilder, prem. Edinburgh, 1954.

The original version of this script, *The Merchant of Yonkers* (1938), was a famous Broadway disaster, flawed, apparently, because director *Max Reinhardt could not persuade his star, Jane Cowl, to take direction. Rather than fight her, he ignored her, setting up a gem of a production that must have been like a cross between Oscar Wilde and Molière. The play leaped to life whenever Cowl quit the stage and sagged when she returned. Out of town in Boston she broke down and begged Reinhardt to save her.

It was too late. But Wilder saved the script, offering his very slight revision a decade and a half later in, finally, a successful new production by *Tyrone Guthrie, with Ruth Gordon in Cowl's role of the versatile finagler who lives on "little pickings" out of other people's affairs. By this era, English-speaking farce tended to the tidy, with small casts of characters all more or less caught up in one plot line. But Wilder's love of antiquing led him to resurrect an older style of farce, with a large cast (seventeen players) and several major plot lines —so much in the way of action that Wilder broke the play into a by then almost unheard of four acts. Indeed, with no time to spare, he jumps right into one of the story threads the moment the curtain rises:

VANDERGELDER: I tell you for the hundredth time you will never marry my niece!

AMBROSE: And I will tell you for the thousandth time that I *will* marry your niece; and right soon, too!

The Matchmaker would almost certainly have remained a mainstay in the American comic repertory, but it was effaced within a decade by the very faithful musical adaptation, *Hello, Dolly!* (1964).

VLADIMIR MAYAKOVSKY

(1894–1930)

A versatile talent and a fanatic of the Revolution, Mayakovsky became one of Russia's major thespians when the Romanovs were overthrown, celebrating the collapse of the old order in *Mistyeriya Booff* (Mystery Bouffe, 1918). Mayakovsky was a designer and director as well as writer, and in all things he liked to experiment. This would eventually have got him into trouble with the authorities, as it did almost all Soviet artists above the level of the mediocre. But somehow Mayakovsky channeled his imagination into "correct" forms, and, in any case, censorship of the arts was relatively lax in the first years of the Revolution, when the economic reorganization of a continent and the annihilation of millions of political dissidents took precedence over the commissars' theatregoing. Even so, Mayakovsky died in his prime, committing suicide shortly after the premiere of his best-known play, *Klop* (The Bedbug, 1929), satirical science fiction in which a pre-Revolutionary bourgeois, frozen alive for fifty years, thaws out in the Soviet era and inadvertently looses upon the nation a similarly pre-Revolutionary bedbug whose bite infects the Soviet citizen with such dangerous signs of deviationist toadyism as smoking, gourmandizing, and dancing the night away.
(See also *Mystery Bouffe*.)

SIOBHÁN MCKENNA (1923–1987)

Irish actress. I have largely avoided standard encyclopediaese in this book—yet what was McKenna *but* an Irish actress? True, her great role was Shaw's *Saint Joan, Irish only by the author's national origins. Still, McKenna delivered a highly Gaelic maid of Orleans, a salty peasant in the first scenes rising, through a dazed, still valiance in the trial scene, to an ecstatic finale, the girl transfigured, universalized, but still resolutely sporting the husky McKenna brogue. (She also played Joan in Gaelic, in her own translation.) Such was McKenna's affinity for Shaw's Joan that her reputation in the part began to pursue that of *Sybil Thorndike, London's first and permanently legendary Joan.

However, McKenna's other great roles were those one would expect of a national heroine— Juno in *Sean O'Casey's *Juno and the Paycock,* the terminally unforgiving wife in Morton Wishengrad's *The Rope Dancers,* and, especially, Pegeen Mike in *John Millington Synge's *The Playboy of the Western World.* Irish women. Over the course of her career, McKenna also played a variety of parts, from Hamlet and Sarah Bernhardt (in John Morell's *Memoir*) to *Bertolt Brecht's very un-Shavian Maid in *St. Joan of the Stockyards.* Aficionados tend to see these as questionable detours. But if the old *star system encouraged the public's favorites to go on and on in their great roles as if they had a portrait curdling in a closet, these days no one can

Siobhán McKenna in her most famous role, Shaw's Joan of Arc.

spend a career playing Pegeen Mike—as McKenna revealed, finally graduating herself to the *Playboy's* subsidiary part of the Widow Quin as a Bernhardt never had to.

MEASURE FOR MEASURE

Christian parable on forgiveness by William Shakespeare, prem. London, 1604.

Like *The Winter's Tale, Love's Labour's Lost,* **Troilus and Cressida,* and *The Tempest, Measure for Measure* is a "dark comedy," though it is also the funniest of this group, its *comic relief spilling over into most of the scenes. Typically for the day, Shakespeare took his tale from another writer— George Whetstone, whose play *Promos and Cassandra* told of a virgin who yields to a judge's lust to save her condemned brother. The judge orders him beheaded anyway, and the head sent to the sister with the judge's compliments—but a sympathetic jailor borrows the head of a convenient casualty and saves the brother . . . and the sister now begs the king to pardon the sadistic judge: she loves and would therefore forgive him.

This is the subject of Shakespeare's play, too, but he suffuses it with a sermon on Christian humility, piety, charity. (The play was written for a Christmas presentation at court.) Whetstone's king has now become a duke, wandering through his city of Vienna in the guise of a friar and playing God, now planning the events, now letting men and women make their free life's choices, for good or ill, a kind of urban Prospero. Shakespeare makes the Duke's allegorical identity plain in his own speech:

DUKE: He who the sword of Heaven will bear
    Should be holy as severe . . .

and in others':

ANGELO: Oh my dread lord
    I should be guiltier than my guiltiness
    To think I can be undiscernible,
    When I perceive your Grace, like pow'r divine,
    Hath look'd upon my passes.

Angelo is the monster who wants to savor the sister —a nun, no less—and still crush the brother. Yet if we are to accept this strangely brooding and all the while exuberant play, we must agree with Shakespeare's insistence that the monster be forgiven—must forgive him ourselves. This difficult notion, as hard to accept as comparable messages in the Gospel, has lamed the history of this delightful and passionate comedy. It is far easier to believe in *The Winter's Tale's* absurdly unfounded jealousy or *Love's Labour's Lost's* delicate chastity than to pardon, as Shakespeare requests, the unpardonable.

MEDIEVAL THEATRE

The fall of ancient Rome meant the temporary disappearance of European theatre—theatre, at least, in the sense of plays written to be staged in playhouses. Professional entertainers remained—the "jugglers" (really all-around thespians who handled everything from acrobatics to singing) who toured from chateau to fairground to castle, or the various local amateurs who might favor a ceremonial occasion with a skit and a dance. The Classical authors slumbered through these Dark Ages, though Rome's Terence inspired a tenth century Benedictine nun of Gandersheim, Saxony to compose six plays in the Terentian manner but on Christian subjects. Named Hroswitha (also spelled Hrotsvitha and Roswitha), she is not only the first known woman playwright but virtually the first known playwright of the early middle ages.

At that, Hroswitha's plays were meant for reading by (and the instruction of) the elite. Like Terence, she wrote in Latin, obviously out of the reach of the bulk of the population even if someone happened to stage her scripts. Yet when the Church instituted what is called "liturgical drama," short plays illustrating Bible tales designed to be performed as a section of the Mass, the texts were in Latin though the "audience" was the commonality, utterly innocent of the learned tongue.

Two developments brought this early form of theatre closer to what audiences of today are used to: the moving of the "productions" out of the churches into less holy venues, outside on the church steps or in the marketplace; and the writing of the scripts in the vernacular. The late twelfth century Anglo-Norman play *Ordo Representationis Adae* (The Rite, By Theatrical Representation, of Adam, generally known by the French title, *Le Jeu d'Adam*) is a famous transitional work, written both in Latin and middle French and clearly planned for performance *outside* holy precincts. The title's use of the churchly "rite" and the secular "representation"—the choice term for theatre projects right into the early development of opera in the seventeenth century—symbolizes the church's ambivalent attitude toward theatre. It might instruct by giving delight: but whatever gives delight must be evil. Throughout the late middle ages, the controversy over the possible benefit or harm of theatre performance ranged up and down the Holy Roman Parish of Catholic Europe.

Nevertheless, rather than attempt to ban theatre, the Church simply retained direct control over it. Feast days seemed to call for recreation, anyway, and by the thirteenth century the "miracle" or "mystery" plays (from *ministerium,* "holy office") became a major, even spectacular civic event, directed by the Church, sponsored by city authorities, and staged by craft guilds and stimulated amateurs. The subject matter remained religious, but the scope of the undertaking was now so broad that entire cycles were raised up, to treat all the world from heaven to hell, all man's journey from Eden to Judgment Day. Later, in the fourteenth century, the form known as the "morality" play became the favored form, as an allegory on the human condition in which a mortal *protagonist shared the stage with embodiments of the virtues and the temptations. The most famous and most enduring of the morality plays is *Everyman,* apparently based on a Dutch original, *Elckerlijk,* in which the hero, faced with the Last Journey, asks Fellowship, Beauty, Kindred, Goods, Discretion, Knowledge, and such to accompany him in death. All draw back. Only Good Deeds is ready to support him.

THE MEININGERS

The popular name of the theatre company run in the late nineteenth century by George II, Duke of Saxe-Meiningen (1826–1914) in Thuringia, Germany. The Duke planned the productions in the overall, emphasizing historical accuracy in the decor, an innovation in this time. The Duke's actress wife Ellen Franz served as *dramaturg and acting coach, and Ludwig Chronegk directed the stage action, especially that of the detailed, naturalistic chorus work. Though contemporaries found the Meininger lead actors stolid and unadventurous, the crowd play dazzled—as when, in *Julius Caesar*'s assassination scene, the masses let out one terrifying cry in unison after Casca's dagger struck. Later, the Romans reacted so wildly to Marc Antony's funeral oration that one spectator wrote, "One feels oneself present at the beginnings of a revolution."

It was a theatre revolution, because the Meiningers toured to thirty-eight cities between 1874 and 1890, teaching the new style of ensemble from London to Moscow. Other theatres of the day respected the *star system as practiced by the stars themselves; the Meiningers observed a clarity of production as developed by the stage director. Such organizational elements as a full-scale rehearsal schedule, realism of portrayal, and authenticity of scenic atmosphere, common today, are novelties of the Meininger style.

MELODRAMA

Literally "a play with music," denoting the nineteenth century's fondness for performing plays with full-scale scores of incidental accompaniment, intermezzos, dances, and songs (as witness Mendelssohn's settings for Shakespeare's *A Midsummer Night's Dream* or Bizet's for Daudet's *L'Arlésienne*). Melodrama also referred to plays or scenes mimed to an orchestral "narration," especially useful in the many plays dealing with magic or horror. By the end of the nineteenth century, the scene of revelation or intrigue, spoken or emoted to a clobbering agitation in the orchestra pit, had become so routine that Gilbert and Sullivan could use it seriously in *Princess Ida* (1884) and burlesque it in *Ruddigore* (1887)—three years later, note—in music that does not switch styles: the serious had become its own burlesque.

Actually, the word *melodrama* had already taken

on a historically important meaning back in the second quarter of the century. *Managers in London sought to challenge the three "patent theatres," *Drury Lane, *Covent Garden, and (in summers only) the Haymarket. These "Theatres Royal" had held a monopoly on theatre performance in town since 1737, so the rival managers opened private theatres on the technicality that they were giving not plays but musical entertainments—"melodramas." These melodramas were fast-moving and violent, emphasizing the war of good against evil through the unrelieved heroism or villainy of stock types. Sudden, coincidental, or even incredible turns of plot led, almost as a rule, to a happy ending. This was a somewhat debased form of *Sturm und Drang tragedy, akin to the work of *Pixérécourt, to Gothic horror, and to crime thrillers. When British Parliament revoked the patents monopolies in 1843, the musical accompaniment was no longer legally necessary, and London theatres either dropped it or gradually limited it to a few effects like those in the Gilbert and Sullivan shows mentioned above. Thus the term "melodrama" now referred not to any musical association but to the contrivedly sensational, romantic, moralistic, and sentimental genre of playwrighting.
(See also *The Robbers* and *Uncle Tom's Cabin*.)

MENANDER (See Greek Theatre)

THE MERCURY THEATRE (See Orson Welles)

DAVID MERRICK (1912–   )

As Broadway's best known and most active producer from the late 1950s virtually to the present writing, Merrick symbolizes an era. Merrick's shows were *the* shows: generally classy, somewhat challenging, and even important, but seldom dar-

ing. Merrick seemed as much the disciple as the teacher, presenting the playwrights, genres, and stars just becoming or promising to become prominent, rather than discovering anything himself. He was fast on the mark, particularly in nailing down the rights to London hits—typically, it was Merrick who brought over *John Osborne's *Look Back in Anger,* the play that notoriously launched the "angry young man" epoch of Britain's theatrical resurgence. Also typical was Merrick's championship of the Big Broadway Musical, especially in his partnership with director-choreographer Gower Champion, king of the super-production; but Merrick rushed Champion only after Champion had established himself with *Bye Bye Birdie* (1960).

Merrick had a flair for creating excitement through controversy. His feuds and even physical battles with performers were the talk of The Street. He was even more celebrated for his PR tactics, as when he hyped an ailing show with blurbs credited to obscure New Yorkers who happened to have the same names as the newspaper critics, or when he paid a woman $250 to leap onstage during *Look Back in Anger* to slap actor Kenneth Haigh during one of his *tirades.

THE METHOD

An American version of coaching formulas developed at the *Moscow Art Theatre by Konstantin Stanislavsky around the turn of the present century. Correcting the artificial approaches of his day, Stanislavsky urged actors to develop a personal relationship with their characters, virtually to become their characters through inward identification. (The key term here is "emotional memory" or "affective memory," through which the actor brings into play feelings he has actually experienced, to develop an empathic presentation of his character.) The approach is the opposite of that of the typical actor of Stanislavsky's day, who presented his character externally, through artifice—as when, in discussing his craft, *John Gielgud says, "Of course, acting is pretense." Stanislavsky's "system" (as it is now called, to separate it from the Method, though the original Russian term *sis-*

tyema covers both words) aimed to dispense with pretense, with the virtuosity of the star, to replace it with the intensity of the realist.

The Method as an American institution begins in the 1930s, when the idealists of Broadway's *Group Theatre, led by Lee Strasberg, emphasized the actor's personality over the character's—and, because the Group rejected classic repertory for contemporary work, it also neglected such other aspects of training as diction and movement. After all, its mandate was to create a performing style for modern-dress naturalism, with the born diction and clumsy movement of the natural. But in the 1950s, Strasberg's school, the Actor's Studio, further dissociated its teaching from Stanislavsky's by encouraging, or at least tolerating, actors' wholly projecting themselves into their characters, giving their portrayals an admirable naturalism but limiting these performers to a single portrayal in play after play.

Method actors have thus been drawn away from the classics, where diction and movement, among other things, matter. Ironically, the Actor's Studio suffered a terrible disaster in London in 1965 in Strasberg's production of Chekhov's *The Three Sisters*—one of the plays that Stanislavsky's teaching originally brought to life. Strasberg's approach, then, both strengthened and weakened two generations of American actors, not only those who sat at his feet but others, who were subsumed by the Method osmotically. "The Method is in the air," says *Arthur Miller. "The actor is defending himself from the Philistine, vulgar public. I had a girl in *After the Fall* I couldn't hear . . . I kept on saying, 'I can't hear you.' She finally got furious and said to me, in effect, that she was acting the truth, and that she was not going to prostitute herself to the audience. That was the living end!"

VSYEVOLOD MEYERHOLD
(1874–?1940)

One of the twentieth century's directing geniuses. Meyerhold began as an actor, playing Tryeplov in Chekhov's *The Sea Gull* with the *Moscow Art Theatre. After four years with the company, Meyerhold left to forge a free-lance career as a director.

Had he learned from Stanislavsky? They were supposedly close, even Master and Pupil: yet Stanislavsky does not mention Meyerhold in his memoirs, and in fact Meyerhold's concept of the director ran exactly contrary to Stanislavsky's. The latter built his theatre on portrayal, on the acting ensemble. Meyerhold built his theatre on spectacle, decor, production. Thus Meyerhold failed utterly to come to terms with the prima donna Vyera Komissarzhevskaya (1864–1910) when he assumed direction of her company in 1906. Although most of Meyerhold's productions for the star were star *vehicles—Henrik Ibsen's *Hedda Gabler,* Maurice Maeterlinck's *Pelléas et Mélisande* and *Sister Beatrice* —Meyerhold upheld a *Gordon Craig–like view of the theatre as entirely a director's and designer's medium, the actors to serve as their puppets. "I see clearly into the future," Komissarzhevskaya told Meyerhold, "and I say that you and I will not be traveling the same road together." She handed her company's direction to her brother Fyodor (later, in America, Theodore) Komissarzhevsky (1882–1954).

All for the better, for a director as visionarily epic as Meyerhold could not tolerate star actors. It is true that his players were treated as marionettes —but they were the marionettes of a spectacular stage. Meyerhold was similarly cavalier with his public, anticipating the "performing versions" of Shakespeare, Chekhov, or Brecht typical of the present-day super-director. Politically committed to the Bolshevik Party, Meyerhold embraced the political theatre, seeing the treatment of contemporary history as a first principle of his art. Take for example *R. Y.* (1924), a look at a failed attempt by Western capitalists to defeat the Revolution. (The title refers to the Westerners' subversive syndicate, known as *Razrusheniya Yevropi,* "For the Destruction of Europe.") Typically, this was less a written text than a commission to order, worked up by Mikhail Podgayetsky under Meyerhold's supervision, from an assortment of science fiction and social problem novels. Meyerhold's decorative concept for *R. Y.*'s production comprised a group of wooden screens, continually in motion as the capitalist soldier Jens Boot agitated for the syndicate and a united proletariat of Europe labors to connect Petersburg (by then Lyeningrad) to New York by a secret tunnel. A characteristic Meyerhold *coup de *théâtre:* Boot, fleeing Russia when his identity is discovered, runs straight upstage as two of the screens rush toward each other. Just before they touch, he squeaks through, and they press on into the wings. Boot has disappeared. (The actor playing Boot simply rode one of the screens into the wings to manage the illusion of having vanished.)

Unfortunately for Meyerhold, *"socialist realism," with its asinine narratives, sentimentalized characters, and simplistically realistic productions, became the only type of theatre that the Party would tolerate. Meyerhold's experimental technique—and his refusal to abandon it when challenged—put him in jeopardy. It was useless for him to defend himself by emphasizing his early support of the Revolution, his insistent staging of Soviet playwrights. Meyerhold was guilty of committing independent art in a totalitarian state. Or perhaps it was because he was Jewish, another capital crime in Stalin's Russia. Like Jens Boot, Meyerhold vanished: arrested, possibly tortured, surely imprisoned and executed. A few weeks after Meyerhold disappeared, his wife was murdered with the most appalling brutality, her eyes gouged out and her body hacked to pieces.

"It must have been burglars," purrs Stalin.

THOMAS MIDDLETON (See Revenge Tragedy)

JO MIELZINER (1901–1976)

The most prolific American set designer for Broadway shows, from the 1930s to the 1970s, Mielziner connects the first American experiments in breaking away from the fixed box set (see Scenery) into more free-flowing and nonrealistic constructions. Before Mielziner, such innovators as *Robert Edmond Jones laid the groundwork for scenery as more than background—as atmosphere, metaphor. Mielziner continued this work: in the literally fabulous view of a bridge hurled into the sky with a slum huddled underneath it in *Maxwell Anderson's *Winterset* (1935), in the sense of work-

*Jo Mielziner in *naturalism and romance. Above, Mielziner's set for *Elmer Rice's* Street Scene—literally a street scene, a recreation of a New York tenement front —and, below, the pageantry of Mielziner, costumes as well as sets, for *Katharine Cornell's 1936 St. Joan.*

ing-class New Orleans hovering around the tenement apartments of *Tennessee Williams's *A Streetcar Named Desire* (1947), in the giant, reproachful bed that dominated Williams's *Cat on a Hot Tin Roof* (1955).

Robert Edmond Jones had very little to work with technologically, but Mielziner's career saw Broadway through astonishing revolutions in the sheer mechanics of set changing. Mielziner became especially adept in the use of light to catch the audience's eye with one set *downstage while the next was being readied *upstage, out of view. This was particularly useful in musical comedy, which by the 1930s was being written around a multiplicity of scenes, as opposed to the single box set still favored at the time in nonmusical drama. Here, in the musical, Mielziner most truly made his mark. He was identified especially with the musicals of *George Abbott and with the biennial Rodgers and Hammerstein musical plays, from *Carousel* (1945) through *Pipe Dream* (1955), but also left his mark on a variety of musicals from *Gay Divorce* (1932) through *Guys and Dolls* (1950) to *1776* (1969).

THE MILK TRAIN DOESN'T STOP HERE ANYMORE

Allegory by *Tennessee Williams, prem. New York, 1963.

Death, evil, and morality preside over the passing of life. In a compound of villas overlooking the Bay of Naples, Flora Goforth dictates her memoirs. Flora has had enough adventures to fill several volumes; now she is dying, attended by her golden rule–abiding secretary and a countess known as the Witch of Capri. They are joined by a handsome

poet, a parasite of the European leisure class who is known as the Angel of Death for his penchant for soothing the last hours of the aged or infirm. Williams deftly allows the symbolism to shine through, never pushes it, and the play works, if one wants it to, simply as a character study.

Unfortunately, the excellent original production failed, and Williams prepared a revision introducing a pair of actors who function as a combination of *Kabuki stagehands and *Greek chorus. Now they are unobtrusively fetching props; then they are commenting on the action as obscurely as possible. The revision was presented on Broadway in 1964 in a completely different production, with Tallulah Bankhead's wildly erratic Flora and Tab Hunter's, uh, indescribable poet. However, even the flawed revision shows Williams's ability to lyricize the fear of aging and death and the yearning for sexual release, to remain tender in the face of terrifying drives. "To be good," Flora announces, "a poem's got to be tough and to write a good, tough poem you've got to cut your teeth on the marrow bone of this world." Note one false note, inevitable on the Broadway of Williams's era: the Witch of Capri is surely meant to be an old queen rather than the oddly bitchy woman that Williams gives us. The film version, entitled *Boom!,* corrected the euphemism, casting *Noël Coward in the part.

ARTHUR MILLER (1915–   )

An accident of time banded Miller with *Tennessee Williams and *William Inge. In fact, Miller, however contemporary his dramaturgy and production associates, relates back to the realistic stage of Henrik Ibsen and George Bernard Shaw, the turn-of-the-century reformers who saw the theatre as a medium of social improvement. Miller's theme is atonement for guilt, preferably in an act of social betterment. Miller's villains selfishly ignore the community—Joe Keller, in *All My Sons* (1947), sends American flyers to doom with inferior equipment in order to honor a war industries contract. Business is business. Eddie Carbone, in *A View From the Bridge* (1955 as a one-acter; 1956 revised to full length), breaks, for a personal grievance, his

Brooklyn neighborhood's taboo against turning in illegal immigrants. Miller's heroes *defend* the community—John Proctor, in *The Crucible* (1953), goes to his death rather than put his name to any writ of the witch-hunting Salem court. Von Berg, in *Incident at Vichy* (1964), gives his Aryan certificate to a Jewish man, saving him through a kind of nationalistic self-sacrifice.

Guilt plays a more personal, less social role in Miller's most successful play, *Death of a Salesman* (1949). Here the *protagonist is a victim of community, a loser in a society run by winners for the other winners. To some, this great postwar success seemed a culmination of the American leftist stage of the 1930s, an artistically experimental domestic drama, socially informed but humanistically based. There is something terribly benighted in the salesman Willy Loman's belief in an American ability to be successful by being liked just because you insist on being likable. Yet there is something terribly believable in it, terribly American—and something terribly final in Loman's suicide, almost the death, symbolically, of the American dream (far more subtly handled here than in *Edward Albee). Typically, Loman's is a remorseful and self-sacrificial death. Thus Miller tells us that Loman is a hero.

Miller made himself the hero, or protagonist, or at any rate the guilty party in *After the Fall* (1964). New York's theatre reviewers could not get past the autobiographical outline in the work, confusing the message with the messenger. Fascinated by Miller's use of his then late wife Marilyn Monroe, critics reviled Miller for doing what every artist does, treating his experiences. This was the beginning of Miller's search for an alternate medium, another Broadway. The impossible dream. What is there for an American playwright but Broadway? Yet what major playwright of our time has enjoyed less support from reviewers and public than Miller? With Williams and Albee the annual unattended flop became almost an event of itself; Miller moved more carefully, weightily, than they. Yet *The American Clock* (1980), an epic retrospective of 1930s culture, lasted two weeks. There was a time when Miller was the kingpin American dramatist, the "intellectual" to Williams's "poet." When *David Merrick met Miller for the first time, Monroe was with Miller—Monroe, the most spectacular woman in the Western world, not to put too fine a point on it. Our Helen. Yet, as the stage-struck Merrick later recalled, "I just couldn't stop staring at Arthur Miller."

(See also *The Crucible* and *A View From the Bridge*.)

MIME (See Pantomime)

MIRACLE PLAY (See Medieval Theatre)

THE MISANTHROPE

Comic tragedy by *Molière, prem. Paris, 1666.

Well, it is a comedy—yet it has a tragic hero, Alceste, doomed to be sensible, direct, and above all honest in a society that deals in diplomacy, flattery, and falsehood. It is Molière's sad aperçu that the admirably impractical Alceste must abandon Paris for the desert. Only there can he practice nobility.

HELENA MODJESKA (1840–1909)

"The Polish Bernhardt." Modjeska maintained one of the largest repertories in the Western world, from Shakespeare to Scribe, Racine's *Iphigénie* to the American melodrama *East Lynne*. She became an American citizen, but is buried in Cracow.

MOLIÈRE (1622–1673)

Jean-Baptiste Poquelin. If Molière had not won the favor of his King, Louis XIV, his work would have been severely compromised, for almost from the first Molière offended many powerful people with his satires. At that, two of Molière's finest plays, *Tartuffe* (1664) and *Don Juan* (1665), were banned, Louis or no Louis, the first before it was even publicly performed complete (the King sat in on a reading of the first three acts), the second in the middle of its first season, when it was the talk of Paris. And while *Tartuffe* got to the stage in six years, *Don Juan* was never given again in Molière's lifetime.

These are the encyclopedist's Molière clichés, as are: his inauspicious beginnings as an upholsterer's son; his thirteen-year tour of the provinces when his first tries in Paris flopped; his return to Paris and controversial, intrigue-bedeviled reign as *manager, player, and star of his own company; his rivalry with the troupe in the Hôtel de Bourgogne (where *Corneille and *Racine were given); his behaving not unlike a character in a play by Molière when he took a wife twenty years his junior; his collapse during a performance of *The Imaginary Invalid* and death that night, unshrived by clergy because both priests sent for refused to come; and his burial in consecrated ground only after the King's intercession. (Even then, a rumor rambled through Paris that Molière's corpse had been secretly exhumed and thrown into an unhallowed mass grave.) To cap this cascade of biographical data is the historical merging, by royal decree, of Molière's troupe (which had already merged with that of the Théâtre de Marais) with that of the Hôtel de Bourgogne, thus creating the *Comédie-Française, the national theatre of France.

What is more important than all this is the ever-surprising theatricality, the vitality and insight, of Molière's plays. They read well enough on the page. But Molière was not just a playwright—Molière was a thespian, wholly of the theatre, and his compositions breach the gulf between literature and performance, between language as its own art and language as a tool of art. As Molière wrote, he plotted the "*business," the touches, the play of personality that his particular actors would bring to the roles. Molière's aesthetic had been colored by popular farce, especially by the improvisational vigor of *commedia dell'arte*. How can mere scripts convey the energy of Molière on stage? We can

*Jean-Louis Barrault and Madeline Renaud in Molière's Le Misanthrope. *Note his bewilderment and her insouciance: everywhere Alceste turns, society horrifies him.*

read Corneille and Racine, imagine their relatively static theatre in our armchairs—but Molière comes to life only in the liveliest performance.

How astonishing he must have seemed in seventeenth century Paris, in comparison with the grave, almost sacerdotal grandeur of heroic tragedy. Molière not only reinvented "popular" comedy as an important form of French theatre; he invigorated the French stage in general. It is fitting that the French national theatre call itself "la maison de Molière" (the house of Molière), for he could not lose his freshness and bite, even after his death, after the absorption of his troupe—even, we now know, after passing centuries have made merely admirable relics of his greatest contemporaries. Today, Corneille and Racine are generally performed only in France, and at least partly as a matter of national honor. Molière remains internationally vital.

The subjects Molière analyzed were contemporary, but they still are: intellectual affectation in *Les Précieuses Ridicules* (The Silly Bluestockings, 1659); jealousy in *Sganarelle; ou Le Cocu Imaginaire* (The Imaginary Cuckold, 1660); the fair man too noble for his frivolous society in the tragically comic *Le Misanthrope* (1666); greed in *L'Avare* (The Miser, 1668); the plebeian plutocrat in *Le Bourgeois Gentilhomme* (1670), one of the many court entertainments that Molière concocted with the composer Jean Baptiste Lully; shallow, know-nothing erudition in *Les Femmes Savantes* (The Learned Women, 1672); hypochondria in *Le Malade Imaginaire* (The Imaginary Invalid, 1673). In these and other plays, Molière delights in testing the obstinacy of delusion to the verge of disaster. He lampoons the poseur and his fools alike.

Perhaps Molière's most enduring satire is that of hypocrisy—specifically that of the religious fake—in *Tartuffe,* often called Molière's masterpiece and possibly the most frequently performed play in French theatre. Of all Molière, *Tartuffe* inspired the most ferocious attacks by his contemporaries, so it must have hit home in the Paris of the 1660s. Yet what could be more relevant today, in the America of the television cleric who professes love and Christian charity yet preaches hatred and grubs for money? *Vive* Molière, literally.

(See also *Don Juan* and *Le Misanthrope.*)

FERENC MOLNÁR (1878–1952)

In his native Hungary, Molnár is almost primarily known as a novelist, but his plays have traveled much better than his fiction. The bulk of Molnár's theatre comprises the equivalent of Parisian *boulevard comedies and romances, such as *A Testör* (The Guardsman, 1911), in which an actor tests his wife's fidelity while disguised as a military man; or *Az Üvegcipö* (The Slipper, 1923), *Cinderella* updated to contemporary Budapest; or *Játék a Kastélyban* (A Performance in the Castle, generally known in P. G. Wodehouse's translation as *The Play's the Thing,* [1924]), in which an adulterous indiscretion is disguised to look like a scene from a play rehearsal. To learn that *Alfred Lunt and Lynn Fontanne launched their wryly sensual partnership with *The Guardsman* on Broadway in 1924 is to understand Molnár's teasing eroticism, effervescence, wit. Yet Molnár's masterpiece was totally out of the Molnár style—*Liliom* (1909), a working-class tragedy with elements of the fantastic.

Molnár has lost his once-encompassing hold on the world stage. But *Liliom* survives, in a way, as the source (faithfully reinvented in a period New England setting) of Rodgers and Hammerstein's musical *Carousel* (1945). The Jewish Molnár fled Europe before World War II, and saw the original *Carousel*. He loved it.

THE MOSCOW ART THEATRE

Konstantin Stanislavsky (1863–1938) and Vladimir Nyemirovich-Danchenko (1859–1943) founded this world-famous company in 1898, after a fifteen-hour conversation in which it was agreed that Stanislavsky would handle the theatrical side of things and Nyemirovich the literary matters. So, one would make the ultimate decision on what plays to stage, and the other would make the ultimate decision on how to stage them. The adoption of *Anton Chekhov as house playwright, more or less, gave the new troupe a solid grounding in composition; and Stanislavsky's direction (and acting) of Chekhov's four masterpieces, *The Seagull,*

The world's acting teacher: Konstantin Stanislavsky as Gaev in Chekhov's The Cherry Orchard.

Uncle Vanya, The Three Sisters, and *The Cherry Orchard,* introduced the Moscow Art's unique ensemble style, naunced and realistic as opposed to the *melodramatic noises raised by more conventional groups. "I like to create deviltry in the theatre," Stanislavsky gloated in his memoirs, claiming to love the passages of "hokum." Yet in fact he helped clear the stage of hokum and deviltry. Before forming the Moscow Art, Stanislavsky had staged and acted in such overripe pieces as *The Bells* (called *The Polish Jew* in Russia, *Polskiy Yevryey*), *Henry Irving's old standby. But once the Moscow Art was set up, Stanislavsky looked for quality of writing and naturalism of character, the two to merge in performance in a very spiritual poetry. Stanislavsky's legacy is regarded as sacrosanct, and even today the Moscow Art performs its Chekhov in what is intended to be a replica of the original productions. However, theatre lives from day to day. Observing "tradition" for nearly a century invariably results in petrification, not fidelity. Nowadays, Moscow's aficionados prefer the Vakhtangov and the Sovryemyennik ("Contemporary") Theatres, younger and bolder.

MOTHER COURAGE

"A chronicle of the Thirty Years War" by *Bertolt Brecht, prem. Zurich, 1941.

In full: *Mother Courage and Her Children.* She has three, lost one by one to the devouring variety of war: the flight before the enemy, the price the noncombatant must pay for moral absolutism, the punishment of a soldier for an act that is called heroic during the hostilities and a crime after the armistice. This in itself makes Mother Courage sympathetic, no matter how she is interpreted; and there is something thrilling in that last sight of Brecht's *protagonist, trundling her wagon of goods to the song of marching soldiers, alone, in despair, and unkillable. She is a survivor, we think, an energy, a heroine. Yet Brecht insisted that she is above all a leech, a capitalist, a war profiteer. *She is not sympathetic.* This is the inherent problem in the epic theatre style. Brecht needs realism of place, action, character, if he is to persuade us of his vision. But realism of character gives us people we are bound to sympathize with. Brecht's program is supposed to "alienate" us intellectually—but his talent attracts us empathically. He outfoxes himself with his own feelings.

True, some actresses defeat him with a cosmetic portrayal, trying to throw away the cynical finagler and embrace the mother and her courage—though in fact Brecht named her ironically. The first Mother Courage, Therese Giehse, infuriated Brecht with her majesty; he vastly prefered his wife Helene Weigel's reading, a staple of the *Berliner Ensemble, even a wonder of the world. Still, while Brecht's disciples harangue us with explanations of the dialectic and the mythos and the logical inevitability and other ten-dollar concepts, we inevitably find more in *Mother Courage* than the Marxist cartoon we are apparently supposed to appreciate. We find one of the most intrepid illustrations of the devastation of war that the theatre has ever produced, dominated by the bitterly sage, humanistically rich, and—sorry—*heroic* figure of Mother Courage herself.

MOURNING BECOMES ELECTRA

(See The Oresteia)

ALFRED DE MUSSET (1810–1857)

One early failure was enough to turn de Musset away from the stage; he took to writing plays to be published and read, not performed. This in itself gave him certain liberties denied the working playwrights, and his best scripts have a dash and diversity of feeling that suggest the amateur genius who needs his own good opinion and has contempt for all other opinions. Critics of his time, had de Musset been writing directly for the theatre, would have shaken their heads at his casual blending of the comic and the heroic, the graceful and the grotesque; they had trouble with Shakespeare for the same reason. The complete set of de Musset's theatre came out under the title *Comédies et Proverbes,* because so many of his titles *are* proverbs: *On ne Badine pas Avec l'Amour* (One Mustn't Trifle With Love, written 1834, prem. 1861), *Il ne Faut Jurer de Rien* (One Must Never Take Oath on Anything, written 1836, prem. 1848), *Il Faut qu'une Porte Soit Ouverte ou Fermée* (A Door Should Be Open or Closed, written 1845, prem. 1848), *On ne Saurait Penser à Tout* (One Cannot Think of Everything, 1849). The "proverb" is in fact an old French theatre genre, a prose one-acter with a small cast in which dialogue (and very little action) illustrates a point of folk or salon wisdom. *Il ne Faut Jurer de Rien,* for instance, teaches a young man not to take an oath that women are fickle— the woman he selects to prove his argument turns out to be incorruptible. Just as well: she's his fiancée. However, *On ne Badine pas Avec l'Amour* upsets the merry atmosphere of the proverb with a bitter *dénouement: Perdican tries to make the coquettish Camille jealous by pretending to love Rosette. Now Camille gives in—but Rosette overhears the two making up and dies of a broken heart.

De Musset was artistically and socially in the very center of the French Romantic movement, an associate or colleague of *Victor Hugo, *Alfred de Vigny, Alphonse de Lamartine, and Charles-Augustin Sainte-Beuve. Thus de Musset's masterpiece, *Lorenzaccio,* probes the dark side of the heroic temperament, the sinner in the saint. The titular hero, Lorenzo de' Medici, determines to assassinate his corrupt cousin Alessandro, ruler of Florence.

To win Alessandro's confidence, Lorenzo must adopt his cousin's sensually lurid ways, and does so with such expertise that he fears he has himself become corrupt. The critic Jules Lemaître, noting de Musset's fondness for the proverb, dubbed *Lorenzaccio "On ne Badine pas Avec la Débauche"* (One Mustn't Trifle with Debauchery), but the play was thought so shocking that, though written in 1834, it was not staged till 1896, with *Sarah Bernhardt playing Lorenzo as a *trouser role. De Musset wrote *Lorenzaccio* on a trip to Italy with his lover George Sand, the empress of the Romantic salon, which makes the play even more important historically than artistically. The trip was a notorious scandal of the day, for de Musset fell ill in Venice and Sand fell in love with his doctor. All three then came to Paris, where they played out the drama in full cry, at soirées, in the theatres, on the boulevards. "The greatest thunderstorms I know of," Sainte-Beuve wrote, describing the episode. De Musset and Sand "spent all this last month in denouncing one another, in being reunited, in tearing each other apart, and in suffering." Swinburne summed it up: "Alfred was a terrible flirt and George did not behave as a perfect gentleman."

MYSTERY BOUFFE

Communist miracle play by *Vladimir Mayakovsky, prem. Petrograd, 1918.

When *Vsyevolod Meyerhold staged the premiere of Mayakovsky's pageant, the Russian Revolution was still so new—exactly one year old—that the old Tsarist Pyetyerburkh (Petersburg) had been Russianized into Pyetrograd but not yet renamed, as it soon would be, Lyeningrad. *Mistyeriya Booff* was the first major act of Soviet theatre, a combination, as the title implies, of medieval fantasy and whirlwind *bouffe* (antic comedy) allegorically proclaiming the new age of Revolution. The scene moves from the North Pole to heaven and hell, and the cast includes Lloyd George, Clemenceau, Tolstoi, Methusaleh, the devil, and a chorus of machines who once oppressed the world's workers but who will now help them build their great universal commune.

THE MYSTERY PLAY (See Medieval Theatre)

N

GEORGE JEAN NATHAN
(1882–1958)

As if he were embarrassed at being a theatre critic, Nathan cultivated the persona of a womanizing dandy who enjoyed slashing plays, playwrights, and actors with the delicious overkill of a ruthlessly nuanced wit. He was a snob, but a perverse one, loftily resisting the politically ideological theatre of the 1930s when it was the hottest thing on Broadway, yet insistently debunking the chic view, popularized in the late 1940s after the *Old Vic's New York visit, that British acting was superior to American. Nathan also shamelessly touted the old-fashioned gags-and-legs musical over the artistic "musical play" developed by Oscar Hammerstein with Jerome Kern and Richard Rodgers.

Yet in an age that took its cultural advice mostly from hack newspapermen who moved up from the sports pages so they could date showgirls, Nathan was an intellectual and a stylist. He wrote many books, including an annual season's retrospective, from 1942–43 to 1950–51, with an essay on every show that played Broadway. It was a dazzling tour de force. Other writers would have run out of ideas by the third flop whodunit, the fourth comeback vehicle, but Nathan's droll mind was inexhaustible. Most important, he had the vision to acclaim *Eugene O'Neill, *Sean O'Casey, and *William Saroyan long before their bandwagons were rolling.

NATIONAL THEATRE

A concept: in the cultural capital of each country, there will be a theatre company, supported by the state, dedicated to an ambitious schedule of classics and new works, and emphasizing native art but taking in Aeschylus, Shakespeare, Racine, Brecht, with the odd foray into Feydeau, Schnitzler, Odets, Stoppard. Ideally, the company might maintain several stages, perhaps a small space for especially experimental work. The stock of productions will be permanent, true *repertory, and the versatile, seasoned acting troupe will trade off roles from night to night, Monday's Orestes playing Mercutio on Tuesday, Wednesday's Mother Courage recovering on Thursday to bounce back as Millamant on Friday. The two of them might join forces for absurd cameos in *You Can't Take It with You on Saturday. The most original directors and designers will superintend, free of the commercial pressures of the unsubsidized, free-market theatres.

Ironically, most attempts to create national theatres from scratch have failed, especially in America. (See entries on The New Theatre, The Civic Repertory Company, and The Lincoln Center Repertory Company.) The great national theatres of the West are more often given state sanction after having established themselves privately. Thus the Old Vic eventually grew into the National Theatre of Great Britain and the Comédie-Française was formed, by royal command, by the merging of competing troupes.

(See also The Comédie-Française, The Old Vic, and The Royal Shakespeare Company.)

NATIONAL THEATRE OF GREAT BRITAIN (See The Old Vic)

NATURALISM

"Naturalism" and "realism" have been used indiscriminately as synonyms for a lifelike presentation: authentic decor, colloquial dialogue, strictly mimetic behavior. However, naturalism in the theatre more correctly denotes a late nineteenth century movement dedicated to the representation of life, as opposed to the artificial dialogue, florid acting styles, and candybox productions in favor at the time. Naturalism sought above all to *reproduce* life—as Hamlet urges the players, "to hold, as 'twere, the mirror up to nature." But different writers see a different nature. Questioned on a rather poetic love scene in his otherwise strictly naturalistic *Before Sunrise,* *Gerhart Hauptmann answered, "Can I help it if nature is sometimes beautiful?"

Realism, at about 1900, was a vague term for a broader ideal, urging playwrights to treat important social issues till then thought unseemly or heretical. Realist playwrights tended to employ naturalism as well, but only up to a point. *Henrik Ibsen, for example, was far more interested in capturing the reality of human feelings and relationships than in exploiting the atmosphere of a city street scene or a family dinner, as Hauptmann was. (But see The Fourth Wall, for a statement by Ibsen that appears to link realism and naturalism absolutely.)

A good example of a naturalistic play in the early stages of the movement is Émile Zola's *Thérèse Racquin* (1873), deliberately written and staged to deal with life as lived. "Make it important," runs Zola's famous warning, "make it simple, make it true."

Even more naturalistic were Stanislavsky's *Moscow Art Theatre stagings of *Chekhov around the turn of the twentieth century, because Stanislavsky, unlike Zola, commanded a troupe of actors straining to create a naturalistic style. On the other hand, a realistic play might be one of *George Bernard Shaw's comedies, artificial in their abundant wit and occasional fantastic touches (the descent into the underworld in *Man and Superman,* for instance), but realistic in their grasp of social theme, such as the subject of prostitution in *Mrs. Warren's Profession* (1902).

Careless use of "naturalism" and "realism" debased them. The productions of *David Belasco were called both naturalistic and realistic because of the photographic persuasiveness of their settings or the evocative power of Belasco's special effects. But in subject matter and writing, Belasco was a fabulist, a rhetorician, a contriver of pageants—anything but a realist. Later, in the 1920s, *Eugene O'Neill was called a realist for the humanist scope of his themes and the documentary atmosphere of his waterfront settings and use of dialects. But by then naturalism had been overrun by experimentally nonrepresentative production, and realism had become a vapid buzz term.

(See also *Awake and Sing!, The Changing Room,* and *Salvation Nell.*)

ALLA NAZIMOVA (1879–1945)

Nazimova was the first of the great theatre talents to be ruined by the movies. Or so it was said. Even while praising Nazimova's Madame Ranyevsky in *Chekhov's *The Cherry Orchard,* critic John Mason Brown couldn't resist a dig at her "exoticism, as it had been tamed since her days in Hollywood." In fact, Nazimova lent an astonishing realism to her stage work and theatricality to her films. She was adaptable. Yet her fame rests on only two very different kinds of parts: classic prima donna leads in *Ibsen, Chekhov, and *O'Neill; and weepie heroines in Hollywood silents.

Nazimova began at the *Moscow Art Theatre, reintroduced Ibsen to Broadway, then went into silent films, including adaptations of Ibsen's *A Doll's House* and *Oscar Wilde's *Salomé* (in flam-

Alla Nazimova, in a PR pose during her early Broadway heyday, before the years of Hollywood decadence and consequent Broadway comeback atonement. Catch her at her best in the 1940 film Escape *some night on the Late Show, for a taste of one of the century's greatest actresses.*

boyant decor with an all-gay cast, in homage to Wilde) amid the treacle. As she had delighted Broadway with her ability to change her face and body language with each character, so did Nazimova enliven the Hollywood scene with her house named the Garden of Alla and her swimming pool shaped like the Black Sea, in tribute to her birthplace, Yalta—not to mention her parties, which included séances and even more advanced drollery. As talkies came in, her vogue was on the wane. She hoped her lustrous voice would save her. She presented herself to Irving Thalberg, MGM's production chief and a buff of Broadway class. But Thalberg remembered an incident years before, in which Nazimova had mistaken the youthful producer for an office boy and uttered an affront. Thalberg never forgave the slight, and more or less ran Nazimova out of Hollywood. She returned to Broadway, a penitent, to redeem herself in great roles, including Lavinia Mannon in the first production of O'Neill's *Mourning Becomes Electra*.

This is the legend of Nazimova: imperious, bizarre, gifted but "ruined." However, the legend obscures Nazimova's impact, in her pre- and post-Hollywood years, as one of the transitional figures who connected the brilliance of the nineteenth century Star to the characterological dexterity of the twentieth century Actor. At her own theatre in the 1910s, then with Eva Le Gallienne's *Civic Repertory and the *Theatre Guild in the 1930s, Nazimova was an inspiration and guide to every committed American actor. So much for the legend; this is the truth.

VLADIMIR NYEMIROVICH-DANCHENKO (See The Moscow Art Theatre)

JOHANN NESTROY (1801–1862)

Theatre history praises this *actor-manager and playwright of the popular Viennese stage grudg-

ingly, on the charge that he was less original than his predecessor, *Ferdinand Raimund. Nestroy had wit, it is said: but Raimund had heart. Then, too, unlike the self-starting Raimund, Nestroy was an enthusiast of the adaptation, rewriting foreign works into his unique Viennese patois and running off burlesque versions of operas (especially Meyerbeer and Wagner) and tragedies. Worst of all for his reputation, Nestroy was amazingly prolific (to a total of some eighty-odd works). Plodders resent the fleet talent.

The truth of the matter is that Raimund's plays are fascinating curiosities, while Nestroy still holds the stage, expecially for *Der Zerissene* (The Jaded Sophisticate, 1844), which looks forward to the Vienna of *Arthur Schnitzler. Nestroy's sources include, most interestingly, Dickens's *Martin Chuzzlewit*, which Nestroy produced as *Die Anverwandten* (The Relatives, 1848). But his most famous adaptation is *Einen Jux Will Er Sich Machen* (He Wants to Frolic, 1842), because *Thornton Wilder and *Tom Stoppard made modern versions of it.

NEWSBOY

*Agitprop sketch developed by the Workers' Laboratory Theatre's Shock Troupe from a poem by V. J. Jerome, prem. New York, 1933.

In under fifteen minutes of choral chanting, jump-cut theme associations, and headline-like text, we see a newsboy hawking the eructations of the establishment press—sex and scandal. At length, the newsboy throws down his papers to join the chorus in their choice of reading matter: the Communist Daily Worker.

THE NEW THEATRE

This was one of New York's few attempts to establish a genuine *repertory theatre, with a revolving schedule of plays and a permanent ensemble (plus guest turns by stars). It was an expensive proposition: a tremendous, opera-sized house was built on Central Park West at Sixty-second Street. It was a classy endeavor: Shakespeare, Sheridan, Arthur Wing Pinero, Ned Sheldon, and Maurice Maeterlinck headed the bills. But it lasted only two seasons, from 1909 to 1911, and its failure was so total that the theatre itself was thought jinxed. Renamed the Century, it hosted a number of one-shot spectacles, including performances by the Metropolitan Opera and *Max Reinhardt's *A Midsummer Night's Dream*. But all Broadway sighed with relief when the structure was demolished in 1929.

What went wrong? Too much ersatz class and too little genuine style was the general opinion. In fact, the New simply didn't offer an alternative to what one could see in the commercial theatres, except some elaborate scenery. It might have recovered from its early setbacks in time, but repertory, like any other Broadway attraction, doesn't have time. In the hit-or-flop system of American theatregoing, you are a hit or you are a flop.

NICHOLAS NICKLEBY (See The Life and Adventures of Nicholas Nickleby)

NŌ THEATRE

Where Japan's *Kabuki theatre is known for its epic flamboyance, this older national form is short and spare. Developed in the late 1300s and early 1400s by Kanami Kiyotsugu and his son Zeami Motokiyu, Nō ("art") theatre uses all-male casts, heavy wooden masks, elaborate costumes, and a highly stylized performing style based on dance and chanting. An evening of Nō drama calls for some five different plays, each of a different genre —the warrior's ghost play, the moralistic play, the noble lady play, the patriotic play, and so on— each separated from the next by comic interludes called kyōgen ("crazy speech"). As with Kabuki, Nō players obsessively maintain their traditions, making this the oldest major theatre type still presented in its original form.

OBLIGATORY SCENE (See *Scène à Faire*)

SEAN O'CASEY (1880–1964)

Here is Ireland's greatest playwright—no, what of *Sheridan, *Wilde, *Shaw, *Beckett? Then: Ireland's most *Irish* playwright. Most native. John Casey, *renominato* Sean with an O' by force of Gaelic commitment, astonished the *Abbey Theatre with his "Dublin trilogy," *The Shadow of a Gunman* (1923), *Juno and the Paycock* (1924), and *The Plough and the Stars* (1926). Here were *naturalistic urban working-class tragedies after two decades of quaint folk fantasies that had sent the Abbey to the edge of bankruptcy. O'Casey was a hero—but whose hero? Hero of the proletariat? of the arts? of Irish culture?

He was all three, and remained so throughout his life. O'Casey's plays are fine art, and politically interested, and a true Ireland, city and country. Like his Abbey predecessor *John Millington Synge, he sees a land charmed by weak men but kept alive by strong women. The central couple in *Juno and the Paycock* is representative, he a wastrel and she a survivor, even when their son is killed (for betraying an I.R.A. comrade), their unmarried daughter pregnant, and their joy in an inheritance blown away. But unlike Synge—unlike anyone—O'Casey wrote of the working class as if nothing mattered but showing on the stage their struggle for life, their war against a sterile, repressive Church and a murderous colonial State. A dazzling man, O'Casey catches one up and spares one nothing. His heroes are cowards. His ideals are beyond reach. His *patria* will never happen. Yet he persuades one that Irish life is worth the struggle, that Church and State may be overthrown, as they are in the late plays *Cock-A-Doodle Dandy* (1949) and *The Drums of Father Ned* (1959).

Historically, O'Casey divides into the Abbey phase of the three famous titles, then into the exile phase so typical of the Irish artist. The disintegrating work is *The Silver Tassie* (1929), a brilliant study of a young athlete who glories in his superiority, suffers a crippling wound in World War I, and returns to his old haunts no more the cynosure but a pathetic waste in a wheelchair. Among O'Casey buffs and critics, *The Silver Tassie* is controversial, for while the Abbey was still doing turn-away business with *Juno* and the *Plough*, *Yeats persuaded the Abbey board to reject *The Silver Tassie* on weak grounds. Yes, the text wanders; yes, the second of the four acts blatantly shifts gears from *naturalism to *expressionism in its look at the battlefield. Still, this is prime O'Casey and no play to reject. As it was, O'Casey had been quarreling with Abbey personnel; so, rather than strive with the board, he declared war on the house and left to live in England.

At this point, O'Casey (1) withered in increasingly pseudo-poetic scripts or (2) reinvigorated his art in fanciful allegories a little less dynamic than his Dublin trilogy—depending on one's critical stance. The second seems more likely. Some of the later plays, such as *The Star Turns Red* (1940), are so intently Communist that they are almost nothing else. And surely O'Casey never again wrote characters as vital as the principals of *Juno and the Paycock* or the many friends, neighbors, and hangers-on in *The Plough and the Stars.* It is a little convenient that, at the *Plough*'s premiere, Yeats faced down a howling mob with the declaration, "This is [O'Casey's] apotheosis"—too convenient because it suggests that all that followed was sequelae and declension. No. Turning away from colloquial naturalism, O'Casey explored symbolism and fable, always less immediately gratifying in theatre than plain storytelling. But wait; his day of glory will come.
(See also *The Plough and the Stars.*)

CLIFFORD ODETS (1906–1963)

"A poet of the decaying middle class," *Harold Clurman called him, "with revolutionary yearnings and convictions." Though a committed leftist, Odets seldom dealt in propaganda; *Waiting for Lefty* (1935) is the notable exception. This one-acter, depicting a meeting of unionized cab drivers deciding whether or not to strike, turns its theatre into a meeting hall, its audience into the union members. Showing us a series of vignettes in which people come one by one to politically radical life decisions, Odets then exposes the union leader, opposed to the strike, as a corrupt hireling of the bosses. Then we learn that Lefty, our hero, has been murdered by goons. How much more do you need to hear? "Well, what's the answer?" Odets cries to the audience—and, in union meeting halls and makeshift theatres across the country in 1935, the public leaped to its feet screaming, "Strike! *Strike!* STRIKE!"

Sheer *agitprop. But for the most part Odets used politics as a factor in the shaping of human destiny rather than as ideology per se. The Communist press came down heavily on *Awake and Sing!* (1935), written before *Lefty* but performed immediately after, for in place of *Lefty*'s stark sketches all reaching toward a clear-cut socialist resolution, the fully rounded *Awake and Sing!* treated the ambiguities and ambivalences of family life. However, the theatre reviewers in the big newspapers began to praise Odets for his ability to reconcile the political stage with incisive, thoughtful composition. Of all the leftist playwrights of the American 1930s, Odets seemed the sole figure capable of universalizing through the specific, of extrapolating art from his lower middle-class and proletarian Jewish characters. Odets was a master of dialect, too. More than one critic has likened Odets's New Yorkese to the Dublin poetry of *Sean O'Casey, and Harold Clurman called *Awake and Sing!*'s dialogue "a compound of lofty moral feeling, anger, and the feverish argot of the big city."

Unfortunately, as the 1930s wore on, Odets seemed to lose his grip on the dynamics of his text, the little guy's search for a place in a system that equates freedom with money. Only *Golden Boy* (1937), about a young Italian violinist who escapes the slums through prizefighting, saw Odets in full strength. He had already begun writing for Hollywood, a move that was regarded as a treacherous sell-out, especially for the prize playwright of the *Group Theatre, Odets's home company since his apprenticeship before *Lefty*. Indeed, *Golden Boy*'s hero, Joe Bonaparte, is killed in a car crash, as if Odets were atoning for his own escape from the "slums" of socialist theatre. Nevertheless, he resumed his screenwriting career. Ironically, his later plays, such as *The Country Girl* (1950)—a commercial success—lack the intensity and insight of Odets's script for *The Sweet Smell of Success* (1957), a film set in the sleazy night world of the gossip columnist and the PR hustler.
(See also *Awake and Sing!*)

OFF-BROADWAY

This informal system of small theatres (299 seats or under, a definition deriving from fire depart-

A typical sight of late-middle off-Broadway: Edward Albee's one-acter The American Dream (1961), so basic to the off-Broadway program that it was revived almost annually through the 1960s—usually, as here, with Sudie Bond as Grandma. Jered Barclay plays the Young Man, the "American dream" of the title and, through Albee's tragic-sardonic symbolism, an analogue of American cultural sterility: big and wonderful but emotionally and intellectually empty. Still, he makes a notable entrance into Albee's bourgeois household of dreary schmudls. "Well, now," says Grandma, "aren't you a breath of fresh air!"

ment regulations), mostly in New York's Greenwich Village and on lower Second Avenue, became prominent in the early 1950s as a response to the increasingly commercial attitudes of Broadway. The big theatres flattered the public; off-Broadway would challenge it. Broadway doted on bourgeois sex comedies; off-Broadway would revel in European *absurdism. Broadway maintained its hit-or-flop ethic; off-Broadway would restage worthy plays that had failed uptown. Broadway worshipped the *star system; off-Broadway would give unknowns a chance at career-making leads. Broadway mistrusted overt political statement; off-Broadway would incline to political rebellion as concomitant with artistic rebellion. Broadway's notion of an important playwright was, say, Paddy Chayevsky; off-Broadway would introduce the dangerous names of the European avant-garde, even the terrifying *Jean Genet. Broadway regarded any departure from traditional *fourth-wall *naturalism as daring; off-Broadway would experiment in mime, improvisation, theatre verité, and nudity.

Off-Broadway's great work, then, included the introduction or reinvestigation of such diverse playwrights as *Ionesco, *Pirandello, *Brecht, *Edward Albee, and *Lanford Wilson; the Circle-in-the-Square's 1952 revival of *Tennessee Williams's *Summer and Smoke,* which made a star of Geraldine Page, and 1956 revival of *O'Neill's *The Iceman Cometh,* which made a star of Jason Robards, Jr; the nurturing of such companies as *The Living Theatre, *The Ridiculous Theatrical Company, and *The Open Theatre; the staging of Barbara Garson's *MacBird!* (1967) and Rochelle Owens's *Futz* (1967), the one a savage Shakespearean spoof of American politics and the other a larky attack on American redneck fascism.

Art, experimentation, rebellion, spoof: this is postwar off-Broadway, perhaps best encapsulated in the 1954 staging of Weill and Brecht's *The Threepenny Opera* in Marc Blitzstein's translation at the tiny Theatre de Lys on Christopher Street, legendary not only for the authenticity of Lotte Lenya's "life is a cabaret and I'm a little bored with the whole thing" survivor persona but for its phenomenal seven-year run. (Even that was too short for the *New York Times'* *Brooks Atkinson: whenever off-Broadway's helter skelter wore him down, he'd close a review with "Bring back *The Threepenny Opera!*") However, off-Broadway only flowered in the postwar era, did not originate then. Many of the Village's theatres are half a century old, relating off-Broadway to the *little theatre movement of the post–World War I years, when idealists first conceived of an "alternate" stage in defiance of the strait commercialism of the big houses uptown. Off-Broadway had its own off-Broadway in "off-off-Broadway," another system of yet smaller theatres, often makeshift "spaces." Off-off is defined not only by cultural rebellion but by its relatively skimpy budgets and nonunion staff.

OH! CALCUTTA!

Nude vaudeville "devised by *Kenneth Tynan," prem. New York, 1969.

The contributing authors ran to the hip—*Sam Shepard, Jules Feiffer, John Lennon, Leonard Melfi, with a touch of prestige in the name of *Samuel Beckett—but the audience tended to petit-bourgeois suburbanites culturally slumming. The title derives from the French ("Oh, quel cul t'as!": roughly, "Gee, you've got a nice butt!") and the nudity was indeed persuasive, from the gracefully defiant opening of the robed cast one by one dropping their robes. At least one scene, a nude pas de deux by (originally) Margo Sappington and George Welbes, drew favorable comment. But was this show an act of artistic liberation or a smutty put-on? When Beckett learned that his nonvisual sketch, *Breath,* was to be staged with apparently copulating bodies, he angrily withdrew it—yet his name remained in the show's credits throughout its original run.

THE "OLD VIC"

One of London's most historic theatres, built in 1818. The fond nickname refers to former titles of this cramped building—The Royal Victoria Theatre, the New Victoria Palace, even The Royal Victoria Hall and Coffee Tavern. It was built across the Thames from the *West End, just southeast of Waterloo Bridge, and so catered to the local work-

Oh! Calcutta!: *George Welbes and Margo Sappington in the famous pas de deux (to Sappington's choreography). The number proved influential within a limited compass, spawning a genre still popular in Las Vegas nightclub revues. I prefer* Nicholas Nickleby *myself.*

ing class more than to the carriage trade. But when Lilian Baylis took over at the start of World War I, she instituted an ambitious repertory emphasizing Shakespeare with, eventually, such notable actors as *Sybil Thorndike, *John Gielgud, and *Laurence Olivier. This formed the basis for The National Theatre of Great Britian, which formally occupied the Old Vic in 1963 and moved to its new home a few blocks north in 1976.

LAURENCE OLIVIER (1907–   )

Olivier may be the century's great instance of the stage actor influenced—not subsumed, not recycled, not ruined—by the movies. The British Olivier came into an age still working out the tensions between the old fustian declamation and post-*Stanislavsky "inward" invention of character. Olivier found the middle road in a kind of outgoing subtlety. His epiphany came about in Hollywood during a crisis on the set of William Wyler's film of *Wuthering Heights* in 1939. The producer, Samuel Goldwyn, had been horrified by the leering, storming Olivier he had seen in the rushes and, under pressure, Olivier found a way to present a larger-than-life character through concentration rather than presentation.

Olivier had already logged a varied stage experience—playing straight man to *Noël Coward and Gertrude Lawrence in *Private Lives* in London and New York in 1930–1931, impersonating (more or less) John *Barrymore in the London production of *George S. Kaufman and Edna Ferber's *The Royal Family* in 1934, and starting in on the big Shakespearean parts, from Mercutio and Henry V to Hamlet and Macbeth. But the experience of working out a plausible Heathcliff in *Wuthering Heights*—that is, recreating a somewhat old-fashioned villain-hero without the aid of the old-fashioned approach—forced Olivier to rethink. By the time of the postwar reorganization of the *Old Vic, where Olivier made his celebrated tour de force of playing *Sophocles' Oedipus and *Sheridan's preening Mr. Puff (in *The Critic*) on the same bill, his heroic characters came off with amazing nuance, his comic characters with exquisite wit. The Old Vic took the double bill to New York on its

first American tour, in 1946, and Olivier's versatility set off a debate on the respective merits of British and American acting. Olivier seemed to typify the British style in his almost ferocious elegance—were not American actors flat and narrow by comparison? But Marlon Brando, in *A Streetcar Named Desire,* seemed to typify the American style at its best in his naturalistic energy. Olivier was palatial, Brando lifelike.

Or so the argument ran. In fact, Brando proved exceptional, despite his many imitators. Olivier proved exponential, and British actors remain more experienced, more dextrous, more poetic than their American colleagues. One reason why might be Olivier's example—his vitality regenerated in delicacy of approach: his Heathcliff. Critic *Kenneth Tynan called him "a player of unparalleled animal powers miraculously crossed with a player of extreme technical acuteness." Thus Olivier startled the Western world with the bellowing terror of Oedipus's cry of recognition; but also bemused his public as Shakespeare's Hotspur (in *Henry IV*), stuttering every time he tried to pronounce the letter 'w'. As England's "first" actor, he accepted the privilege of becoming the first director of the National Theatre of Great Britain, from 1963 to 1973.

EUGENE O'NEILL (1888–1953)

The tense question is, Is he the Great American Playwright? His proponents cite O'Neill's majesty of theme—for instance, as the prophet of genetic doom, of the sins of the fathers inherited by the sons; or as the exposer of that most basic of human frailties, the delusional lie that allows us to pass as "well-adjusted." There is as well O'Neill's greatness as a historical figure, Broadway's acknowledged leader in its experimental 1920s, then insistently pursuing an essential American form, the family chronicle. O'Neill is important, too, as a breakaway figure between America's old-fashioned and modern theatres, literally the child of the old style as the son of actor *James O'Neill but metaphorically the patricide who, absorbing the lessons of *Wedekind and *Strindberg and helping to found the *little theatre movement, guided a generation of insurrectionary playwrights. Their work, along with O'Neill's, called up a new kind of actor, more developed—more honest—than the James O'Neills and their Counts of Monte Cristo.

O'Neill's detractors point out the awkwardness of the writing, the glaring repetitions of thematic phrases and general verboseness, the hopeless flatness of the dialogue, the irritating regional and ethnic dialects. "O'Neill," wrote Mary McCarthy, "belongs to that group of American authors, which includes Farrell and Dreiser, whose choice of vocation was a kind of triumphant catastrophe; none of these men possessed the slightest ear for the word, the sentence, the speech, the paragraph . . . What they produce is hard to praise or condemn; how is one to judge the great, logical symphony of a tone-deaf musician?" Even some playwrights object to O'Neill's playwrighting. "There's no finesse at all," *Arthur Miller said. "He wrote with heavy pencils." O'Neill, in an oft-quoted line from *Long Day's Journey Into Night* (1956), seems to agree with McCarthy and Miller. Father Tyrone (the James O'Neill part) says to young Edmund (the Eugene part), "Yes, there's the makings of a poet in you all right," and Edmund replies, "The *makings* of a poet. No, I'm afraid I'm like the guy who is always panhandling for a smoke. He hasn't even got the makings. He's only got the habit."

Actually, O'Neill's arguable grasp of language improved as he went along. *Lynn Fontanne, the original Nina Leeds in *Strange Interlude* (1928), joked that O'Neill *had* to improve, if only because *Strange Interlude* was so long. Nine acts affords plenty of practice: "By the time he finished *that* he was writing fine." The jest is accurate, in a way: by the time O'Neill finished off his prolific youth, his eagerness to fill the 1920s with his work, he *was* writing fine, detailing character in dialogue that is blunt but telling, seldom lyrical and never witty but increasingly natural, direct, powerful. His critics feel that the Great American Playwright should have more than the *makings* of a poet. But for all O'Neill's struggles with language, he did from the first command the instincts and skills of a great *dramatist*—the ability to build his characters into action, his actions into themes, to raise up compelling theatre. The scripts play better than they read, because his stories serve his vision— "the drama of souls," he called it. Even as one stirs

restively at a dry moment in one of O'Neill's marathons, or shakes one's head at a questionable outburst, O'Neill's stubborn, clumsy majesty carries one along.

Certainly O'Neill is the most written-about American playwright; and, but for a dead spot of neglect in the decade between *The Iceman Cometh* (1946) and *Long Day's Journey into Night* (1956), just before and after his death, he has infinitely outlasted his predecessors, contemporaries, and successors in sheer survival of oeuvre. Their lives were careers; his was a saga. He was actually born on Broadway, right in the middle of the old *star system show shops of his father's world. But O'Neill came up through the new ranks of the artist rebels of the alternate stages. O'Neill emphasized the one-acter, a defiance of the Broadway edict that short pieces aren't popular, aren't worth doing. (Forty years later, they became the stock-in-trade of the young American playwright.) O'Neill defied the star system that had supported and ruined his father—made him successful but drained him of talent. O'Neill swore that he would not sell out when he got to Broadway, and he never did.

He had concentrated his theatregoing on what little of the avant-garde came to Broadway—*Nazimova's *Ibsen, the touring *Abbey Theatre. But he also responded to the best of commercial Broadway—*Edward Sheldon's *Salvation Nell,* for instance. In a way, much of O'Neill's output suggests a Strindberg or Ibsen writing an American *melodrama. Early O'Neill especially conforms to this contradictory paradigm—in, say, the tautly purchased ironies of the domestic drama *Beyond the Horizon* (1920), O'Neill's first full-length play and, some say, the beginning of the modern American theatre; or in the sea-haunted, comically serious *Anna Christie* (1921). The narrative structures and characters are familiar, but the vitality of the relationships and the way the author develops the atmosphere of gripping doom is new to Broadway, at least from an American writer. Furiously churning out his texts, fearful that he'll lose control of one idea while working on another, O'Neill maps out his terrain and themes: the family scene, the war of honor against money, the romance of the idealist and the opportunist, and, especially, the loser's delusion that keeps him looking like a

Three ages of Eugene O'Neill: the observing boy, the highly promising young artist, and, at length, the Great American Playwright.

winner. "The lie of a pipe dream," says someone in *The Iceman Cometh,* "is what gives life to the whole misbegotten mad lot of us, drunk or sober."

By 1920, O'Neill has arrived. Now he must experiment, must bend Broadway away from his father's stage. *Expressionism stimulates O'Neill through its evocative Freudian subtexts. In the early 1920s, O'Neill applies expressionism in *The Emperor Jones* (1920) and *The Hairy Ape* (1922); in the late 1920s, he turns the mind-opening utterances into asides in *Strange Interlude* (1928) and *Dynamo* (1929). Here, particularly, is the O'Neill his detractors laugh at, freezing the action as his characters murmur dire soliloquy. However, *The Great God Brown* (1926) had already proposed a suaver O'Neill, working the expressionistic glosses into the conversation—the feelings into the realism. O'Neill centered his pretensions as a major dramatist in *Mourning Becomes Electra* (1931), a marathon drawn from *Aeschylus. O'Neill expanded his identity in comedy—*Marco Millions* (1928) and *Ah, Wilderness!* (1933), the one a satire on American commercialism (in the figure of Marco Polo), the other sentimental nostalgia. After one more play, *Days Without End* (1934), he fell silent. He continued to write, but refused to be staged.

In about a decade and a half, O'Neill had superintended the reorganization of the American theatre, from his father's stage to his own. From the *actor-manager to the *Theatre Guild, O'Neill's producing firm in his prime. From the ham to Charles Gilpin's Brutus *(The Emperor)* Jones, Louis Wohlheim's Yank (in *The Hairy Ape*), Nazimova's Lavinia Mannon in *Electra.* From melodrama to realism. From *The Count of Monte Cristo* to *The Iceman Cometh.*

O'Neill's return to Broadway after World War II was underappreciated. The *Iceman* is difficult, the production was flawed, and O'Neill's vogue had passed. The last production of his lifetime, *A Moon for the Misbegotten* (1947), drew so poorly on its tryout that it did not come to Broadway. But the 1950s became O'Neill's great decade of enthusiastic, awed reconsideration just as the 1920s saw his time of hell-for-leather arrival. The 1956 Circle-in-the-Square *Iceman* revival, the publication and then production of *Long Day's Journey into Night* that same year, the first Broadway mounting

O'Neill's pencils never bore down more heavily than in the composition of The Iceman Cometh, *repetitive and strident, a forced epic; yet utterly true and noble and overwhelming. Here we look in on the original Theatre Guild production, with James Barton (standing, left foreground) as Hickey the salesman and Dudley Digges (third from right) as Harry Hope (note the typical O'Neillian heavy-handed, yet so appropriate, symbolism), the saloon proprietor. Hope, O'Neill tells us, is lies. But Hickey is the wart on your delusion.*

of *A Moon for the Misbegotten,* in 1957, and the appearance of *A Touch of the Poet* (1958), as well as O'Neill's imposing reputation in Europe . . . all this seemed to reveal O'Neill all over again, but freshly, as, yes, the Great American Playwright. For surely no one who had come forth since challenged the heavy pencils of his drama of souls. With the regional dialects and expressionism of his 1920s put by, we perceived a clean, clear writer of immense power and insight. His style had changed, but not his worldview; on the contrary, his vision seemed surer than ever, especially in his insistent take on life as a series of consequences of

past actions. "The past *is* the present, isn't it?" says Mary Tyrone in *Long Day's Journey.* "It's the future, too. We try to live our way out of it, and can't." Written in 1941, this last major work—so painfully autobiographical that O'Neill wanted it withheld for decades, not the three years between his death and the world premiere in Stockholm— is utterly unlike the sprawling, dense texts of early O'Neill. Yet it is the same O'Neill, and the most basic O'Neill, as if he had been writing this same play over and over until he perfected it. The piece is tight—four acts but one day; virtually four characters, but one family; four stories, but one story, on the essentials of life: loyalty, love, ideals, delusion, honesty; the past as the present. "It's the future, too," isn't it? A timelessly instructive work, unrivaled by any other American play. Who could have written the Great American Play but the Great American Playwright?

(See also *Anna Christie, The Iceman Cometh,* and *The Oresteia.*)

JAMES O'NEILL (1847–1920)

The actor father of *Eugene, supposedly a gifted performer who declined in flash vehicles, especially *The Count of Monte Cristo,* which he played an alleged six thousand times over the years around the country. We of today meet him in the father, James Tyrone, in Eugene's *Long Day's Journey into Night,* looking back on his life's choices with gloom.

THE OPEN THEATER (See Joseph Chaikin)

THE ORESTEIA

Trilogy by *Aeschylus, prem. Athens, 458 B.C.

In this extraordinary work we see the world pass out of barbarism and tribal justice into the modern voting democracy. Before the action begins, the House of Atreus is playing out a curse stemming from adultery, blood-murder, and cannibalism. As the action proceeds, we encounter yet more murder, wife's of husband and son's of mother. The young prince Orestes is caught in the kind of trap the Greeks loved: if he doesn't avenge the slaying of his father Agamemnon, the Eumenides—the Furies—will torment him. But Agamemnon's killer was Agamemnon's wife; and if Orestes slays his mother, the Eumenides will torment him. He is damned whether he does or doesn't.

He does. The Furies immediately swarm about him and set to driving him mad, but the immortals intervene. Orestes is tried for matricide,

Athena breaking a tie vote to acquit him in the name of Athenian democracy. The Atrean family curse is broken and no more will families make law unto themselves. The passionate "justice" of slayings and counter-slayings will be replaced by the compassionate courts of the enlightened city-state. Thus Aeschylus gives his fellow Athenians a glorification of their reason, clarity, nobility. This is self-congratulation. (It might also be a warning to Athens not to let its democratic structures fall to tyranny.) But, after all, was not Athens the mother of democracy and—better yet—the mother of Western theatre?

While scanning the resolutions and disruptions of the idea of "community," Aeschylus created a thrilling confrontation of character. Each of the three plays centers on a trial. In *Agamemnon,* Clytemnestra "tries" her husband for the ritual murder of their daughter. In *The Choephori* (also called *The Libation Bearers*), Orestes similarly treats Clytemnestra for Agamemnon's murder. Last, *The Eumenides* presents the more formal trial of Orestes. Thus, in a way, the *Oresteia* has no single *protagonist. The central player varies from play to play.

Nominally, Orestes is the protagonist. And of course it is he whose choice—dishonor his father or kill his mother—forms the very basis of the work. However, only Clytemnestra of the entire cast appears in all three plays (in *The Eumenides,* of course, she is a ghost, exhorting the Furies to haunt her son), and hers is surely the greatest role —one of the greatest in all Greek theatre. On her entrance, tending her altar fire as a chorus of old men intone an exposition of foreboding, she endures an entire scene in silence, as if her rage for revenge must be ritually mastered before she can trust herself to speak. When she does, it is to give voice to the only thing that has occupied her for ten years: the Trojan War is over and Agamemnon returns! Thrusting aside "unity of time," Aeschylus jumps ahead a few days to show the homecoming, a stupendous scene: Clytemnestra tensely veiling her intent, Agamemnon contemptuous, suspicious . . . and at length accepting, to parade into his palace to be slaughtered in his bath. Hear, then Clytemnestra's war cry as he steps over the threshold: "Eleleleleu!"—not literally in the manuscript, but referred to by Cassandra, Agamemnon's war booty, a bit later. As many commentators have noted, Aeschylus sees Clytemnestra virtually as a man. Her motherhood outraged by the sacrifice of her daughter, she refuses the role of wife and assumes that of warrior, even taking for her lover the weak Aegisthus much as Agamemnon takes Cassandra. Given Aeschylus's interest in the individual's struggle against the demands of society and the subsidiary role women played in the Greek world, his Clytemnestra is a fascinating conception—a "villain" who is in the right.

The *Oresteia* is not only the outstanding masterpiece of the Greek stage, but the only Greek play cycle that has come down to us with its three narrative sections intact. (The fourth section, the usual comically refreshing *satyr play, *Proteus,* has vanished, although Paul Claudel wrote a *Protée* [1929] to accompany his French translation of the *Oresteia.*). Thus this trilogy bears an epic weight that outmatches other surviving Greek versions of the tale, *Sophocles's *Electra* and *Euripides's *Orestes, Electra,* and his two *Iphigenia* plays, which develop the alternate reading of the legend: Iphigenia is not sacrificed, but spirited away by the immortals.

Many modern playwrights have offered their own versions of the saga of the House of Atreus—*Racine, *Goethe, *Giraudoux, and *Sartre among them—some in mere allusion to the characters, others faithfully reinterpreting. *T. S. Eliot's *The Family Reunion* (1939), like all his drawing room plays, claims a Greek antecedent, in this case Aeschylus's *Oresteia* itself. So Eliot said. But his Orestes, Harry Monchensey, may or may not have murdered—he isn't sure—and it is his *wife* who is dead, lost overboard on a cruise. His mother is very much on the scene, especially in *Peter Brook's 1956 London revival, when she was played by the redoubtable *Sybil Thorndike. Eliot included a (silent) chorus of Furies, but experiments in naturalizing an essentially fantastic convention failed. Visible, they were absurd. Dimly glimpsed, they were . . . absurd. Brook turned them into great featureless bird-like visions filling the set's huge windows, a valid compromise. Still, but for the occasional use of the principals as a chorus, murmuring their lines now in solo, now in ensemble, Eliot totally misses out on the hieratic splendor of Aeschylus, even the basic turns of his plot.

*Gerhart Hauptmann's *Die Atriden-Tetralogie* (1940–1944) accords with the Iphigenia-as-survivor legend, indeed makes her the protagonist. The first and fourth plays, *Iphigenie in Aulis* and *Iphigenie in Delphi,* are the "heavy ones," almost ecstatically meaningful, while the middle two, *Agamemnons Tod* (Agamemnon's Death) and *Elektra,* run—rather quickly, too—through the action of Aeschylus's first two Atreus plays. As Hauptmann's final work it disappoints, more impressive during the bloodshed than in the poetic *Iphigenia* plays.

There is no Iphigenia at all in *Eugene O'Neill's *Mourning Becomes Electra* (1931), the most faithful modern rendering of Aeschylus. But Electra, now, is the protagonist. Moreover, O'Neill's three plays, *Homecoming, The Hunted,* and *The Haunted,* correspond with Aeschylus's trio only in their first two thirds. There is no climactic trial of the matricide in O'Neill, no exaltation of the development of community justice. For O'Neill's major break with Aeschylus is the American's total disregard of the sociopolitical background that so impelled the Greek. What attracted O'Neill to the *Oresteia* was its depiction of a curse haunting a family through its generations, of inevitable inheritance passed from youth to age, past to present, reckless times to pensive times. It was O'Neill's obsession that you cannot "laugh at your ghosts," as his Electra puts it. Or, as the hired hand Seth phrases it, "There's been evil in that house since it was first built in hate—and it's kept growin' there ever since." The curse of the House of Atreus. If O'Neill parts company with Aeschylus's broader historical theme, he partakes of the Greek's psychology of genetic doom.

The literal correspondence between Aeschylus and O'Neill are fetching. We move from Argos to a small New England seaport town. In place of the Trojan War, O'Neill gives us the Civil War—slyly cuing in the period's typical Greek-Revival architecture. In the *Theatre Guild's original production, designer *Robert Edmond Jones drew up the curtain on a portico of columns that drew a muffled gasp from the audience, as if, expecting a drawing room or boudoir, they had sighted the Parthenon. Agamemnon becomes Ezra Mannon, Clytemnestra Christine, Electra Lavinia, Orestes Orin, Aegisthus the sea captain Adam Brant. For a chorus, O'Neill uses a few townspeople and the Mannon handy man Seth, who punctuates the action with snatches of the folk song, "Shenandoah."

JOE ORTON (1933—1967)

This British playwright's unique blend of the facetious and the macabre made him notorious. Orton is a moralist of the amoral, a comic of the brutal. He defaces the walls of the culture with lubricious graffiti—much as he defaced library books with his lover Kenneth Halliwell, a prank for which the pair spent six months in jail. This is Orton, a jester running the blade. Authority figures are his villains, bourgeois values his targets; and business as usual is his scene—as he reveals the lying and arranging that authority usually indulges in. The usual, then, is in fact the unusual in hiding.

In Orton, those not guilty of crimes of passion would like to be. *Entertaining Mr. Sloane* (1964), Orton's first produced play, looks in on a middle-class household playing host to an attractive drifter who, by curtain's fall, is set up as the unwilling boyfriend of the man (for six months) and his sister (for the other six)—though the deliciously entertaining Sloane has murdered their father. The dialogue is flat yet strange, a naturalized *Pinter:

KATH: Isn't this room gorgeous?
SLOANE: Yes.
KATH: That vase over there comes from Bombay.
  Do you have any interest in that part of the
  world?
SLOANE: I like Dieppe.
KATH: Ah . . . it's all the same. I don't suppose
  they know the difference themselves.

The odd tilt of this humor made Orton difficult to stage, at first: directors kept trying to match his sense of spoof with a "put on" staging, whereas Orton insisted that his texts would work only in the most realistic productions.

He was gone before he came into his prime. *Loot* (1966) was a mock thriller, *What the Butler Saw* (1969) a blend of *Oscar Wilde's social comedy with *West End sex farce. But Orton was already over, his head bashed in by Halliwell, who then drugged himself to death. Horrible though it be

to say, it was a finish that, in his plays, Orton might have giggled at.

JOHN OSBORNE (1929—   )

"I doubt if I could love anyone who did not wish to see *Look Back in Anger*," wrote *Kenneth Tynan, expressing the stimulated amazement theatre people felt on its premiere in 1956. "It's the best young play of its decade." It was better: the universally acknowledged start of a new era in British theatre. Osborne was the playwright of the moment with the work of the age. However, *Look Back in Anger* broke with tradition not in form but in tone. The vehemently articulate Jimmy Porter —the avatar of the "angry young man"—seemed to gather unto himself the rage of the working class, the unprofessioned college man, the restless husband, and, ultimately, the raving intellectual: all of which Jimmy Porter is. It was his point of view rather than the somewhat familiar triangle romance in the seedy midlands flat that made *Look Back in Anger* the best young play. After seeing it, the drawing room playwright *Terence Rattigan predicted that a new generation of dramatists would sweep in in Osborne's wake saying, "Look how unlike Terence Rattigan I'm being."

Osborne redoubled his advance with a decade and a half of plays in various styles, usually with belligerently egotistical male *protagonists as alienated as Jimmy Porter: *The Entertainer* (1957), alternating naturalistic family scenes with Archie Rice's onstage music hall act to symbolize fading England in a metaphor of vaudeville; the *Brechtian *chronicle play *Luther* (1961); the modern-dress *Inadmissable Evidence* (1964), about a lawyer; *A Patriot for Me* (1965), another chronicle play, this one on the secret homosexual life of Austro-Hungarian officer Alfred Redl; *The Hotel in Amsterdam* (1968), a conversation piece; the even more *Chekhovian *West of Suez* (1971). Already, Osborne had lost his hold on critics and public. Where once his plays, invariably premiered at London's *Royal Court Theatre, were rushed to Broadway, the last few were not imported. Osborne had at least claimed the services of some of the greatest actors of the day—Kenneth Haigh's Jimmy Porter, *Laurence Olivier's hollow, strutting Archie Rice, *Albert Finney's Luther, Nicol Williamson in *Inadmissable Evidence,* Paul Scofield in *The Hotel in Amsterdam,* and Ralph Richardson in *West of Suez.*

OTHER PLACES

Four one-acters by *Harold Pinter, prem. London, 1982.

Both in London (at the National Theatre, directed by Peter Hall) and in New York (at the Manhattan Theatre Club, directed by Alan Schneider), only three plays were given, each a different set. Interest has centered on *A Kind of Alaska,* about a woman who fell into a trance at the age of sixteen and wakes up (just as the play begins) thirty years later on the very Pinteresque line, "Something is happening." However, the quartet as writ-ten forms a unit, each play about a character or characters more or less helplessly displaced. In *Victoria Station,* a taxi controller tries to make contact with a disoriented driver. In *Family Voices,* a mother and her late husband try to reclaim their wandering son. In *One for the Road,* a police-state interrogator terrorizes a liberal and his family. Further to unite the plays, a line in one piece will relate to another piece, or all the others: as when *Victoria Station*'s driver reveals that a woman is sleeping in his back seat (recalling *A Kind of Alaska*), or when *Family Voices'* young wanderer speaks of a "secret policeman," cuing in the Orwellian velvet of *One for the Road. Other Places* reminds us how strongly Pinter depends on his actors, for there is almost no decor, no movement, even—*Family Voices* consists entirely of three isolated people. The inarticulate alienation of individuals, however technically related they might be, is one of Pinter's most constant themes, and the one-acter a constant form in his work. A very . . . Pinteresque evening.

PANTOMIME

Generally, this word refers to the silent art by which the performer conveys his subject entirely through nuanced body language and facial distortion. (The older term for this is "dumb show.") In a more limited use, pantomime denotes a British form of musical comedy popular at Christmas, using fairy-tale plots, low comedy, and audience participation.

JOSEPH PAPP (1921–   )

As head of the New York Shakespeare Festival, which he founded in 1954, Papp is as central to the world of modern *off-Broadway as *Charles Frohman was to turn-of-the-century carriage trade pop or *David Merrick was to postwar anglophile, big musical Broadway. Despite its name, derived from Papp's insistence on producing free summer Shakespeare (despite city honchos' disdain and even hostility), the Festival puts on everything—classics, new work, staid and experimental productions, staged readings, even musicals, including *A Chorus Line* (1975) and *The Mystery of Edwin Drood* (1985). Papp's critics declare that he lacks taste, that he unselectively abounds in theatre. Papp's

defenders reply that he is keeping the New York stage fresh and vital: that he *abounds* in theatre.

PASSION PLAY

A medieval form portraying events leading up to the Crucifixion, especially popular in German-speaking countries. The Bavarian town of Ober-ammergau still gives one every ten years, its cast and staff drawn entirely from local amateurs.

ROBERT PATRICK (See *Kennedy's Children*)

PEER GYNT

Picaresque fantasy in verse by *Henrik Ibsen, prem. Oslo, 1876.

This bizarre and episodic work, a folk tale with interruptive disquisitions in its third quarter, is one of the theatre's great challenges. It is often done, but seldom well—there is too much in it, too many important small parts, too much in decor and special effects, too many themes for the director to juggle. Ibsen published it in 1867, to be read as poetry, as so many nineteenth century verse plays were. Still, it is a play, a strangely affecting one, for its solipsistic *protagonist, one of the first of the modern anti-heroes, pursues his selfish destiny with an almost Christlike concentration. And he dies in a Pietà picture, his head in the lap of his now ancient village sweetheart, as she sings a lullaby and the Button Molder, a kind of collector of souls, warns that he and Peer shall meet "at the final crossway." Edvard Grieg wrote the famous music to accompany the original production.

"PENNY PLAIN, TWOPENCE COLOURED"

A vendor's cry, in nineteenth century London, offering artwork representing the characters and scenery of the latest stage success, or some star actor costumed for his great roles. Printed on rectangular sheets—in black and white for a penny, the same in color for twice that—the sets and characters were designed for use in the toy theatres popular in Victorian and Edwardian times. By cutting out the figures and mounting them in long-handled metal braces one could set the stage and put on one's own plays.

PERIAKTOI

In the ancient *Greek theatre, these were three-sided polyhedrons painted to depict locations of scene (a city, a harbor, and so on) and revolved on their bases as the scene changed. The Classical revival of the late Renaissance saw the reinstitution of the *periaktoi*, as theatres of the day used standing street scene sets of no particular context. In the late 1500s, the introduction of decor unique to each play made the *periaktoi* redundant.

PERIPETEIA

Greek for "reversal": the sudden change of fortune that overwhelms the *protagonist in tragedy; or invigorates him in comedy.

ARTHUR WING PINERO (1855–1934)

Like most playwrights of his day, Pinero began as an actor. He first gained note in the 1880s for comedy, yet the work that made his reputation was a "woman with a past" melodrama (a genre very popular at the time), *The Second Mrs. Tanqueray* (1893). A look at a woman tragically failing to redeem a liberal past with marriage to a respectable man, the play drew notice as much for *Mrs. Patrick Campbell's performance of the title role as for the realistic sensitivity with which Pinero told her story. Paula Tanqueray became one of the era's great star parts, a perennial for Campbell but also for *Eleonora Duse, Olga Nethersole, Madge Kendal, Ethel *Barrymore, and Tallulah Bankhead.

Other Pinero titles are dimly familiar to the theatre buff—*Dandy Dick* (1887), *The Notorious Mrs. Ebbsmith* (1895), *The Gay Lord Quex* (1899). But his most enduring work is the comedy *Trelawney of the "Wells"* (1898), on Pinero's favorite theme, the romance of an aristocrat and a commoner. Because the commoner is an actress, Rose Trelawney, the misalliance is doubly reprehensible to the aristocrat's family. But Pinero's real concern here is the opening of the backstage to show his public the rarer romance of the theatre, even of the third-rate suburban company he envisioned. (The "Wells" was originally a fictitious theatre; Pinero later said outright that he had always thought of it as the real-life *Sadler's Wells.) In fact, *Trelawney* worries less about Rose's love for Arthur Gower than about whether or not the obscure and unstaged playwright Tom Wrench will ever break through to glory. He does—and did: the character is based on Pinero's predecessor, the "father of English realism," *T. W. Robertson. *Trelawney*'s final moment pulls all this together, as the company is about to begin work on Wrench's new play, *Life*. (Note the allusion to Robertson's fondness for one-word titles.) Gripping Arthur's hand and leaning on Rose's shoulder, Wrench cries, "Oh, my

dears! Let us—get on with the rehearsal!" Real *Life* is about to begin; and the curtain falls.
(See also The Royal Court Theatre.)

HAROLD PINTER (1930–   )

Pinter's first full-length play, *The Birthday Party* (1958), presents a loser named Stanley. To the boardinghouse where he lives come two men who menace and interrogate him, then take him away. In 1967, when *The Birthday Party* was playing Broadway, a woman wrote to the New York *Times,* asking Pinter to explain "the meaning of your play." She went on, "These are the points which I do not understand: 1. Who are the two men? 2. Where did Stanley come from? 3. Were they all supposed to be normal?"

Pinter's reply was . . . well, Pinteresque. He wanted his correspondent to explain "the meaning of your letter." He went on, "These are the points which I do not understand: 1. Who are you? 2. Where do you come from? 3. Are you supposed to be normal?"

Pinter has never been forthcoming in "explaining" the "meaning." There is no meaning as such, we are led to believe, no subtext, no key. The play means what the play is. Certainly, Pinter's action is always clear. In *The Caretaker* (1960), a man brings an old bum to stay in his house. The man's brother harasses the bum; the bum tries to play brother against brother. The bum is told to leave. Or, in *The Homecoming* (1965), a man brings his wife from America to meet his London family—father, uncle, and two brothers. The wife fits into the strangely troubled family scene. Her husband leaves, but she stays behind to support the family as a prostitute.

One is reminded of the famous last line of *Ibsen's Hedda Gabler:* "People don't do such things!" But it is not Pinter's plots that made the word "Pinteresque" necessary as much as it was his dialogue—spare, volatile, and so laden (apparently) with Meaning that requests for Explanations are necessary, too. The action is always clear, yes; but the dialogue is oblique. This is partly because Pinter gives us people, as he has said, "on the extreme edge of their living"—but also because he sees much of the spoken language as evasion: "a violent, sly, anguished, or mocking smokescreen." The aimless excursions, the outbursts, the velvet baiting of friends, family, and strangers alike, the perfectly rational delivery of non sequiturs, the neurotic tirades about commonplace things—all this is not just a stunt of verbal blitz, but a kind of *expressionistic *naturalism. Pinter's dialogue is eloquent not in what it says but in what his characters hope to avoid having to confront. There are the Pinteresque silences, too, as in the famous beginning of *The Homecoming*'s second act, an elaborate post-lunch ritual in which cigars are lit and coffee is poured and passed without a word uttered. This scene invariably fascinates yet embarrasses audiences, used to navigating through the spoken word, even as spoken by Pinter's curious characters.

It's usual to think of Pinter as something of an *absurdist. Martin Esslin, who coined the term, has placed Pinter with—this is *very* mixed company—*Samuel Beckett, *Arthur Adamov, *Eugène Ionesco, and *Jean Genet. Critics have found sources for Pinter in music hall comedy, in *August Strindberg's misogyny, even in *Maurice Maeterlinck, another exploiter of silence and pauses. But in all, Pinter seems very much his own invention. Whatever the historical and artistic input, nothing was Pinteresque till Pinter. He is remarkably consistent, too, guarding his terrain with plays that vary in length but not in scope, in setting but not in inflection. And unlike many of his contemporaries, especially the absurdists, Pinter is unarguably actable—"the player's playwright," as one critical casebook calls him. Pinter began his career as an actor (under the name David Baron), and he has provisioned some excellent ensembles, even pulling a bit of the old *West End into new times in *No Man's Land* (1975), first produced with *John Gielgud and *Ralph Richardson. *No Man's Land* may well be the most Pinteresque of all Pinter's works, almost a retrospective of his plays—*The Caretaker*'s shabby intruder, invited in and then disowned, *The Homecoming*'s all-male household, and especially the games of memory and fabrication explored in *Old Times* (1971). The action, still and always, is clear. But what are these people trying not to say?
(See also *The Dumb Waiter* and *Other Places*.)

A trio of great English actors in famous Pinter portrayals. Above, Paul Rogers in The Homecoming. Below, Richardson and Gielgud in No Man's Land.

LUIGI PIRANDELLO (1867–1936)

As with *Bertolt Brecht and *Harold Pinter, this playwright's name has become a common-use adjective. But where "Brechtian" and "Pinteresque" summon up a clear image of the experience these writers deliver, "Pirandellian" oversimplifies the world of Pirandello. What is Pirandellian? An inquiry into where we can place the border between art and life, or between objective truth and perception. A play in which "real life" seems less real than theatrical fiction. Games of identity, of recognition, of explanations that make the comprehensible unbelievable.

Sei Personaggi in Cerca d'Autore (Six Characters in Search of an Author, 1921), Pirandello's best-known work, lies at the center of this conception of what is Pirandellian. A family of six bursts into a play rehearsal. (The play they interrupt is, amusingly—and how Pirandellian the joke!—one of Pirandello's own, *Il Giuoco delle Parti* [1918], known in English as *The Rules of the Game*.) They demand that their story be enacted instead—but as they demonstrate what this entails, they apparently not only reenact their tale but re-undergo it. It actually happens.

Or did it?

This is "Pirandellian." However, in his native Italy (his native Sicily, in fact, as any Sicilian will insist), Pirandello is much more than this "Pirandellian" shadowboxing with existential conceits. Pirandello is one of Italy's great men of letters, a Nobel laureate, born to a fast, witty pen that left behind seven novels, eight volumes of poetry, countless articles and short stories, and some forty-five plays. There is a great deal more to Pirandello —even in his most famous plays alone—than the stunt of blurring the line between the stage and reality. The identity rebuses in Pirandello are often merely the facade of a moralistic parable. In *Come Tu Mi Vuoi* (As You Desire Me, 1930)—the source, by the way, of the 1932 Greta Garbo vehicle of the same name—a cabaret dancer is recognized as a man's long-lost amnesiac wife, restored to him, and rehabilitated. She is an imposter. Yet she accedes to the impersonation out of love for her "husband." Then she realizes that his happiness depends not on her love but on the fortune "she" represents. Now the real wife, an insane wretch, turns up. Everyone would rather deny *her* and play along with the imposter: but she spurns the easy life and goes back to her cabaret underworld, leaving the husband with his poor demented thing of a wife. On the surface another "Pirandellian" game of facsimiles, *As You Desire Me* (more literally, *As You Would Like Me to Be*) is an attack on the husband's hypocrisy and greed, on *his* sham.

Still, we mustn't let the solemnly moralistic Pirandello obscure his cleverness and dexterity, his ability to veer from the "experimental" shape of *Six Characters* or the bizarre spontaneity of *Questa Sera Si Recita a Soggetto* (Tonight We Improvise, 1930) to the conventional *naturalism of *Enrico IV* (Henry IV, 1922) or *L'Uomo dal Fiore in Bocca* (The Man with the Flower in his Mouth, 1923), a one-acter not unlike *Edward Albee's *The Zoo Story*. We should note as well the breezy colloquialism of Pirandello's titles, very avant-garde for their day: *Pensaci, Giacomo!* (Think Of It, Giacomo!, 1916), *Ma Non è una Cosa Seria* (But It's Not Serious, 1918), *Come Prima, Meglio di Prima* (The Same Only Better, 1920), the sadly autobiographical *Quando Si è Qualcuno* (When One Is Somebody, 1933). Pirandello was Somebody in the 1920s, when *Six Characters* enjoyed a worldwide success. Toward the end of his life, most theatres were closed to him, including those in Berlin, site of his most imposing successes, where *Max Reinhardt staged a moody, *expressionistic *Six Characters* that broke house records. Even Italy shrugged him off; the critics found him dangerous and the public was bored with his intellectual intensity. Today Italians regard him as their greatest playwright. (See also *Henry IV* and *Right You Are {If You Think You Are}*.)

ERWIN PISCATOR (1893–1966)

One of the first modern super-directors, whose productions sometimes overwhelmed the plays as compositions. Piscator anticipated many of the century's trends, including mixed-media presentation, costuming classics in modern dress, mechanized sets, improvisational rehearsals, and the *alienation effect of the *epic theatre. A German, Piscator thrived in the open arts world of post-World War I Berlin. His subjects—so one may well call the plays he staged—included the classic (*Schiller's *Die Räuber*), the modern title of renown (*Gorky's *The Lower Depths*), new work (Ernst Toller's *Hoppla, Wir Leben!*), and oddities (Piscator's own epic theatre version of Tolstoy's *War and Peace*). Fleeing the Nazis in 1933, Piscator came to New York and left his mark on the local avantgarde, counting among his disciples Judith Malina, co-founder of *The Living Theatre. After the war Piscator returned to Germany, living long enough to work with such important new dramatists as *Rolf Hochhuth, Heinar Kipphardt, and *Peter Weiss—all of whom have adapted Piscator's epic style into the new form called *documentary drama.

GUILBERT DE PIXÉRÉCOURT (1773–1844)

"I write for people who cannot read," he declared, more or less defending the violent and sentimental character of his scripts and contrived turns of his narrative. Pixérécourt was the king of Paris's popular stage, the first of the great *boulevard playwrights and the founder of *melodrama. So vicious were his villains, so sinned against his innocents, that the Boulevard du Temple, the *Broadway of post-Revolutionary Paris, was known as the "Boulevard of Crime." But then the Revolution had made a theatre of execution; only through overkill could Pixérécourt hold the interest of his largely working-class public. His first success was the Gothic tale *Victor, ou L'enfant de la Forêt* (Victor; or, The Child of the Forest, 1798), his first smash hit *Coelina, ou L'Enfante de la Mystère* (1800), on the lurid adventures of an angelic but rich orphan. But it's difficult to distinguish titles in an oeuvre so unvaried, so overflowing with *coups de théâtre, coincidences, and tableaus of no special context. What distinguishes Pixérécourt, the "*Corneille of the Boulevards," is his literally fabulous international success in a form that scarcely any historian can praise, let alone bear.

PLAUTUS (See Roman Theatre)

THE PLAYBOY OF THE WESTERN WORLD

Ironic comedy by *John Millington Synge, prem. Dublin, 1907.

The "world" is Ireland's far western wilds and the "playboy" is Christy Mahon, a stranger who arrives in a village claiming to be a patricide. Taken with his charm and thrilled at his rebellion, the villagers adore him till his father blunders in. The hoax thus exposed, all turn on Christy, especially Pegeen Mike, till then his fiancée. "Oh, my grief," she cries, all the same. "I've lost him surely. I've lost the only Playboy of the Western World." Curtain.

The public turned on the play on its premiere at the *Abbey Theatre, fulfilling Synge's idea of Irish tolerance. This is the people who made exiles of James Joyce, *Sean O'Casey, and *Samuel Beckett, a touchy people who resent the slightest depiction of themselves as anything less than heroic and lovable. Synge's wistfully poetic brogue ennobles his characters, but their actions reflect the petty, querulous self-interest of the Irish rustic, and first-nighters greeted the piece in cool silence. Then, toward the end of the last act, the Christy, William Fay, came to the line, "What'd I care if you brought me a drift of chosen females, standing in their shifts itself, maybe"—and the rest of the speech was drowned in a fury of jeers and shouts. Technically, it was the use of "shifts" (undergarments) that set off the riot. But in truth, Synge had come too close, all evening, to capturing a sense of Irish life as lived. This the Irish can never forgive. Even in America, when the Abbey took the *Playboy* on tour, Irish audiences tried to yell the play off the stage. New Yorkers let off stink bombs; and the Philadelphia police arrested the cast. George Bernard Shaw, asked for his opinion, observed, "All decent people are arrested in the United States."

Sean O'Casey's The Plough and the Stars: *"Here, where are you goin' with that?" Dublin has broken out in open war and both Bessie Burgess (Siobhán McKenna) and Mrs. Gogan (Angela Newman) want the use of the absent Mrs. Sullivan's pram in the looting of the shops that is sure to come. "Steppin' from th' threshold of good manners," says Mrs. Gogan, "it's a fat wondher to Jennie Gogan that a lady-like singer o' hymns like yourself would lower her thoughts from sky-thinkin' to stretch out her arm in a sly-seekin' way to pinch anything dhriven asthray in th' confusion of th' battle our boys is makin' for th' freedom of their counthry!"*

THE PLOUGH AND THE STARS

*Naturalistic tragedy by *Sean O'Casey, prem. Dublin, 1926.

"You have disgraced yourselves again!" said *William Butler Yeats, in dinner clothes, from the stage of the *Abbey Theatre at the premiere of O'Casey's look at a group of individuals caught up in Dublin's 1916 Easter Rebellion. The audience was storming in protest, as it had been at *Synge's **The Playboy of the Western World* nineteen years before. Then, the public had rejected Synge's satire of Irish hero worship; now, it rejected O'Casey's nuanced view of Irish heroism, with too many self-doubting or even cowardly Catholics and a surprisingly courageous Protestant, shot as she tries to wrest a demented Catholic woman from an exposed window. "I've got this through . . . through you . . . Through you, you bitch, you!" The dying woman begs for company; the worthless young bride she saved calls for her husband, does not move. The dying woman begs for assistance, a drink of water, a doctor, a friend. "Blast you, stir yourself before I'm gone!" Nothing. The woman dies singing a hymn. (O'Casey dedicated the play "To the gay laugh of my mother at the gate of the grave.") Such pictures of a real Dublin life, never idealized and at times brutally revelatory, amazed much of the public but offended a faction. It was the latter whom Yeats addressed. "Is this to be an ever-recurring celebration of the arrival of an Irish genius?" he asked. Synge, O'Casey, Joyce, Beckett. The Dublin artist held in contempt at home with such a racket of antagonism that the world turns to hear. "Dublin," said Yeats, "has once more rocked the cradle of genius."

PRODUCER (See Manager)

PROLOGUE

A scene or act preceding the main action of a play, considered preparatory either because it encapsulates the play's theme or because it takes place significantly earlier than the rest of the work. The original *prologos* (literally "before the word"), in *Greek tragedy, referred to the opening five or ten minutes leading up to the entrance of the chorus. In *Agamemnon,* the first play of *Aeschylus's *Oresteia,* the prologue consists simply of the Watchman's speech, setting up the time, the place, and the barest outline of the situation. In *Euripides's *Medea,* however, the prologue takes in a long scene between the Nurse and the Tutor, punctuated by cries from Medea, offstage ("Do I not suffer? Am I not offended? Should I not weep?"), thus laying out the background in some emotional detail.

In Shakespeare's day, the prologue became a speech delivered by one character, similarly informing the audience of preceding events—for instance, the thirty-one line prologue of *Troilus and Cressida:* "In Troy there lies the scene . . ." In *Restoration theatre, however, the prologue became sport, the author's and star actor's fribble of teasing wit. Instead of filling in the background of the action, the prologue now served as the thespian's warning to the public to be alert and appreciative. Epilogues, too, were favored, from the Greek *epilogos* ("after the word"), these to send the public home with a last appeal to their sensibilities. Thus *William Congreve's *The Way of the World* begins with a Prologue "Spoken by *Mr. Betterton":

> Of those few fools who with ill stars are curst,
> Sure scribbling fools, called poets, fare the worst:
> For they're a sort of fools which Fortune makes,
> And after she has made 'em fools, forsakes . . .

And closes with an Epilogue "Spoken by *Mrs. Bracegirdle":

> . . . So Poets oft do in one piece expose
> Whole belles-assemblies of coquettes and beaux.

PROMPT CORNER (See "Stage Left")

PROSCENIUM

The arch that frames the stage in modern Western playhouses, a convention of theatre architecture from the *Restoration to the present day.

PROTAGONIST

The central character: Sophocles's Oedipus, Shakespeare's Hamlet, Beaumarchais's Figaro, Goldoni's Truffaldino (in *The Servant of Two Masters*), Ibsen's *Peer Gynt, Edmond Rostand's *Cyrano de Bergerac, Shaw's John Tanner (in *Man and Superman*) and *Saint Joan, O'Neill's Nina Leeds (in *Strange Interlude*), Brecht's *Mother Courage, Miller's John Proctor (in *The Crucible*). Not all plays have clearly designated protagonists. Who is the central figure in Beckett's *Waiting for Godot?* The play focuses on the two tramps, Vladimir and Estragon, in equal portion. (Perhaps the inaccessible Godot is the protagonist, given Beckett's worldview.) Who is the protagonist of O'Neill's *Long Day's Journey into Night?* Surely all four members of the Tyrone family bear the dramatic weight in comparable measure.

Yet technically there can be only one protagonist. The very word takes us back to the early days of *Greek tragedy, when the cast consisted of one player and the chorus. That player was the *protagonist* (literally "first contestant"). Successive authors introduced the second, then the third player —the *deuteragonist* and *tritagonist.* Virtually all surviving Greek texts put forth one all-basic lead character as protagonist. But later eras broadened the perspective of action, projected a world with a center wide enough to depend on more than one person, one will, one destiny.

THE PROVINCETOWN PLAYERS

A *little theatre group founded in 1915 by a band of idealists led by George Cram Cook and his wife Susan Glaspell. As if in geographical as well as artistic rebellion, the company made its headquarters in Provincetown, Massachusetts, on the tip of Cape Cod. But one cannot make American theatre history away from New York, and the company soon moved to the city, eventually settling in a converted stable just south of Washington Square on MacDougall Street, still in use today. The players were determined to establish a stage primarily for playwrights. Said Cook, "There ought to be one theatre for American writers to play with— one where, if the spirit move them, they can give plays which are not likely to be produced elsewhere." Movements of artistic rebellion need more than a credo: they need a unique talent to draw attention from the opinion makers and the public —as *Sean O'Casey did for Dublin's *Abbey Theatre, or *John Osborne did (with *Look Back in Anger*) for the *Royal Court's English Stage Company. Other little theatre groups died for lack of this talent. But the Provincetowners put the movement on the map: it was they who discovered Eugene O'Neill. Interested students may glimpse a valid reconstruction of the original group in rehearsal up on Cape Cod (along with unreliable editorial comments from senile "witnesses" of the place and time) in Warren Beatty's film *Reds.* Jack Nicholson plays O'Neill.

THE QUARE FELLOW

Gallows humor by *Brendan Behan, prem. Dublin, 1954.

Like Behan's *The Hostage,* two years after, *The Quare Fellow* was mounted by *Joan Littlewood at her Theatre Workshop, and thus bears her influence. But if the wildly colorful, multi-toned *Hostage* is virtually a vaudeville tragedy, *The Quare Fellow* is more consistent in style, gray naturalism treating the last twenty-four hours before a hanging in an Irish prison. (At that, Littlewood's production was hailed for an unusually keen discipline of her habitual theatrical gamesmanship.) Behan had spent something like a third of his adult life in prisons for political offenses, including conspiracy in an IRA terrorist bombing; thus he captures the flavor of prison life with a penetrating reality. The play has been taken as an argument against capital punishment, but it does not argue: it simply presents. We get the mild curiosity of the other prisoners, the business-as-usual cool of officials, and a not unsympathetic hangman, moonlighting from his usual occupation of running a pub. Only the prison warder Regan strongly questions the righteousness of the punishment. When "Holy" Healey, of the Justice Department, points out that the condemned get "the priest and the sacraments" and suggests that they may thus die "holier deaths than if they had finished their natural span," Regan

ironically replies, "We can't advertise 'Commit a murder and die a happy death,' sir. We'd have them all at it. They take religion very seriously in this country." Behan's acid jesting runs right up to the moment of doom, when an unseen prisoner yells out an eyewitness report on the procession to the scaffold in the form of a racetrack narration: "We're ready for the start, and in good time, and who do I see lined up for the off but the High Sheriff of this ancient city of ours . . ." For a final joke, Behan never shows us the condemned man, an ax murderer.

QUARTO (See Folio)

THE QUEEN'S MEN

The term given to several English acting companies, each holding special appointment as entertainers to Elizabeth I, Anne, and Henrietta. The most famous was the first troupe, formed in 1583 and performing in, among other places, the very first playhouse erected in London, James Burbage's Theatre.

QUINTERO, SERAFÍN AND JOAQUÍN (See Álvarez Quintero)

JOSÉ QUINTERO (1924—   )

In a time when the florid and allegedly self-advertising style of *Elia Kazan signaled an emergence of the director-as-auteur in American theatre, Quintero appeared to offer an alternative in his more introspective approach. Kazan, on Broadway, had his Arthur Miller and Tennessee Williams. Quintero, on off-Broadway, directed the famous 1956 Circle-in-the-Square revival of Eugene O'Neill's *The Iceman Cometh, which led O'Neill's widow Carlotta to give Quintero the plum assignment of staging Long Day's Journey into Night on Broadway. Since then, Quintero has remained America's alleged O'Neill specialist. He and Kazan crossed paths historically when both worked for the *Lincoln Center Repertory Company in its first years in the early 1960s, when Kazan's earthy approach made a mess of the Elizabethan *revenge tragedy The Changeling and Quintero inadvertently questioned O'Neill's reputation with a lifeless Marco Millions. The two share another credit in Thornton Wilder's *The Skin of Our Teeth: Kazan staged the 1942 Broadway premiere, Quintero Broadway's Bicentennial revival, in 1976. Kazan's production was highly charged, Quintero's (with Elizabeth Ashley, Alfred Drake, Martha Scott, and Steve Railsback) strangely underpowered for so theatrical a work.

DAVID RABE (See *Hurlyburly*)

RACHEL (1820—1858)

The outstanding actress of mid—nineteenth century France. Originally Élisabeth Félix, born to poverty, Rachel was singing in the streets for small change at the age of twelve, or so the fable runs. Certainly, she did make her debut at the *Comédie-Française at the age of eighteen, as Camille in *Corneille's *Horace.* This is a statistic, not a legendary performance, for the house was nearly empty and no note taken of the debutante. However, the heavyweight critic Jules Janin praised Rachel the following season, and Paris began to follow her progress through the classics: Corneille's *Cinna;* *Voltaire's *Tancrède;* *Racine's *Iphigénie, Andromache, Bajazet,* and, above all, *Phèdre.* Fittingly, Rachel created the title role of *Scribe and Legouvé's *Adrienne Lecouvreur* (1849), based on the life of another great interpreter of Racine. Traditionalists regarded Rachel as a national heroine for her revitalization of the seventeeth century repertory, in disrepair since the 1820s. However, behind the scenes Rachel was something less than a heroine, throwing her fame around and upsetting the Comédie's time-honored *communitas* of talent. The Comédie-Française was above all a company; but Rachel was above all a star.

JEAN RACINE (1639—1699)

Corneille's successor and Molière's contemporary in the founding of the Classical French stage. Racine's output counts twelve plays, one comedy called *Les Plaideurs* (The Litigants, from Aristophanes's *The Wasps,* 1668) and eleven tragedies, these built generally on the lines that Corneille observed—the *alexandrine metre, the "rules," and so on. (See Corneille for a discussion of this form.) However, the two playwrights are very unalike in feeling: Corneille—in the famous critics' comparison— painting people as they should be, Racine as they are. There is another distinction, emphasized in Corneille's dictum that "the dignity of tragedy requires some important interest of state, some passion nobler and more virile than love, such as ambition or vengeance." Love takes "second rank in the poetry" to weightier affairs. Honor, in Corneille, is most often purely that: a matter of self-esteem and public regard. In Racine, everything is a matter of the heart.

This in part explains Corneille's preference for historical subjects, Racine's for mythological ones, presented with the imperative *vraisemblance*—a believable sequence of events—but nonetheless of a *Euripidean tang, a magic called up by the names and places of imaginary antiquity. Thus, in *Andromaque* (1667), Racine builds the action entirely around unrequited loves—the heroine's for her dead husband, Hector, Pyrrhus's for Andromaque, Hermione's for Pyrrhus, and Orestes's for Hermione. Where Corneille focuses on masculine drives, Racine's heroes are women. The *protagonist of *Bajazet* (1672) is not the title role but the extraordinary Roxane, as ferocious in love as in hatred; and in Phèdre (1677) Racine created perhaps the greatest tragedienne's role in all French theatre in the Queen of Athens, struggling against a passionate desire for her stepson Hippolyte. In Paris, they say, a good Andromaque can make a reputation—a good Phèdre can make a career.

Unfortunately, Racine has traveled beyond the borders of France no better than Corneille has. The unique slant of the alexandrines makes translation difficult; and if Corneille's high-flown discourse seems absurd outside its chevaleresque context, Racine's penetrating directness loses its poetry, its intimacy. Take these two lines from the second act of *Phèdre,* as the heroine approaches her stepson:

PHÈDRE: He is here. Toward my heart all my
    blood draws away.
  Seeing him, I forget what I came here to say.

My translation is clumsy, even idiotic. But it's the best I can do, keeping to Racine's language and the alexandrine rhythm. How beautifully simple the original is, how honest, precise, fair:

PHÈDRE: Le voici. Vers mon coeur tout mon sang
    se retire.
  J'oublie, en le voyant, ce que je viens lui dire.

FERDINAND RAIMUND
(1790—1836)

As actor and playwright, Raimund is considered one of the major figures of Vienna's popular theatre (as opposed to the pretentiously noble drama ensconced in the Burgtheater, the royal stage).

Working in the "suburban" theatres—those in the small towns outside the medieval ramparts that surrounded the old city center—the popular thespians dealt largely in farce and sentiment. Raimund, however, preferred a uniquely Viennese form related to English *pantomime, Italian *commedia dell'arte,* and what would later turn into a simplistic form of musical comedy, the Zauberposse (literally "Magic skit"). Vienna best enjoyed this last form, a blend of reality and fantasy, of the beautiful and the grotesque, when it was set to music—Mozart's *Die Zauberflöte* (The Magic Flute, 1791), for instance. Raimund dutifully included ditties, ensembles, and incidental accompaniments. But he was celebrated above all for the vital humanity of his characters and stories—*Der Barometermacher auf der Zauberinsel* (The Barometer Maker on the Magic Island, 1823); *Das Mädchen aus der Feenwelt, oder der Bauer als Millionär* (The Maid from the Fairy World; or, The Peasant as Millionaire, 1826), a treatise on the dispiriting nature of greed; *Der Alpenkönig und der Menschenfeind* (The King of the Alps and the Misanthrope, 1828). A major operetta theatre in present-day Vienna bears Raimund's name.

TERENCE RATTIGAN (1911—1977)

In the early 1950s, when Rattigan had long been established as a *West End master of *boulevard theatre, the playwright baited progressive critics with the invention of "Aunt Edna." This was Rattigan's ideal playgoer, a bourgeoise with strong opinions, certain limits, and good instincts. "Aunt Edna has existed for more than two thousand years," Rattigan explained. "Shakespeare and Sophocles had to satisfy her, too."

Rattigan certainly did, not only had to satisfy her but was glad to. A work such as *Separate Tables* (1954) is prime Rattigan and first-rate entertainment, two one-act plays set in a seaside hotel and employing the same minor characters as connective background. The two lead actors flatter the conceit by playing completely different roles in each one-act, first as a couple of somewhat faded glamour, former lovers about to rekindle their intense affair; second as a mousey spinster and a pathetic old

Margaret Leighton and Eric Portman in Terence Rattigan's Separate Tables. *Aunt Edna loved it.*

bachelor who is in trouble for molesting women in a movie theatre. The evening's excitement thus turns on the *tour de force of the starring couple's playing all four parts—Margaret Leighton and Eric Portman dazzling London and New York in the original productions.

We cannot put Rattigan down as a mere *boulevardier, pandering to the conservative taste of the Aunt Ednas. First of all, his plays gave splendid opportunities to a number of distinguished actors, not only Leighton and Portman but the*Lunts, *Paul Scofield, *Peggy Ashcroft, Margaret Sullavan, *Laurence Olivier and Vivien Leigh, *Alec Guinness, and John Mills. Second, Rattigan often stole beyond his genteel cover to touch upon realistic subjects—a young woman's sexual obsession in *The Deep Blue Sea* (1952), the homosexual panic of T. E. Lawrence in *Ross* (1960). Third, Rattigan's lifelong interest in the strong woman whose sense of honor overwhelms practical considerations amplifies the flat psychology of the typical boulevardier. In *The Winslow Boy* (1946), our interest in the innocence of a cadet expelled from military school for theft is gradually intercepted by admiration for his feminist sister. Even the charming trifle, *The Sleeping Prince* (1953), turns on a young American musical comedy chorus girl's solving the problems, political and emotional, of a Ruritanian royal family. Rattigan once said that he wrote his plays to please himself—"I am Aunt Edna." However, while amusing her with sound construction and startling curtain lines, Rattigan offered, on at least a few occasions, to enlighten Aunt Edna's sensibility, perhaps beyond even his expectations.

REALISM (See Naturalism)

THE REDGRAVES

Michael Redgrave (1908–1985), father of the clan, married Rachel Kempson (1910–   ). Their children, Vanessa (1937–   ), Corin (1939–   ),

and Lynn (1943–   ), also took to the stage, the first two to the political advantage, the third in the United States, where the Political Actress position was already held by Jane Fonda. Anyway, Lynn didn't want it. Corin is little celebrated, but Vanessa has been called one of the few outstanding actresses of her generation, even by those who loathe her politics. She is versatile, moving from *The Taming of the Shrew*'s Katherina to *The Seagull*'s Nina, from *Brecht's Polly Peachum in *The Threepenny Opera* to *Noël Coward's Gilda (in *Design for Living*). Vanessa is as well an absolute professional, never allowing her personal feelings to intrude on her work. Lynn is more delightful. Father Michael counted a heavy *curriculum vitae,* including not only the expected Shakespeare but arresting turns in Chekhov and Ibsen and his own adaptation of Henry James's *The Aspern Papers* (1959), which Maurice Evans played in New York, to Wendy Hiller's deviously bashful heroine. All this theatre in the blood, this dynasty of presentation! Here is talent enough for Vanessa, the least accommodating of the family, to turn out to be the most impressive. What an absorbing Mary Tyrone (in Eugene O'Neill's *Long Day's Journey into Night*) she would make.

MAX REINHARDT (1873–1943)

One of the greatest directors of the twentieth century. By a paradox, Reinhardt was known to the public as a stager of spectacles, to the profession as an "actor's director." Austrian, centered in Berlin, Vienna, and at the Salzburg Festival, Reinhardt was in fact *both* a stager of spectacles and an actors' director: ambitious in concept but careful of detail. Even his crowd scenes seemed to pulse not with balletic motions but with countless individual portrayals. "These crescendi of mass ecstasy," Reinhardt's son Gottfried wrote, "these huddling diminuendi, the ritardandi of dawning, slowly paralyzing horror, the breathlessly expectant accelerandi, the catatonic rests and vivaciously surging alla breve passages, the muted fadeouts and predestined doom were symphonic. But Reinhardt was not only the conductor of this unwritten symphony. He was its composer."

Max Reinhardt's Oedipus Rex—*spectacle, yes, but note the calmly superintendant *protagonist, Alexander Moissi.*

Reinhardt has been linked with *Gordon Craig for his highly structural approach to set design and crowd control—and Reinhardt did try to lure Craig to Reinhardt's Deutsches Theater (in Berlin) several times, in vain. However, Craigism is but one facet of Reinhardt, whose style, from the visuals to the treatment of the actors, changed from work to work. Sophocles's *Oedipus Rex,* with Alexander Moissi, became a nightmare of heaving, clamoring crowds. *Sumurîn,* a mime play drawn from the Arabian Nights, borrowed *Kabuki stylistics, even unto the *hanamichi, the runway connecting the stage to the back of the theatre. *The Miracle* (1911) was the ultimate religious pageant, a passion play beyond Oberammergau. And the first of Reinhardt's many stagings of Shakespeare's *A Midsummer Night's Dream* raised up a real forest that turned on a revolve as the fairies and mortals ran through it—and Puck was costumed in grass. These productions were extensively toured or remounted from Russia to the United States, and the *Midsummer Night's Dream* that Reinhardt staged in the Hollywood Bowl in 1934 was preserved in a Warner Brothers film the following year. It sounds dire—Dick Powell and Olivia de Havilland are among the lovers, James Cagney takes Bottom, and Mickey Rooney tries Puck. In fact, Cagney and Rooney are very engaging, and the magical production supports Reinhardt's legend.

RÉJANE (1857–1920)

Gabrielle Réjane built her career as an entrancing light comedienne in plays by Georges de Porto-Riche—most notably *Amoureuse* (A Woman in Love, 1891)—and *Victorien Sardou, especially *Madame Sans-Gêne* (1893), by popular consent Réjane's greatest role. Queen of the *boulevard theatre in her prime at the turn of the century, she was nonetheless overshadowed by the ferocious *Sarah Bernhardt, with whom Réjane shared the Sardouvian heroine parts.

MADELEINE RENAUD (See

Jean-Louis Barrault)

REPERTORY

A much abused word. Most loosely, it refers to the plays in a given field, for instance "the classic German repertory" or "the Italian comic repertory." More specifically, it refers to the stock of productions maintained by a resident or touring company, from Aeschylus through Molière to Pinter. Ideally —and all too seldom—the repertory consists of such productions presented in nightly alternation, with any part covered by several actors over the course of the season.

This was standard practice in the old stock companies. At the turn into the twentieth century, the free-lance one play–one theatre approach replaced revolving repertory, for plays were running longer. A nineteenth century stock company might give at most twenty-five performances of its most popular title in even the largest city. By 1900, a hit could last well over a hundred performances, and the longest runs approached the four hundred mark. Thus repertory became unfeasible, technically cumbersome and economically unsound. However, the concept of a permanent stock of productions and a fixed acting company has survived at the great European *national theatres. Most American "repertory" companies run one production with a set cast, then drop it for the next production. This is repertory by wishful thinking.
(See also Stock Company.)

RESTORATION THEATRE

England's Civil War of 1642 put an end to *Elizabethan theatre, at least to legal performances open to the public. This was a Puritan England, run by prudes. There were scofflaws here and there, and the nobility underwrote private performances. But not till the monarchy was restored in 1660 did the English theatre as such revive: thus the "restoration." However, the stage of Christopher Marlowe, William Shakespeare, and Ben Jonson was not restored as much as reinvented. The accession of Charles II directly influenced the new stage, for the Stuart party had spent its exile in France, and wanted the London theatre less like that of Elizabeth's subjects and more like that of Paris. In place of the young male adolescents in women's parts, England welcomed its first actresses—Margaret Hughes, who launched the new tradition as Shakespeare's Desdemona, *Mrs. Betterton, *Nell Gwyn, Elizabeth Barry, *Anne Bracegirdle. In place of the huge open-air circular structures like the Globe, Restoration theatre buildings were smaller, rectangular, and entirely enclosed. (The Elizabethan *thrust stage, however, remained in use, along with the doors in the *proscenium.)

One aspect of Parisian theatregoing that Charles did not miss was the intellectuals' politicization of each premiere, the pamphlets and faction wars. In Paris, the theatre was a temple of state policy. In London, the theatre would be a home *away* from court—and indeed, Charles II was the first English ruler to attend public performances. (Elizabeth I loved the stage too; but limited her theatregoing to private ceremonies.) Charles gave out exclusive patents to two playwrights, Thomas Killigrew

(1612–1683) and William D'Avenant (1606–1668), to form separate companies, respectively the King's Men and the Duke's Men—the founding, in effect, of the forces that were to result in the Theatres Royal, *Drury Lane and *Covent Garden.

There were other differences between Elizabethan and Restoration theatre. What poetry was to the one, wit was to the other; this was an age not of tragedy but of comedy. The Restoration enjoyed serious subjects, of course, but not great ones. The summit of Restoration dramatic poetry was *All for Love; or, The World Well Lost,* a retelling of Shakespeare's *Antony and Cleopatra* by John Dryden (1611–1700). *All for Love* has its passages of beauty, but where Shakespeare gives us sweep, Dryden is tidy. Worse yet, even Shakespeare himself was "tidied up" in these years, his savagery tamed and his blunt humor sweetened. To cite only the most famous instance, Nahum Tate's edition of *King Lear* dropped the Fool, married Cordelia off to Edgar, and spared Kent, Gloucester, and even Lear.

No, it was comedy that made the Restoration era, a peculiarly licentious, very contemporary, London-based comedy quite unlike the romances and farces of Shakespeare's day. Perhaps some of Ben Jonson's work inspired the Restoration humorists; but Jonson's "comedy of humours" hardly anticipates the bawdy insinuation of the Restoration's three presiding wits, George Etherege (?1634–1691), William Wycherley (1640–1716), and William Congreve (1670–1729), in their comedy of manners.

None of the three was a professional thespian. Like their heroes, they were dandies and jesters, duelling—if we take their heroines as representative—with women no less fluent in jest, and as salacious, as themselves. Love and seduction, along with the odd family crisis, provision the plots, and it is not in form or tone that Restoration playwrights distinguish themselves, but in brilliance of language. To move from Etherege's *The Comical Revenge; or, Love in a Tub* (1664), *She Would if She Could* (1668), and *The Man of Mode; or, Sir Fopling Flutter* (1676), thence to Wycherley's *The Country Wife* (1675) and *The Plain Dealer* (1676), and finally to Congreve's *The Old Bachelor* (1693), *Love for Love* (1695), and *The Way of the World* (1700) is

to meet the same essences of society over and over: the wise and the foolish, the enamored and the flirtatious, the honest and the hypocritical. Thus the vocational nomenclature so typical of the era, the Fopling Flutters, Lady Fidgets, and Sir Wilful Witwoulds. Moreover, other than in certain slants of tone—especially Wycherley's wicked relish of bawdry or Congreve's exceptional beauty of language—the three writers resemble each other. Their comedies are "of manners" because they take their particular society as a model for the world, a microcosm of human virtues and failings.

All Restoration comedy, then, treats a conflict between nature and style: between knowing the truth and telling it, between what love wants and what marriage yields, between honor and vanity. The emphasis on intrigue and deception suggests that Restoration dramatists took Shakespeare's "All the world's a stage" literally. Almost everyone in these comedies *is* acting in some way or other. These are virtually plays-within-the-play, using glamour of vice and opulence of wit to lure the spectator toward the mirror.

(See also Comedy of Manners and *The Way of the World*.)

REVENGE TRAGEDY

A genre popular in Elizabethan and Jacobean England, originated by Thomas Kyd (1558–1594) in *The Spanish Tragedy* (?1586) and pursued by such dramatists as Cyril Tourneur (?1580–1626) in *The Revenger's Tragedy* (?1606) and Thomas Middleton (1580–1627) in *The Changeling* (1622), a collaboration with William Rowley (?1585–1626). The old tragedies of Seneca (see Roman Theatre) provided the formal base, especially in the figure of the ghost who launches the action by telling a descendant of his most foul murder and demanding vengeance. Thus Shakespeare's *Hamlet* (?1601) is regarded as the paragon of revenge tragedy. In its last few moments, Hamlet's friend Horatio gives an apt description of this genre to the just-arrived Fortinbras and the English Ambassador, as they view a stage cluttered with corpses:

HORATIO: Let me speak to th'yet unknowing
world

How these things came about. So shall you hear
Of carnal, bloody, and unnatural acts;
Of accidental judgments, casual slaughters;
Of deaths put on by cunning and forc'd cause;
And, in this upshot, purposes mistook
Fall'n on th'inventors' heads—all this can I
   Truly deliver.

RHINOCÉROS

Cautionary *absurdism by *Eugène Ionesco, prem. Paris, 1959.

In a provincial French town, rhinoceroses rampage in the streets, more and more of them. Where have they come from? It appears that the population is undergoing metamorphosis—as they do, perhaps, when the Fascists take over, or the Communists, or the Buddhists, or whoever's next to seize power. As Ionesco's perennial *protagonist Bérenger looks on in horror, his friends and neighbors turn into monsters, till finally only he and his girlfriend Daisy are left:

BÉRENGER: Listen, Daisy, there's something we can do. We'll have children, our children will have other children. It will take time, but it's up to us to regenerate humanity.

DAISY: Regenerate humanity?

BÉRENGER: It's been done before.

DAISY: Long ago. Adam and Eve . . . They must have been very courageous.

Listen as Daisy frames her argument:

DAISY: I don't want to have children. It sounds boring.

BÉRENGER: How else would you save the world?

DAISY: Why save it?

BÉRENGER: What a question! . . . Do it for me, Daisy. Please let's save the world.

DAISY: After all, perhaps we're the ones who need saving. Perhaps we're the ones who are abnormal.

BÉRENGER: Daisy, you're raving. You're feverish.

DAISY: Well, you don't see anyone else like us, do you?

BÉRENGER: Daisy I won't listen to you!

(Daisy looks all about them at the rhinoceroses.)

DAISY: Really. See: they're happy. They feel good in their skins. They don't seem crazy. They seem very natural. They're the ones in the right.

BÉRENGER: (Desperately) We're the ones in the right, Daisy, I assure you.

DAISY: What nerve!

BÉRENGER: You know I'm right.

DAISY: There is no absolute right. It's the world that's right, not you or I.

Daisy joins the animal party, and, as the curtain prepares to fall, Bérenger is the last man alive. "I won't surrender!" he shouts. And there Ionesco leaves him.

Rhinocéros stands out in Ionesco's output, as his most "relevant" full-length work, an important international success. Unlike most Ionesco, *Rhinocéros* treats a natural setting, characters, dialogue, and action—which makes the notion of people turning into beasts all the more imposing. In Act Two, Bérenger's best friend turns into a rhinoceros more or less in front of the audience. A fantasy. A description—life in France under the German occupation. A parable. A prediction—the society of the future? The text is so open-ended that the French premiere and the first London production were comic, the first New York staging tragicomic, and most German productions starkly terrifying.

ELMER RICE (1892–1967)

Trained for the law, Rice was still twenty-one when his first play, *On Trial* (1914), made him rich and famous—and a professional playwright. Though he often drew on his experience of courts and contracts, most notably in *Counsellor-at-Law* (1931), Rice decided he could advance his liberal sympathies better in the theatre, and left the bar.

Rice had an erratic career, suffering his worst defeat with his most outspoken and heartfelt scripts, often compromising his originality in collaborations with other writers (including Dorothy Parker and *Philip Barry), and never coming to terms with the limitations of the commercial theatre, or even of the idealist theatre—as when, having steered the New York unit of the *Federal Theatre toward the audaciously polymorphous-perverse Living Newspaper, Rice resigned in fury when the government closed the first Living Newspaper after the dress rehearsal.

Erratic. Now Rice was making Broadway take *expressionism in *The Adding Machine (and making Broadway virtually like it). Now he was working the outdated format of slice-of-life *melodrama in Street Scene (1929), so flagrantly sentimental and violent that Kurt Weill turned it into an opera with very little alteration. And then Rice was shepherding a huge cast through the twenty scenes of We, the People (1933), a look at the authoritarian repression of free speech. Headstrong, self-willed, uncompromising. But erratic. The Adding Machine remains a fascinating document of the historic avant-garde, and Street Scene won the Pulitzer Prize. But We, the People closed quickly and lost a fortune.

RALPH RICHARDSON (1902–1983)

One of the great English actors, a colleague of *Laurence Olivier and *John Gielgud—yet somehow not consistently their equal in heroic parts. Even in Shakespeare, Richardson had more failures than successes, though his 1944 Falstaff for the *Old Vic is legendary. That same season, Richardson played a fascinating *Peer Gynt under *Tyrone Guthrie with a brilliant cast—*Sybil Thorndike as Mother Åse, Joyce Redman as sweetheart Solveig, Margaret Leighton as the Troll King's Daughter, Vida Hope as Anitra, and Olivier as the Button Molder. In modern dress character comedy, Richardson was matchless (a superb General St. Pé in *Jean Anouilh's The Waltz of the Toreadors), quirky and quizzical, always halfway between deliberation and mockery. He once said that he went on stage "to dream."

Richardson was, by all accounts, an utter eccentric. It came through in his acting, and served him especially well in *Restoration comedy. Richardson made a most touching Sir Peter Teazle in *Sheridan's *The School for Scandal to Geraldine McEwan's Lady Teazle, with Gielgud directing and playing Joseph Surface. This bent for the un-

Two PR portraits of Ralph Richardson: in youth, the all-purpose leading man, game for nearly anything from Shakespeare's Prince Hal to Ibsen's Peer Gynt; then, in maturity, the beloved crackpot, not quite of this world and most apt as looney bin sages, from General Sir William Boothroyd in William Douglas Home's Lloyd George Knew My Father to Ibsen's John Gabriel Borkman.

conventional led Richardson, late in life, to a series of senile cranks, most notably in William Douglas Home's *Lloyd George Knew My Father* (1972), and, again with Gielgud, *David Storey's *Home* (1970) and *Harold Pinter's *No Man's Land* (1975), not to mention Richardson's cameo as the old servant Firs in Chekhov's *The Cherry Orchard* at the National Theatre in 1977, with Dorothy Tutin, Albert Finney, Robert Stephens, and Ben Kingsley.

Richardson made a pretty spry eccentric in youth, too. In a famous thespians' tale, an early middle Richardson, on the night of the final dress rehearsal, is called to question by an unusually sadistic director. Till now, the director has vented his rages upon the rest of the cast. Now it's Richardson's turn. Apparently, the actor has made an exit that offends the director's sense of style. "Mr. Richardson," he says, having called the actor back from the wings. "Do you suppose it all to be looked for that you might condescend, between now and tomorrow night, to learn how to walk out of a room like a gentleman?"

"Oh, yes," says Richardson, with intense but delicate conviction. "I'm quite sure I can." And he proceeds to do so: he goes, like a gentleman, off the stage, out of the theatre, away from London, and never comes back to that play or that director as long as he lives.

THE RIDICULOUS THEATRICAL COMPANY

One of the few instances of an avant-garde troupe's managing to stay avant-garde—and first-rate—for twenty years. The Ridiculous Theatrical Company, founded in 1967, was a mainstay of New York's off-off-Broadway scene, offering varied fare that observed an aesthetic of delicate camp mixed with cultural satire, show biz spoof, and parodistic vaudeville. The RTC's titles alone describe the firm's unique tone: *Conquest of the Universe, or When Queens Collide* (1967), *Eunuchs of the Forbidden City* (1971), *Professor Bedlam's Educational Punch and Judy Show* (1974), the Wagnerian takeoff *Der Ring Gott Farblunget* (1977), *The Elephant Woman* (1979), *Secret Lives of the Sexists* (1982).

Like *Henry Irving's Lyceum Theatre and *Joan Littlewood's Stratford East, the RTC, ensconced after some early wandering in its own little house in Sheridan Square, was a one-man operation. The genius of the place was Charles Ludlam (1943–1987). As founder, director, playwright, and star of the company, Ludlam *was* the Ridiculous Theatrical Company, though he troubled to build up an acting ensemble adept in his peculiar style of high-tech Manhattan facetia, players like Lola Pashalinski, Everett Quinton, Black-Eyed Susan, and Ludlam's occasional writing collaborator, Bill Vehr, who could complement Ludlam's over-the-top absurdities, not to mention having to play straight to a heroine in drag. (At times, Ludlam went all the way with the travesty, as in his *Salammbô,* the devastating sex queen of Carthage. However, in one of his most famous roles, as *Alexandre Dumas's Camille, Ludlam blithely flourished chest hair above his décolletage.) Because so much of Ludlam's drollery commented on the importance of physical appearance, he made casting surprises an element of his craft. *Anti-Galaxie Nebulae* (1978) was written for puppets, *The Mystery of Irma Vep* (1984) offered only Ludlam and Quinton sharing a multitude of characters in a quick-change marathon, and *Salammbô* (1985) filled out Flaubert with a live bird, a platoon of posing bodybuilders, and a grotesquely obese person of indeterminate sex and terrifyingly scanty costume. At the height of his powers, planning a play about Houdini and a production of Shakespeare's *Titus Andronicus* for the New York Shakespeare Festival, Ludlam died of AIDS.

RIGHT YOU ARE (IF YOU THINK YOU ARE)

Comedy by *Luigi Pirandello, prem. Milan, 1917.

The above is but one of several English translations of Pirandello's title, *Così è (Se Vi Pare),* which literally means *So It Is (If It Seems So To You):* truth is subjective, infinitely variable. This was one of Pirandello's earliest successes, dating from the time when he was still thought a folklorist and a satirist of country ways. The big city folk laughed to see such sport. But with this work Pirandello

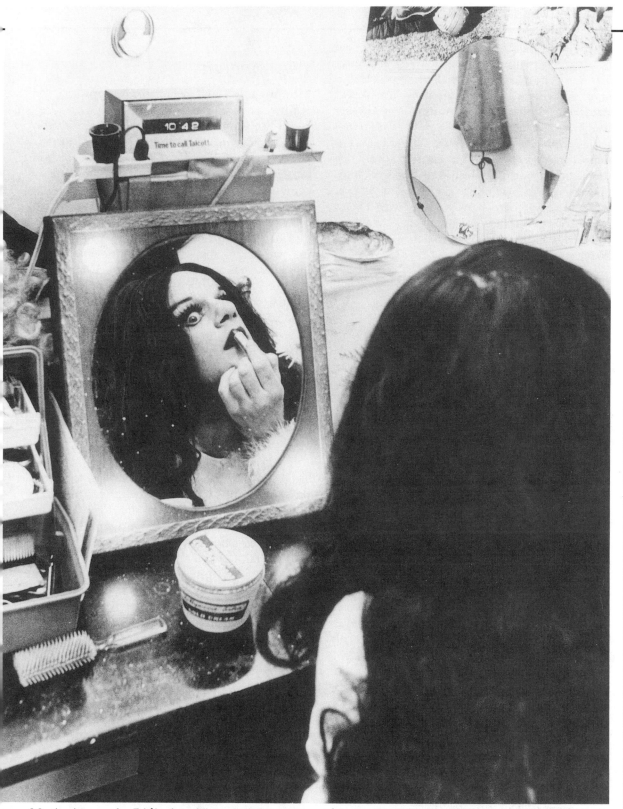

Magic time at the Ridiculous Theatrical Company: making up with Charles Ludlam.

broke away from rustic dialect comedies and launched his inquiry into the relativity of reality. Town gossips question Signor Ponza's odd household of secluded wife and social mother-in-law. Ponza claims that the old woman is mad. Her daughter died, and now she has mistaken Ponza's second wife for the deceased daughter. The mother-in-law says no, it's *Ponza* who's mad. He thinks his wife died, so she had to "remarry" him, pretending to be someone else. At last Signora Ponza herself appears, heavily veiled, with a third explanation: she is both daughter and second wife. But who is she herself? the town gossips ask. "Nobody," she replies.

JASON ROBARDS (1922–   )

Robards still bore a Jr. after his name (to distinguish himself from his actor father) when he made his reputation as a Eugene O'Neill stylist. This was in 1956, when O'Neill himself was making *his* reputation all over again after years of neglect. Playwright and actor were bound together, first on off-Broadway in Robards's Hickey in the Circle-in-the-Square revival of *The Iceman Cometh,* a few months later on Broadway in Robards's creation of the older brother, Jamie Tyrone, in the first American production of *Long Day's Journey into Night.* Robards went on to other O'Neill, in *Hughie, A Touch of the Poet,* as the senior Tyrone in *Long Day's Journey,* and, most successfully, in *A Moon for the Misbegotten* on Broadway with *Colleen Dewhurst.

Robards's dry, quizzical manner and deceptively casual delivery yields a very American artist, contemporary, densely projected, avoiding the classics but for a touch of Shakespeare. Robards's roles beyond O'Neill included a character modeled on F. Scott Fitzgerald in *The Disenchanted* (1958), looking back on his life from his last fading years in Hollywood; the neurotically pampered brother in Lillian Hellman's southern Gothic *Toys in the Attic* (1960); the wry loafer hero of Herb Gardner's comedy *A Thousand Clowns* (1962); the despairingly autobiographical hero of Arthur Miller's *After the Fall* (1964); and, perhaps most effective of all, the complacently exploited captain of a small circle of losers in Hugh Wheeler's touching *Big Fish, Little Fish* (1961).

THE ROBBERS

*Sturm-und-Drang *melodrama by *Friedrich von Schiller, prem. Mannheim, 1782.

Schiller wasn't yet "von" when he wrote this iconoclastic romance on the brutality of aristocratic power. As *Die Räuber* views the world, a nobleman can either be harmfully ineffectual, murderously aggressive, or a bandit: because in such a world only the outlaw is righteous. The text spills out every which way, full of coincidences and lacking explanatory transitions; but this very passion made it a wonder of the day. The Sturm und Drang movement was above all impetuous. A French adaptation of the play in 1792 led to Schiller's being granted honorary French citizenship for his revolutionary ardor—and to Robespierre's banning the dangerous work in 1799. Among several operatic versions is Verdi's unfortunately neglected *I Masnadieri,* written for Jenny Lind.

T. W. ROBERTSON (1829–1871)

Thomas William Robertson was born into a large theatrical family. His sister Madge (1848–1935), billed by her married name as Mrs. Kendal, was to be named a Dame of the British Empire and survives in the modern repertory in Bernard Pomerance's *The Elephant Man* as the actress who champions the miserable hero. But Robertson holds major fame as an instigator of the modern English theatre. As playwright, he began as an eclectic, but found a unique metier in six succinctly titled comedies for Squire Bancroft's company at the Prince of Wales' Theatre, produced annually in the years just before Robertson's death: *Society* (1865), *Ours* (1866), *Caste* (1867), *Play* (1868), *School* (1869), and *M. P.* (1870). Known as "cup and saucer drama" for their bourgeois *naturalism (and most especially for *Caste*'s elaborate kitchen tea party scene), the sextet promoted a liberal examination of society's received notions, bold not for our day but certainly for Robertson's. For instance, in *School,* hearing one Lord Beaufoy dilating on the preposterous concept of women's suffrage, the Robertsonian spokesman ironically replies:

JACK: I agree with you there. If women were admitted to electoral privileges, they'd sell them for the price of a new chignon. Man, as the nobler animal, has the exclusive right to sell his vote for beer.

Thus opening the way for *Henry Arthur Jones, *Arthur Wing Pinero, and *George Bernard Shaw, Robertson as well began a much-needed reform in production. Loathing the artificial decor and stand-and-deliver monotony of staging, he launched a check of the reckless power of the *actor-manager, virtually inventing the figure of the writer-director who alone had the ability to bring his scripts to life. We see a loving portrait of Robertson on the verge of his reforms in the character of Tom Wrench in Pinero's *Trelawny of the "Wells."*

ROMAN THEATRE

The ancient Romans based their theatre on the *Greek model, apparently with infusions from local traditions in comic *pantomime that, on their own, eventually blossomed into Italian *commedia dell'arte.* Roman theatre structures, at the height of Rome's glory, were smaller, tighter, and almost entirely enclosed versions of the Greek outdoor amphitheatre, and the texts were drawn from classic Greek tragedy and New Comedy, suaver and less bawdy than the Old Comedy of Aristophanes. However, the atmosphere of the performances was vastly different from that of the Greek play contest. In place of an audience partaking of a central civic function, the Roman stage gives us a pleasure-seeking elite in a city that takes spectacle and sadistic sport for granted.

Three playwrights above all stand out in this arena, the jaunty Plautus (254–184 B.C.), the Hellenophile stylist Terence (?195–159 B.C.), and the tragedian Seneca (?4 B.C.–65 A.D.). All three left plays that proved very influential in the Renaissance and after—Shakespeare based *The Comedy of Errors* on two plays of Plautus, and the heavy-

weight critic *Gotthold Lessing declared Plautus's *Captivi* (The Prisoners) the perfect comedy, a model for moderns. But then, of all Roman forms, it was the freewheeling Plautan *farce, with its screwball contingent of lecherous old man, braggart soldier, shrewish wife, cunning slave, and so on, that most thoroughly left a mark on Western theatre. Terence was thought somewhat sedate (though this in itself recommended him in the prudish Middle Ages), and Seneca's copies of Aeschylus, Sophocles, and Euripides lack the vitality of the originals. It is believed that Seneca's plays were purely literary exercises, to be read by his friends, not staged even privately: Seneca did enjoy a vogue in sixteenth century Spain and in England during the Elizabethan era; scholars have enjoyed a field day in picking through Shakespeare, John Webster, and Ben Jonson for Senecan hommages, line by line. More important, it was Seneca's overall structure, lit by a blazing new poetry, that helped create Elizabethan tragedy. However, of the three Romans, only Plautus remains eminently actable today, agelessly droll.
(See also Roscius.)

THE ROPE DANCERS

Domestic tragedy by Morton Wishengrad (1914–   ), prem. New York, 1957.

A totally forgotten but very beautifully written piece, quite unlike the typical Broadway fare but, shockingly, a Broadway hit. Set in a New York City tenement apartment at the turn of the century, *The Rope Dancers* concerns a broken Irish family: good-for-nothing charmer of a father, implacably unloving mother, and a daughter cursed with a sixth finger on one hand—"the finger of God's wrath!" the mother cries. The young *Peter Hall directed Art Carney (in his Broadway debut) and Siobhán McKenna fresh from her off-Broadway *Saint Joan;* Joan Blondell played a slovenly neighbor and Theodore Bikel a Jewish doctor. All told, this is a mildly surprising but not implausible lineup for post–World War II Broadway. What was surprising was the success of an essentially sombre and despairing work, as angry as the thwarted mother, as helpless as the wistful father, very naturalistic, very poetic. McKenna orders

Carney out of the apartment, offering him fifty cents for lodging, but their daughter begs him to go without it:

MARGARET: He can't, Lizzie. Shall I tell you why? Because your father knows that fifty cents is forty-nine cents more than pride. James Hyland, you stand there dumb! Where are all the books you read, the stories, the jokes, the bragging! Did you brag to Mrs. Farrow and make her laugh! I will pay fifty cents to laugh. A dollar. Make me laugh, James. Tell me one of your stories. (Shouting it) Well . . . Did you spend it all on Mrs. Farrow? Is there nothing left for me? (She goes to him, close . . . her body taut like a drawn bow.) Where are all the words?

JAMES: You choke me, Margaret.

MARGARET: Good. Tell me a story full of your choking words.

JAMES: What you do to me.

MARGARET: I'll tell you what you do to me . . . my fastidious James Hyland who always had to carry two clean handkerchiefs . . . you choke me. (He reaches to her, touching her lips, and her body arches at his touch, her eyes close; then, with rage, she swings her arm down like the blade of a guillotine.) I am no rag doll for your fingers to touch. . . . I am five flights above the street. These are my four walls. My rent is paid in advance. So you go! And let me shut the door! And turn the key! And draw the chain across!

ROSCIUS (?120–62 B.C.)

Quintus Roscius was not only the most famous actor of the *Roman theatre, but a thespian buzz word two milleniums later. Numerous actors were hailed as "The Irish Roscius," "The American Roscius," and so on—though, ironically, the truly immortal actors were seldom so honored. The best-known modern Roscius was the black American *Ira Aldridge, but the most typical was *Master Betty, the child prodigy who took London by storm for a season and then fell into obscurity.

EDMOND ROSTAND (See *Cyrano de Bergerac*)

THE ROYAL COURT THEATRE

One of London's most historic theatres, though located way off the *West End, in Chelsea. The first of two Royal Courts, a converted church, opened in 1870; in the 1880s it played host to a series of comedies by *Arthur Wing Pinero, the so-called "Court farces" that established a new level of ensemble playing in this form. The structure was demolished in 1887 and a new Royal Court opened the next year, when Pinero capped his series with the "comedietta" *Trelawney of the "Wells"*, a huge hit at least partly because of its polished cast, which took in the young Gerald du Maurier (who was later to create *Peter Pan*'s dual lead of Captain Hook and Mr. Darling), Dot Boucicault (son of the eminent actor and playwright *Dion Boucicault, and sister of the original Peter Pan, Nina Boucicault) as the crabby Sir William Gower, and, as heroine, the great Irene Vanbrugh.

More ambitious fare saw the Royal Court through the early 1900s, including a great deal of *George Bernard Shaw (who first became popular in England through these productions) in the famous joint managership of *Harley Granville-Barker and John Vedrenne. After two decades as a movie theatre and a casualty of the blitz, the renovated house reopened in 1952. Four years later, George Devine (1910–1965) settled his English Stage Company there, and with *John Osborne's *Look Back in Anger* in 1956, Devine proceeded to stimulate, harass, and enlighten West End placidity with an extraordinary parade of "angry young" writers, including *Arnold Wesker and *John Arden, with *Eugène Ionesco and even *Noël Coward spliced in to texture the revolution. (And this was unreconstructed, *well-made, and once-over-lightly Coward, an adaptation of Georges *Feydeau called *Look After Lulu*—with Vivien Leigh, no less. The progressive writers were scandalized.)

After Devine's death, the theatre retained its

special status as the forum of the iconoclastic writer, at the same time drawing in many of Britain's most important actors, eager to try their talent on something with bite. *Laurence Olivier, Joan Plowright, *Paul Scofield, *John Gielgud, and *Ralph Richardson have dropped in, as have numerous touring troupes even more avant-garde than the house teams.

THE ROYAL SHAKESPEARE COMPANY

Major cultural-capital theatre companies usually form *before* they occupy their permanent home: the National Theatre of Great Britain, the *Comédie-Française, *Habimah, and the *Berliner Ensemble all existed before they found ultimate housing. *This* company started with a building—at that in a cultural backwater, however historic—the Shakespeare Memorial Theatre in Stratford-on-Avon. Opened in 1879, the project of Charles Flower, a stage-struck brewer, the theatre first played host to free-lance production, then assembled a company. However, the out-of-London location forced a second-class status on the company, especially in relation to the Shakespeare put on at the *Old Vic in the golden days of *Olivier and *Gielgud.

In 1960, when *Peter Hall took over the company, the present name was adopted, a London home established at the Aldwych Theatre, and a program implemented: to blend the eponymously mandated Shakespearean productions with a wider repertory, including new works. This stimulated a pungent rivalry with the Old Vic, especially in the 1970s, when the latter took official residence directly across the Thames from the Aldwych in its private palace as the National Theatre of Great Britain. The two troupes competed not only for talent but for government subsidy, for the long independent Shakespeare Memorial Theatre had expanded beyond a simple box office economy. It was, in effect, a second (or first?) national theatre, with its own traditions, personalities, goals—not least when Hall crossed the river to take over *the* National Theatre, choosing Trevor Nunn (1940–   ) as his successor. Hall's move seemed to bind and separate the two companies all at once. His style and taste were binding factors; his entry into the more officially "national" house was a distinction. More distinctive yet is the National's struggle to unite its arts (on three stages) while the RSC calmly revels in diversity of projects. As witness, its varied roster of major productions: *The Wars of the Roses* (from Shakespeare's *Henry VI* trilogy along with the consecutive *Richard III*); *Harold Pinter's *The Homecoming;* *Peter Brook's stagings of *Marat/Sade, King Lear* (with Paul Scofield—the "Beckett version"), and *A Midsummer Night's Dream;* John Barton's accordion of tragedies entitled *The Greeks; *The Life and Adventures of Nicholas Nickleby;* and even musicals, including a delightful *pantomime spoof called *The Swan Down Gloves,* a viciously ironic pantomime spoof (on British imperialism in China) called *Poppy,* and an adaptation of a French pop opera, *Les Misérables.* Amusingly, the RSC—the theatre that created a company—became the company that created a theatre in 1982, when it moved into the Barbican arts complex far to the east of the *West End theatre district, near Moorgate.

S

SADLER'S WELLS

Though there have been auditoriums of one sort or another on this suburban North London site since 1685, Sadler's Wells lacks the epic historical grandeur of *Covent Garden and *Drury Lane. As Theatres Royal, those two houses held the monopoly on drama as such. Non-"patent" theatres like Sadler's Wells had to get along on concerts, musical plays, pantomimes, and an early nineteenth century fashion, "aquatic drama."

The "Wells," as it eventually came to be called, was named after a mineral spring that one Thomas Sadler discovered on his property. It came into its own as a neighborhood *repertory house after Parliament disbanded the patent monopoly in 1843, with a bill taking in everything from Shakespeare to murder thrillers. (This is just the company that *Arthur Wing Pinero had in mind when he wrote *Trelawney of the "Wells".) By the early 1900s, the theatre's various eras had ended and it sat on Rosebery Avenue empty and forgot. Then Lilian Baylis took over the site, building a new (the present) playhouse to match the *Old Vic, the theatre that Baylis had inherited from her aunt, Emma Cons. The two houses were to alternate performances by a drama company and an opera company; but by the mid-1930s the thespians held the Old Vic and the musicians Sadler's Wells. Everything was sung in English—"Vesti la giubba" as "On with the motley," Carmen's Habañera as "Love resembles a wilful bird"—and important opera history was made in 1945 at the world premiere of the work that launched a glorious era in which composers, librettists, singers, conductors, and stage directors made English opera a byword of excellence on the international level: Benjamin Britten's *Peter Grimes.* In the summer of 1968, the opera troupe moved into the center of London, taking over the Coliseum in *John Gielgud's production of *Don Giovanni.* This is the English National Opera; the New Sadler's Well's Opera, back on Rosebery Avenue, specializes in operetta.

SAINT JOAN

*Chronicle play by *George Bernard Shaw, prem. New York, 1923.

Jean Anouilh's version of the same events, *The Lark,* sees Joan as a victim of Church fascism and national politics. She is a maid, a sprite, a visionary. Shaw sees her as a warrior, a revolutionary, a genius. And like all geniuses, she is too good for her time. The world is run by tyrants for the benefit of mediocrities. A daredevil phenomenon like Joan of Arc (and, Shaw surely implies, like Shaw) would destroy established civilization. In a comic epilogue, the dead Joan confronts the major figures of the play and learns from a clergyman in modern dress that she has been made a saint. Her murderers have become her admirers. But the world is still not ready to face up to genius. At Joan's suggestion that she "rise from the dead, and come back to you as a living woman," the cast recoils in panic. Indeed, Shaw warns us, they would burn her again. Alone, Joan prays, "O God that madest this beautiful earth, when will it be ready to receive Thy saints? How long, O Lord; how long?"

Though it lacks the color and fun and action of the more typical Shavian plays, *Saint Joan* has become one of his most enduring works, often called his greatest.

SALOMÉ

Art nouveau one-acter by *Oscar Wilde, prem. Paris, 1896.

So scandalous in subject and approach that Wilde wrote it in French, *Salomé* was the first of his mature plays, published in 1892. Sarah Bernhardt was to have created the Judean princess that year, but the authorities banned the play. It was not seen in London till 1905—privately, at that. In exquisitely overwrought language—not only in the spoken lines but in the detailed stage directions as well, as if Wilde knew that more people would read than see the play—Wilde pictures a world of poetic licentiousness, wherein a princess must have a prophet beheaded before she can relish his kiss. Two historical points: the play has been overshadowed by Richard Strauss's operatic setting of the text (1905); and Wilde was in prison for being a homosexual when *Salomé* was first performed.

SALVATION NELL

Social-realist soap opera by *Edward Sheldon, prem. New York, 1908.

Sheldon's study of life among New York's proletariat helped mark the emergence of the American *naturalistic style, from *melodrama into character drama—"a real theatre," the grateful Eugene O'Neill wrote to Sheldon, years later, "as opposed to the unreal—and to me then, hateful—theatre of my father [*James O'Neill], in whose atmosphere I had been brought up."

Salvation Nell concerns a scrubwoman who abandons her criminal boyfriend for life in the Salvation Army, at length to take him back upon his promised reformation. *Mrs. Fiske played the heroine; it became one of her great roles. But the play's most noteworthy feature was its persuasive representation of the slums, from the argot of the streets to the despair of life on the bottom of the system. The opening of Christmas Eve in a teeming bar, an orchestration of the voices of real city people, left a memory upon a generation of American playwrights. O'Neill used something very like it to launch *The Hairy Ape,* in the firemen's forecastle of a transatlantic liner, "crowded with men, shouting, cursing, laughing, singing—a confused, inchoate uproar swelling into a sort of unity." This, removed to a tavern, was precisely the effect of Sheldon's opening tableau in *Salvation Nell.*

VICTORIEN SARDOU (1831–1908)

"Why need plays be so brutally, callously, barbarously immoral as this?" asks George Bernard Shaw of Sardou's *Fédora* (1882)—immoral not because the heroine is an adulteress, but because Sardou wrote of life without writing of life, because he scanned life's mysteries not for understanding but for sensation. Shaw terms it "Sardoodledum"—note the compliment in the insult. For Sardou was no mere playwright, but The Playwright of the Age, a one-man kingdom of drama. Sardou's *"well-made plays" had immense influence on the English theatre—to an extent, they had influence even on Shaw, in the plot contrivances of his earliest pieces. Moreover, the greatest actresses of the day loved Sardou's ability to build his pieces around the faceted glories of the prima donna. This also made them ideal subjects for opera settings. Puccini adapted Sardou's *La Tosca* (1887), dropping the article, but not before La *Bernhardt had toured the show to and fro in the West, and up and down in it, like Satan looking over the human

One of the great stars of all time in one of the all-time great star parts: Sarah Bernhardt as Sardou's Tosca.

race, and finding nothing to respect or believe in. Sardoodledum.

WILLIAM SAROYAN (1908–1981)

Saroyan's is a world of tender souls forever menaced by professional villains, economic hardship, and small-minded neighbors; but his folk survive through optimism and naiveté. An Armenian-American raised in northern California, Saroyan blended the immigrant's fervor for his (new) homeland with a Californian amiability, in both fiction and theatre. Unfortunately, Saroyan never found the right theatrical structure to house his worldview, and the promise made in *My Heart's in the Highlands* (1939) was never kept, though the immediately following *The Time of Your Life* (1939) remains a kind of fitful classic, revived just when everyone thinks it must be beyond revival. A look at various drifters and dreamers in a San Francisco waterfront bar, *The Time of Your Life* is basic Saroyan, sweet and innocent and a little shabby till evil confronts good, when for a moment, it becomes tough, still shabby but heroic. The play's theme—"In the time of your life, *live*"—recalls *Thornton Wilder. But the writing lacks Wilder's control, blossoming out here and there as Saroyan sifts the barflies for moods and tempos. The public lost patience with Saroyan's approach in the ensuing decades, though *Hello Out There* (1941), a one-acter about the wan romance between a jail slavey and a young man framed on a rape charge, became a fixture of the American high school repertory.

JEAN-PAUL SARTRE (1905–1980)

More a philosopher than a playwright, Sartre used the theatre to explore his view of the world. His oeuvre, then, is almost entirely comprised of *pièces à thèse* ("thesis plays," more commonly called "problem plays," as with Ibsen and Shaw). Sartre proved an able dramatist, so versatile that his forms and tone change along with his "problems." Thus, *Les Mouches* (The Flies, 1943) is a reinterpretation of Greek tragedy, specifically the aftermath of Orestes's murder of Clytemnestra, the flies being Sartre's version of the Furies. *Huis-Clos* (No Exit, 1944) is a black parody of a drawing room comedy, the "drawing room" a chamber in the underworld where the light never goes off and three people are trapped in each other's company forever. "L'enfer," says one of them, "c'est les autres": Hell is other people. *Les Mains Sales* (Dirty Hands, 1948) is a murder thriller, *Le Diable et le Bon Dieu* (The Devil and the Good Lord, 1951) a costume drama.

At the heart of all Sartre's "problems" is an at times savage existentialism, exhorting the public to renounce traditional Western institutions, especially religion. Instead, each man must become his own institution. To be alive is to exercise one's will. Awareness of free choice and responsibility for the actions chosen are Sartre's most intent themes. Even in comedy, in *Kean* (1953), adapted from *Alexandre Dumas *père*, Sartre asked his actor *protagonist to separate himself from the alluring imagery of his stage roles, to objectify his perceptions. Sartre's only other comedy, *Nekrassov* (1955), begins with one man jumping into the Seine to drown and another man pulling him out —not because suicide is wrong, but because *half-hearted* suicide is questionable. The rescued man furiously insists that he wanted to die, but his rescuer corrects him: "You were swimming." (See also *Kean*.)

SATIRE

The use of comedy to expose faults in the social system, for example George S. Kaufman and Marc Connelly's *Beggar on Horseback* (1924), an attack on the American commercialization of art, or Alan Bennett's *Forty Years On* (1968), an ingeniously insidious deprecation of establishment England through the device of a boys' school pageant. Satire is a higher form than mere spoof; satire, whatever its tone, has a moral purpose. We may note the difference by comparing the best *Restoration comedies with most of Kaufman's. Restoration comedy is sharply observed social critique, gritty and anti-sentimental. It does not forgive its villains. Kaufman's collaborations, such as *The Man Who Came to Dinner* and *You Can't Take It With

You, are just sharp entertainments, sentimental-ized and forgiving—and Kaufman liked it that way. "Satire," he notoriously said, "is what closes Saturday night."

(See also *The Importance of Being Earnest, The Mis-anthrope, The School for Scandal,* and *The Way of the World.*)

SATYR PLAY

In *Greek theatre, the great all-day tetralogies of the spring *Dionysia comprised three intercon-nected serious plays followed by a low comedy on the same theme or story, utilizing a chorus of sa-tyrs. This so-called satyr play, apparently a some-what civilized version of an ancient psycho-sexual ceremony, was considered far less important as literature than as song-and-dance-rite. For while some twenty-five Dionysian tragedies have sur-vived, we have only one complete satyr play, Eu-ripides's *Cyclops.*

THE DUKE OF SAXE-MEININGEN

(See The Director and The
Meiningers)

SCÈNE À FAIRE

French for "obligatory scene." In the *"well-made play," a carefully balanced structure of plot in-trigues made certain scenes necessary—the con-frontation of two antagonistic characters, for instance, or the revelation of a character's shocking past, known to the audience but not, till the Big Moment, to the other characters. Though these were the key scenes, the high points of the drama, their contrived nature only reaffirmed the artificial quality of the well-made form as a whole. By the end of the nineteenth century, more *naturalistic writers such as Ibsen and Chekhov were revamping or wholly doing away with the well-made play; and the first thing that they did away with was the larger-than-life falseness of the *scène à faire.*

On the other hand, the notion that certain ac-tions lead up to a certain climax is basic to the very idea of theatre, any kind of theatre. One might call the moment in which Sophocles's Oedipus learns that he has killed his father, married his mother, and called down the plague upon Thebes the *scène à faire,* even the Revelation Scene. George Bernard Shaw, who used the well-made play as a form (while giving it different content), was well aware of the uses of the obligatory scene, and actually added one into the *film* version of *Pygmalion*—Eli-za's debut at the Embassy Ball. Indeed, he had left it out of the original play only to spare *Pygmalion's* companies the expense of a dressy crowd scene. One might discern the survival of the *scène à faire* in the age even of *absurdism, in Samuel Beckett's *Waiting for Godot.* By teasing our interest in seeing the mysterious title character and at length never presenting him, Beckett is using the concept of the obligatory scene by omitting it, making his point by playing off the audience's expectations. Perhaps it is best to think of the "obligatory scene" as an ageless concept of theatre, and "scène à faire" as merely a term that came along thousands of years after the fact.

SCENERY

Until the Renaissance, the physical appearance of theatre production lay entirely in the movement and costuming of the players, not in the dressing of the stage. The *Greeks and *Romans saw no scenery as such, only the permanent architectural facade of the back wall. *Medieval European the-atre developed the importance of props, or portable accessories, but thought the front steps of a church, without decoration, a valid stage. Eastern theatre placed far more importance on costume than any style thus far mentioned, even the Greeks, whose elaborate, almost ritualistic masked outfits were, but for the masks, rather standard-ized. However, even in the East, theatre concen-trated on the look of the players, not on the look of the stage.

The notion of shifting pictures mounted behind the actors was not introduced till the Elizabethan masque, a court entertainment taking in music, poetry, dance, and an exhibitionistic attitude toward decor; and, in the sixteenth century, Italian theatres, built with the express intention of setting up a series of all-purpose settings—a meadow, city streets, the gardens of a palace—behind a framing *proscenium. Special effects were provided by "transformation" scenes, for instance as a wasteland gave way to a fairy bower.

The masque proved an ephemeral form. But Italian theatre design strongly influenced all European theatre architecture, especially as the Italians emphasized facilities for the production of opera, and Western theatres of any importance had to accommodate this universally popular entertainment. Italian technology in the devising of the famous "perspective" views that gave the illusion of distance and density were influential even beyond the borders of the theatre world, and by the late eighteenth century all Western theatres were organized along similar lines: a painted backcloth far *upstage, flats of painted canvas mounted on light wooden frames strapped together as standing pieces and secured in grooves, the framing side- and top-pieces hanging in the overhead flies for use as needed, and perhaps a scrim up front, solid when lit from the audience's side and transparent when lit from behind. Ninteenth century *naturalism favored the box set for interiors, virtually a room with the *fourth wall (the "curtain side," so to say) left open to the spectators. The twentieth century revolt against naturalism, however, favored the impressionistic vistas made possible by the cyclorama, a curved blank wall at the back of the theatre, very suggestible to plays of light and shadow. The revolving stage, which allows for very fast and fluid changes of scene, proved one of the early twentieth century's most useful innovations, and developments in nonrepresentational decor have freed the contemporary stage of the slavish duplication of a "real life" that had been pressing on the theatre since the mid-1800s. For instance, the *Royal Shakepeare Company's 1985 staging of Christopher Hampton's Les Liaisons Dangereuses—on sexual intrigue in late eighteenth century France—could move blithely from one location to another without changing Bob Crowley's "unit set" arrangement of suffocating drapery, louver doors, a huge bureau overstuffed with linen and jewelry, and salon furniture.

Thus, from an essentially bare playing area, ef-fortfully filled over the centuries with increasingly lifelike settings, the theatre has lately developed an evocative pseudo-realism, sophisticated and flexible.

(See also Adolphe Appia, the Galli-Bibiena Family, Robert Edmond Jones, Sean Kenny, Jo Mielziner, Periaktoi, Proscenium, Thrust Stage, Wings.)

FRIEDRICH VON SCHILLER
(1759–1805)

One of Germany's greatest playwrights, the equal of his contemporary *Goethe and the superior of all who followed till *Bertolt Brecht and the twentieth century. Schiller was the outstanding exponent of the *Sturm und Drang movement, tensely collating the Romantic's medievalism and nature painting with revolutionary politics. Schiller makes heroes of a bandit, a musician, a rebellious prince, Joan of Arc, William Tell—and Schiller himself, at the age of twenty-three, had to flee his home in Württemberg to seek asylum in Mannheim, though twenty years later he was elevated into the aristocracy, skeptically but willingly.

Such is the air of tragic exaltation in Schiller that Rossini, Donizetti, and Verdi found his characters irresistibly operatic. (Better yet, their Schiller adaptations brought out their very best in, respectively, Guillaume Tell, Maria Stuarda, and Don Carlos.) Yet if most of these plays end in the death of the defeated, Schiller's glory overwhelms Schiller's doom. Perhaps it is Schiller's youthfulness above all that marks his work, the reckless, bold energy of the naive icon breaker. Schiller's plays abound in father roles—Count von Moor in Die Räuber (The Robbers, 1782), Miller in Kabale und Liebe (Intrigue and Love, 1784), King Philip II in Don Carlos (1787), Thibaut d'Arc in Die Jungfrau von Orleans (The Maid of Orleans, 1801), and the *protagonist of Wilhelm Tell (1804). Still, except for the freedom fighter Tell, all these fathers, even the sympathetic ones, seem to symbolize stifling conservatism. Fathers uphold the old order; young heroes strive for a better world. Thus, Philip II of Spain actually hands his son over to a dark age Church for execution, and Joan's father denounces her as a witch before King and people in the cathedral square of Rheims on coronation day.

Thus, too, in *Maria Stuart* (1800), the monarch in power (Elizabeth I) is the one Schiller fears; the monarch stripped of power (Mary Stuart) is Schiller's heroine, in a questionable reading of the historical data. This was almost habitual with Schiller. Though he led the movement to reopen the case of Joan of Arc, exploited and destroyed by her coevals and defamed by Shakespeare and Voltaire as a bitchy whore, Schiller's Carlos is a dauntless hero where the real Carlos was apparently a demented cretin. So Schiller's Mary is poetic and admirable, Elizabeth a neurotic tyrant: and of course Schiller must bring the two noble rivals together for a confrontation scene. History tells us they never met.

No matter. This is historical theatre, not history, and Schiller's belief in heroes, in the heroism of a brotherhood battling for liberty, invigorates the public yet today. Again: this is a *young* writer's theatre, fitting work for the man who became a European celebrity in his mid-twenties, as a result of the international sensation created by *The Robbers*. It contrasts nicely with the "grand old philosopher" guise of Goethe, who eventually befriended Schiller and made him his colleague in the important cultural capital of Weimar, putting the court theatre at the disposal of Schiller's output, starting with the opening of the new city playhouse with *Das Lager* (The Camp, 1798), the first part of Schiller's *chronicle trilogy on the Thirty Years' War, *Wallenstein*. In this great work, Schiller completed his growth from the format of insurgent *melodrama to a Shakespearean majesty. The switch from prose dialogue to verse, introduced in *Don Carlos,* marked the start of Schiller's development from Wunderkind to Meister. But *Wallenstein*'s astonishing scope, blending heroic tragedy into a fresco of historical events, gives us the playwright of the age.

(See also *The Robbers.*)

AUGUST VON SCHLEGEL
(1767–1845)

This playwright and critic, outraged that his work was getting no attention, ironically left his mark on the repertory as the major German translator of Shakespeare. From 1797 to 1801, Schlegel published sixteen titles—*Romeo and Juliet, Hamlet, The Merchant of Venice, The Tempest, Twelfth Night* (under its subtitle as *Was Ihr Wollt:* What You Will), *A Midsummer Night's Dream, Julius Caesar, As You Like It,* and the most notable of the history plays. Nine years later, Schlegel added *Richard III,* but the remaining titles he handed over to the playwright Ludwig Tieck (1773–1854), known for his *Carlo Gozzi–like fairy-tale plays. Tieck collaborated with his daughter Dorothea and Count Wolf von Baudissin, and the complete Schlegel-Tieck Shakespeare was published in 1839–1840.

These translations stand as the most imposing such undertaking in theatre history. Their fidelity to Shakespeare's spirit, if not invariably to the Shakespearean letter, is amazing; and poor neglected Schlegel became, by proxy, one of the most frequently performed playwrights of the Romantic era in German-speaking nations. Today, his Shakespeare outdraws Germany's two "national poets," Goethe and Schiller, and rivals Bertolt Brecht.

ARTHUR SCHNITZLER (1862–1931)

This Austrian physician, something of a Sunday playwright, belongs to the *fin-de-siècle* Vienna of Jugendstil (the German term for art nouveau) painting and expressionistic music, when late-Romantic art seemed to decline into psychotic delirium: the Vienna of Gustav Klimt and Arnold Schoenberg, of Peter Altenberg and Gustav Mahler, even of Hugo von Hofmannsthal, the Classic-Romantic playwright, with his fresh views of Greek myth and his famous collaboration with the opera composer Richard Strauss. Schnitzler was especially associated with the literary circle called "Young Vienna," and the Vienna that Schnitzler portrays in his theatre is not only young but intimate, melancholy, and sensual, a place where the aristocratic dandy of the great world and the *süsses Mädel* ("sweet maiden") of the suburbs meet as equals through the democracy of sex.

Schnitzler, in short, was trouble. He was Jewish in an increasingly anti-Semitic environment, a bold artist in the most conservative culture in Eu-

Lady Teazle (Geraldine McEwan) and Joseph Surface (John Gielgud) in Gielgud's 1962 production of Sheridan's The School for Scandal. *This is Act Four, scene three, the Seduction: "Now, my dear Lady Teazle, if you would but once make a trifling faux pas. . . ."*

rope, and a truth-teller in a society made of expedient lies. Throughout his life, his plays did battle with censors; even one of his published scripts was banned as pornography. Most typical of this side of Schnitzler is *Reigen* (The Round Dance, written 1900, prem. 1912, in Hungarian), generally known by the title of the French adaptation, twice filmed, *La Ronde. Reigen* gives us a social cross section: the soldier, the prostitute, the poet, the actress, the husband, the wife, and so on, of course including the ever-essential dandy and *süsses Mädel*. In ten scenes, each for a different couple, the "round dance" passes from man to woman to man to woman, right through the cast, with a little dialogue and a little sex for each pairing. Indeed, each scene is built around an act of copulation, an amazingly daring premise for 1900. But then Schnitzler was less a man of the theatre than a writer who used the convention of dialogue. Many of his plays seem born for the library rather than the playhouse—not because they lack a sense of drama, but because they defy what was considered practical on German-language stages of Schnitzler's time. He seemed fascinated by the possibilities of the small piece, concentrating on one-acters, even on cycles of one-acters, to be performed as one might unstring a strand of pearls. Most typical of *this* side of Schnitzler is the series of seven more or less consecutive dialogues known collectively as *Anatol* (written 1893, prem. as a whole 1910), each dialogue self-contained but gaining in effect when read or performed complete. The storyline follows the shifting amours of a young bachelor, a first-rate showcase for Schnitzler's enlightening insights into the character of sex relations.

THE SCHOOL FOR SCANDAL

*Comedy of manners by *Richard Brinsley Sheridan, prem. London, 1777.

If Sheridan generally stands out in his day for his satiric pungency, this play stands out in Sheridan's output for its perfection of technique. From William Congreve to Oscar Wilde, British social comedy reads well enough on the page, but this work more than most really springs to life in the theatre, with its salon of gloating gossips; its "old man took a young country wife" quarrel scene, delightful but disturbingly realistic as the two agree to maintain peace then, step by step, break out the war all over again; its historical use of the "delayed entrance" for the lovably roguish secondary hero, Charles Surface, constantly mentioned through the first and second acts and therefore as fascinating when he finally opens his mouth as Puccini's Turandot, launching her first line after the opera is half over; and the famous Screen Scene, another historical precedent in what was to become a cliché of *farce, though of course Sheridan uses the unmasking of the hidden party for climactic *peripeteia* rather than for laughter. In fact, the moment is *terrifyingly* comic—antic, but honest.

So is the play in general—too honest, almost, for its good. Hypocrisy and malice are exposed, yes; but the villains are always with us, and Sheridan wants us to know that. His play, luckily, is always with us, too, as the most endearing English title of the eighteenth century. Unlike most of his coevals, Sheridan retained the old *Restoration style of nomenclature—his hypocrite is Joseph Surface, his chief gossip is Lady Sneerwell, her confidant and familiar is Snake, and the bantering young country wife is Lady Teazle. But Sheridan's plot and characters, so Restoration in overall appearance, lack the Restoration's appetitive bawdiness. On the contrary, this is an abstemious play, in which marriage is a matter of affection and dalliance a matter of style. The two young lovers, Charles and Maria, do not even have a love scene. Some commentators take this for a fault in Sheridan's dramaturgy; it seems to me more an element of his distinctly anti-sensual atmosphere.

We cannot leave this masterpiece without quotation. Here's the first of the Scandal Scenes, with that unstoppable locomotive of dish, Mrs. Candour:

MRS. CANDOUR: People will talk—there's no preventing it. Why, it was but yesterday I was told that Miss Gadabout had eloped with Sir Filagree Flirt. But, Lord! there's no minding what one hears; though, to be sure, I had this from a very good authority.

MARIA: Such reports are highly scandalous.

MRS. CANDOUR: So they are, child—shameful, shameful! But the world is so censorious, no character escapes. Lord, now who would have suspected your friend, Miss Prim, of an indiscretion? Yet such is the ill-nature of people, that they say her uncle stopped her last week, just as she was stepping into the York mail with her dancing-master.

MARIA: I'll answer for't there are no grounds for that report.

MRS. CANDOUR: Ah, no foundation in the world, I dare swear: no more, probably, than the story circulated last month, of Mrs. Festino's affair with Colonel Cassino—though, to be sure, that matter was never rightly cleared up.

JOSEPH SURFACE: The license of invention some people take is monstrous indeed.

MARIA: 'Tis so; but, in my opinion, those who report such things are equally culpable.

MRS. CANDOUR: To be sure they are; tale-bearers are as bad as the tale-makers.

PAUL SCOFIELD (1922–   )

"This is the best Hamlet I have ever seen," critic Kenneth Tynan wrote of Scofield in 1948, in director Michael Benthall's production for the Shakespeare Memorial Theatre (later the *Royal Shakespeare Company) in Victorian decor. There was Olivier. There was Gielgud. Now Scofield would join them in transatlantic proclamations of Shakespeare, Marlowe, Sheridan, Shaw, Ibsen, Chekhov. What no one could have foreseen, not even Tynan, was the coming revolution in English playwrighting, the John Osbornes, Arnold Weskers, and Harold Pinters who would challenge the classics in the ensuing generation. Suddenly, new British plays were not merely graceful placeholders, maintaining an actor's career between the Othellos and Shylocks. Some new plays presented roles of such contemporary bite and power that important actors had no choice but to redefine their importance in them—Olivier, perhaps most prominently of all, as Osborne's shabby vaudevillian in *The Entertainer*. Gielgud was slower to respond to the changed climate. His new roles counted Noël Coward or Peter Ustinov, of an older fashion, though he did play Edward Albee's *Tiny Alice* in New York and, later, finally tried Pinter and David Storey.

Scofield's road was the widest. True, his most famous contemporary portrayal was Thomas More in Robert Bolt's *A Man for All Seasons* (1960), a *chronicle play very much in the classical line, even admitting the *Brechtian interlocutor figure that Bolt calls the Common Man. And Scofield's icily tragic reading of the titular anti-hero of Peter Shaffer's *Amadeus* (1979) is another performance of the kind that Scofield could easily have rendered in a classic. But in Charles Dyer's *Staircase* (1966), about two aging gay lovers; John Osborne's *The Hotel in Amsterdam* (1968), playing a garrulous screenwriter "relaxing" in the company of other moviemakers; and Christopher Hampton's anti-colonialist *Savages* (1973) moved Scofield into the world of present-day British stagecraft. Then, too, the *King Lear* that Scofield took on tour from Russia to the United States in the early-middle 1960s (and later filmed) was the ultimate in modernist Shakespeare, staged by *Peter Brook with an eye on *Samuel Beckett. To top it all, Scofield is one of the very few elite English actors of his time to have appeared in a musical in an all-out song-and-dance role, as the cynical agent of a rock and roll star in *Expresso Bongo* (1958).

EUGÈNE SCRIBE (1791–1861)

The presiding playwright of early nineteenth century Paris, celebrated in his lifetime and increasingly execrated in the last quarter of the century for the invention of the "*well-made play," deftly plotted rather than realistically characterized. Because Scribe worked with collaborators, it was said —fairly—that he ran a "factory," especially of opera librettos. Scribe's operas, in both the lighter form of *opéra comique* and the dense majesty of grand opera, are musical expansions of the well-made formula, depending on surprise and the picturesque rather than on mimetic truth. But Paris was the center of the opera world in Scribe's day, and he was immensely influential, running up texts set by such masters as Verdi, Rossini, Donizetti, Bellini, Meyerbeer, Gounod, Halévy, and, most constantly, Auber. None of Scribe's plays survives in performance, unless one counts Cilèa's opera *Adriana Lecouvreur,* based closely on Scribe's *Adrienne Lecouvreur* (1849), a biographically imaginative recollection of an eighteenth century star of the *Comédie-Française. Scribe wrote *Adrienne Lecouvreur* (with Ernest Legouvé) for *Rachel and the Comédie, and it became an insistent vehicle for such other stars as *Sarah Bernhardt, *Eleonora Duse, and *Helena Modjeska. Despite his wide popularity, Scribe had his detractors even when he was alive and at his height. As the poet Heinrich Heine was fading on his deathbed, someone asked him to rally, to make an effort to live, to *breathe.* If not a breath, then at least a hiss. Could he not even *hiss?* "No," gasped Heine. "Not even something by Scribe."

SENECA (See Roman Theatre)

ANDREI SERBAN (1943–)

As a disciple of *Peter Brook, the Romanian Serban unites the distinct traditions of physicalized theatre and what we may call "dialogue theatre." However, Serban's oft-cited debts to Antonin Artaud's *Theatre of Cruelty and to *Jerzy Grotowski's pantomime workshops are exaggerations, or true, at most, only part of the time. No devotee of these men's highly eccentric approaches to the notion of a written and enacted text could have done as well with Chekhov's *The Cherry Orchard* as Serban did—albeit controversially—with the New York Shakespeare Festival in 1977. On the other hand, Serban's *Fragments of a Greek Tragedy,* a compilation of scenes from Sophocles's *Electra* and Euripides's *Medea* and *The Trojan Women,* first presented at off-off-Broadway's La Mama in 1974, strongly suggests the occult ritual theatre propounded by Artaud and implemented by Grotowski. No English is heard in Serban's *Fragments;* he uses the original Greek (and some Senecan Latin). The audience is not conventionally seated by ushers but portentously led into the ceremony by the actors themselves. Nudity, violence, pan-

tomime, music (by Elizabeth Swados at the very top of her form), chanting, dance, and stark decor combined as they seldom if ever do on Broadway. The production was the talk of the town—*Electra*'s Aegisthus, spectators dazedly reported, entered wearing a live snake around his neck. Critic Stanley Kauffmann, noting the lack of narrative communication that such a staging inevitably must accept, nevertheless applauded Serban's ability "to scrape down to the psychic-tribal essences that made these legends material for tragedy in the first place."

THE SERPENT

"A ceremony" created by the Open Theater under the direction of *Joseph Chaikin, "words and structure" by Jean-Claude van Itallie, prem. Rome, 1968.

Actually, *The Serpent* had been performed privately for two years before the Open Theater almost grudgingly put on a single public performance at the Washington Square Methodist Church. This in itself suggests the arcane reaches of this uniquely off-off-Broadway, Vietnam-era piece—and, indeed, though the theme is technically drawn from Bible stories from Adam and Eve (thus the "serpent" of the title) through Cain and Abel to the Begats, the variations ring in images of death, murder, war. The show began (after the performers' warm-up exercises and welcoming parade around the "space") with a doctor's autopsy punctuated by an assassin's gunshots, and ended, to the reciting of the Begats, with a stylized mime of sex, birth, aging, and expiration. (That is, of course, not counting the performers' final march through the audience out of the space, singing "On Moonlight Bay.") Yet the general effect of the piece was not a fear of mortality but an exaltation in being alive—as if *The Serpent* were meant to contradict *Thornton Wilder's *Our Town,* which despairs of being able to convince its public that life is to be savored, all of it, each moment. As Chaikin himself said, "The thing about theatre—more than anything else—is that the people are actually there. You can't confront being alive without confronting that you're mortal."

Four stills of Andrei Serban's 1974 La Mama production of Fragments of a Greek Tragedy. *Compare them with the rigorously traditional look on* *Tyrone Guthrie's* Oedipus the King *on page 133.*

WILLIAM SHAKESPEARE (See Elizabethan Theatre)

GEORGE BERNARD SHAW

(1856—1950)

Playwright, critic, prophet, jester, and crank. His most immediately notable quality, dazzling wit, obscures the somewhat dangerous intent of his philosophy. At first glance—even after a lifetime of attending such popular Shavian titles as *Arms and the Man, The Devil's Disciple, Candida, Man and Superman, The Doctor's Dilemma, Pygmalion, Androcles and the Lion,* or *Saint Joan*—we perceive an oeuvre of socially reformative plays aimed toward economic fairness and sexual equality and against privilege and hypocrisy, bound into mystical urges toward spiritual evolution of the human species. In fact, a thorough exploration of Shaw reveals as well a worldview so impatient with democracy that nothing less than violent revolution and a dictatorship by "experts" will serve society's future—a dictatorship, lest we forgive a possibly impish notion of what this word implies, with full powers to dispose of "troublemakers" by judicial execution. However, this darker, callously totalistic Shaw is obscured by a facade of radiant charm. Shaw was perhaps the only artistic egomaniac who spoofed egomania. Thus, taking his bow at the end of the successful premiere of *Arms and the Man,* Shaw heard someone hiss through the general ovation, turned to his heckler and said, "I quite agree with you, sir, but what can two do against so many?"

Shaw got settled in the theatre late in life. An Irish Protestant removed to London, he educated himself at the British Museum and became a critic, of music from 1888 to 1894, of theatre in the late 1890s. He who cannot, teaches. (A Shavian maxim, by the way.) But Shaw could. Shaw wrote plays. He even served, at first, as their director. Yet he was not a thespian by vocation. Theatre was merely his engine of content. Shaw himself admitted that he had no interest in theatre per se, and but for his posts as critic would never have visited a playhouse. The art held no enchantment for him, which made him a highly erratic critic in drama and music alike—though many reviewers, thrilled to point out one who teaches who also can, praise Shaw's reports on theatre and opera. His achievements reprieve them, they hope. Yet Shaw's drama reviews are distinguished only by his agitations for vital composition and lifelike acting; and musicians then and now regard the "musical" Shaw as an ignorant buffoon, disdaining Verdi because he failed to affirm Shaw's socialist politics and hailing Wagner because Wagner flattered them. Verdi was —Shaw thought—old style, willingly inheriting the world of our fathers. Revolutionary Wagner shattered the old style, the old world.

Ironically enough, Shaw based *his* forms on old style, on the plays of our fathers. "My stories," he wrote, "are the old stories; my characters are the familiar Harlequin and Colombine, clown and pantaloon; my stage tricks and suspense and thrills and jests are the ones in vogue when I was a boy, by which time my grandfather was tired of them." Old stories, old settings, old characters, old plotting devices, yes.

But the *topics* are new: "The fashionable theatre prescribed one serious subject: clandestine adultery." Think of the fallen women of *Arthur Wing Pinero, the "Bunburying" of *Oscar Wilde. "I," says Shaw, "tried slum-landlordism, doctrinaire Free Love [which he terms "pseudo-Ibsenism"], prostitution, militarism, marriage, history, current politics, natural Christianity, national and individual character, paradoxes of conventional society, husband hunting, questions of conscience, professional delusions and impostures, all worked into a series of comedies of manners in the classic fashion."

Bravo! Here is the matrix for early Shaw—*Widowers' Houses* (written 1887, prem. 1892), on the slum landlord; *Arms and the Man* (1894), on militarism, and, like any *"well-made play," bound around the macguffin of a telltale portrait in the pocket of a coat; *Mrs. Warren's Profession* (written 1893, prem. 1902, in private), on, yes, prostitution, and firmly supportive of it as a way for a woman to outfox capitalist gender oppression;

Candida (1895); *You Never Can Tell* (1898); *The Devil's Disciple* (1897), set during the American revolution; *Caesar and Cleopatra* (written 1898, prem. 1906, in Berlin under *Max Reinhardt); *Major Barbara* (1905), *The Doctor's Dilemma* (1906), on the humbug of the medical profession.

In these early works, Shaw socialized the well-made formula. He exploits its conventions to new ends, working out not mechanics of plot or personality as much as a dialectic of theme. Shaw was shocking, subversive—which is why some of his plays were ready to stage before his culture was ready to see them staged. (*Mrs. Warren's Profession,* which was closed by the police in New York, was not seen publicly in England at all until 1925, thirty-two years after it was written.) Nevertheless, Shaw proved to be irresistible, because of his avid wit. But this, too, is shocking, even today. Thus, in *Major Barbara,* the munitions tycoon Undershaft tells Adolphus Cusins, an idealistic academic, that "there are two things necessary to Salvation." Well, of course:

CUSINS: Baptism and—
UNDERSHAFT: No. Money and gunpowder.

The timing is that of comedy, but the statements are offensive:

CUSINS: Excuse me: is there any place in your religion for honor, justice, truth, love, mercy, and so forth?
UNDERSHAFT: Yes: they are the graces and luxuries of a rich, strong, and safe life.
CUSINS: Suppose one is forced to choose between them and money or gunpowder?
UNDERSHAFT: Choose money and gunpowder; for without enough of both you cannot afford the others.

Undershaft, a self-made man, undercuts even the righteous fury of the exploited:

PETER SHIRLEY: Who made your millions for you? Me and my like. Whats kep us poor? keepin you rich. I wouldn't have your conscience, not for all your income.
UNDERSHAFT: I wouldn't have your income, not for all your conscience, Mr. Shirley.

It is said that Shaw's lack of interest in characterization blunts his realism; too many of his people sound like either Shavian mouthpieces or straight men for them. In fact, Shaw was often cavalier about the invention and development of his characters—but, just as often, delightfully inventive, observant of the human condition. *Pygmalion* presents very persuasive characters, not only in Henry Higgins, Eliza Doolittle, and her father, but in the people who surround them—so persuasive that for seventy years audiences have vigorously rejected Shaw's insistence that there is no lasting romance in the Higgins-Eliza elocution lessons. The public feels it knows these characters so well that romance is not conventionally indicated but *emotionally* inevitable. Thus the satisfaction in the happy, anti-Shavian ending of the *Pygmalion* film, carried over into the musical adaptation, *My Fair Lady:* this is not sentimentality but consummation. Moreover, it must be said that many of Shaw's heroines have given gifted actresses a main chance, even a basis for legend—*Mrs. Patrick Campbell's Eliza, *Katharine Cornell's Candida, *Sybil Thorndike's and *Siobhán McKenna's Joan. Would they have done so well in parts that were not fully characterized?

The individuality of Shaw's women in general adds to his distinction—but not as lovers, as heroines. Director *Peter Hall dismissed *Pygmalion* as "romance with no balls," and writer Frank Harris, noting Shaw's largely ascetic life, argued that such an existence could only—and did—produce "a text-booky, sexless type of play." And does not Shaw invite such judgments when he writes, "I lived a continent virgin . . . until I was twenty-nine"? Some adventures followed, but of his marriage he admits, "We found a new relation in which sex had no part." Critic Eric Bentley replies to all this by outlining another aspect of Shaw's revolutionary thinking: "Instead of the emotions of lover and mistress," Bentley writes, Shaw "renders the emotions of parents and children, particularly the emotion of the child rejecting the parent." Thus Bentley finds *Pygmalion* sensible as Shaw wrote it, "for Henry Higgins is the progenitor of the new Eliza, and that is why she must break free of him."

Breaking free is essential Shaw, not only of the father—of the old system, so to speak—but into a new self. This is Shaw's Nietzschean, Bergsonian

St. Joan: *naturally, Shaw's version of Joan of Arc will center on the confrontation of the extraordinary individual with the mediocrities of the status quo. Left, Joan (Katharine Cornell) and the reluctant Dauphin (Maurice Evans); above, Joan biting the bullet against the officials of Smother Church in the Trial Scene.*

Creative Evolution, evolution by act of will (the "life force") rather than by Darwinian selection. Thus Shaw delivers unto us *Man and Superman* (1903), which initiates a new Shavian form, the "disquisitory extravaganza," as he called it, conversational rather than plotted. The play itself is half old style and half new, but it contains (a removable) one-acter known as *Don Juan in Hell* that is all talk, in the new Shavian manner. Shaw pursued the disquisitory format in *Getting Married* (1908), *Heartbreak House* (1920), *Back to Methusaleh* (1922), *Saint Joan* (1923), *The Apple Cart* (1929), and *Too True to Be Good* (1932), arguably the last decent play before Shaw's dismal, halfhearted final phase.

Man and Superman contains not only an "extra" play but, in the published text, *The Revolutionist's Handbook,* which tenders such Shavian nuggets as "Beware of the man whose god is in the skies," "Home is the girl's prison and the woman's workhouse," and "The love of fairplay is a spectator's virtue, not a principal's." The disquisitory aspect of Shaw lies not just in his increasing distaste for plotting, but in his career-long relish of the preface, the dedication, the appendix. Shaw's exuberant prefaces not only extrapolate the theme of each play but give him a chance to dilate upon any number of subjects, often at great length—the preface to *Androcles and the Lion* is longer than the play itself. Moreover, Shaw took great care in the writing of his stage directions, further enhancing his scripts and thus helping to popularize the reading of plays, encouraging the emergence of a published text independent of the variables of theatre production.

However, the outrageous quipster with the limitless supply of quirks is still only the facade of Shaw, his front. The Fabian Socialist promoting a new phonetic alphabet for English—*Androcles and the Lion* was published in it—suggests a quixotic liberal. Shaw was anything but. *The Apple Cart* virtually denounces the democratic principles that allow businessmen and the press to manipulate an impressionable population. Better a dictator, says Shaw—even Mussolini, whom Shaw openly admired; even Hitler, for whom Shaw apologized. The preface to *Geneva* (1938), published in 1945, dismays the Shavian who knew only *Candida, Man and Superman,* and *Saint Joan:* dismays with its

blithe excuses for the Nazi death camp. Torture? Gas chambers? Holocaust? Shaw passes these off as a routine of "every war when the troops get out of hand." It is this side of Shaw, perhaps, that Frank Harris and Peter Hall are responding to in the quotations cited above. It is not merely Shaw's sexlessness that they dislike, but the man's utter lack of warmth, heart, compassion. Like many reformers who speak of the disadvantaged, Shaw has no more sympathy for them than for their oppressors. He doesn't want to rationalize the world's paradoxes; he wants to flourish his own. Shaw was a joking Jeremiah, a sexless romantic. Shaw was a professional grotesque, unpredictable, self-righteous, and flamboyant. Shaw was George Bernard Shaw rolled into one.

(See also *Back to Methusaleh, Heartbreak House,* and *Saint Joan.*)

EDWARD SHELDON (1886–1946)

Sheldon was but twenty-two years old at the opening of his first produced script, *Salvation Nell* (1908), one of the classics of American social-realist *naturalism. Sheldon followed *Nell* with *The Nigger* (1909), *The Boss* (1911), and *The High Road* (1912), all similarly important in their day as social inquiries, and he branched into mad, sad, bittersweet charm in *Romance* (1913), using the familiar trope of the man of God who falls in love with a woman while trying to reform her. Handsome, debonair, and incredibly youthful for a man of such purpose, even wisdom (he looked about sixteen at the time *Nell* swept the country), "Ned" Sheldon seemed destined to become America's Great American Playwright. Sadly, in 1915, he began to suffer from a stiffness of the joints that made even ordinary tasks difficult. His health steadily deteriorated. By 1928 he was paralyzed from the neck down, by 1932 blind.

Yet Sheldon's work—his influence, better—did not end. He was forced to retire as a working thespian, but he went on sharing his natural gifts as a craftsman, in collaborations with playwrights and in the glittering cultural salon he maintained in his New York apartment. Paul Robeson and Geraldine Farrar sang, Alexander Woollcott doted,

*The classic Eliza Doolittle between *Mrs. Patrick Campbell and Julie Andrews: Gertrude Lawrence faces off with Raymond Massey's Henry Higgins in Broadway's 1945* Pygmalion. *By reinventing Eliza's speech, Higgins will rehabilitate her socially. Language is class.*

"The Nigger."

Garraway-Byron Studio
New York
'07

Annie Russell and Guy Bates Post in Edward Sheldon's The Nigger: **melodrama turning into social-problem theatre.*

*Thornton Wilder and *Robert E. Sherwood read their scripts and took advice, and virtually every important actor and actress working on Broadway performed scenes or even whole plays for Sheldon, from *Edith Evans and Katharine Cornell to Beatrice Lillie and Joan Crawford. Lillian Gish called Ned Sheldon "the Pope of the theatre."
(See also *Salvation Nell*.)

SAM SHEPARD (1943–   )

What other major American playwright has got so far on such flat writing?:

SLIM: I tried to make a dam once in a river. It was just a little river. I put a whole bunch a rocks and sticks and shit in that river. I even put a tree in that river, but I couldn't get it to stop. I kept coming back day after day putting more and more rocks and mud and sticks in to try to stop it. Then one day I stopped it. I dammed it up. Just a little trickle coming out and a big pool started to form. I was really proud. I'd stopped a river. So I went back home and got in bed and thought about what a neat thing I'd done. Then it started to rain. It rained really hard. All night long it rained. The next morning I ran down to the river, and my dam was all busted to shit. That river was raging like a brush fire. Just gushing all over the place. Gushing up over the sides and raging right into the woods. I never built another dam again.

This comes from *Cowboy Mouth* (1971), which might easily serve as Shepard's nickname. He has presented himself as a kind of western punk hero, slow to speak and quick to quarrel, a casual master of argot, an adherant of jazz and rock, almost a jazzrock dramatist, extemporizing on the self through the language of hip. Drifters, loungers, down-and-outers, crooks, and families at war provide his characters; his actions arise out of thwarted hungers and unchanneled aggressiveness. Eugene O'Neill built such subjects into epics; Shepard is tidy. Yet he bears comparison with O'Neill for a shared clarity of theme—an ability to develop his poetic insights from within the flow of dialogue. Indeed, Shepard may do it better than the marmoreal O'Neill, whose thematic repetitions are sometimes awkward. Shepard's bent for colloquial American English keeps him spare, self-conscious but easy-real, a showboater who always goes *just* too far *enough*. His fellow playwright Jack Gelber calls Shepard "a New World shaman." An exorcist, a genie, a fire priest—but a contemporary one. As one of Shepard's characters observes, "You gotta be a rock-and-roll Jesus with a cowboy mouth."

Shepard is prolific and, within his set confines, versatile. *La Turista* (1967), his first full-length play (named for "Montezuma's Revenge," the dysentery American tourists pick up in Mexico, which the natives call "la turista"), is wildly anti-realistic. *Operation Sidewinder* (1970), to this day Shepard's only big-house Broadway entry (for the *Lincoln Center Repertory Company), is sternly realistic, with between-the-scenes rock interludes and a *slightly* apocalyptic finale. *The Mad Dog Blues* (1971), an "adventure show," wanders merrily across the continental United States (on a bare stage) with Marlene Dietrich, Mae West, Captain Kidd, Paul Bunyan, Jesse James, and two cowboy mouths, Kosmo and Yahoodi. "Leads with his cock," Shepard advises us on the casting of Kosmo. "Hates politics, philosophy, and religion." And Yahoodi "strikes like a serpent. Perfected a walk that cuts through the pavement . . . Trades his mojo for a bag of coke and disappears in the night."

Shepard can wax colorful when he feels the urge, but a plainness of intent and presentation is more typical. *Killer's Head* (1975), first performed at New York's American Place Theatre with Richard Gere, is a very short one-acter for one player, yet it seems more essential in Shepard's canon than many of his evening-length pieces. *Killer's Head* presents a young man in jeans and a t-shirt, blindfolded and strapped into an electric chair, speaking in a "clipped, southwestern rodeo accent" about a pick-up truck he's planning to buy. His monologue takes in the varying quality of certain breeds of horse, cuts off for a full minute of silence, then returns to the plan to buy the pick-up. When he again stops speaking, the lights very slowly dim;

as they hit black, the chair lights up with the electric shock and the play is over.

Thus Shepard takes us inside his killer's head, his outlaw rap. His killer, called Mazon, is the ultimate Shepard hero, everything stripped away but the look and the style and the cowboy mouth. Plot is not Shepard's forte; here he can dispense with it entirely. Nor does he care for conventional heroism, or for the solid citizenry. He gives the yuppie couple in *La Turista* sunburn and dysentery. He outfoxes the government heavyweights in *Operation Sidewinder*. He turns the 4-H Club daughter in *Curse of the Starving Class* (1977) into a prostitute and blows her up in a car she was planning to steal. He bedevils the screenwriter of *True West* (1980) with a lawless slob of a brother, then forces them to change places, the slob turning Hollywood mastermind and the screenwriter liberating the neighborhood homes of their toasters. But these last two plays usher us into a new era in Sam Shepard, one of major fame, of a movie actor's career, of a series of domestic dramas that bend Shepard's true west mythology into the American family scene. *Buried Child* (1978), *Fool for Love* (1983), and *A Lie of the Mind* (1985) also deal with blood ties—father and son, brother and brother, brother and sister, parents and children. This is a more mature Shepard, his form settled on lower-middle-class naturalism and his take relentlessly honing in on his subjects. The mañana attitude and formal experimentation of some of the earlier plays have vanished. From *Curse of the Starving Class* on, Shepard is no longer hymning the libertarian doom of his cowboys and sidekicks, but analyzing their psychology ontologically, at its very root of being. Early Shepard was trips and motels: places we get to. Later Shepard is kitchens and living rooms: places we come from.

(See also *Curse of the Starving Class*.)

RICHARD BRINSLEY SHERIDAN

(1751–1816)

Because Sheridan's best known plays, *The Rivals* (1775) and *The School for Scandal* (1777), bear the verve and satiric bite of *Restoration comedy, this playwright is often mistaken for a Restoration figure. In fact, Sheridan was born a half century after the Restoration peaked, with William Congreve's *The Way of the World*. Moreover, Sheridan was much more a thespian than the notable Restoration dramatists, who were primarily gentlemen of leisure who primarily wrote for amusement. Sheridan was the son of an actor, Thomas Sheridan (1719–1788), and became a *manager as well as a playwright, absolutely of the theatre.

As an Irishman, Sheridan's father was most active in Dublin, but the son moved to London, where he took over the management of *Drury Lane in 1776, only to neglect his duties shamefully when he was elected a Member of Parliament in 1780. What sets Sheridan yet further apart from the Restoration writers was his versatility, typical of a day that saw the stage as a medium of varied forms of entertainment—not only spoken drama, but opera, "ballad opera" and "comic opera" (both early forms of musical comedy), *pantomime, and burlesque spinoffs of earlier works. Sheridan wrote in most of these forms: *The Duenna* (1775) is a comic opera, *Robinson Crusoe* (1781) a pantomime.

ROBERT E. SHERWOOD

(1896–1955)

Playwright Sherwood represents Broadway's progressive-liberal wing in the 1930s, his significant decade. Even in his first play, *The Road to Rome* (1927), ostensibly a *vehicle for Jane Cowl, Sherwood took a passionately antiwar reading of Hannibal's march on Rome, especially for an essentially comic work; and Sherwood gained his maturity in *The Petrified Forest* (1935), a killer-on-the-loose *melodrama allegorically debating the roles of the pacifist and the warmonger. *Idiot's Delight* (1936), for the *Lunts—Alfred as a cheap nightclub hoofer and Lynn as a phony Russian countess—took an actively anti-pacifist position in a look forward to the next world war. Sherwood clearly saw that there would be one, and followed up his parables on how to take a moral stand in wartime with further messages: the *chronicle play *Abe Lincoln in Illinois* (1938) and a look at Finland under attack in *There Shall Be No Night* (1940), again with the Lunts, in one of their few serious and contemporary pairings. Sherwood then left the theatre to write speeches for Franklin Roosevelt. By the time Sherwood returned to Broadway, after the war, his era was over. His last (posthumously produced) play, *Small War on Murray Hill* (1957), a slyly cold-war–related comedy about enemy relations during the American Revolution, was an ignominious flop.

SARAH SIDDONS (See The Kembles)

THEATRE OF SILENCE (See The Theatre of the Unexpressed)

NEIL SIMON (1927–   )

Though he has written a half-dozen musical comedy books (and reportedly "doctored" many others during tryout emergencies), Simon is mainly known for his extraordinarily successful comedies, generally light looks at contemporary social and sexual mores set in New York City. Farce impelled early Simon, heavily plotted in *Come Blow Your Horn* (1961) and merely situational in *Barefoot in the Park* (1963) and *The Odd Couple* (1965). Simon introduced a slightly unusual form in the trilogy of one-acters bound by a setting, most obviously in *Plaza Suite* (1968) and *California Suite* (1976), but also in *The Last of the Red-Hot Lovers* (1969), presented as a three-act comedy, but actually three one-acters on the unsuccessful attempts of a married loser (James Coco in the original production) to commit adultery in his mother's apartment. His first nonpartner is a tough broad, his second a scatterbrained "actress." His third, however, tests the Simon lightness in the character of a woman of the

*protagonist's own community, in fact a friend of his wife.

This pointed to a new, somewhat darker Simon, and the succeeding *The Gingerbread Lady* (1970) affirmed the bent in a study of an alcoholic cabaret singer. In the pre-Broadway tryout, the heroine, having chased away her daughter and closest friends, was seen tippling into oblivion. Public resistance convinced Simon to doctor his own play and concoct a more optimistic ending—but the flaw lay not in the dramaturgy but in the casting of Maureen Stapleton as the singer. The role needs a *singer*—Elaine Stritch, for instance, who played it in 1974 in London.

Nevertheless, Simon had begun to touch nerves, to strive for honesty as well as gags. Adaptations of *Chekhov's stories in *The Good Doctor* (1973) and of the Book of Job in *God's Favorite* (1974), again with James Coco, though commercially unsatisfying, led Simon on to a third period. First we had the jester, then the dark comic. Now, with *Chapter Two* (1977), *Brighton Beach Memoirs* (1983), *Biloxi Blues* (1984), and *Broadway Bound* (1986), the autobiographically intense Simon appears. (See also *Come Blow Your Horn.*)

THE SKIN OF OUR TEETH

The history of mankind as a pre-*absurdist *farce by *Thornton Wilder, prem. New York, 1942.

The absurdism inheres not in worldview but in style—collapsing scenery, one performer consistently breaking out of character to appeal and complain to the audience, pantomime animals, and so on. True absurdism believes that the world is meaningless. Wilder stands to the contrary. Thus, despite an ice age in Act One, the Flood in Act Two, and a world war in Act Three, Wilder sees a purpose in human life. Note that Wilder's own deflating *Our Town,* on mortality, ends with the same two words as this exhilarating work, on survival: "Good night."

SLAPSTICK

Rough, physical comedy named after the slapsticks of *commedia dell'arte:* two long, flat pieces of wood fastened at one end to make a slapping sound at the other end when the wood is used as a paddle.

MAGGIE SMITH (1934–   )

Here is one of the most vivaciously versatile British actresses of the day, from Shakespeare to Chekhov, Coward to Ionesco, *Hedda Gabler* to *Peter Pan.* Increasingly mannered, Smith has lately fared best in roles of brittle wit, especially *Private Lives'* Amanda, Millamant in *The Way of the World* in London in 1985, and, again in London, as the eccentrically well-meaning heroine of Peter Shaffer's *Lettice and Lovage* (1987).

SOCIALIST REALISM

A Communist term denoting artwork stripped down to simplistic happy-ending tales of golden revolutionary heroes and black counter-revolutionary villains, as opposed to art free to deal with the world as it is. The Soviets' insistence on socialist realism on their stages virtually destroyed the Russian theatre.

"SOCK AND BUSKIN"

A theatrical buzzterm referring to the footgear of the *Greek theatre. The sock (*soccos*) was the slipper worn in comedy, the buskin (*kothurnos*) the high-soled shoe used in tragedy. The combination of the two is quaint, a usage popular with early twentieth century American dramatic clubs.

SOLILOQUY

A longish solo speech. "To be or not to be . . ."

SOPHOCLES (496—406 B.C.)

Where his predecessor *Aeschylus rose to prominence in a truly democratic Athens, Sophocles gained his maturity in Periclean Athens, still democratic but governed by an aggressive president-king. Just as late Aeschylus suggests some admonition of those in power not to abuse it, Sophocles often seems to be warning Pericles that strength of reason is not enough: strength of mercy is necessary, too. We wonder what was running through the public's mind as it sat through Sophocles's *Antigone* (?442 B.C.)—did they see in the almost recklessly rational Creon a facsimile of Pericles? Is Sophocles's *Oedipus the King* (c. 430) an ambivalent eulogy for the recently deceased tyrant of Athens, admiring his good intentions while damning his arrogance? Worse yet, after Pericles, democracy collapsed in Athens, and Sophocles's last plays were written in more and more oppressive times. In *Oedipus at Colonus,* Sophocles's last play, produced posthumously in 401, the author is clearly yearning for a vanished golden age in the noble character of Theseus. With biting irony, Sophocles set the play in the very town where Athenian citizens voted to abolish their democratic traditions.

As dramatist, Sophocles is less interested in building a poetry on the familiar stories he adapted than in developing their characters as individuals. Aeschylus shows us the universe; Sophocles fills in the details. His *Electra* (c. 420–415) is one of the greatest of Greek plays for the brutalized splendor of its heroine. Yet Sophocles is above all philosophical, detached, understanding. As contestant playwrights, Aeschylus was magnificent: Sophocles was popular. Crabby Aristophanes, who jeered at *Euripides and even at Aeschylus, dealt gently with Sophocles. This suggests an encompassing prestige. Perhaps Sophocles earned his unique position through an ability to handle the most savage subjects with a soothing magnanimity. Sophocles's seven surviving plays (out of over a hundred) deal with the very notion of tragedy as a kind of consolation for the public, an attempt to reconcile the spectator to the hard truths of human life. If Aeschylus asks us to comprehend the world and if Euripides insists that we understand it, Sophocles

simply invites us to forgive it.
(See also Greek Theatre.)

GEORGE SPELVIN

A Broadway insider's joke. There is no George Spelvin. The name has been used in programs for half a century, as billing for corpses, walk-ons, and in various emergencies. In the early 1950s, *Theatre Arts* magazine ran a column reviewing the follies of the first-night critics' writing, under the byline of "George Spelvin."

"STAGE LEFT"

That is: to the *actor's* left, as he stands facing the audience. Stage right, obviously, is the other side. These are the American designations. The British theatre uses "prompt corner" and "opposite prompt," referring to the prompter, who traditionally sat, script in hand, in the wings to the performers' left.

KONSTANTIN STANISLAVSKY
(See Moscow Art Theatre)

STAR SYSTEM

This was the prevailing condition of the Western theatre during the eighteenth, nineteenth, and very early twentieth centuries: play production revolved around the star centrifugally, throwing all else to the side. The star, usually an *actor-manager, chose the repertory, hired the company, ran the business, and staged the shows. Staging, most often, consisted of keeping the other actors out of his way and chopping up their parts; but then the audience's interest, most often, lay in the star, not in the work or in any possible ensemble of production. The emergence of the integrated production in such companies as the *Meiningers and the *Moscow Art Theatre doomed the fascism of the star, though it held on into the 1900s in, for instances, the touring packages put together by and for *Sarah Bernhardt, perhaps the last of the truly solipsistic actor-managers. Stars—or let us say Important Actors—remained essential in the theatre, but now their work was more fairly blended into the ideal of production as a comprehensively developed unit. The term *star system* is still in use, but now it refers simply to the employment of headline actors, whether in an outright *vehicle (Rosalind Russell in *Auntie Mame,* say) or in a piece of artistic integrity (such as an O'Neill revival with *Colleen Dewhurst or *Jason Robards).

STICHOMYTHIA

Greek for "alternating dialogue." Stichomythia is a form of repartee in which two speakers echo the patterns of each other's lines in conflicting observations. The classic instance is from *Hamlet:*

QUEEN: Hamlet, thou hast thy father much offended.
HAMLET: Mother, you have my father much offended.
QUEEN: Come, come, you answer with an idle tongue.
HAMLET: Go, go, you question with a wicked tongue.

Stichomythia works best in verse drama, thus its popularity with Elizabethan writers. However, Samuel Beckett uses a lean form of it in *Waiting for Godot:*

VLADIMIR: We could do our exercises.
ESTRAGON: Our movements.
VLADIMIR: Our elevations.
ESTRAGON: Our relaxations.
VLADIMIR: Our elongations.
ESTRAGON: Our relaxations.
VLADIMIR: To warm us up.
ESTRAGON: To calm us down.

STOCK COMPANY

Whether permanently housed in a major playhouse of a cultural capital or forever on tour, and whether giving the most illustrious performances of the day or barely surviving the walk-in business of a heedless public, the stock company was the standard form of theatrical organization in the Western world from about 1700 to the early 1910s. Because even the most popular plays could support a minimal number of performances, companies had to be prepared to present a variety of titles to keep the customers coming back and the personnel employed. Thus the actors had to be prepared to play a variety of parts. This was the stock company, organized by type—the First Tragedian, the Heavy Father, the Low Comedian, the Walking Lady and Gentleman, the Singing Chambermaid, and so on. So many plays were written to accord with convention that a given actor or actress might run an entire career playing hundreds of roles cut to the same fit, and most troupes adhered to a homogeneous repertory, or bent the plays—even Shakespeare—to suit the available talent.

The talent was often more a matter of assignment than endowment, for the bulk of the stock companies built outward from a nucleus of family members to take in friends, in-laws, and chance acquaintances. This is where such acting dynasties as the *Kembles and the *Drews (and their descendants, the Barrymores) originated. It was not that every relative was talented, but that every relative was related. In the hard life of the actor, nothing was more dependable in the long haul of a season than a . . . dependent. "I am in the theatrical profession myself," *manager Vincent Crummles tells Charles Dickens's *Nicholas Nickleby, "my wife is in the theatrical profession, my children are in the theatrical profession. I had a dog that lived and died in it from a puppy; and my chaise-pony goes on in Timour the Tartar." This is not to mention the pony's mother: "She ate apple-pie at a circus for upwards of fourteen years . . . fired pistols, and went to bed in a nightcap; and, in short, took the low comedy entirely."

Crummles's theatre, in Dickens's fond spoof, is the world of the third-rate provincial English stock company, the kind that promptly mounts a play featuring "a real pump and two washing tubs" simply because the manager bought them at a bargain. The kind that kept the hoary varieties of *"business" alive long after London had booed them off the stage. The kind that runs a series of Absolutely Guaranteed Last Farewell Performances; as Crummles explains to Nicholas: "We can have positively your last appearance, on Thursday—re-engagement for one night more, on Friday—and, yielding to the wishes of numerous influential patrons, who were disappointed in obtaining seats, on Saturday. That ought to bring three very decent houses." Nicholas is amused at the idea of making "three last appearances," but Crummles calls it short weight: "It's very bungling and irregular not to have more, but if we can't help it we can't, so there's no use in talking. A novelty would be very desirable. You couldn't sing a comic song on the pony's back, could you?"

TOM STOPPARD (1937–   )

Our *absurdist *Sheridan. Not since George Bernard Shaw has a British dramatist so invigorated the language and so elegantly phrased his ideas. Yet Shaw was an old-fashioned playwright with dangerous ideas. Stoppard is a writer of new schools here to reprimand the revolutionaries—as James Joyce reprimands the *dada proselytizer Tristan Tzara in Stoppard's *Travesties* (1974): "You are an over-excited little man, with a need for self-expression far beyond the scope of your natural gifts. This is not discreditable. Neither does it make you an artist."

Stoppard thundered onto the scene with *Rosencrantz and Guildenstern Are Dead* (1967), almost a *Samuel Beckett version of *Hamlet,* a new play reviewing the old one through the eyes of two of its most minor characters. (If nothing else, Stoppard has made productions of *Hamlet* impossible without some reference to the existentialist wonder of these two bit players.) Stoppard was tighter, more nimble, in *The Real Inspector Hound* (1968), a short piece burlesquing mystery plays and critics, as two of the latter watch one of the former, commenting ("There are moments, and I would not begrudge it this, when the play, if we can call it that, and I think on balance we can, aligns itself uncompromisingly on the side of life. *Je suis,* it seems to say, *ergo sum* . . . And here one is irresistibly reminded of Voltaire's cry, 'Voilà!") and even getting drawn onto the stage-upon-the-stage.

This is Stoppard the *boulevardier, and he does show the aspect of the entertainer that Shaw never did. But Stoppard, when he cares to, grows trenchantly political, as if admitting that a political viewpoint is inescapable in contemporary playwrighting—that where Shaw was an inconoclast simply by having a politics, Stoppard has to grapple with his politics, admit to having opinions, apply himself to developing them . . . and ends up an iconoclast all the same. Shaw challenged the establishment, however: Stoppard challenges the anti-establishment, as in *Every Good Boy Deserves Favour* (1977), on the totalitarian oppression we can expect from the left no less than from the right. (Stoppard, Czech by origin, is in effect a refugee from the Soviet bloc.) Similarly, *Night and Day* (1978), a look at newspaper coverage of a volatile African situation, comes off almost as a reproach of the play that most of Stoppard's fellow British playwrights would have made of the subject. But then comes *On the Razzle* (1981), a farce adapted from *Nestroy, in purely artistic adventurism, for *Thornton Wilder adapted the same text into *The Merchant of Yonkers,* which subsequently became *The Matchmaker* (not to mention *Hello, Dolly!*)—and Nestroy had based *his* text on an English play in the first place. Not only does Stoppard resist every opportunity to engage in political dialogue with the worldview of Nestroy's imperial Vienna: Stoppard respects his archeology enough to disinter (as Wilder did not) Nestroy's line, "Das ist klassisch" (It's classic), which became a catchphrase in mid-nineteenth century Vienna. This is resolute orthodoxy.

On The Razzle was followed by *The Real Thing* (1982), a highly literate, almost dreamy dissection of a marriage, and Stoppard's biggest success since *Rosenkrantz and Guildenstern Are Dead.* Clearly, this is not a typical writer of the era that began with *John Osborne's *Look Back in Anger.* Even though English is not his native language, Stoppard has revived the moribund love of language on the transatlantic stage. He has as well wrestled with the existentialist paradoxes that the age of *Beckett made essential in theatre. Most personally, he has struggled to redefine the playwright's objectives in a time that often seems interested mainly in manias and hatreds.

(See also *Travesties.*)

DAVID STOREY (1933–   )

Among British playwrights of the present, Storey has carved his niche as a master of *naturalism—not the sometimes hectic social problem naturalism of the turn of the century, but an almost artless naturalism that captures the "everyone's got a story tucked away within" *real* life that hides behind the day-to-day of business-as-usual. True, *Home* (1970) first produced in London and New York with *John Gielgud and *Ralph Richardson, has the somewhat fantastic flavor of a Pinter-edged Chekhov, all the more so in that what seems at first like an absent-minded house party turns out to be an afternoon in a madhouse. And Storey's more recent plays, especially *Mother's Day* (1976) and *Sisters* (1978) have led him to try out plotting technique. But his reputation grew upon *The Contractor* (1969), *The Changing Room* (1971), *The Farm* (1973), and *Life Class* (1974): a few hours spent with the people of a given place, a certain culture, more or less as they look, sound, and act when we're not watching.

(See also *The Changing Room.*)

LEE STRASBERG (See The Group Theatre and The Method)

GIORGIO STREHLER (1921–   )

This Italian director is primarily known for his leftist readings of classic operas, and for Il Piccolo Teatro della Città di Milano, which Strehler founded in 1947 with the *capocomico* Paolo Grassi. The Piccolo Teatro's productions run from Shakespeare to Chekhov, from Carlo Goldoni and Luigi

Pirandello to new Italian playwrights. But Strehler has distinguished himself above all in the work of Bertolt Brecht—who himself attended Strehler's staging of *Die Dreigroschenoper* (The Threepenny Opera) and declared himself satisfied.

AUGUST STRINDBERG
(1849—1912)

As playwright, Strindberg is best known for the passionate gender war of *Fadren* (The Father, 1887), *Fröken Julie* (1888), and *Dödsdansen* (The Dance of Death, 1901). Passionate by temperament himself, a borderline psychotic who nearly went over the top in his tempestuous marriage to Siri von Essen, Strindberg seemed to revel in castration anxiety and love-hate games. To understand how shocking Strindberg was in his time, consider that *Edward Albee's very Strindbergian *Who's Afraid of Virginia Woolf?* disturbed many a theatregoer—seventy years later. Strindberg was the first to do what Strindberg did, building *The Father,* for instance, around the methodical destruction of a man by the women in his life. It is not enough that he is driven literally mad; for a crowning touch, Strindberg has the man's childhood nurse soothe him in motherly tones as she straps him into a straitjacket. At this moment, in a performance in Copenhagen, as Strindberg gleefully reported to Friedrich Nietzsche, "The audience rose as one man and ran from the theatre bellowing like mad bulls!"

This sensational aspect of Strindberg, however, has obscured a very faceted talent. The most obvious reason why Strindberg was so major a figure in the late–nineteenth century transition into the isms of modern art is the power of his *naturalism. Even *Henrik Ibsen, so influential in the act of bringing the perceived world into the playhouse, could not equal the sting, the directness, the encompassing honesty, of Strindberg. The two warily noted each other's gifts—the Norwegian Ibsen's clarity of social topic, the Swedish Strindberg's vehement theatricality. Publicly, they hated each other. But Ibsen hung Strindberg's picture in his study, and told visitors, "*There* is the one who will be greater than I."

A second reason for Strindberg's importance is the opposite of the first: not his realism but his fantasy. Anticipating the revolt against naturalism that would succeed *Chekhov's patiently lifelike conversations, *Belasco's photographic sets, and *Shaw's dogged pamphleteering, Strindberg first investigated the *chronicle play to interpret Swedish history, then moved on to a series of dreamlike plays that point through *symbolism toward *expressionism and even *absurdism. The allegorical *Ett Drömspel* (A Dream Play, 1902), the fairytale *Svanevit* (Swanwhite, 1902), and the naturalistically fantastical *Spöksonaten* (The Ghost Sonata, 1907) are only the best known of this last group, for Strindberg left an astonishing body of work—the history plays alone number twenty-one texts. Sine qua non on the Scandinavian stage, ceaselessly reinvestigated, Strindberg has yet to be wholly encountered in the English-speaking theatre. He is a buzzword more than a playwright.

THE STURM UND DRANG
MOVEMENT

The term derives from the play *Der Wirrwarr, oder Sturm und Drang* (Confusion, or Storm and Stress, 1776), by Friedrich von Klinger (1752–1831). Note the politicized contemporaneity of the work: Klinger's setting was America during the brandnew Revolution. Turbulence of rebellion both social and emotional characterized the movement that sprang up around Klinger's piece, so reverberant that when the text of the play was published, the title had been dropped and the subtitle stood alone: *Storm and Stress*. Other figures of Sturm und Drang include Jakob Michael Reinhold Lenz (1751–1792), whose *Die Soldaten* (The Soldiers, 1776) indicted the callously licentious Prussian military caste; and Heinrich Leopold Wagner (1747–1779), whose *Die Kindermörderin* (The Infanticide, 1776) exposed the gender double standard: a seduced woman suffers but her seducer goes free. By far, the two most potent dramatists of the trend were *Johann Wolfgang von Goethe and *Friedrich Schiller (not yet von at the time), though only their early works belong to the style. (See also *Götz von Berlichingen* and *The Robbers*.)

SURREALISM

Playwright and poet *Guillaume Apollinaire coined the term in 1917 to describe the gathering movement—in poetry and painting especially, but also in the theatre—that sought to create a new "realism," not mimetically but in the abstract. Realism had become a labored photography of life, a cheap copy. Surrealism would explode life, stimulate while discovering it: in its most profound psychology. Surrealism would unearth the truth, no limits, no brakes, no lies. Surrealism would liberate mankind from civilization and its rationalisms. Besides, how "realistic" could realism hope to be in the first place? "The theatre is no more the life it represents," Apollinaire explained, "than the leg is a wheel."

Thus the surrealists' interest in "automatic writing," in which the pen would be guided not by plan but by instinct, detailing the secrets of the unconscious. Thus the movement's strong associations with *dada, *expressionism, and Antonin Artaud's *Theatre of Cruelty. Thus René Daumal's *En Gggarrde!*, written in 1924, is set, among other places, inside a snail's shell and on the raft of the Medusa "or something of that sort," and includes in its cast Napoleon, Cleopatra, the Author ("Moi!," Daumal helpfully adds), and a Toothbrush. And thus surrealism was more successful in poetry and painting; most surrealist theatre was too elaborately strange to be practical. (See also *The Breasts of Tiresias*.)

SYMBOLISM

If *naturalism was the reaction to Romanticism, symbolism was one of the reactions to naturalism. Instead of the everyday, the dreamscape; instead of vernacular dialogue, poetry; instead of social polemic, fairy tales about love and death. Above all, the action must be centered thematically on the use of evocative verbal images—the onion that *Ibsen's *Peer Gynt* peels away to nothing (as if revealing his own lack of substance), or Oswald's syphilis in Ibsen's *Ghosts*. Rooted in the work of the French poets Stéphane Mallarmé, Charles Baudelaire, Paul Verlaine, and Paul Valéry, symbolism moved into the theatre in the 1890s and early 1900s, in the work of *Hauptmann, *Maeterlinck, *Chekhov, *Yeats, and *O'Neill, among others.

SYMMETRICALS

The tailored tights worn of old by the heroic actors of *melodrama and Shakespeare, padded and shaped to show off a well-turned leg—or create one artificially.

"THE SYNDICATE"

Also known as "The Trust." This was the theatre's equivalent of the business monopolies that grew up in America during the very late 1800s. The Syndicate, a group of *managers and theatre owners (including *Charles Frohman, Al Hayman, and the ironically termed "Honest Abe" Erlanger), was formed in 1896. Taking control of nearly all major American theatres, the Syndicate caught the stage in a vicious commercial vise, blacklisting its enemies and banning any play that did not accede to bourgeois artistic standards. Thus the breakthrough American dramas tended to be, however intensely written, conventional in form and plot, as if they were trying to sneak past the Syndicate —*Edward Sheldon's *Salvation Nell*, for example. Thus also the more avant-garde breakthrough works, especially those by *Ibsen, tended to be staged by those outlawed by the Syndicate—*Mrs. Fiske, for example. Heroic resistance by the Fiskes, *David Belasco, and *James O'Neill, among others, broke the Syndicate by about 1910.

JOHN MILLINGTON SYNGE

(1871—1909)

It was Synge who insisted that Ireland's *Abbey Theatre must not imitate the cosmopolitan *national theatres of the continent, mixing Molière, Shakespeare, and Schiller: but must treat only native art. And it was Synge who drafted himself to become the playwright at the service of that art. From 1902 to his early death (from Hodgkin's disease), Synge wrote only six plays, mostly comedies on the lives of village folk—publicans, peasants, fishermen, and their wives, mothers, and sisters. The short *Riders to the Sea* (1904), Synge's first play, is wholly tragic, and the unfinished *Deirdre of the Sorrows* (1910), Synge's last play, dwells in Irish legend. But the bulk of Synge's work endows his country scenes with a robust humor in a unique diction that bends the native brogue to an almost *Elizabethan majesty of phrase. Synge's best known piece, *The Playboy of the Western World* (1907), deals entirely with village people, yet their expressive dialogue makes them avatars of a wild poetry, realistic and mythic at once.

(See also *The Playboy of the Western World*.)

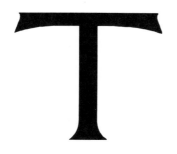

FRANÇOIS-JOSEPH TALMA
(1763–1826)

This French actor was the outstanding interpreter of Classical tragedy in Revolutionary and Napoleonic France. His days of glory at the *Comédie-Française made him something of a national symbol, especially of the restrained heroism of *Pierre Corneille—yet Talma tired of the case-hardened old style and longed for something bold and fresh. As it was, he instituted a number of reforms at the Comédie, especially in a more realistic, less declamatory approach to the presentation of dialogue and in a more appropriate sense of costume. In the last year of his life, still active, Talma begged the rebellious young Romantic *Victor Hugo for a new kind of play, something with the breadth and vigor of Shakespeare, perhaps. Hugo was just the man, and he had the play in mind, *Cromwell.* Unfortunately, Talma died before Hugo could complete it.

TAMBURLAINE THE GREAT

Pageant in two parts by Christopher Marlowe, prem. London, ?1588 and ?1589.

Marlowe's first important play, on a Scythian shepherd who sets out to conquer the world, *Tamburlaine* marks the rise of poetic energy in the *Elizabethan theatre. Before *Tamburlaine* came fustian and makeweight; after *Tamburlaine* came Shakespeare.

These are actually two plays, the second part having been written in response to the success of the first. In Part One, Tamburlaine is victorious. In Part Two, maddened by warlust and despairing over his wife's death, he falls before the united front of his enemies. Yet this is not the *peripeteia,* the classic reversal in fortune, of the tragic hero. Tamburlaine is as monstrous as he is noble, not a gallant warrior: a terrifying one. Amid a spectacular procession of victories, surrenders, and betrayals, Marlowe bends his poetry to assimilate love of heroism and beauty with love of power and savagery. There is aggression in romance, cruelty in strength. All these qualities intermingle in the hero: "For *will* and *shall* best fitteth Tamburlaine," as he himself observes. Near the close of Part One, he celebrates his triumph over the Turkish emperor Bajazeth by locking him in a cage like an animal. Refusing to survive under such a condition, Bajazeth kills himself by smashing his skull against his prison bars. In the climax-upon-climax that the Elizabethans loved, Marlowe immediately sends Bajazeth's empress Zabina on stage. Her speech, "What do mine eyes behold?," leads to a mad scene that anticipates twentieth century stream of consciousness. So penetrating is the sense of errant word association that Marlowe abandons his "mighty line" of iambic pentameter for a paragraph of wild prose:

ZABINA: O Bajazeth, my husband and my lord! O Bajazeth! O Turk! O Emperor! Give him his liquor? Not I. Bring milk and fire, and my blood I bring him again.—Tear me in pieces—give me the sword with a ball of wildfire upon it.—Down with him! Down with him!—Go to my child! Away! Away! Away!—Ah, save that infant! save him, save him!—I, even I, speak to her.—The sun was down—streamers white, red, black—here, here, here!—Fling the meat in his face—Tamburlaine.—Tamburlaine!—Let the soldiers be buried.—Hell! Death, Tamburlaine, Hell! Make ready my coach, my chair, my jewels.—I come! I come! I come!

Zabina, too, brains herself to death on the bars of the cage. All of *Tamburlaine* is so bloody that after the closing of the theatres by the Puritans in 1642, the play vanished from the professional stage till *Tyrone Guthrie's 1951 London revival with *Donald Wolfit at the *Old Vic.

A TASTE OF HONEY

Semi-comic *naturalism by Shelagh Delaney (1939–   ), prem. London, 1958.

Nineteen years old, Delaney saw a play by *Terence Rattigan and thought she could do better. What she did, better or not, was certainly different, a character study of a young working-class woman's relationships with her whorish mother, the black sailor who impregnates the girl, and the gentle gay man who cares for her. Delaney's fine ear for dialogue so impressed *Joan Littlewood that within two weeks of receiving the script she put it into rehearsal at her Theatre Workshop in London's East End. The production, with the typical Littlewood emendations, including a jazz trio and choreographed entrances and exits, was moved to the *West End. New York saw a different staging, by Tony Richardson and George Devine, with Joan Plowright as the heroine, Angela Lansbury as her mother, and Billy Dee Williams as the sailor.

LAURETTE TAYLOR (1884–1946)

Here was one of the oddest careers in American acting: a forty-three-year reign in, for the most part, cheap popular fare, bounded near the start by a gigantic hit in utter treacle and at the very end by one of theatre history's most famous performances in a work of subtle poetry. The early hit was *Peg O' My Heart* (1912), about an American waif forced to live with snobbish English relatives. Its author, J. Hartley Manners, became Taylor's husband and professional partner, and when he died in 1928, Taylor was so shattered that she retired to alcoholic seclusion. Barring a few isolated appearances, she was off the stage for seventeen years. Then, noting, "Well, that was the world's longest wake, wasn't it?," Taylor stepped into Tennessee Williams's *The Glass Menagerie* (1945) and legend. Her almost gratingly radiant portrayal of the nagging, nostalgic mother remains the great farewell performance, for she died shortly after the original run.

THE TENTH MAN

Jewish exorcism by Paddy Chayevsky (1923–1981), prem. New York, 1959.

Chayevsky made his name in television (especially for *Marty,* 1954) and then on stage for contemporary middle-class naturalism. Here he pushed the everyday into the supernatural, in the tale of a young Jewish woman apparently possessed by a dybbuk, in Jewish folklore the spirit of a late mortal denied eternal rest. During a ritual of exorcism, however, it is not *her* dybbuk that screams out in terror, but that of a young man possessed by professional-class urban paranoia. In this boy-meets-girl—rather, dybbuk-meets-dybbuk—romance, the young man gets the girl, for in Chayevsky, love is the cure for all ailments. One might call it typical Broadway fare but for Chayevsky's emphasis on Jewish mysticism, lightened by a

The legendary Laurette Taylor in her legendary role as the Mother in The Glass Menagerie, *with Julie Haydon as the Daughter. As many actresses observed, while Williams's contemporary *Arthur Miller wrote his most challenging parts for men, Williams composed his poetry for women.*

group of old kibitzers who bridge the two worlds of religious ecstasy and everyday realism:

SCHLISSEL: So how goes it with a Jew today?

ZITORSKY: How should it go?

SCHLISSEL: Have a pinch of snuff.

ZITORSKY: No, thank you.

SCHLISSEL: Davis won't be here this morning. I stopped by his house. He has a cold. His daughter-in-law told me he's still in bed.

ZITORSKY: My daughter-in-law, may she grow rich and buy a hotel with a thousand rooms and be found dead in every one of them.

SCHLISSEL: My daughter-in-law, may she invest heavily in General Motors, and the whole thing should go bankrupt.

TERENCE (See Roman Theatre)

ELLEN TERRY (See Henry Irving and Sybil Thorndike)

THE THEATRE GUILD

This producing organization was the pride of Broadway from the early 1920s into the 1950s. Yet it began, in 1915, as a *little theatre, the Washington Square Players, offbeat and without celebrity. The Players only lived around Washington Square; they performed at the Bandbox Theatre, a cabaret-sized house on East Fifty-Seventh Street, in the shadow of the Third Avenue El. (This is the present site, bearing a new structure, of the Sutton movie house.) Military service called the Players's men away and the group disbanded in 1917. But by 1919 some of the original members and a few newcomers were reforming as the Theatre Guild.

The Guild was very much a communal organization. Lawrence Langner (1890–1962) and Theresa Helburn (1887–1959) more or less administered a board composed mainly of designer Lee Simonson, actress Helen Westley, director Philip Moeller, and all-arounder Rollo Peters. But everyone did everything at the Guild, from reading submitted scripts to painting the scenery. Nor did the Guild adhere to the *star system, as other managements did. There were no "stars" at the Guild at all, at least in terms of billing, for posters proclaimed only the title and author. The rest of Broadway observed a management-labor segmentation; not the Guild. This in itself saved the fledgling group from financial crisis. Sworn to produce artistically rather than commercially, the Guild was struggling along till its fortune was made by —ironically enough—the Actors' Equity strike of 1919. Broadway's producers had refused to talk terms with the union, even to recognize it. But the Guild *had* recognized Equity and believed in profit-sharing salaries and thus was permitted to run St. John Ervine's *John Ferguson* right through the strike, making it virtually the only show in town for an entire month. The Guild was established: solvent and even a little famous.

As for the artistic value of the Guild's offerings, this is debated by many. As the major American producer of George Bernard Shaw, Eugene O'Neill, Maxwell Anderson, Robert E. Sherwood, Ferenc Molnár, Philip Barry, and S. N. Behrman, the Guild clearly has claims to importance, but also to a midcult complacency. Shaw's controversies next to Molnár's romantic trifles? Anderson's verse drama next to the salon quibbling of Barry and Behrman? And even the great O'Neill has his detractors, who see the ambition to be great substituting for true greatness. Then, too, was not the Guild the house of the bon ton *Lunts, for whom the no-stars rule had to be retired? Did not the Guild produce the first three Rodgers and Hammerstein "musical plays," *Oklahoma!* (1943), *Carousel* (1945), and *Allegro* (1947)?

Perhaps one may say if the Guild was not as vital as it might have been, it was bolder and more idealistic than the rest of Broadway. It *did* mount a great deal of Shaw, including world premieres; if O'Neill is not our greatest playwright, who is?; and Rodgers and Hammerstein's form revolution-

A typical Theatre Guild event, from its early years as Broadway's "art house" company: Goethe's
*Faust in 1928, with Dudley Digges (above, on table; below left on riser) as the Devil and George
Gaul (above in background) as Faust. To encompass Goethe's mercurial scene plot, designer Lee
Simonson conceived a medieval unit set that could be changed from a garden to a prison in an instant
by changing the backdrop behind the arch, shifting the "wall" pieces, and replacing the furnishings
and props on the front stage, as we see here: above, a tavern; below the witch's kitchen. This blithe
rejection of the detailed, realistic presentations of the *David Belasco era and the emphasis on European
masters old and new are what marked the Guild as Broadway's official Idealists in Residence.

ized that salient American theatre genre, the musical. These are heavy credentials. The Guild was innovative, too, in stagecraft, especially in the 1920s. By the following decade, it may have become too secure to be truly challenging. Daring is the province of the upstart. Certainly, the Guild failed to assimilate the leftist political art of the 1930s, preferring simply to encourage a spin-off of some of its rebellious youngsters as the *Group Theatre. Nor did the Guild attempt to reassert itself in the 1940s, though it is possible that *Oklahoma!*, on paper an allegedly dubious project, would not have been produced but for Guild sponsorship. By the late 1950s, though still relatively active, the Guild had virtually ceased to matter in the history of the American theatre.

THEATRE WORKSHOP
(See Joan Littlewood)

THESPIAN (See Greek Theatre)

SYBIL THORNDIKE (1882—1976)

"Surely the best-loved English actress since Ellen Terry," John Gielgud called Thorndike in *An Actor and His Time* (1979). "These two great players shared many of the same fine qualities—generosity, diligence, modesty, simplicity." They had more in common. Both were importantly associated with an acting partner, Terry with *Henry Irving, not only her onstage vis-à-vis, but, it was thought, her lover; and Thorndike united her career with that of her husband Lewis Casson (1875–1969), who like Irving was both an actor and a director. Moreover, both Terry and Thorndike

were honored by having roles written expressly for them by *George Bernard Shaw: Terry's Lady Cicely Waynflete in *Captain Brassbound's Conversion* (1906) and Thorndike's Maid of Orleans in *Saint Joan* (1924).

Here the resemblance ends, for Terry's Shaw part emphasizes her reputation for bantering comedy. She was no tragedian—a splendid Portia (in Shakespeare's *The Merchant of Venice*), for instance. Thorndike, on the other hand, had the weight, the concentration, the dangerous grandeur, for serious roles. "I hate pathos," she once said. "It's soft and weak. But tragedy has fight." So, surely, does Shaw's Joan, which became Thorndike's great role, constantly revived and always the key association in the Thorndike legend.

Thorndike was versatile. She balanced Euripides's Medea and Hecuba (in *The Trojan Women*), Shakespeare's Lady Macbeth, and Beatrice in Percy Bysshe Shelley's *The Cenci* with Shaw's Candida, the American murder farce *Arsenic and Old Lace*, and even a musical, playing Miss Crawley in Julian Slade's monumental *West End disaster *Vanity Fair*, after Thackeray's novel. Indeed, Thorndike plumed herself on versatility, thriving on a challenge. "Oh, Lewis," she told her husband—so Gielgud reports—"if only we could be the first actors to play on the moon!"

THRUST STAGE

Avant-garde theatre design in the post–World War II years favored the pushing out of the stage "apron" into the auditorium, thus bringing the players closer to the spectators and breaking the centuries-old segregation of art and public. Ironically, when the modern Western playhouse was founded, in Shakespeare's London and later in the Restoration era, the thrust stage was a convention.

LUDWIG TIECK (See
August Schlegel)

TIRADE

The windy speech given to heroic characters in Classical French drama, traditionally executed with a variety of virtuoso effects—violent fortissimos followed by opulent whispers, fluctuations in tempo and vocal color, and so on. In short: an aria without music. By the nineteenth century the tirade had degenerated into a mere noise of *boulevard *melodrama. In its pure form, it could be heard only in revivals of *Corneille and *Racine at the *Comédie-Française—or, for purposes of spoof, in musicals and farces. But *Jean Anouilh revived the convention, with loving bemusement, for the character of the Prince in *Léocadia*, and *Samuel Beckett lampooned it in Lucky's speech in *Waiting for Godot*.

ERNST TOLLER (See

Expressionism)

TO-NIGHT AT 8:30

"Acting, singing, and dancing vehicles for Gertrude Lawrence and myself" by *Noël Coward, prem. London, 1936.

An ingenious idea: ten one-acters to be performed in rotation in groups of three, in a miniature version of *stock company *repertory. (One of the ten, *Star Chamber*, proved so disastrous on its sole appearance that it was snatched from the set and never even published.) *To-night at 8:30* demonstrates Coward's bundle of specialties better than any other of his works, counting everything from romantic melodrama (*The Astonished Heart*) and screwball comedy (*Hands Across the Sea*) to working-class naturalism (*Fumed Oak*) and a musical backstager ("*Red Peppers*").

TORCH SONG TRILOGY

Profound comedy by Harvey Fierstein (1954–   ), prem. New York, 1982.

These three one-act plays—*The International Stud, Fugue in a Nursery,* and *Widows and Children First!*—came to light on off-off-Broadway at La Mama in 1978 and 1979. Revised and unified (given their heterogeneous formats), they moved to a small Broadway house for a three-year run, a remarkable record for a gay play that confronts the straight public with defiant nonconformism and the gay public with identity conflicts, maternal homophobia, and the murder (by straight teenagers on a thrill trip) of the perfect lover. *The International Stud* is a series of monologues and conversations for two punctuated by a torch singer's ballads, *Fugue* a structure of dialogues for two couples, constantly shifting "partners" to orchestral commentary, and *Widows and Children First!* flows naturalistically. All follow the love life of the drag artist Arnold Beckoff—author Fierstein himself, in an already legendary performance—from bar sex to a failed affair with a bisexual man, thence to a successful romance with a "shamefully beautiful" eighteen-year-old, and last, after the latter's murder, to the legal adoption of a more or less homeless waif and reconciliation with the bisexual. The desperately touching saga might have been unbearable without the flood of humor, especially as generated by the prideful yet fiercely self-mocking Fierstein:

ARNOLD: Did you say "Oops"? No, Ed. "Oops" is when you fall down an elevator shaft. "Oops" is when you skinny-dip in a school of piranha. "Oops" is for accidentally douching with Drāno. No, Ed, this was not an "Oops." This was a (ghastly strangled scream)!

TOTAL ECLIPSE

Art history by Christopher Hampton (1946–   ), prem. London, 1968.

Hampton built his view of the love affair of the French poets Paul Verlaine and Arthur Rimbaud on the historical record, filling out the data with an imagination of what the two, and their associates, and their times and places, were like. Documentary fiction of this kind became extremely popular in the second half of the twentieth century, but *Total Eclipse* stands out for its lack of political reading and its intimate presentation: a couple of people and how they felt rather than a historical act.

TOUR DE FORCE

French for "turn of strength": the composition or performance that fully exploits one's talent(s). A classic *tour de force* was *Laurence Olivier's playing Sophocles's Oedipus and *Sheridan's *The Critic* on a double bill, blithely jumping from the depth of tragedy to the utmost in mannered burlesque. Perhaps even more of a *tour de force* was Olivier's studied bewilderment at the excitement he was creating, the signals of egocentric modesty—as if actors should pull off such stunts as a matter of routine, or, at least, as if Olivier should.

CYRIL TOURNEUR (See Revenge Tragedy)

TOY THEATRES (See "Penny Plain")

TRAVESTIES

Anti-*absurdist absurdist *farce by *Tom Stoppard, prem. London, 1974.

Zurich, 1917. The revolutionary writer James Joyce, the revolutionary stylist Tristan Tzara (a founder of *dada), and the revolutionary politician Lenin all figure in this farrago of parody, disguise, collusion, and spoof on the subject of art versus politics, even art versus art. No other play of Stoppard's better illustrates his wit and ingenuity, whether he is mimicking the languid dandyism of *Oscar Wilde's *The Importance of Being Earnest, satirizing the traditions of xenophobia ("What a bloody country," a Briton says of Switzerland, "even the cheese has got holes in it!"), or explaining the character of dada though Joyce's cross examination of Tzara, performed to Joyce's magic act. Tzara has cut up Shakespeare's eighteenth sonnet, to rearrange the words in the typical anti-art of dada. The cut-up bits of paper were in Joyce's hat. Joyce, making an exit, puts the hat on. Joyce returns, covered in bits of paper:

JOYCE: What is the meaning of this?
TZARA: It has no meaning. It is without meaning as Nature is. It is Dada.
JOYCE: Give further examples of Dada.
TZARA: The Zoological Gardens after closing time. The logical gardenia. The bankrupt gambler. The successful gambler. The Eggboard, a sport or pastime for the top ten thousand in which the players, covered from head to foot in eggyolk, leave the field of play.

As this expansive game of Twenty Questions continues, Joyce puts the papers back into the hat one by one, then pulls out a paper carnation. Silk handkerchiefs and tiny flags appear as well, till Tzara gives a demonstration of applied dada by smashing everything in sight. Now Joyce replies:

JOYCE: An artist is the magician put among men to gratify—capriciously—their urge for immortality. The temples are built and brought down around him, continuously and contiguously, from Troy to the fields of Flanders. If there is any meaning in any of it, it is what survives as art, yes even in the celebration of tyrants, yes even in the celebration of nonentities . . . and if you hope to shame the world into the grave with your fashionable magic, I would strongly advise you to try and acquire some genius and if possible some subtlety before the season is quite over. Top o' the morning, Mr. Tzara!

At which Joyce produces the traditional live rabbit and makes his exit as well as his point.

Better yet, at the close of Act One, we learn that, to the question, "And what did you do in the Great War?" Joyce replies, "I wrote *Ulysses.* What did you do?"

TROILUS AND CRESSIDA

Metaphysical comedy by William Shakespeare, prem. London, 1602.

Troilus is unique in Shakespeare's canon: a comedy, yes, but so disenchanted and bitter that it disturbs rather than pleases; a tale of heroes in which heroism is scathingly ridiculed; a romance that spits on the very idea of romance. It was not given at the Globe Theatre, Shakespeare's home base, but at a private showing, presumably at one of the Inns of Court, where its densely intellectual contentions on love, war, and time might be better appreciated than by the rowdy pleasure seekers of the public theatres. The scene, of course, is Troy during the great war for Helen, a perfect setup for the dualistic confrontations on Shakespeare's thematic motifs, one side battling the other as character battles character for first rights to wisdom and insight on what love is, what war is for, what time does. It is Shakespeare's most difficult play, and one of his least appreciated.

THE TROJAN WOMEN

Antiwar tragedy by *Euripides, prem. Athens, 415 B.C.

Two plays, *Alexander* and *Palamedes,* preceded *The Trojan Women* in the usual Greek tetralogy, followed by the *satyr play *Sisyphus.* It's hard to imagine the Athenian audience enjoying the comic finale directly after this harrowing look at the aftermath of the decisive battle that separates the winners from the losers. Troy is a ruin, its men killed

and its women to be divvied up as slaves among the conquerors. Hecuba, queen of the fallen city, is Euripides's *protagonist, leading the chorus of Trojan women in lament, most pointedly over the body of her grandson Astyanax, thrown from the walls of Troy at the order of Odysseus to ensure that the boy would not grow up to collect blood vengeance against the Greeks.

We of today naturally view the play as a timeless argument against the horror of war. But Euripides's contemporaries knew that he was referring to Melos, an island neutral to Athens that was attacked by Athenian forces much as Troy was, one year before the presentation of *The Trojan Women.* Note that, while Greek plays technically treated old tales, they were quite capable of commenting on contemporary matters, even—in Euripides's case especially—of confronting Athenians with more reality than they could bear. Not surprisingly, Euripides failed to win a first prize in the play contest that year. *Edward Bond, too, confronts his public, in another version of the same tale, *The Woman.*

TROUSER PARTS

Also called "breeches parts": male characters played by women, usually in tights for the display of a shapely limb. They were particularly popular in England and America in the nineteenth century, and have survived to the present day in the "principal boy" hero of the British *pantomime.

KENNETH TYNAN (1927—1980)

One of the few critics who dignified the profession, even decorated it. Tynan was brilliant, fearless, and well-grounded in his subject: not an opportunist but an aficionado, and not a hack but a wit. He admitted in so many words that he regarded it as his vocation to "commemorate" the great portrayals of his day for posterity. (Conversely, his account of productions as wholes was skimpy. He was an actor's critic rather than a director's.) Tynan was progressive in roundly welcoming the "angry" generation of playwrights that entered in the wake of *John Osborne's *Look Back in Anger* and writing his review of the conservative *Terence Rattigan's *Separate Tables* in the form of a dialogue between Rattigan's own creation "Aunt Edna" and "A Young Perfectionist" to slice the *"well-made play" to bits. ("And what do you say to a comic Cockney maid?" asked the Young Perfectionist, outlining the characters with relish.) Tynan could appreciate the comparably conservative *Noël Coward—though here Tynan may have been responding to a star worship that confounded his critical probity. Tynan adored the famous. Better —worse—Tynan emulated the famous; he chased chic and stars all his life. He became controversially leftist, apparently in order to live in harmony with his idol, *Bertolt Brecht, and though Tynan maintained a solid body of work in his nineteen years at the London *Observer* (with two years off at *The New Yorker*) and became *Laurence Olivier's *dramaturg at the National Theatre of Great Britain, leaving at the insistence of Olivier's successor, *Peter Hall, Tynan really found himself as the perpetrator of the nude revue, *Oh! Calcutta!,* cast with unknowns. Tynan was, for once, the famous name in the play.

U

UBU ROI

Indescribable burlesque by *Alfred Jarry, prem. Paris, 1896.

King Ubu began as a schoolboy prank, a spoof of a risible professor nicknamed "Père Hébé" (roughly, "Father Stupefying"), which eventually turned into "Père Ubu." Jarry performed it with marionettes. The expanded version, unveiled at *Lugné-Poë's Théâtre de l'Oeuvre, inspired one of the greatest on-the-spot protests in theatre history. After all, the first word of Jarry's text is an expletive never spoken on a stage before then: "Merdre!" —a schoolboy prank in itself, as this untranslatable term, used throughout the play, is "Shit!" *(Merde!)* with a flip on it, "Shit!" saying, "Look at me!" This *merdre* fairly captures Jarry's whimsical recklessness. "The players are supposed to be dolls, toys, marionettes, and now they are all hopping like wooden frogs," wrote *William Butler Yeats, in the house on that historic night. "The chief personage, who is some kind of king, carries for a sceptre a brush of the kind that we use to clean a [toilet]." The plot concerns Father Ubu's cowardly, pompous, and casually bloodthirsty usurpation of the Polish throne; the bizarre turns of plot, the use of French adolescents' argot, and the mock-simple staging style make the work not horror but fantasy, frolic, and revolt against the sensible.

Yeats was disturbed. Had not art already reached some sort of apex with Mallarmé, Verlaine, Moreau, and with Yeats himself? *Ubu Roi* proposed a new age, but an age of what? "After us," Yeats mused, "the Savage God."

He was right. *Ubu Roi* was most directly succeeded by two other *Ubu* plays, *Ubu Cocu* (Ubu Cuckolded) and *Ubu Enchaîné* (Ubu in Chains). Despite Jarry's attractive notoriety, neither was performed in his lifetime. But *Ubu Roi* did more generally make way for the savage god of *surrealism, with its relative, *dada, and its descendant, *absurdism.

UNCLE TOM'S CABIN

*Melodrama by George L. Aiken (1830–1876), prem. Troy, New York, 1852.

This was the most popular of several stage versions of Harriet Beecher Stowe's abolitionist novel. Aiken combined sentimentalism, cheap piety, violent villainy, and spectacle, all haphazardly, and in writing that is ruthlessly poor even for the standards of old-time melodrama. The action follows that of the novel, with the kindly slaveholder St. Clare facing off the dastardly overseer Simon Legree as the slave Eliza outruns her pursuers and their bloodhounds over the icy Ohio River, the black pixie Topsy capers and "dances a breakdown," and St. Clare's saintly daughter, in a tableau of apotheosis, materializes in heaven perched on a milk-white dove flanked by her murdered father and the equally murdered and if possible even more saintly old slave Uncle Tom.

The insistent note of Christian transcendence made the piece popular with a huge segment of the population that normally avoided theatres as hostels of sin. But it was the spectacle above all that kept *Uncle Tom's Cabin* a mainstay of the touring circuit for half a century, as competitive "Tom shows" promised ever more lavish versions of "The Escape Over the Frozen River" and the "Allegory" finale in heaven. Yet there were those who attended the piece to be uplifted, perhaps by Tom's tender quotations of Scripture (expanded over the years to accommodate popular demand) or even by Simon Legree's scene of (temporary) repentence, brought on by a lock of hair that recalls to him— no! *yes!*—his mother, who seems to have been at least as saintly as little Eva and Uncle Tom put together:

CASSY: Has aught on this earth power to move a soul like thine?
LEGREE: Yes, for hard and reprobate as I now seem, there has been a time when I have been rocked on the bosom of a mother, cradled with prayers and pious hymns, my now seared brow bedewed with the waters of holy baptism.
CASSY: (aside) What sweet memories of childhood can thus soften down that heart of iron?
LEGREE: In early childhood a fair-haired woman has led me, at the sound of Sabbath bells, to worship and to pray. Born of a hard-tempered sire, on whom that gentle woman had wasted a world of unvalued love, I followed in the steps of my father . . . I drank and swore, was wilder and more brutal than ever. And one night, when my mother, in the last agony of her despair, knelt at my feet, I spurned her from me, threw her senseless on the floor, and with brutal curses fled to my ship.
CASSY: Then the fiend took thee for his own.
LEGREE: The next I heard of my mother was one night when I was carousing among drunken companions. A letter . . . told me that my mother was dead, and that dying she blest and forgave me! (Buries his face in his hands.)

THE THEATRE OF THE UNEXPRESSED

The stage's counterpart to the baroque intersections and arabesques of art nouveau, and of the same era, the early 1900s. In the Theatre of the Unexpressed, the most telling moments yield not confrontations, *tirades, or even gala exits, but silence: a character striving to project emotion through mime. This is acting between the lines. The playwright *Maurice Maeterlinck introduced the style, but Jean-Jacques Bernard, Maeterlinck's successor in the 1920s, was most closely identified with the term, also called the Theatre of Silence.

THE UNITIES

Of action, place, and time. A much misunderstood concept, traditionally the weapon of critics who couldn't write a play to save their lives. *Aristotle supposedly discerned the unities in analyzing Greek tragedy: one plot, set in one place, occurring within the span of one day. In fact, Aristotle only spoke of the unity of action; Greek playwrights exploited place and time at will. *Aeschylus's *Eumenides,* the third part of the *Oresteia,* moves from Delphi to Athens without the least apology for the jostling of unity of place. Not till the day of *Corneille and *Racine in seventeeth century France did "the unities" become an obsession—again, only with those who judged rather than created the work. Over the eras, fascination with this essentially irrelevant structuring system has flagged, though many a contemporary play—Jason Miller's *That Championship Season,* for instance, or *Simon Gray's *Butley*—observes the three rules.

UPSTAGE

Back, away from the public.
(See also Downstage.)

PETER USTINOV (1921–)

Fantasy, satire, history, and politics are the stuff of Ustinov's plays, the best of which Ustinov directs and stars in himself. He is a sharp director, a sharp actor. He is a sharp playwright, as persuasive when he mixes a kind of *Shavian *Chekhov as when he separately mocks their styles. Yet his oeuvre seems to have paid its way and faded, the more ambitious along with the tidy. His modest burlesque *Romanoff and Juliet* (1956), on cold war confrontations in the capital of a jaded European Graustark ("In 1471 we attracted the attention of the world by failing to stop the Turks in a bloodless battle not two streets away from here . . . in the suburbs"), may prove Ustinov's most enduring piece. Its postwar timeliness of course dates it, but it is rich in Ustinov's most notable quality: charm.

JOHN VANBRUGH (1664–1726)

This English architect, the builder of Blenheim Palace, was also a dramatist—the last, perhaps, of the *Restoration playwrights in tone and style. The London stage was already turning back from the gloating licentiousness of William Wycherley and William Congreve for a more "moral" approach, but Vanbrugh could not conform. He wrote his masterpiece, *The Relapse; or, Virtue in Danger* (1696) as a corrective sequel to *Colley Cibber's comedy *Love's Last Shift; or, The Fool in Fashion,* presented earlier that same year. Cibber told of a reformation of a rake, and Vanbrugh didn't buy it. Rakes don't reform; pleasure is not a phase of their existence, but its permanent motivation. Using Cibber's principals and adding in a delicious parade of Restoration characters—Lord Foppington, Sir Tunbelly Clumsy, Foppington's fiancée Hoyden, Tom Fashion (younger brother of Cibber's Sir Novelty Fashion)—Vanbrugh kept the bawdy spirit of the Restoration alive, though *Richard Brinsley Sheridan was to recorrect *The Relapse* in a prudish revision as *A Trip to Scarborough* in 1777. To complete the bowdlerizing of Vanbrugh, Cibber himself completed and tamed Vanbrugh's *A Journey to London,* left unfinished at his death, as

The Provok'd Husband (1728)—a reference to Vanbrugh's other outstanding play, *The Provok'd Wife* (1698).

JEAN-CLAUDE VAN ITALLIE (See Joseph Chaikin and *The Serpent*)

LOPE DE VEGA CARPIO (1562–1635)

The "Spanish Shakespeare," as he is sometimes called, is the most prolific playwright known to history, having left some 1800 titles. (About five hundred are extant.) Lope de Vega's likeness to Shakespeare stems from their comparable positions in the theatres of their time. They are almost exact contemporaries, born two years apart, each coming to his maturity just when the theatre of his native culture had burst into flower; and each developed the somewhat raw materials of the available forms into perfect artistic compounds; and each is now regarded as *the* dramatic poet of his place and era.

There the resemblance ends. Lope de Vega's output is far more diverse than Shakespeare's, despite the latter's formal experiments in darkening comedy and personalizing the chronicle play. Lope's works defy such relatively easy classification as the Shakespearean Comedies, Tragedies, and Histories. Indeed, it was Lope who set up the classifications of Spanish theatre simply by writing so many different kinds of plays. However, he was particularly known for expanding the possibilities of the comic *gracioso character, and for the genre known as the *comedia de capa y espada,* the "cloak and sword drama." (*Comedia,* like the Italian *commedia* and the French *comédie,* refers generally to drama, not to comic drama specifically. Thus the name of the *Comédie-Française, meaning roughly "the French [national] Theatre.") Further to separate Lope from Shakespeare, we should note that Lope has no *Hamlet,* no *Henry IV,* no *Midsummer Night's Dream*—no titles that stand out for citation in books like this one. We should at least consider *Fuente Ovejuna* (?1614), perhaps the most popular of Lope's plays today (under the title *The Sheep-Well* in English) for its surprisingly advanced view that justice is more important than law. The play bears the name of an Andalusian village that, in 1476, killed an oppressively corrupt nobleman; Lope's piece chronicles—and defends—the rebellion. Elsewhere, however, Lope is very much a Spanish Catholic, upholding the dogma of Mother Church. He was himself a functionary of the Inquisition, and is believed to have tortured heretics to death.

VEHICLE

The star rides his "vehicle" as the conquistador his horse: the play becomes simply the means by which the performer engages his talents. The notion of a play thus supporting the leading player dates back to the *star system that prevailed during the nineteenth and early twentieth centuries. Not till the star system broke down in the post–World War I years—when integrity of production or brilliance of composition became more important than beauty of star charisma—did the word "vehicle"

come into use, to distinguish the stars' theatre from the playwrights' or the troupes'.

The vehicle has largely disappeared, as most European stars favor classics or important new plays and most American stars disdain the stage for film work. Yet the idea of an appearance centered on the player in an otherwise useless work has held on—in for instance Katharine Hepburn's Broadway appearances in the musical *Coco* (1969) and the comedies *A Matter of Gravity* (1976) and *The West Side Waltz* (1981). That these plays have authors, even well-known ones, is beside the point. Received opinion held that "the play is so-so, but it's worth it for *her.*"

However, it is a paradox of the vehicle syndrome that quite excellent plays may also serve as a star's showcase—that certain box office names are so big that they overwhelm even Shakespeare as the genius of the evening. Laurence Olivier's smashing performance in *John Osborne's *The Entertainer* did not so overwhelm the work, for, one, Osborne was England's hottest and most controversial new playwright and, two, Olivier did not "do" vehicles. Similarly, Dustin Hoffman's New York revival of *Arthur Miller's *Death of a Salesman* was no vehicle, as the play is a solemn American classic and Hoffman is perceived as too dedicated to believe in vehicles. Indeed, the very materialization of a movie star on a stage is regarded as dedication in itself. On the other hand, Al Pacino's 1981 Broadway appearance in a Long Wharf production of *David Mamet's *American Buffalo* is questionable, if only for the air of respectful support on the part of Pacino's colleagues. The original Broadway *American Buffalo,* with Robert Duvall, Kenneth McMillan, and John Savage, was acted in balance by a three-man ensemble. Pacino's *American Buffalo* felt somewhat like a Motown trio, with a lead singer and two backups.

(See also *Auntie Mame, The Beauty Part,* and *Cyrano de Bergerac.*)

VERFREMDUNGSEFFEKT (See Alienation Effect)

VIEUX CARRÉ

Autobiography by *Tennessee Williams, prem. New York, 1977.

Had Williams produced this piece early rather than late in his career, it might have enjoyed a huge success, for it is funny, true, and very touching. This look at the young Williams's sojourn in a rooming house in New Orleans in 1938 and 1939 brings forth what would seem to be the originals of Williams's most constant character types—the flurried, intelligent, guiltily sensualist woman (here called Jane) who wants something better than good sex but can't find a way to believe that anything *is* better; the lawless stud (Jane's boyfriend Tye), the grumpy beldame (Mrs. Wire, who runs the boarding house), the failed artist and wretched, angry queen (Mr. Nightingale), and Williams himself, here a shy young man called The Writer. Unfortunately, Williams had worked these characters and their wistful spasms of loneliness and self-deception too long for the reviewers to support him in his era of officially recognized Failure, and the abysmal New York production virtually demanded to be destroyed.

It was. Still, *Vieux Carré* remains one of Williams's most finished texts, especially in the revision made for the 1978 London staging with Vera Miles as Mrs. Wire (Sylvia Sidney's role in New York). Of all his plays, this is the one—even considering the "memory play" *The Glass Menagerie*—that most heavily bears Williams's thought on who he was and what he saw. "They're disappearing behind me," The Writer says as he leaves the rooming house at the play's end. "Going. People you've known in places do that; they go when you go. The earth seems to swallow them up, the walls absorb them like moisture, they remain with you only as ghosts. Their voices are echoes, fading but remembered."

A VIEW FROM THE BRIDGE

Near-*melodrama by *Arthur Miller, prem. (as a one-acter) New York, 1955; (revised and expanded to full-length) London, 1956.

From the Brooklyn Bridge: looking into a waterfront Italian-American community. These are people of fast passions and an absolute code of behavior, which makes this Miller's only brush with the old-fashioned threats-and-confrontations melodrama, reclaimed, of course, by Miller's thematic grip, rounded characterization, and authentic ear for subcultural argot. As Miller's hero, Eddie Carbone, says, warning his niece about the world beyond their ethnic ghetto, "Most people ain't people." It is a cliché that Miller's plays are about guilt: alternatively, one might say that they are about honor, especially loss of honor because of a guilty act. *The Crucible's John Proctor dies to regain his honor. Eddie Carbone dies because he throws honor away, because he cannot "settle for half" and accept the Code over his personal code. Eddie Carbone is his own people. "He was as good a man as he had to be in a life that was hard and even," says the narrator figure, the ghetto's lawyer. Thus, "Something perversely pure calls to me from his memory . . . for he allowed himself to be wholly known." Yet, "I mourn him—I admit it —with a certain . . . alarm."

ROGER VITRAC (See Dada)

VOLTAIRE (1694–1778)

François-Marie Arouet juggled the letters of "Arouet l. i." (for Arouet le ieune, "Arouet the younger") to arrive at a pseudonym. The rest of Voltaire's self-invention, as poet, playwright, historian, philosopher, wit, and overall, the outstanding celebrity of the eighteenth century, took a bit more time. Voltaire was long ahead of his days of eminence when he began to write for the stage, at the time suffering a decadent era energized only by revivals of *Corneille and *Racine. Voltaire leaned toward the Racinian construct, in tales in which passion disorders the social contract. But Voltaire was as well a Shakespearean at the time (later, he recanted his youthful Romantic impressionability), and sought to bend "the rules" (see The Unities) of French tragedy to suit a more expansive format.

Nevertheless, Voltaire's masterpiece, *Zaïre* (1732), is ultra-Raciniste, but for a touch of on-stage violence. The titular heroine is a Christian raised in Jerusalem by Moslems, engaged to a sultan. Her crusader father and brother attempt to reclaim her, her sultan mistakes the brother for a rival and kills Zaïre and himself. Onto this rather contrived scenario, Voltaire tacked scenes of intense feeling. The poetry is not up to Racine's level, no—but in this impoverished era, *Zaïre* became the play of the day and has survived as an undisputed classic, standard material in the academic syllabus and the nationalist thespian repertory. Except for *Mérope* (1743), Voltaire's other plays are considered third-rate, though he did open up the French tragic form to discussions of ethnic and religious bigotry, and, in operatic adaptation, his scripts attracted composers from Rossini to Verdi. Bellini left the most famous *Zaïre* opera, as *Zaira* (1829), but there were at least thirteen other versions, demonstrating the work's appeal in Voltaire's lifetime and the decades following his death.

W

WAITING FOR GODOT

"Tragicomedy" by *Samuel Beckett, prem. Paris, 1953.

Two acts, five characters. "A country road. A tree. Evening." In Act One, two tramps wait for the mysterious Mr. Godot. Two strange men appear, master and servant. The servant delivers a Joycean parody of the classical French *tirade:

LUCKY: Given the existence as uttered forth in the public works of Puncher and Wattmann of a personal god quaquaquaqua with white beard quaquaquaqua outside time without extension who from the heights of divine apathia divine athambia divine aphasia loves us dearly with some exceptions for reasons unknown but time will tell and suffers like the divine Miranda with those who for reasons unknown but time will tell are plunged in torment plunged in fire whose fire flames if that continues and who can doubt it will fire the firmament that is to say blast hell to heaven so blue still and calm so calm with a calm which even though intermittent is better than nothing . . .

The two strangers pass on. A boy comes in to tell the tramps that Godot will come not today but tomorrow. The second act mirrors the first except: the tree is now slightly in flower and the two strangers now claim to be respectively blind and dumb. "Well?" says one tramp. "Shall we go?" "Yes," says the other, "let's go." So they had said at the end of the first act. Beckett has the last word: "They do not move."

Who is Godot? Many have guessed; but Beckett says *he* doesn't know himself—"If I knew, I would have said so in the play." We had best leave it at that. Will Godot come? If *Clifford Odets's *Waiting for Lefty* is any clue—no, he won't. Lefty is dead and Godot is . . . not there. The play was slow to achieve its now encompassing success as a central existential statement, but it is noteworthy that audiences of convicts at performances given in prisons respond to the play immediately, seeing in it an articulation of the empty, hopeless isolation of their lives. At least one prisoner thus became a Beckett disciple: Ron Cluchey, sentenced to life without parole, felt so stimulated by a *Godot* production in San Quentin that he became the *actor-manager of a theatre troupe. Declared rehabilitated, Cluchey was freed, met Beckett, and, after study with The Master, launched an acting career as a Beckett specialist. Perhaps Beckett is wrong: there is a Godot after all; and he does keep (some of) his appointments.

Waiting for Godot *in Paris and New York: above, the premiere in 1953 at the Théâtre Babylone under Roger Blin, with Blin (far right) as Pozzo. Right, the first New York staging, in 1956, with Bert Lahr and E. G. Marshall. Note that the tree, bare in Act One (above) has sprouted, as the author directs, "four or five leaves" during the intermission, though the second act (right) takes place, in typically spare Beckettian instructions, "Next day. Same time. Same place."*

WALK-ON PART

One of the theatre's most foolish clichés holds that there are no small parts, only small actors. There most certainly are small parts, and the walk-on is the smallest, counting just enough motion (and possibly a line or two) to be bigger than a member of a crowd scene: listed by name and character in the program but of tenuous value in terms of an actor's talent and self-respect. Yet a walk-on can be essential in its limited way. A classic instance is the role termed A Visitor in *Neil Simon's *Come Blow Your Horn. Throughout the play, the characters have repeatedly referred to an Aunt Gussie, unseen but a strong presence because of her totemic importance in Simon's loving spoof of Jewish middle-class tribalism. Aunt Gussie is the looming figure small boys kiss under parental duress. As the play nears its final curtain, the central plot lines tied up and a young man awaiting a hot date, the doorbell rings. "Coming, my snowflake," the young man coos, dimming the lights. He opens the door, and in walks A Visitor. "Aunt Gussie!" the boy squeals in panic.

Curtain.

THE WATER ENGINE

"An American Fable" by *David Mamet, prem. Chicago, 1977.

As if stressing his extraordinary ear for the American vernacular, Mamet first wrote *The Water Engine* as a radio play, packing his art into the purely verbal. The stage version, set in a radio station during the performance of *The Water Engine,* games with the visual in that the actors sometimes deliver their lines into microphones (as radio players) and sometimes play to each other naturalistically, as their characters would if *The Water Engine* were not a play but a real-life event. Surely it couldn't be real: an obscure man has invented an engine that runs on distilled water. In the artful jumble of dialogue, passing conversations, announcer's narrations, mottos, warnings, and other aural confetti that Mamet hurls at us, cutthroat businessmen attempt to steal the plans for the water engine, torturing the inventor and his sister to death. But the inventor has mailed his plans to a science-minded teenager. "All people," one of the announcer's homilies runs, "are connected."

THE WAY OF THE WORLD

*Comedy of manners by William Congreve, prem. London, 1700.

This is the summit of *Restoration comedy, the last and greatest in a line of plays that, for all their delightful ribaldry and satire, depend on brilliance of language more than anything else to defend their longevity. Yet here wit is not only the weapon but the very cause of the war, for it was Congreve's stated aim to replace the typical fools and knaves of Restoration comedy with "characters which should appear ridiculous, not so much through a natural folly . . . as through an affected wit." Thus even our hero and heroine, Mirabell ("handsome to look at") and Millamant ("of a thousand suitors"), err in putting style and brilliance before substance and feeling. And of course the rest of the cast *are* the typical fools and knaves, though Congreve sets them off in language far more beautiful than they deserve: Mrs. Fainall, Mrs. Marwood, Millamant's servant Mincing, Sir Wilful Witwould, and, best of all, the grotesque beldame Lady Wishfort, even more grateful than *The Importance of Being Earnest*'s Lady Bracknell for comediennes of seniority.

The Way of the World is not often revived because its extraordinarily tangled plot makes it difficult for even the advanced theatregoer—enough story to fill three or four modern comedies has occurred *before* the curtain rises, as if *The Way of the World* were an evening-length Fifth Act. Still, for the aficionado it remains the most delightful of its kind, replete with absurd inventions, as when Lady Wishfort tells her servant Peg to bring her some brandy. Peg takes a bit too long for milady's taste, and she rails at Peg:

PEG: Madam, I was looking for a cup.
LADY WISHFORT: A cup, save thee! and what a
  cup hast thou brought! —Does thou take me

for a fairy, to drink out of an acorn? Why didst thou not bring thy thimble? Hast thou ne'er a brass thimble clinking in thy pocket with a bit of nutmeg? —I warrant thee. Come, fill, fill! —So—again.

(Knocking at the door.)

See who that is. —Set down the bottle first —here, here, under the table. —What, wouldst thou go with the bottle in thy hand, like a tapster? As I am a person, this wench has lived in an inn upon the road, before she came to me, like Maritornes the Asturian in *Don Quixote!*

Or consider the famous Marriage Contract Scene, in which Mirabell and Millamant make their peace and arrange to wed:

MILLAMANT: I won't be called names after I'm married; positively I won't be called names.
MIRABELL: Names!
MILLAMANT: Ay, as wife, spouse, my dear, joy, jewel, love, sweetheart, and the rest of that nauseous cant, in which men and their wives are so fulsomely familiar—I shall never bear that—good Mirabell, don't let us be familiar or fond, nor kiss before folks . . . Let us never visit together, nor go to a play together; but let us be very strange and well-bred: let us be as strange as if we had been married a great while; and as well-bred as if we were not married not all.
MIRABELL: Have you any more conditions to offer? Hitherto your demands are pretty reasonable.
MILLAMANT: Trifles! —As liberty to pay and receive visits to and from whom I please; to write and receive letters, without interrogatories or wry faces on your part . . . to have no obligations upon me to converse with wits that I don't like, because they are your acquaintance: or to be intimate with fools, because they may be your relations. Come to dinner when I please; dine in my dressing-room when I'm out of humour, without giving a reason. To have my closet inviolate; to be sole empress on my tea-table, which you must never presume to approach without asking. And lastly, wherever I am, you shall always knock at the door before you come in. Those articles subscribed, if I continue to endure you a little longer, I may by degrees dwindle into a wife.

JOHN WEBSTER (See Elizabethan Theatre)

FRANK WEDEKIND (1864—1918)

Coming onto the scene as *naturalism was giving way to more experimental, nonrealistic modes, such as *symbolism and *expressionism, this German playwright (also cabaret performer and actor) made his work transitional, drawing on all the available forms. Thus, Wedekind's realistic plays have dreamlike, even nightmarish effects that distinguish his work from that of his colleagues. This is especially true of *Frühlings Erwachen* (Spring's Awakening), Wedekind's most enduring piece, so shocking in its time that, though written in 1891, it was not staged till 1906 (by *Max Reinhardt in Berlin). A tale of young people harassed to insanity and death by the bourgeois repressiveness of their elders, it runs a relatively naturalistic course but for two scenes, a broadly burlesqued meeting of bloodless academics, and an expressionistic fantasy set in what was to become a favorite expressionistic locale, a graveyard.

Actually, Wedekind's frank view of human sexuality made a number of his plays shocking and banned—but also ageless. Like *Spring's Awakening,* the two "Lulu plays," *Erdgeist* (Earth Spirit, written 1895, prem. 1898) and *Die Büchse der Pandora* (Pandora's Box, 1905), startle with their persuasive candor even today, though adaptations for cinema (the famous G. W. Pabst silent with our own Louise Brooks) and opera (Alban Berg's *Lulu*) challenge the originals for public attention. Wedekind is often compared to *August Strindberg for their shared view of love and marriage as gender war. However, Strindberg's masochistic misogyny is less convincing, in the end, than Wedekind's more forgiving womanizing. Strindberg sees the female as devouring and castrating, an artistically useful paranoia in his era, perhaps, but not a message most people can seriously consider. Wedekind's battle of the sexes faults the male's egomania and acquisitiveness more than the female's aggressiveness, and thus makes a more telling impression on his public.

HELENE WEIGEL (See The Berliner Ensemble)

PETER WEISS (1916–1982)

"I learned most from *Brecht," this German dramatist claims. "I learned clarity from him, the necessity of making clear the social question in a play." Yet Weiss's plays are not at all like Brecht's, at least experientially, for the spectator. True, some of the plays employ song spots, as Brecht's do, and, like Brecht, Weiss likes to write plays around historical figures, as in *Trotzki im Exil* (Trotsky in Exile, 1970), sympathetic to the revolutionary, and in *Hölderlin* (1971), which pictures the poet undergoing an exile of the mind into madness, while *Goethe, *Schiller, and Hegel come off as opportunists who stay sane by selling out to bourgeois, even totalitarian, interests. But Weiss's free verse and his very various use of experimental staging techniques set him apart from Brecht, who used the *epic theatre principle far more consistently. Moreover, if Weiss shares with Brecht a didactic leftist orientation, Weiss's personal record shows none of the temporizing, "do as I say, not as I do" stunts of the Brecht who ran a theatre company in the Soviet block yet retained a West German publisher and a Swiss bank account.

Like Brecht, Weiss left Germany when the Nazis took over. German-Czech (and Jewish) on his father's side and Swedish on his mother's.

Weiss went to Sweden. Brecht did, too, but only as a stopover on the exile that took him, like Trotsky, to the Western hemisphere. Weiss settled in Sweden, assumed Swedish citizenship, and remained in Sweden, writing in German because German subjects occupy him more than any others. His outstanding success is set in revolutionary France: *Die Verfolgung und Ermordung Jean Paul Marats Dargestellt Durch die Schauspielgruppe des Hospizes zu Charenton Unter Anleitung des Herrn de Sade* (The Persecution and Murder of Jean-Paul Marat as Performed by the Theatre Troupe of Charenton Hospital under the Direction of the Marquis de Sade, 1964), though we should note that the formal title of Geoffrey Skelton's English translation of the play is slightly less faithful: *The Persecution and Assassination of Jean-Paul Marat as Performed by the Inmates of the Asylum of Charenton under the Direction of the Marquis de Sade*. We note, too, that *Marat/Sade*'s madhouse setting lends the piece to flamboyant, grotesque, terrifying stagings that draw attention from Weiss's message. However, a more clarified Weiss puts forth his "social question" in *Die Ermittlung* (The Investigation, 1965), a *docudrama taken verbatim from transcripts of the trial of officials and guards of Auschwitz concentration camp. *The Investigation* is so basic to an understanding of German history—by the Germans themselves—that the play was premiered simultaneously in seventeen German theatres. If *Marat/Sade* is as entertaining as it is harrowing, the very simple, very direct, very straightforward *Investigation* is one of the most horrifying shows ever mounted, made entirely of the testimony of witnesses, the denials of the accused, and the interjections of the legal team. Weiss has also dealt with colonialism in Africa in *Gesang vom Lusitanischen Popanz* (Song of the Lusitanian Bogey, 1967), and with Vietnam in a play whose title is even longer than *Marat/Sade*'s: (to keep to the English translation) *Discourse on the Background and the Progress of the Prolonged War of Liberation in Vietnam as an Illustration of the Necessity for Armed Struggle of the Oppressed Against Their Oppressors as well as on the Attempts of the United States of America to Destroy the Foundations of Revolution*, 1968, known in German as *Vietnam/Diskurs* and in English as *Discourse on Vietnam*.

(See also *Marat/Sade*.)

ORSON WELLES (1915–1985)

"It was an astonishing performance, wrong from beginning to end," wrote one of Welles's first critics, "but with all the qualities of fine acting tearing their way through a chaos of inexperience. His diction was practically perfect; his personality, in spite of fantastic antics, was real and varied; his sense of passion, of evil, of drunkenness, of tyranny, of a sort of demoniac authority, was arresting. A preposterous energy pulsated through everything he did." So thought *actor-manager Micheál MacLiammóir of the sixteen-year-old Welles's audition for Dublin's *Gate Theatre, his first professional engagement, in Lion Feuchtwanger's *Jew Süss,* in 1931.

Back in his native America, Welles maintained this mixture of the brilliant and the erratic. In the mid-1930s, he joined the New York outfit of the *Federal Theatre, directing the notorious *Voodoo Macbeth* (1936), Shakespeare reset in the Caribbean, and Marc Blitzstein's *Brechtian musical *The Cradle will Rock* (1937), politically so dangerous that the government tried to shut it down—or, rather, up—before it opened. In 1937, Welles and his assistant John Houseman formed the Mercury Theatre, presenting an unusual bill of classic repertory from Shakespeare (*Julius Caesar*) to Shaw (*Heartbreak House,* with Welles as Captain Shotover) in a neglected old 687-seat house on West Forty-first Street. The productions were venturesome. The Mercury gave *Julius Caesar* in the costume of Mussolini's Italy, the chorus a troop of skulkers in overcoats and fedoras; and *Georg Büchner's *Danton's Death* unfolded the Terror of the French Revolution before a permanent backdrop of five thousand Halloween masks painted to look like grinning death's heads.

Welles was making himself known as Broadway's most promising actor and director. By mid-1939, unfortunately, he was in Hollywood, making films for RKO. His work there included one of the greatest American movies, *Citizen Kane* (1941), but thereafter Welles spent more time in film than in the theatre. He stayed in touch with the stage, typically for very unusual projects—preparing,

staging, and starring in a *Gesamtkunstwerk adaptation of Jules Verne as *Around the World* (1946) for Broadway, taking in everything from acrobats, a belly dancer, and a magic act to a miniature railroad train and a Cole Porter score; or devising a stage version of Herman Melville's *Moby-Dick* (1955) for London, directing and now even designing the show as well as playing the Narrator and a vast Captain Ahab.

Sadly, none of Welles's post-Mercury theatre stints paid off commercially. *Around the World* was thought too loosely organized. It had everything; yet it was nothing. *Moby-Dick* also failed, though *Kenneth Tynan, admitting the uncomfortably overwhelming grandeur of Welles's Ahab, cheered for the show's "sheer theatrical virtuosity." The Duke of York's Theatre, Tynan wrote, was "a house of magic." Yet the 1960 Broadway staging, a two-week flop, did not even retain Welles's original production, and offered Rod Steiger as Ahab.

Wells did at least film himself in some important Shakespearean roles, most notably his monstrous, touching Falstaff (to a very young Keith Baxter's Prince Hal) in *Chimes at Midnight* (1967). However, most people today probably remember Welles as the implausibly portly spokesman for television wine commercials, grimly warning that "Paul Masson will sell no wine . . . before its time."

THE "WELL-MADE PLAY"

The dominant popular form of drama in the nineteenth century. Plot and theatricality were its main features, using such conventions as An Episode in Her Past, His Dastardly Step-Brother, The Missing Will, and so on, to run the action not on believable characterization but on a succession of arresting incidents. Since the incidents were rather unrealistic, so were the characters.

The well-made play was especially prevalent—and influential—in France, where playwrights *Eugène Scribe and *Victorien Sardou made it not only popular but essential, the very model of dramatic construction. Thus we find *Anton Chekhov referring derisively to "French scenes" when he abandons the Scribe-Sardou approach for a more naturalistic program. Other playwrights of the very late 1800s similarly denounced the "French" approach, particularly *George Bernard Shaw, who termed the world of the well-made play "Sardoodledum." Yet Shaw blithely borrowed Sardou's construction as a setting for sociopolitical themes that the well-made play very seldom tackled. *Henrik Ibsen also found the "French" form useful—though Ibsen built it around character rather than plot. In short, the well-made play was in fact made well: sensibly structured. What was wrong with it was its disregard for reality.

(See also *Scène à Faire*.)

ARNOLD WESKER (1932–   )

Wesker was one of the earliest of the "angry young" playwrights who came into prominence in the wake of *John Osborne's *Look Back in Anger*. *Chicken Soup with Barley* (1958) defined Wesker's territory: socialist *naturalism intent on the need for humanitarianism in politics—for communication, understanding . . . love. As one of the characters says near the end of *Chicken Soup*, "You've got to care or you'll die." *Roots* (1959) and *I'm Talking About Jerusalem* (1960) completed what is known as "the Wesker Trilogy." The three plays are tied together by the character of Ronnie Kahn, Wesker's autobiographical invention, who serves as *protagonist of the first play, an unseen but much mentioned "presence" in the second, and the interlocutor in the third—though by far the most fetching moment of the original stagings at the Belgrade Theatre in Coventry and the *Royal Court in London was Joan Plowright's performance of *Root*'s heroine, Beatie Bryant. Ronnie Kahn's fiancée and "student," she quotes his wisdom to her unhearing family until, the engagement broken off, she realizes that she has become her own person, no longer quoting but articulately original. There's a bit of the feeling of *Clifford Odets's *Awake and Sing!* in Wesker's trilogy, particularly in the dialect realism of working-class Jewish life. However, Wesker broke off in a new direction in *The Kitchen* (1959), a microcosmic allegory, and especially in the military *Chips With Everything* (1962), a despairing look at how class solidarity (in the Royal Air Force) overwhelms ecumenical fair-ness: even the aristo who wants to befriend the prole is warned away by his fellow aristos, virtually restrained by force. The first productions of all the above plays were directed by *John Dexter, a notable collaboration comparable to that of *Jean Giraudoux and *Louis Jouvet. Wesker has also been extremely active in Centre 42, a project designed to popularize the arts for a working-class public.

THE WEST END

London proper, The City, adhering to the outline laid down for Londinium in Roman Britain, is but a section of the metropolis now known as "London." Running roughly from The Tower (on the east) up to the Guildhall (in the north) and across to St. Paul's (in the west), this is a place of lawyers and bankers, a daytime city of offices. In Shakespeare's day, the theatres were deliberately built beyond the city limits, especially across the Thames in Southwark (where the *Old Vic and the National Theatre of Great Britain stand today). When the *Restoration brought public theatre performances back to England, new theatres were built within civic jurisdiction—but still not in The City: to the west, past St. Paul's and Ludgate, the western entrance to The City through the old Roman fortifications. *Drury Lane stands just to the west, *Covent Garden farther west, and the Haymarket yet farther west, halfway to Westminster, seat of the royal and church authorities, where the Abbey, Parliament and Big Ben, 16 Downing Street, and Scotland Yard are located.

Drury Lane, Covent Garden, and the Haymarket approximately map out the territory long known as the West End, largely aristocratic estates in Shakespeare's day but, since the nineteenth century, London's theatre district. Geographically, "The West End" exactly corresponds to New York's "Broadway": it's where the theatres are. Professionally, however, the terms are not equal. "Broadway" suggests a standard of thespian excellence supposedly not equaled elsewhere in the nation. But "the West End" refers only to England's front-rank *commercial* stages. Its two notable repertory companies, the National and the *Royal Shakespeare, though associated with West End playwrights, actors, directors, and techies, stand apart, especially now that the Royal Shakespeare has joined the National in adversary location, having moved far from its West End home at the Aldwych for the distant reaches of the Barbican complex, way off to the east.

WHAT PRICE GLORY?

Comic war play by Laurence Stallings and *Maxwell Anderson, prem. New York, 1924.

What Price Glory? is many things. First of all, it's a play about World War I, not of battle and life in the trenches, but of American Marines relaxing, joking and swearing during a peaceful interlude in France. Second, it's a triangle: two soldiers and the French girl they both chase. Third, it's a study in male camaraderie, for the two are old acquaintances thrown together again by chance, antagonists as much as buddies. Fourth—and here's where war veteran Stallings and the pacifist Anderson made their history—it's a notable statistic in the American theatre's battle against state censorship. The 1920s was the decade in which prudes and fascists made their last great attempt to clamp down on free expression on Broadway. They threatened everything from trash to Eugene O'Neill. But *What Price Glory?*'s vitality and honesty helped defeat them. The general public didn't much care if art or smut was closed—but to threaten a play that everyone and his sister thought the funniest and most touching event of the decade was to encourage popular resistance to censorship, turn opinion against the bluenoses. This play was just too amusing to kill, as witness a taste of the opening scene, three marines deep in bull session:

LIPINSKY: When there's women around the skipper's got trick eyes like a horsefly.

KIPER: The old man? Say, he can't look at a mam'selle without blushing. Compared to me he's an amateur. He don't know the difference between a Hong-Kong honky-tonk and a Santo Domingo smoongy.

LIPINSKY: No, oh, no! I suppose women is an open book to you. You're damn well right—a code book.

KIPER: Yeah, you're damn well right . . . When I was in Spain the king of Spain put an ad in the paper offering a reward for the return of the queen.

GOWDY: What did you do?

KIPER: Took her back for the reward.

(See also *Journey's End.*)

WHEN WE DEAD AWAKEN

A "dramatic epilogue" by *Henrik Ibsen, prem. Oslo, 1900.

Ibsen's last play, an epilogue both artistically and autobiographically. Its *protagonist, sculptor Arnold Rubek, speaks of his past in terms that describe Ibsen's. Rubek's life's work, *The Resurrection Day,* begins as an exquisitely beautiful woman, pure and glorious (not unlike Ibsen's early verse plays). Then, growing worldly, Rubek adds other figures to the piece, realistic and impure (like the famous "social problem" plays of Ibsen's middle years). Then Rubek adds himself to the group, "a man burdened with guilt . . . for a forfeited life" (like the protagonists of the late plays: like this same Rubek, wise and "dead"). As the play moves from naturalism into a symbolical second act and finally a nearly mythological third, Ibsen reviews his art, seeking escape from the hollow needs that spurred him in youth. And when we dead awaken? "We see that we have never lived."

OSCAR WILDE (1854–1900)

"Oh! Life is terrible," says a character in Wilde's *Lady Windermere's Fan* (1892). "It rules us; we do not rule it." Yet Wilde spent his career doing battle with life—with society, really—and its intolerant greed for conventions and presenting acceptable appearances. Despite the prickly dandies who fill Wilde's stage to mouth frivolous epigrams, Wilde actually wrote to unmask the lies behind the conventions, the corruption in the notion of an "appearance." *Lady Windermere's Fan,* for instance, under the *Sardouvian facade of the

A portrait of the aesthete as a young man: Oscar Wilde on his American tour in 1882, in the famous sessions photographed by Napoleon Sarony. As always in public, Oscar is Heavily Posing. He based his theatre aesthetics on the art of posing as well. Claiming that *Hugo and Shakespeare had used up all the worthy subjects and that it was impossible to be original, Wilde said of his tragedy The Duchess of Padua *(1891) that "there are no emotions, just extraordinary adjectives."*

"woman with a past" melodrama, attacks the double standard of gender morality. Indeed, the "fallen woman" of the play, Mrs. Erlynne, is by far the most admirable character—far more than those who are quick to judge her, including her own unwitting daughter.

The secret identity, the fatal letter, and other contrivances of the *well-made play mar others of Wilde's stage works—the ironically titled *A Woman of No Importance* (1893), ironic because it is the man in the case who turns out to be "of no importance"; and *An Ideal Husband* (1895). But these bows to standard procedure were Wilde's only such. In all else he slashed—in his languid way—at Britain's self-appointed conservors of status quo. He baited his critics with his self-advertising bons mots, his outrageous affectations, his delight in himself. It seemed genuine. Yet "Public and private lives are different things" runs a line in *An Ideal Husband.* "They have different laws, and move on different lines." No one knew this better than Wilde, husband and father but homosexual rhapsodist and lover of Lord Alfred Douglas. Wilde wrote his masterpiece on this very theme: *The Importance of Being Earnest* (1895) might as well have been called *The Importance of Having a Second Identity*—of having a country to flee the town for, a town in which to do things the country wouldn't tolerate. In the very year that *Earnest* opened, Douglas's father the Marquess of Queensbury denounced Wilde, in a notorious solecism, as a "somdomite." Wilde sued for libel and lost. By English law, Wilde thus laid himself open for prosecution for sodomy, virtually for making his private life public. Wilde was sentenced to two years' hard labor and retired at last to Paris, penniless and in broken health. "I was as much a landmark of the *West End as the Savoy Hotel," a fictional Wilde writes in Peter Ackroyd's *The Last Testament of Oscar Wilde.* "I built castles of gold which I would then enter." But then: "I was trapped in some flat, phantasmagoric nightmare." And finally: "I had descended into Hell through my own vanity." Let Wilde himself have the last word, true wit under pressure in a very public dishonor, as he was led in handcuffs to Reading Gaol. "If this is how Her Majesty treats her prisoners, she doesn't deserve to have any."

(See also *The Importance of Being Earnest.*)

THORNTON WILDER (1897–1975)

American playwrights tend to the conservative or the experimental. Wilder was both: conservative in his worldview but experimental in form. We note his style in miniature in three one-act plays of 1931, *The Long Christmas Dinner, Pullman Car Hiawatha,* and *The Happy Journey to Trenton and Camden:* narrator, bare stage, simple family people engaged in family things like car trips and letting time pass and observing the ceremonies of life— and, in *The Long Christmas Dinner,* of death, as a series of holiday meals expands into one great festival of the generations. The erudite Wilder drew on many sources. As Woody Allen closes *Manhattan* with an *hommage* to Charlie Chaplin's silent film *City Lights,* so does Wilder accumulate Molière, Gertrude Stein, Pirandello, Ibsen; and two James Joyce scholars, apparently eager to find fame in a controversy, attacked Wilder's *The Skin of Our Teeth* (1942) for its associations with Joyce's novel *Finnegans Wake.* "Literature," Wilder commented, "has always more resembled a torch race than a furious dispute among heirs."

But then, Wilder's conservative outlook made enemies. The left attacked *Our Town* (1938) for its seemingly complacent view of American bourgeois life. The production develops the allegorical simplicity of the one-acters, especially *The Long Christmas Dinner:* as the Stage Manager takes us, on a nearly bare stage, through Grover's Corners, New Hampshire, we witness the epic of life in symbolic passage. The children of the first act marry in the second; in the third act, the wife dies, and, before taking a permanent place in the churchyard, invisibly revisits her youth only to draw back in agony at the failure of the living to appreciate the *act* of life, the simple administration of the experience of being among loved ones, friends, neighbors. One recalls that notable moment of *The Long Christmas Dinner,* when a woman, grieving for her late mother, cries, "I never told her how wonderful she was. We all treated her as though she were just a friend in the house. I thought she'd be here forever."

Our Town is a masterpiece of American drama. But its hugeness depresses many spectators, dwarfs

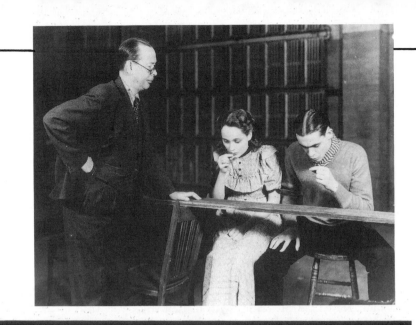

The original *Jed Harris production of Wilder's Our Town *illustrates the show's celebrated bare-stage look. Top left, the Stage Manager (Frank Craven) plays counterman for the soda shop date of Emily Webb (Martha Scott) and George Gibbs (John Craven, Frank's son). The youngsters marry, but Emily dies young; below, she joins the dead souls of Grover's Corners (seated at left) as the mourners (right) pay their last respects in the rain. When they go (above), the young widower throws himself across his dead wife's grave.*

their self-esteem. *Our Town* (=Our World) says each person is a moment in the endless panorama of human time. Its theme directly opposes those of such socially individualistic American plays as *Salvation Nell* or *The Crucible*. These two, and countless others like them, insist that the present is all the time there is, and that one has the free choice to influence the world, be more than a moment. *Our Town* says, You don't matter, and even if you did, you'd never realize it, because time runs by so fast. Even Eleanor Roosevelt, one of the largest figures of the era, felt diminished by the play —"moved," she admitted, but "depressed."

Wilder quickly followed *Our Town* with a comic complement, *The Merchant of Yonkers* (1938), which engagingly urges one and all to seize the day and *matter,* at least to oneself. Production problems silenced it till the 1954 revision (really more of a retouched revival) as *The Matchmaker,* with Ruth Gordon as the dizzily ontological arranger of life's ceremonies, another Wilderian Stage Manager. Unfortunately for the stage, Wilder's careers in academia and fiction limited his theatrical output. (See also *The Matchmaker* and *The Skin of Our Teeth.*)

TENNESSEE WILLIAMS

(1911–1983)

Mike Nichols's spoof of Williams, as "Alabama Gross," found him chortling over the misadventures of his latest heroine, as she deliciously falls prey to "drink, prostitution, and puttin' on airs." That captures the paradox of Williams the dramatist, at once sensualist and tragedian, poet and voyeur. His arena is the south, his genre is the cross section of personal relationships, and his archetypes are the somewhat cultured (but inbred and shy) gentlewoman and the brutish male who shatters her flimsy pretenses: in essence, Blanche DuBois and Stanley Kowalski of *A Streetcar Named Desire,* but, in variation, the Daughter and the Gentleman Caller of *The Glass Menagerie,* she terminally unsensual and he more breezy than brutish; or Maggie and Brick of *Cat on a Hot Tin Roof,* she, for once, the stronger of the two and he the bruised half-survivor. Almost always, however,

Williams deals with the confrontation of the dreamer and the realist, his sympathies lying with the dreamer but the victory, in the end, always going to the realist. Thus Stanley sends Blanche to the lunatic asylum; the Gentleman Caller does not, as was hoped, stay on to comfort the Daughter; and Maggie forces Brick to give her the child that will secure them his father's estate.

Realists and dreamers: and Williams may have been both, a gifted and prolific writer drifting through the usual American bohemia of fame and pleasure. At times, he seemed like the greatest writer on Broadway, more colorfully theatrical than *Arthur Miller and more profound than *William Inge. Yet Williams's was another of those American careers without a sound final act. In his first years of success, *The Glass Menagerie* (1945), *A Streetcar Named Desire* (1947), *Summer and Smoke* (1948), and *The Rose Tattoo* (1951) proposed a unique talent. But Williams's second period was erratic. *Camino Real* (1953) found Williams botching *absurdist *symbolism. *Cat on a Hot Tin Roof* (1955)—the playwright's favorite of his plays—returned him to good form. But *Orpheus Descending* (1957) and *Sweet Bird of Youth* (1959) seemed retreads of old material, the further adventures of Stanley and Blanche. *Period of Adjustment* (1961) at least discovered a novel Williams in a sunny comedy about two spatting couples; and *The Night of the Iguana* (1961), if another restatement of familiar themes and characters, was one of Williams's most finished works.

But the third period saw consistent commercial failure, virtually one disaster after another, at that in productions much less honorable than, for instance, those that introduced *The Glass Menagerie* (*Laurette Taylor, Julie Haydon, and Eddie Dowling, staged by Dowling and Margo Jones), *A Streetcar Named Desire* (Marlon Brando and Jessica Tandy, staged by *Elia Kazan), or *Sweet Bird of Youth* (Geraldine Page, Paul Newman, and Rip Torn, again under Kazan). Typical of Williams's third period Broadway style was *Vieux Carré* (1977), seen for the very short run typical of Williams's last years in a production so perfunctory that the published text cites the cast of the later British staging (with no reference to any Broadway appearance) and is dedicated to the British director, Keith Hack.

Moreover, a cult of celebrity had overtaken Williams in those last two decades, a cult more amused by his alcoholic antics than impressed by his talent. When his critical and popular following deserted him, Williams found other ways to get attention —or to fail to get it. "I was always falling down," he later recalled, "and would always say 'I'm about to fall down,' and almost nobody ever caught me." A curious observation from the author of the line, "Whoever you are—I have always depended on the kindness of strangers." (This is Blanche's statement, her last in *Streetcar,* to the doctor who has come to take her away.) Still, revivals of the best of Williams's plays have shown him to be one of America's greatest playwrights. Only Eugene O'Neill can claim a larger bibliography, a sign that Williams's personality, like O'Neill's, is as fascinating as his characters: to write about the work is to observe the life. But was Williams a dreamer or a realist? The airs he himself put on suggest a dreamer defying the realists: or perhaps a realist desperately wishing to believe in the dream.
(See also *The Milk Train Doesn't Stop Here Anymore* and *Vieux Carré.*)

LANFORD WILSON (See Circle Repertory Theatre)

ROBERT WILSON (1941–   )

A century from now, encyclopedias like this one will either hail Wilson as the archon of the American post-Vietnam avant-garde, or omit him entirely as a figure of transitory chic. For the present, Wilson is very much hailed; this is a time in which Americans are reveling in their avant-garde, as long as the artists generate an air of swank, of splendid eccentricity. Wilson obliges. Unlike many adventurers cited elsewhere in these pages—the desperately political playwright Georg Büchner, the scabrous *absurdist Alfred Jarry, or the

designer Adolphe Appia—Wilson need not fear neglect. Most critics dote on him. The foundation money pours in. Yet whether he is mounting a fourteen-hour, one hundred fifty–person spectacle such as *The Life and Times of Joseph Stalin* (1974) or the mere (by comparison) *A Letter for Queen Victoria* (1975), Wilson's substitution of very, very slow-moving pictures for plot, character, and dialogue is of questionable value. Wilson has been called the heir to *dada and *surrealism. But their rapid-fire kaleidoscope of words and images always leaped to the most compact sort of art, not the most expansive. More appropriately, Wilson has been associated with the current ism, minimalism, partly because even his biggest shows usually employ only a very few performers and a simple decor at any given point. (*Joseph Stalin* was exceptional here, especially in its famous "Mammy Dance," a pride of performers costumed as southern mammies, entering one by one to whirl to Johann Strauss's "On the Beautiful, Blue Danube" waltz.) Even more telling is Wilson's collaboration with the minimalist composer Philip Glass. Music plays so important a part in Wilson's works that he has called them "operas," though they weren't anything like operas till *Einstein on the Beach* (1975), to Glass's raptly doodling accompaniment.

WINGS

The far left and right sides of a *proscenium stage, out of public view, where the actors and technicians stand during a performance.

PEG WOFFINGTON (?1717–1760)

A worthy feminist work of fiction or theatre might be made of this life, for here was what appears to be a proud and fair Irish actress who was disfigured by sexist legend into a harlot (are not all actresses sluts?), a fortune hunter (were her suitors not aristocrats?—some of them, anyway), and a shrew (did she not call a bore a bore, even if he was a man of estate?). In fact, Peg was none of these things—

and, unlike *Nell Gwyn of *Drury Lane, the other great "actress-whore" of the British theatre between Shakespeare and Shaw, Peg Woffington was an unquestionably talented thespian, especially known for comedy. Uncontested in most of her roles in Dublin and London (at *Covent Garden, but for one season at Drury Lane), Peg especially registered in *trouser parts. This gave birth to one of the most repeated anecdotes in theatre lore. Coming into the Drury Lane *greenroom after an especially uproarious turn as Sir Harry Wildair in *George Farquhar's *The Constant Couple,* Peg declares, "By heaven, I say half the audience now thinks me to be a man!" Whereupon Peg's tempestuous rival Kitty Clive snaps back, "By heaven, madam, the other half already knows you to be a woman!"

DONALD WOLFIT (1902–1968)

"There has never been an actor of greater gusto than Wolfit," wrote critic *Kenneth Tynan. "He has the dynamism, energy, bulk, and stature, and he joins these together with a sheer relish for resonant words, which splits small theatres as Caruso shattered wine glasses." Wolfit was sometimes dismissed as a ham, but Tynan was quick to check this. Wolfit had the command, judgment, and subtlety that the ham lacks. But: "He's a middle-aged *actor-manager who goes on provincial tours with an unimpressive supporting cast."

This in itself identifies Wolfit, and it does suggest the ham, in the implied vanity of the big fish–little pond stardom, the rough-and-tumble performances setting off the suavely centered star. Apparently, Wolfit was too self-directed to be able to suffer anyone else's management for long. He would occasionally bring his touring Shakespeare into London, and did at odd times hire out as a freelance, scoring for instance a great triumph in Christopher Marlowe's *Tamburlaine the Great at the *Old Vic under *Tyrone Guthrie in 1951. Yet less than a year later, Wolfit had broken with the company and gone off on his own again. Thus he locked himself out of the halls of fame occupied by

Laurence Olivier, John Gielgud, Ralph Richardson. Perhaps Wolfit simply wasn't able to share a stage. Like these three colleagues, Wolfit was knighted, and he appears—apparently—in the character of the Shakespearean "Sir" in Ronald Harwood's play *The Dresser* (1980), filmed with Albert Finney as the imperious Sir and Tom Courtenay (from the stage original) as the touchingly worshipful dresser.

THE WOMAN

"Scenes of War and Freedom" by *Edward Bond, prem. London, 1978.

The woman of the title is Hecuba, Queen of Troy, who in Bond's version of the Trojan War works with the wife of one of the Greek commanders to call the war off. But officials on both sides defeat them, as Bond compares the astonishing brutality of men with the patient reason of women. Typically, Bond makes the situation disturbingly theatrical, as when the Greek wife, Ismene, tries to make the Greeks face the horror of war for both victors and the defeated. Stamping, clapping, and shouting "Hooooo! Hooooo! Hooooo!," the Greeks drown out her wisdom, leaving her to call out to no one:

ISMENE: Priam's city has nothing to give you but a grave and rubble to fill it! Soldiers, nothing but a grave and rubble to fill it! A grave and rubble! Soldiers, a grave and rubble!

Troy falls. But to this freely retold *chronicle play, Bond adds a What Happened Next, on an island where Hecuba and Ismene confront the Greek commander and turn his brutality against him. A grave and rubble to fill it.
(See also *The Trojan Women.*)

WILLIAM WYCHERLEY (See Restoration Theatre)

Y

WILLIAM BUTLER YEATS
(1865–1939)

Irish playwrights fall into two groups: those who left Ireland and largely or entirely avoided Irish subjects and characters, like *Richard Brinsley Sheridan and *Oscar Wilde; and those who stayed local, ethnic, *Irish*. Like Yeats. Primarily a poet, Yeats joined Lady Augusta Gregory and *John Millington Synge in founding the *Abbey Theatre, Ireland's fundamental stage. Besides running the company, all three provisioned its texts, Yeats building on his pre-Abbey folk plays *The Countess Cathleen* (written 1892, prem. 1899), *The Land of Heart's Desire* (1894), and, with Lady Gregory, *Cathleen ni Houlihan* (1902)—complementing *On Baile's Strand* (1904) as one of the two plays that opened the Abbey. This one-acter launched Yeats's series of Chuchulain plays, on the hero of Ireland's ancient Ulster cycle of sagas: *The Green Helmet* (originally known as *The Golden Helmet,* 1908), *At the Hawk's Well* (1916), *The Only Jealousy of Emer* (1919), and *The Death of Chuchulain* (1939). This much was Yeats pursuing his self-imposed mandate to erect a "popular theatre" at the Abbey, a poetry of Irish life and lore. Yet Yeats was unable to reconcile his genius to the demands of a stage aimed at everybody. "I want to create for myself," he wrote to Lady Gregory, "an unpopular theatre and an audience like a secret society with admission by favour . . . I want so much—an audience of fifty, a room worthy of it (some great dining-room or drawing-room), half-a-dozen young men and women who can dance and speak verse or play drum and flute and zither."

Throughout Yeats's twenty-six plays runs an encompassing, a *historical* vision of theatre, the palpable influence of the Greek, Oriental, and French *symbolist styles. It was a noble dream; but it is perhaps too ideal for anything above an audience of Yeats's secret fifty. As of this writing, at least, Yeats is a minor figure in theatre compared with his compatriots Sheridan and Wilde; and Yeats's unpopular theatre cannot compete with the three popular Abbey plays of his junior colleague, *Sean O'Casey, *The Shadow of a Gunman, Juno and the Paycock,* and *The Plough and the Stars.*

YOU CAN'T TAKE IT WITH YOU

*Farce by *George S. Kaufman and Moss Hart, prem. New York, 1936.

This is the classic form of American farce, with the humor spread evenly over the three acts, as

A day at the Vanderhofs': You Can't Take It with You, *perhaps the greatest of all the screwball farces so popular in American theatre and film in the 1930s. Grandpa (Henry Travers, center) is relaxing, but the rest of the gang are demonstrating the Great American Screwball Credo: enjoy life while you can.*

opposed to the French form, emphasizing the middle act. Then, too, European and English farce build the premise on sexual situations. Here the topic is that American idyll of Having a Good Time. The setting is a house of screwballs, the problem a very serious daughter of same who falls in love with the son of a pompous Wall Streeter. Thus, Kaufman and Hart present a war of styles. The screwballs win, of course. Yet this is in all a very cynical play, the *joie de vivre* a front of bravado in the face of frustration and entropy. Grandpa Vanderhof, head of the screwball clan, habitually attends university commencement exercises:

GRANDPA: You take a good Commencement orator and he'll drown out a whole carload of fireworks. And say just as much, too.
PENNY: Don't the graduates ever say anything?
GRANDPA: No, they just sit there in cap and nightgown, get their diplomas, and then along about forty years from now they suddenly say, "Where am I?"

ZANNI

The servant characters of *commedia dell'arte,* forerunners of the modern "zanies." The word itself is Venetian argot for (Gio)vanni, or John. Thus the *zanni* were "Johnnies," shrewd and two-faced characters forever duping their bourgeois bosses.

FRANCO ZEFFIRELLI (1923–   )

Beginning as a set designer for Luchino Visconti's play productions and in opera, the Florentine Zeffirelli spent the 1950s growing into a more important role as director-designer in opera, especially of the burgeoning *riesumazione* ("exhumation") movement devoted to reconstructing nineteenth-century opera not only musicologically but theatrically. This background in the grand manner made Zeffirelli's work in the spoken theatre startlingly operatic—lyrical, florid, picturesque. Zeffirelli's *Romeo and Juliet* for the *Old Vic in 1960 with John Stride, Judi Dench, and Alec McCowen (as Mercutio) startled for its blend of realism and passion, for its facetious view of Mercutio's duel with Tybalt, Mercutio killed not out of hot blood but apparently by accident; for its very Italianate Verona, crowded with merchants, idlers, children; for its breathlessly adolescent lovers' poetry. Similarly, a *Much Ado about Nothing* at the same house five years later with Albert Finney, Maggie Smith, Robert Stephens, Ian McKellen, Derek Jacobi, and Frank Finlay (with music by Federico Fellini's collaborator, Nino Rota) reaffirmed Zeffirelli's operatic welding of spectacle and subtlety. Zeffirelli's Italian work with such writers as Arthur Miller and Edward Albee has been smaller-scaled; but his Shakespeare made important theatre history, and has been especially influential in American Shakespearean productions. As someone commented to *Kenneth Tynan during an intermission at the *Old Vic *Romeo,* "Every director in the audience is biting his nails and wondering why he never thought of this before."

EMILE ZOLA (See Naturalism)

THE ZOO STORY

One-acter for two men and park benches by *Edward Albee, prem. Berlin (in German), 1959.

In New York's Central Park, north of the zoo, a rundown bohemian encounters a sedate bourgeois whom he befriends and then baits into a fight to the death. Albee's first play (not counting "a three-act sex farce" he wrote when he was twelve), *The Zoo Story* had to take the stage in Europe in translation before it could return home. It was produced on *off-Broadway in 1960 (with George Maharis and William Daniels) on a bill with *Samuel Beckett's *Krapp's Last Tape.* This proved a historical pairing. Beckett, by then the senior *absurdist, compatriot of James Joyce and creator of Godot, conjured up the disjunct, hollow-man world of post–World War II fantasy *Angst,* while Albee's fresh voice explored, in his bohemian *protagonist, a very contemporary and realistic Upper West Side hollow man, intelligent, clever, humorous, attractive, yet mysteriously unhappy. Two such different styles of writing seemed an unlikely fit. In the event, they complemented each other so well that Albee was hailed as America's emerging absurdist. There is a touch of *Godot* in Albee's title, in that the bohemian has apparently pulled some wild stunt in the park zoo that is bound to show up on the evening news, a stunt he keeps promising to discuss. We wait hungrily for the "story," but he never gets to it, just as the expected Godot never shows up. However, what makes *The Zoo Story* compelling is less Albee's use of the resonantly open-minded dialogue of modern theatre than his ability to shatter the appearance of reality—the benches in the Park on a summer afternoon—with the nightmarish reality of his psychology.

ABOUT THE AUTHOR

Ethan Mordden was born in Heavensville, Pennsylvania, and educated at the Locust Valley, New York, Friends Academy and the University of Pennsylvania. He has worked as: an off-Broadway musical director, a copywriter for *TV Guide,* the editor of the romance division of DC comics, and the assistant editor of *Opera News.* He has also taught at Yale University. He is the author of twenty books: non-fiction on theatre *(Broadway Babies, The American Theatre)*; opera *(Demented, A Guide to Opera Recordings)*; film *(The Hollywood Musical, The Hollywood Studios)*; and fiction, including the novel *One Last Waltz* and a trilogy of story cycles, *I've a Feeling We're Not in Kansas Anymore, Buddies,* and *Everybody Loves You.* He has been a lifelong theatregoer, dating back to *The King and I* with Gertrude Lawrence, which he saw on his third birthday.